C0-AVN-677

BRITAIN AND THE WAR FOR YUGOSLAVIA, 1940-1943

Mark C. Wheeler

EAST EUROPEAN MONOGRAPHS, BOULDER
DISTRIBUTED BY COLUMBIA UNIVERSITY PRESS
NEW YORK

1980

EAST EUROPEAN MONOGRAPHS, NO. LXIV

Mark C. Wheeler is Senior Lecturer in History
at the University of Lancaster

Library of Congress Card Catalog Number 79-56523
ISBN 0-914710—57-5
Printed in the United States of America

TABLE OF CONTENTS

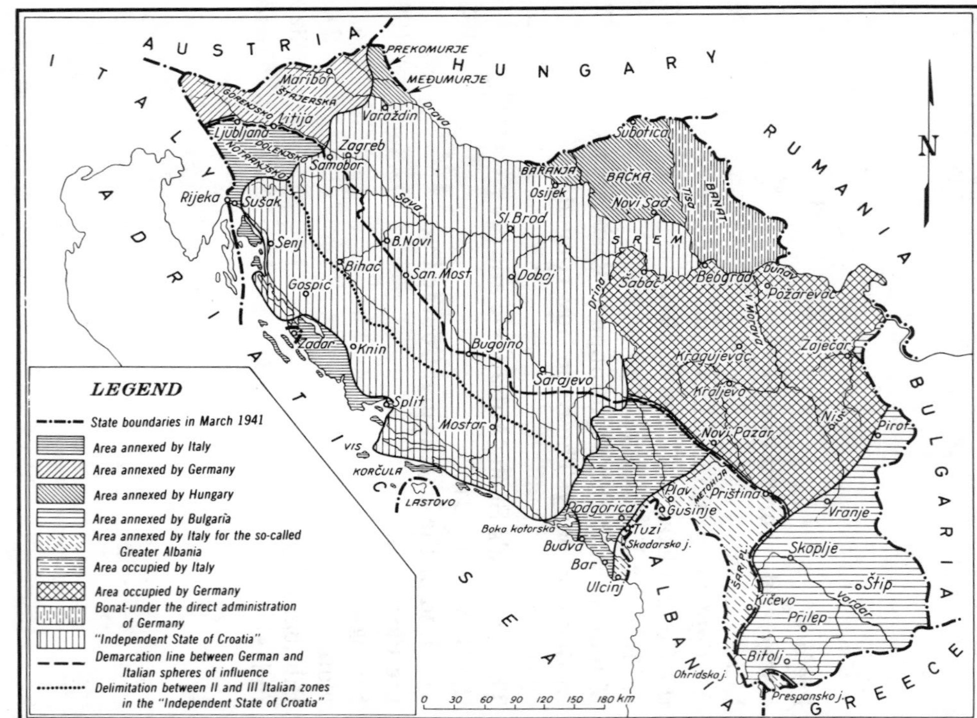

Dismemberment of Yugoslavia by Germany, Italy and their allies in April 1941

Source: Josip Broz Tito, *Selected Works on the People's War of Liberation* (Bombay: Somaiya Publications Pvt. Ltd., 1969), fig. 1.

PREFACE

This book is about Britain's wartime relations with the old Yugoslavia - so called despite being neither very old nor very Yugoslav. It was a state dominated by the institutions and ethos of the pre-existing Serbian kingdom: the Karadjordjević dynasty, the Serbian officer corps and Serbian nationalism. The book charts the rise and fall of official Britain's predilection for an hopes from all three, but especially their armed exponent in the homeland after the occupation of April 1941, General Draža Mihailović. The detailed narrative ends in the spring of 1943 with the establishment by the British of relations with the standard-bearers of a new, communist Yugoslavia, Tito and the Partisans.

A great deal has been published about Yugoslavia during the Second World War since this project was conceived. It is certain that there is much more yet to come. The subject - if not the patience of the intended readership - appears inexhaustible. My debtsto those historians and memoirists who have already had their say are evident in the notes. These same voluminous notes will also make it obvious to the reader that this book had its origins as a Ph.D. thesis. My first expression of appreciation must therefore be to my supervisor, F. H. Hinsley, Master of St. John's College, Cambridge. Without his encouragement, patience and counsel there would have been no thesis worth re-writing. There are three other scholars to whom I owe much: to John V. A. Fine, Jr., of the University of Michigan for introducting me to Balkan history; to Kosta St. Pavlowitch of the University of Cambridge for teaching me Serbo-Croat and answering endless questions about the exile government he served; and to Jovan Marjanović of Belgrade University for sponsoring my work in the Yugoslav archives.

I have also been fortunate in having friends and colleagues who were ready to read and criticize all or part of the work at various stages in its progress. My thanks go to Elisabeth Barker, Michael Laffan, Sir Cecil Parrott and Dušan Puvačić. Elisabeth Barker has been especially kind in sharing with me both her insights and the private papers of George Taylor which are under her control. Given the controversy that surrounds nearly everything about wartime Yugoslavia, it needs be said that none of the people mentioned above would necessarily wish to be associated with my interpretations, and certainly not with my errors.

Finally, I must record my gratitude to those persons and institutions that facilitated my work. Trinity Hall, Cambridge, the Yugoslav-American Commission for the Fulbright Program and the University of Lancaster Research Grant Fund all provided financial assistance for research. My head of department, Zbyněk Zeman, was generous in his encouragement and in the extraordinary claims he permitted me to make on his secretary, Joan Armitstead. Her help in typing and re-typing the manuscript has been invaluable. The book has been brought to publication with the assistance of a subvention from the British Academy.

USAGE AND ABBREVIATIONS

I. The spelling of Yugoslav names has been standardized in this work in accordance with proper Serbo-Croat forms using diacritic marks. Thus Draža Mihailović appears as such - even in quotations - and not in one of the many disguises which transliteration, phoenetic spelling or misspelling have cloaked him over the years. The names of authors and their works are, however, rendered as published. Similarly, the titles of works in Serbo-Croat are cited in the original.

Place names have also been made to conform to modern Serbo-Croat usage with the exception of those for which accepted English versions exist, e.g. Belgrade instead of Beograd, Croatia rather than Hrvatska. Where there is reason to doubt whether or not a commonly accpeted English version exists (e.g. Sandjak or Sandžak), I have used the Serbo-Croat spelling or something approximating it (e.g. Četniks instead of Chetniks).

Citations of documents in archives are designed to be helpful rather than consistent. Thus merely the reference number is cited in the case of British Foreign Office and Cabinet papers, but more extensive information is provided for documents from other, less well-ordered collections. Books and articles with lengthy titles are cited in shorthand form after the first reference.

Extracts from Crown-Copyright records in the Public Record Office appear by permission of the Controller of Her Majesty's Stationery Office. English translations of passages and documents in Serbo-Croat are mine.

II. The following abbreviations are used in the text and/or notes:

AD	SOE sign for George Taylor
AD3	SOE sign for Lord Glenconner
AFHQ	Allied Force Headquarters, Mediterranean
A/H31	SOE sign for Draža Mihailović
AJ	Arhiv Jugoslavije (Archive of Yugoslavia, Belgrade)
AVII	Arhiv vojno-istorijskog instituta JNA (Archive of the Military History Institute of the Yugoslav People's Army, Belgrade)
BBC	British Broadcasting Corporation
C	Head of SIS (or MI6), sometimes used to refer to the organization
CAB	Cabinet Papers, Public Record Office, Kew
CD	Executive head of SOE
CIGS	Chief of the Imperial General Staff
COS	Chiefs of Staff
C-in-C,ME	Commander or Commanders-in-Chief, Middle East
D	Section of MI6, predecessor of SOE
D/H2	SOE sign for S. W. Bailey
DMI	Director of Military Intelligence
DMO	Director of Military Operations
FO	Foreign Office Papers, Public Record Office, Kew
FRPS	Foreign Research and Press Service, Chatham House

FRUS	*Foreign Relations of the United States; Diplomatic Papers*
Glasnik	*Glasnik srpskog istorisko-kulturnog društva 'Njegoš'*
HSS	Hrvatska seljačka stranka (Croatian Peasant Party)
KPJ	Komunistička partija Jugoslavije (Communist Party of Yugoslavia)
MEW	Ministry of Economic Warfare
MI3	Military Intelligence (European Country Section)
MI5	Military Intelligence (Security Service)
MI6	Military Intelligence (Secret Intelligence Service)
MI(R)	Military Intelligence (Research)
NDH	Nezavisna država Hrvatska (Independent State of Croatia)
OSS	Office of Strategic Services
PREM	Prime Minister's Office Papers, Public Record Office, Kew
PWE	Political Warfare Executive
SIS	Secret Intelligence Service (MI6, C)
SOE	Special Operations Executive
SSIP	Savezni sekretarijat inostranih poslova - Arhiv (Archive of the Federal Secretariat of International Affairs, Belgrade)
WO	War Office Papers, Public Record Office, Kew
Zbornik	*Zbornik dokumenata i podataka o Narodno-oslobodilačkom ratu naroda Jugoslavije*
ZP	SOE sign for the Foreign Office

N.B. — dates are abbreviated day/month/year. Thus 6/4/41 is 6 April 1941.

CHAPTER I

INTRODUCTION

In the years between the two World Wars the new Yugoslav kingdom was neither regarded with favour nor invested with strategic significance by successive British governments. Situated north of the Mediterranean lifeline that lent importance to Greece, west of the Middle Eastern sphere of influence that predicated close relations with Turkey and east of a continental commitment that rarely extended so far as the Rhine, Yugoslavia existed beyond the pale of vital and defensible British interests. The contention among powers closer at hand for predominance in Yugoslavia and the Balkans was observed by the British with interest - and usually with regret - but not until war loomed did the British see cause for involvement in so remote and intractable a region.

The Yugoslavs suffered, as did their Balkan neighbours, from a British tendency to view their independence as something of a menace and their exercise of it as more than a little absurd. Balkan diplomats were insufferably tiresome, Balkan politicians invariably tortuous, Balkan intrigues impenetrably deep and Balkan disputes inevitably insoluble. Like the other Balkan states, Yugoslavia was an uncivilized land of peasants and poverty. Its political life was chaotic, corrupt and occasionally violent. Neither its Serbian royal family nor its financial and political establishment was quite respectable: the Karadjordjević scions were too ruthless in their exercise of power, the Belgrade *čaršija* too rapacious in its pursuit of gain. What passed for parliamentary democracy in interwar Yugoslavia gave way to royal dictatorship in 1929, but the new regime was no more congenial to the British than the old. Both the trains and the politicians remained unreliable.

If the Balkan peoples were "trash" - a proposition which found adherents in Whitehall as well as in the Reich Chancellery[1] - then Yugoslavia was especially damned. It contained more nationalities and national minorities than any European state except the Soviet Union. In the face of tactless, self-interested and centralized Serb rule from Belgrade, this heterogeneity made for disunity and discontent. Among the South Slav peoples the Croats and the Macedonians proved least reconciled to their status in the interwar years, but the others too had their grievances. Disaffected Yugoslavs, as well as national minority groups (Albanians, Germans, Hungarians, Italians, etc.), used and were used by the five (out of seven) neighbouring states that coveted Yugoslav territory. Even the Serbs, inheritors and executors of the mantle of state, were deemed susceptible to that old bugbear of the Foreign Office, Pan-Slavism. From the British government's point of view there was little political profit to be derived from close association with a country so insecure and so reviled. Such disincentives did not inhibit British investors from seeking profits of another sort in Yugoslavia, and in fact the British share of foreign investment in the country was second only to that of the French between the wars. But however important the British financial stake in their underdeveloped country was to the Yugoslavs, it was scarcely of comparable significance to the British. Moreover, what political importance it had was vitiated by the absence of a correspondingly high level of Anglo-Yugoslav trade. As the Germans demonstrated in the 1930's, trade could be a more potent political lever than ownership.[2]

The French pursued political as well as financial profits in Yugoslavia between the wars, but their interest in the country was no recommendation to the British. Its inclusion, albeit somewhat marginally, in the French security system caused the British government more disquiet than satisfaction. Nor was the lively interest of the few Britons who had plumbed the mysteries of South-Eastern Europe appreciated. Students of the region might emerge with a more sympathetic understanding of its peoples than that which obtained in the Foreign Office, but they also often became champions of one or another of the unredeemed national causes that agitated them. It was perhaps fortunate for Anglo-Yugoslav relations at the official level that the Foreign Office found few things so obnoxious as fervour allied to expertise in the service of small and remote peoples' national grievances.

Despite a nutual lack of sympathy and affection the Yugoslavs - and particularly the Serbs - ought to have been the natural allies of the British. They had fought side by side in the Great War (a war which the South Slavs helped start) and presumably shared a common victors' interest in the maintenance of the peace that followed (a peace which the British helped dictate). The British had been late converts to the idea of a Yugoslav state, but they had nonetheless responded to the call. The trouble was that while the British began to doubt both the moral foundations and the practical effectiveness of the Paris peace, the Yugoslavs came to question the ability of their former comrades in arms and the League of Nations to preserve it - and them. If Yugoslavia, like Poland, soon epitomized for the British the incapacity of the successor states to provide a stable order in East Central Europe, then Britain's wavering commitment to the status quo indicated to the Yugoslavs that they might have to look elsewhere for guarantors of their security.

The French appeared for some time more resolute in their determination to defend the order established at Paris (and to ensure that France did not bear alone the brunt of any future war in Europe), but their affiliation with the Little Entente in the early 1920's and their proposals of an Eastern European grand alliance against Germany in the early 1930's were not wholly reassuring to the Yugoslavs. Unlike the French alliances with Poland, Czechoslovakia and Romania, the friendship treaty signed with Yugoslavia in 1927 bore no military convention. And while the Yugoslavs and their small power allies were capable of containing Bulgarian or Hungarian revisionism, the Yugoslavs were disadvantaged by the fact that their most implacable enemy was Italy, a would-be great power which the French, almost as consistently as the British, wished to wean away from the revisionist camp. What was more, although Germany might be the obvious threat to Britain and France, to the Yugoslavs Germany represented both a possible counterweight to Italy and the only ready customer for their agricultural and mineral surpluses. Rather than lend support to the Yugoslavs against the Italians, the French sought to unite them against the Germans. This was never possible and in the end the French succeeded only in confirming the enmity of the Italians while shaking the confidence of the Yugoslavs.[3]

Even before King Alexander's assassination in Marseilles in 1934, and the lesson in League of Nations futility that followed, Yugoslavia had begun to chart a more flexible course in its international relations.[4] Subsequent demonstrations of the inability or unwillingness of Britain and France to stand up to the German and Italian challenge confirmed the Yugoslavs in their new commitment to neutrality and manoeuvre. Reconciliation with Italy was the most pressing requirement, but efforts were also made to improve relations with Hungary and Bulgaria. Such success as these moves had was largely attributable to Milan Stojadinović, the Prince Regent Paul's nominee as Premier and Foreign Minister from 1935 to 1939. Stojadinović's fascist inclinations, fawning regard for Mussolini and willingness to serve as a junior partner in Italian imperialism allowed for an abatement in even the Duce's inveterate hostility towards Yugoslavia.

By the summer of 1939 Prince Paul and his ministers appeared unlikely either to insist upon or long enjoy any existence save on sufferance of the Axis powers. They presided over a country still divided within and increasingly isolated without. The Little Entente was dead, along with Czechoslovakia; the Balkan Pact dying, along with its member states' faith that common interest implied common strength. Both revisionist and anti-revisionist states - in the first instance Hungary and Romania - were beginning their scramble to align themselves with the Axis; the former out of gratitude for revisionism rewarded, the latter out of terror lest revisionism unregulated wipe them off the map of Europe. In their respective categories Bulgaria and Yugoslavia seemed next in line. Germany now possessed not only a stranglehold on the Yugoslav economy, but a common frontier in former Austria as well; while in the south, Italy had just acquired a potential second front in Albania. Both Stojadinović and Prince Paul had already been called upon to journey to Berlin to bear witness to the majesty of the Third Reich and to proclaim their devotion to Germany, if not yet their readiness to withdraw from the League of Nations or sign the Anti-Comintern Pact. Britain and France seemed ever more remote.

Yet as war drew near neither power accepted that the South-Eastern European states were necessarily lost to them. Guarantees against Axis aggression were offered to Greece and Romania in April 1939, although without any idea on the part of their authors as to how they might be honoured. In Yugoslavia there were hopeful signs. The pro-Axis Stojadinović was dismissed by Prince Paul in February. His successor as Primier, Dragiša Cvetković, was regarded as a none too honest opportunist, but he was at least favourably disposed towards Britain and France.[5] Moreover, he had been expressly charged by the Prince Regent with the task of reaching an accommodation with the Croats which would defuse their separatism and reconcile them, even at the eleventh hour, to continued membership in the Yugoslav community. Such an agreement, known as the *Sporazum,* was signed at the end of August. It provided for a Croatian *Banovina* (province) with wide autonomy and permitted Vladko Maček, leader of the Croatian Peasant Party and tribune of his people, to enter the Cvetković government as Vice-Premier. With the Croats apparently conciliated and Yugoslav unity seemingly placed on firmer foundations the British and French could feel greater confidence that the independent spirit and anti-German sentiment of the majority of Serbs would serve to deny the country to the Axis. That the presence of the Croats in the government might compel Prince Paul and Cvetković to take into account their perhaps differing views on foreign policy and national defence was not immediately appreciated.

For the British, however, the most encouraging factor, once the threat of war caused them to look with new interest at Yugoslavia, was Prince Paul himself. Educated at Christ Church, Oxford, married to the sister of the Duchess of Kent and speaking English and reading *The Tatler* at home with his family, Prince Paul was that great rarity among Balkan statesmen: a civilized gentleman whom London could both understand and trust.[6] He accorded to British ministers in Belgrade the same ease of access and close personal relations as he naturally enjoyed among official and court circles in Britain. And since the Cvetković government did his bidding, the British seemed assured that their interests would not go unregarded. Yet it was a measure of Britain's objective weakness in South-Eastern Europe that so much reliance had to be placed on Prince Paul's Anglophilia. As the Foreign Office appreciated once they began seeking to bolster Yugoslav resistance to Axis dragooning, they had few other cards to play; they could neither effectively threaten nor materially aid the Yugoslavs, they could only appeal to Prince Paul to "do the right thing".[7]

Prince Paul returned from a state visit to Hitler in June 1939 convinced that a European war was both inevitable and imminent. He and his future War Minister, General Petar Pesic, set out soon thereafter for Paris and London to investigate the intentions of the western powers and to explain to them Yugoslavia's position. They maintained that Yugoslavia would be unable to enter the war on the side of

Britain and France at the outset; rather, they would proclaim their neutrality, keep their country and army intact and only become belligerents at the moment of maximum benefit to themselves and the Allies. General Maurice Gamelin, Chief of the French General Staff, did not like the Yugoslavs' scenario. They would not, he told Pešić, be able to maintain their neutrality in the face of inevitable German exactions. Instead they should enter the war as soon as Britain and France seized Salonika, as he hoped they would do when war broke out. The British, whose military preparedness impressed Pesic less than that of the French, were on the other hand more sympathetic towards the idea of Yugoslav (and Balkan) neutrality.[8]

And indeed when war came in September the Yugoslavs immediately declared their neutrality. To the Western Allies this was represented as a temporary expedient, necessitated by the country's military unpreparedness and exposed position, but not the product of any doubts as to the outcome of the war; while to the Axis powers it was portrayed as the best guarantee of their pre-eminent economic and political interests in the region: to the former as neutrality with a mask, to the latter as neutrality with a tilt.

The different reactions with which Pešić and Prince Paul had met in Paris and London in the summer of 1939 pointed to a continuing divergence in French and British attitudes towards the role of the South-Eastern European countries. With the onset of war the two Allies' disagreement was transformed into a strategic debate which continued through the spring of 1940. As in 1915 the French ministers and generals itched to open a Balkan front based on Salonika - a front which would provide their restive population with the reassurance of action and themselves with the reassuring diversion of German troops away from the west. The British argued instead for the formation of a neutral Balkan bloc, including or even led by Italy, which would keep war from the area and obviate the need for a merely diversionary Salonika front.[9]

Reflecting the importance to the Serbs of Salonika as a port for the supply and, if need be, for the evacuation of their army, Prince Paul was initially enthusiastic about the French plan; until, that is, he realized that the Western Allies did not dispose of the troops required to make a Salonika front Yugoslavia's effective protector, and not simply the means by which the country would be drawn into the war.[10] Since General Maxime Weygand, principal proponent and would-be commander of a Balkan campaign, had at his base in Syria only one division that might be sent to Salonika (and could hold out the hope of securing just two more) it became obvious to the Greeks and Yugoslavs that the French regarded their own contribution as merely the catalyst which would bring the large Balkan armies into play.[11] The Greeks and Yugoslavs wanted protection, especially from Italy, not precipitation into a war against Germany. The British stand against Balkan adventures with inadequate forces thus met with Prince Paul's aproval, although the underlying premise of the British strategists that continued Italian nonbelligerency was the main prize caused the Yugoslavs to worry that concessions might be made to Mussolini in the Balkans which would prove to be at their expense.[12]

Given the inability of the French to mount a Balkan operation unaided, the consistent opposition of the British and the trepidation of the Greeks, Yugoslavs and Turks ensured that French plans came to naught before France itself went down in defeat. To the end, however, the French sought to provoke a conflagration in the Balkans. In the first days of June their Minister in Belgrade, Raymond Brugère, implored Prince Paul to order his armies to fall upon the Italians in Albania as soon as Mussolini entered the war. The Foreign Office felt that the French in their desperation were both exaggerating the Italian threat and neglecting to consider the likely consequences for Yugoslavia were Prince Paul to intervene in Albania - an act which would probably set off a general Balkan land-grab. But the disapproval of the Foreign Office was tempered by the realization that the British Chiefs of Staff were coming to share the French view that a flare-up in the Balkans was desirable.[13]

In May London had declined to assure the Yugoslavs that an attack upon them by Italy (which then appeared imminent) would be met by a British declaration of war, despite pleas to this effect from Ronald Ian Campbell, the Minister in Belgrade.[14] But in June, with the situation critical in the west and the Italians obviously bent upon hostilities, the Chiefs of Staff began to reassess their stand against an extension of the war to South-Eastern Europe. In a report to the Chiefs of Staff Committee on 8 June the Joint Planning Committee contended that Balkan policy should be modified: the Germans would now be hurt and the Allies helped by the creation of a diversion in the Balkans. Arguing that the only means of denying the Axis powers eventual dominion over the entire region was to get Greece and Yugoslavia into the war before France fell, the Joint Planners concluded that both states should be urged to declare their belligerency, that Turkey should be prodded to play a more active role and that Yugoslavia should be given an Anglo-French guarantee against attack by Italy.[15] The Foreign Office disagreed, discounting the effectiveness of a guarantee to Yugoslavia ("since we could in fact give her little if any direct support in the event of Italian aggression against her"), as well as the likelihood of the Greeks or Yugoslavs intervening on the Allied side unless and until their own territories were violated.[16] These realistic arguments were brushed aside, however, when on 11 June the Chiefs of Staff Committee embraced the Joint Planners' recommendations. Italy having declared war the previous day, the Chiefs maintained that "we feel that there is little doubt that any military relief, however small, which we could obtain from a diversion in the Balkans would be to our immediate advantage."[17]

The hope that some relief might be forthcoming from the Balkans was of course illusory, and evaporated completely with the fall of France and the refusal of the Turks to play their assigned part and enter the war against Italy.[18] Nonetheless in the days following the French armistice the Foreign Office and the military continued to keep open the admittedly "somewhat academic" question of whether or not the Balkans should be set alight. The verdict that emerged in early July was positive. In no position to strike the match themselves, the British could only resolve to do their worst to exploit the rivalry between Germany and the Soviet Union that had opened up with the Russians' seizure of Bessarabia and Northern Bukovina in June. British satisfaction at the development of Russo-German tension in the Balkans was tempered only by concern lest the machinations of the Soviets completely terrorize the Turks.[19]

Despite their previous reluctance to join the contest in South-Eastern Europe - and their present inability to do more than egg on third parties - the British had inherited a good measure of their defeated ally's Balkan activism. With Churchill now at the helm (and he had been more favourably inclined than his colleagues towards the Balkan strategy of the French) and with Italy at war, both personal and strategic obstacles to British involvement in the region had been removed. Only the strength to take the initiative continued to elude, in the Balkans as everywhere else. During the next eight months the British nonetheless stepped-up their campaign to encourage Prince Paul, his government and the Serbian people to stand firm against German blandishments as these became more importunate; until in the end, in February and March 1941, the British were to find themselves adopting the same provocative policy formerly promoted by the French: despatching a weak expeditionary force to Greece and then demanding of the Yugoslavs that they make the British commitment more tenable by attacking the Italians in Albania. What the Foreign Office had felt tempted to decry as selfish and irresponsible when urged upon the Yugoslavs by the French was to appear a moral imperative once British and Commonwealth forces were at risk.

CHAPTER II

A FIGHT FOR BRITAIN: PRINCE PAUL AND THE COUP D'ETAT OF 27 MARCH 1941

(i)

If the original British objectives of creating a neutral Balkan bloc, maintaining Italian nonbelligerency and preventing spread of war to South-Eastern Europe had been imperilled by the French and then abandoned to the logic of total war, Hitler's plans for the peaceful incorporation of the region in the Axis economic and political orbit were ultimately frustrated by his allies, the Italians, and that same inexorable logic.

South-Eastern Europe was not an area which Hitler envisaged as playing anything but a subsidiary part in the new German empire. Located on "the right wing of German expansion", the region was an important source of oil, nonferrous metals and foodstuffs, but it need not be occupied or annexed.[1] The exercise of political leadership in the states bordering the Adriatic and Eastern Mediterranean could be left to Mussolini, or at least the prospect of such hegemony dangled before him as bait with which to secure his compliance with German wishes. On one occasion, in August 1939, Hitler urged the Italians to settle accounts with Yugoslavia, but

Mussolini, unready for war, demurred.[2] From then until the Italians' failure to subdue Greece in late 1940 compelled Hitler to decide to settle accounts himself, the Germans sought to restrain Mussolini from attacking Yugoslavia or from unleashing his Ustaše proteges to foment a separatist rebellion in Croatia. The Duce was repeatedly assured that dominion over Yugoslavia would one day be his, but not just yet. Any premature move to seize Dalmatia or detach Croatia, he was warned, would set off a general Balkan conflict which might drive the Russians and British into each others' arms.[3]

However remote that prospect in 1940, the Soviets' unwillingness to renounce an interest in the fate of the Balkan states had become obvious. While the effect of the Russians' depredatory attentions was to drive Romania irrevocably into the Axis camp, in the case of Yugoslavia the Soviets' new involvement in the region seemed to hold out to Prince Paul and his government the hope of enlisting a powerful counterweight to Germany and Italy, and so maintaining their neutrality. Sacrificing his dynasty's longheld anti-Bolshevik principles, Prince Paul had ordered the opening of direct contacts with the USSR in early 1940. Passing from discreet feelers in Ankara in March to negotiations for a trade agreement in April, the Yugoslav initiative culminated in the establishment of full diplomatic relations on 24 June, two days after France left the war.[4]

The bewilderment felt by the Serbs at the crushing defeat inflicted upon their traditional ally and the disappointment that was openly expressed at the French failure to continue the struggle from their colonies were allayed to some extent by the prospect of new support from the east. Campbell reported from Belgrade in July that although Britain's resolution to fight on alone had produced a noticeable rise in British prestige in Yugoslavia, "Until we can show military successes to our credit against Germany and Italy it is likely that many hopes will be turned to the Soviet Union as the only possible saviour of Balkan independence."[5]

The Foreign Office understood, but regretted these sentiments. Not only was the Yugoslavs' implicit judgment on

Britain's strength wounding, but the Foreign Office was certain that Belgrade's new-found faith in the USSR was misplaced.[6] And so it was; but in the second half of 1940 the Russians did not simply echo British entreaties that Yugoslavia not submit to Axis pressure, they also on two occasions promised arms. Though their offers remained unfulfilled and Prince Paul ceased before long to expect deliverance from this quarter, the British rather resented Soviet intimations of largesse. In no position themselves to meet Yugoslavia's military requirements, they preferred to avoid the subject altogether.[7]

Campbell described the Yugoslav attitude towards the Axis following the fall of France as one of pliability masquerading as subservience.[8] The government was discriminating in favour of Axis propaganda in the news budgets of the controlled press and was dutiful in its obeisance to Nazi sensibilities, even making the occasional anti-Semitic gesture.[9] It was resolved to meet Axis economic demands, even to the extent of producing food shortages in the home market and clogging the railways with shipments bound for Germany.[10] And the composition of the cabinet and administration was being manipulated so as to present a pro-Axis facade. The government's efforts, Campbell wrote in July, represented "a balancing act at a milestone nearer the Axis camp."[11] Yet neither he nor the Foreign Office questioned that the Yugoslavs were pro-British at heart and could be relied upon to side with Britain in the end.[12] No disagreement was expressed with the Yugoslav government's continuing conviction that the greatest service which it could render the British war effort was the save itself until such time as the tide began to turn. If there was a contradiction between the British commitment - at least in principle - to stir up trouble in the Balkans and the Yugoslavs' dependence upon its avoidance in order to maintain their neutrality, then that was resolvable with time. As Philip Nichols of the Southern Department suggested in August, Britain might later incite the Italians to make demands upon the Yugoslav government which would force it off its fence. That it would come down on the right side was not yet in doubt.[13]

In the meantime, unable either to deliver arms or to promise naval and air support in event of Italian attack, the British resorted to endeavouring to sustain Prince Paul's morale. The method chosen by the Foreign Office was to draft encouraging letters to the Prince Regent for despatch under the signature of King George VI. The idea of a royal correspondence had originated in April, when the Foreign Office considered using the King's good offices to convince Prince Paul that Tsar Boris of Bulgaria was both trustworthy and a potential recruit to a neutral Balkan bloc.[14] Events had proved otherwise, but the tactic was revived in mid-June when, in the midst of the French collapse, the fear grew that Prince Paul's anxiety might lead him to abandon neutrality for abject subservience towards the Axis powers. The first letter testifying to Britian's faith in him and portraying the growth in the United Kingdom's armed might was sent on 3 July.[15]

Whatever tonic effect the King's message may have had, it was only temporary, for a month later Prince Paul was again showing signs of despair. He told Campbell on 9 August at his summer residence on Lake Bled that he expected Italian territorial demands at any moment and that he no longer held out any hope of Russian help. "He always told everyone, especially the Germans, Yugoslavia would fight, but he clearly did not see of what use it could be," Campbell reported. The country might lose two million men and still be overrun in a fortnight. The Prince Regent's gloom elicited on 22 August another Foreign Office message on the progress of the British war effort, detailing the increase in munitions production and pointing to the firm American commitment to Britain (a point excised from the first message sent on behalf of the King).[16]

The next initiative in the campaign of regal evangelism was suggested in mid-October by Sir Orme Sargent, Deputy Permanent Under-Secretary of State. Reasoning that Prince Paul must "be feeling very lonely and unhappy" after the movement of German troops into Romania, and with a similar penetration of Bulgaria in prospect, Sargent canvassed the idea of another brotherly letter from the King. Pierson Dixon of the Southern Department opined that arms and not letters were what was required, but Campbell reported from Belgrade that another royal message would be heldful, provided it were truly personal and sympathetic in tone.[17] The drafting was put into abeyance however by the Italian invasion of Greece on 28 October.

No doubt relieved that Mussolini had found another victim for his frustrated machismo, the Yugoslavs promptly declared their neutrality. There were some in the Foreign Office who regarded this attitude toward their former ally as craven and wished somehow to push them into the conflict, but it was soon decided that the risk of involving the Germans in the Greek war at this stage was greater than any advantage which the Yugoslavs might render the Greeks.[18] The Yugoslavs would be asked only to make their neutrality as benevolent as possible towards Greece, especially by denying transit rights across their territory to either Axis power.[19]

Then as now there was debate over the extent to which Mussolini acted independently of Hitler in attacking Greece, but it was clear to the Foreign Office that the Germans would have to extricate the Italians if they got "into a mess". It was thus resolved, in Cadogan's words, "to make the mess as bad as possible so as to cause the Germans the maximum of embarrassment".[20] Eventually this was to be accomplished by lending Athens all the military support it was in Britain's power to provide - and in the Greeks' interest to accept. Meanwhile the second and more personal letter of encouragement from King George VI was transmitted to Prince Paul on 15 November.[21]

That the war was closing in on Yugoslavia was attested by others during November with heavier emphasis than the British were able to bring to bear in their now reiterated demands that transit rights be denied the Axis powers. On 5 November Italian aircraft bombed the Macedonian city of Bitola, offering an object lesson in the perils of either assisting the Greeks or contemplating the pre-emptive occupation of Salonika.[22] While from the Germans there came on 25 November a summons to Foreign Minister Cincar-Marković to wait upon Ribbentrop in Austria two days later.

Hitler had already decided to invade Russia in the spring of 1941. It was thus necessary to put an end to the stalemated war in Greece as early as possible in the new year. This would prevent (or eliminate) any reestablishment of British forces on the continent within striking distance of the vital Romanian oilfields and, at the same time, put German bombers within range of British bases in the Eastern Mediterranean. Yugoslavia was not to be allowed the luxury of remaining an imponderable in Hitler's calculations for much longer. As Cincar-Marković was told when he met with Ribbentrop and Hitler at Fuschl and Berchtesgaden on 27 and 28 November, "the time had now come when every European state had to take a stand". Yugoslavia was offered a place in the new order in the shape of a three-sided non-aggression pact in which Italy and Germany would undertake to guarantee its present frontiers, would promise not to demand any military aid or transit rights for their troops and would express their intention to remember Yugoslavia's special interest in Salonika.[23] The terms were generous - and indicative of the importance which Hitler accorded the peaceful incorporation of Yugoslavia in the Axis fold before mounting his invasions of Greece and the USSR. Yet Hitler could afford to be generous; it was Mussolini who was to foot the bill. As instructed by Prince Paul (and doubtless against his own inclinations), Cincar-Marković was non-committal in his responses.

The crisis in Yugoslavia's relations with the Axis in late November came at a time when the Foreign Office was otherwise encouraged by what was seen as a recent stiffening of the Yugoslavs' resolve to resist any German or Italian violation of their territory and to insist upon their special claims on Salonika.[24] The resistance of the Greeks and British support for them were credited with influencing this firmness, despite the likelihood that the prolongation of both would soon force the Yugoslavs into a showdown with Hitler.[25]

When Campbell realized on 23 November that demands from Germany were imminent he appealed to London for another stiffening message for Prince Paul and - a significant addition -

for "other staunch elements". He asked for a formal communication that would not only counsel resistance to any Axis demands incompatible with Yugoslav sovereignty, but would also promise all possible British assistance should the Yugoslavs feel called upon to defend their independence. Though he found Campbell's accompanying draft text circumlocutory, Churchill agreed that "the moment is appropriate and the action needful". Anticipating, however, the reaction of the Chiefs of Staff to any suggestion of armed help, he went on, "If we cannot promise any effective material aid, we can at any rate assure them that, just as we did last time, we will see their wrongs are righted in the eventual victory".[26] The Chiefs reported on 24 November that indeed there was little Britain could do to help defend Yugoslavia, save to continue doing what was already being done for Greece. Depending upon the attitude of the Bulgarians, Salonika just might be held, while a few submarine raids into the Adriatic and some air cover over southern Macedonia could perhaps be arranged, but no direct support on the ground would be possible.[27]

Besides exhorting the Yugoslavs to resist Axis pressure the resulting message was confined to offering the vague assurance that Britian would "make common cause with them" if they decided to fight: "Yugoslavia will be fighting side by side with us and our allies, and we could look forward once again to achieving a victory by our joint effort that would secure to Yugoslavia all her rights and interests." Prince Paul, who doubtless realized how little this actually meant, nonetheless expressed himself "deeply touched" when Campbell delivered the text to him on 25 November.[28] For as he informed the British Minister, the expected call from Berlin had just arrived.[29] The reaction of Campbell's "other staunch elements" can only be surmised; but for them "common cause" with the mighty British Empire would necessarily have implied more than a submarine foray into the Adriatic.

Romania having signed the Tripartite Pact on 23 November, the Foreign Office was upset by the news that Cincar-Marković was journeying to meet Ribbentrop and hastened to offer

Prince Paul yet more advice - advice now coupled with a warning. Although the British government understood his predicament, they counted upon him to give nothing away to the Germans. No treaty or pact which facilitated German or Italian military aims in the Balkans, especially the Tripartite Pact, could be countenanced.[30] Thus the ante was raised; no longer was denial of passage to Axis forces the only requirement were Prince Paul and his government to prolong their neutral state of grace. Accession to the Tripartite Pact was now expressly forbidden them.[31]

Prince Paul reported to Campbell several days later that Hitler and Ribbentrop had not demanded adherence to the Tripartite Pact, although they had thrown out hints. A subsequent and explicit request would not surprise him. The Southern Department was sceptical that this was all that had transpired, but could see no alternative for the time being but to give Prince Paul the benefit of the doubt.[32]

The Russians, also distributed by the prospect of German advances in the Balkans in the autumn of 1940, again entered the lists. Unlike the British, however, they did not demand of the Yugoslavs a leap of faith unsustained by material support. Without any preliminaries the Soviet government on 23 November offered the Yugoslav Military Attaché in Moscow the opportunity to buy all the war matériel his government required at whatever price it chose to pay. The only reservation was that the equipment might not be of the most modern design. The offer was accepted with the alacrity demanded, but as the immediate danger passed the Soviets lapsed into enigmatic and unforthcoming silence.[33] With the Yugoslav government evidently resolved during the remainder of the year to withstand German pressure, it probably seemed unnecessary to Moscow to risk arousing German ire by overly demonstrative support.[34] On the other hand, after January 1941 the signs that Prince Paul's government was succumbing to German blandishments no doubt convinced the Russians that the game was not worth the candle.

(ii)

Despite their inability to provide arms or promise protection, the British did not rely exclusively upon missionary diplomacy to deter Prince Paul from aligning his country with the Axis powers. The record of the activities of Britain's intelligence agency - known variously as SIS (Secret Intelligence Service), MI6 and "C" - is understandably obscure. But the activities of Section "D" and MI(R), the special operations agencies set up by SIS in 1938 and taken over by the Special Operations Executive (SOE) upon its formation in July 1940, have been more fully reported.[35] Although documentary evidence about SOE is also sparse - and likely to remain so - the recollections of former operatives have become almost voluminous in recent years. Thus the workings of their upstart organization, which had to struggle to achieve recognition for both its role and accomplishments against an oftentimes hostile military and civilian bureaucracy (not to mention a sceptical posterity), have become better known than those of its theoretically non-existent rival, SIS.[36]

In part the efforts of the secret services were designed to reinforce the work of the diplomats, creating by the use of subsidies, bribes and propaganda a pro-British climate of opinion in Yugoslavia (and especially in Serbia) that would make it difficult for Prince Paul and his ministers to knuckle under to the Axis. Implicit in this campaign was an interest in maintaining contacts with and influence over such elements as might prove ready and able to overturn the Prince Regent and lead the nation into war should he betray Britain's trust. The third task of the secret organizations was more far-reaching yet: to prepare the ground for wartime sabotage and post-occupation resistance - activities that then fell under the rubric of "economic warfare".

Although in other countries in the region, notably Hungary and Bulgaria, the diplomats found it difficult to support, or even to tolerate, the activities of their heterodox colleagues,[37] in Yugoslavia there was less friction between the Legation and the secret organizations. This was the case despite the fact that

Campbell remained charged with maintaining the closest possible rapport with Prince Paul's government even after other British agents had begun endeavouring to subvert it - and that their activities in this direction were far from secret among the loquacious Serbs.[38]

Although some links were maintained with Slovene irredentist groups, for the British secret services operating in Yugoslavia anti-Axis activity meant, first of all, work among and cooperation with Serb nationalists.[39] The other peoples of Yugoslavia were generally discounted, as was the political left.[40] The vehicle which proved most amenable to the purposes of SOE was the small Serbian Agrarian Party (*Zemljoradnička stranka*) of Dr. Milan Gavrilović. While various individual Serb politicians and government officials cooperated closely with the British (most notably Jovan Djonović, a former diplomat and a Republican Party leader from Montenegro, and Stojan Gavrilović, a senior official in the Ministry of Foreign Affairs*), the Agrarian Party as a whole became associated with the British effort. The Party was represented in the Cvetković-Maček cabinet, but also had close relations with the traditional Serbian parties - the Radicals and Democrats - in "opposition" since the imposition of the dictatorship in 1929. The Agrarians' leadership, in the person of Miloš Tupanjanin (Gavrilović's deputy during his posting as Minister in Moscow), requested and was provided with financial subsidies from July 1940. These were intended to enable the Party to maintain an anti-Axis line both in public and in the councils of state to which it had access. Less realistically, the British also expected the Party to offer leadership in any campaign of sabotage of guerrilla warfare that might follow upon the country's occupation. Thus besides money (£5,000 monthly), the Agrarians were provided with small arms and wireless transmitters.[41]

In addition to their close relationship with the Agrarian Party, SOE established contacts in 1940 with the legandary Serbian nationalist association *Narodna Odbrana* (National Defence), the organization accused by Vienna - incorrectly but

*Stojan Gavrilović was no relation to Milan Gavrilovic.

plausibly - of plotting the assassination of Archduke Franz Ferdinand. Its president, *"Vojvoda"* Ilija Trifunović-Birčanin, a celebrated *Komite* leader in the Balkan and First World Wars, became a prized contact of the British; and the *Narodna Odbrana* was also alloted a subsidy. As early as May 1940 MI(R) singled out Trifunović-Birčanin's *komite* veterans as a readymade guerrilla cadre whose plans ought to be coordinated with those of the British in anticipation of hostilities spreading to the Balkans.[42] Nationalist-minded bishops of the Serbian Orthodox Church were also canvassed for support for some success.[43]

While such links were maintained on the basis of common interest and a shared commitment to the defeat of the Axis, other British activities depended upon Yugoslavs of a more mercenary cast of mind. Notable among these were the Sokić brothers, owner-editors of the Belgrade newspaper *Pravda*. In the spring of 1940 they were awarded a "douceur" from the British; but growing more greedy, they demanded a regular monthly subsidy of 150,000 dinars in order to maintain their paper's pro-British line. Apparently they did not get it, for *Pravda* went over to the Axis in the course of the summer.[44] Bribes, however, were nonetheless considered later on as the surest means by which important Yugoslav generals might be induced at the proper moment to cooperate with the British forces in Greece and to sabotage strategic mines.[45]

Most of Britain's cloak and dagger work in Yugoslavia was entrusted to a small band of amateurs recruited from the ranks of British businessmen, mining engineers, journalists and junior diplomatic personnel already in the country. Section "D" 's operations were directed initially by Julius Hanau, a South African-born arms dealer long resident in Belgrade; and after November 1940 (as SOE) by Tom Masterson, sent to Yugoslavia under the guise of serving as First Secretary at the Legation.[46] Agents of SOE in Belgrade included Julian Amery, John Bennett, Peter Boughey, Alexander Glen, A. Dunlop Mackenzie, Hugh Seton-Watson and George Taylor - all formally on the staff of the Legation - the journalists Terence Atherton, Basil Davidson and Ralph Parker, and the mining engineers S. W. ("Bill") Bailey and D. T. ("Bill") Hudson. Other operatives were contributed by Chester Beatty, the mining magnate and friend of Section "D"'s founder, Colonel Lawrence Grand. Beatty was persuaded to second several of his employees from Selection Trust's Yugoslav subsidiary, Trepča Mines, for service with Section "D"/SOE at no expense to the British taxpayer.[47]

Any such roster of SIS agents in Yugoslavia is impossible to compile. Their chiefs, however, may have been the resident service attachés.[48] They appear to have recruited operatives from the same small pool of Britons as did Section "D"/SOE, as well as from among Yugoslav citizens. Whatever their affiliations, the attachés were directed in the spring of 1940 to reassign their routine duties to their assistants and to take on the tasks of maintaining liaison with expected co-belligerents, gathering intelligence and plotting sabotage and guerrilla warfare under the "cover" of their Legation posts. MI(R) christened the retreaded service attachés "Shadow Missions" and asked the Foreign Office in May to facilitate their new role.[49] While neither the division of personnel nor responsibility between Section "D"/SOE and the "Shadow Missions" (MI(R)/SIS?) was very clear cut at this time, generally the attachés seem to have concentrated on maintaining liaison with anti-Axis elements in the Yugoslav armed forces, while Section "D"/SOE concerned itself with civilians of a similar persuasion.[50] Both, however, interested themselves in sabotage (particularly of Danube shipping), in fomenting rebellions in Albania and Bulgaria from Yugoslavia and in the identification and encouragement of potential Yugoslav resistance leaders - whether against Prince Paul's government or an eventual Axis occupier.

The first report that Serbs with whom the British were in contact were considering a coup d'état against Prince Paul was sent by Campbell to the Foreign Office on 25 July 1940. Campbell reported that the Serbs proposed to utilize the growing discontent with the government's pro-Axis policy to overturn the Prince Regent and to declare common cause with Great Britain. The *Narodna Odbrana,* the Orthodox Church, significant sections of the army and "the peasants" supported the plan according to Campbell's informants. It was their intention that simultaneous coups take place in Yugoslavia and Bulgaria (the latter to be led by the Bulgarian Agrarians with whom SOE also maintained relations) and that a South Slav federation be proclaimed. Violence against both Prince Paul and Tsar Boris was foreseen. The time for action would come, they believed, when Britain had amassed large forces in the Mediterranean and Middle East. The plan's sponsors also maintained that, if successful, they would attack the Italians in Albania and defend their frontiers against any resulting German invasion.

Campbell was dubious both as to the conspirators' ability to carry out their plan and its timeliness. He warned London that with Germany's military might unshaken a coup in Yugoslavia was unlikely to enhance Britain's chances of promoting Russo-German conflict in the Balkans. Nor did he believe that Britain should tolerate the use of violence against Prince Paul. He reported that he had ordered the Legation staff to give no encouragement to the proposal which had, he emphasized, come from the Serbs themselves.

Disregarding like Campbell the plotters' own condition that British strength in the area must be increased, the Foreign Office agreed that a coup d'état would at present be premature. However, it was felt that such a movement might later prove to be "of first class importance to H.M. Government". Hugh Dalton, Minister of Economic Warfare (and hence responsible for SOE), was reluctant to let any such promising opportunity slip by, but agreed that the time for an anti-Axis revolt had not yet come. A draft reply for Campbell along these lines was prepared and, after being sanctioned by the Chiefs of Staff, was despatched on 3 August. Campbell was to inform the Serbs that their plan did not "at present" meet with British approval, but that,

> the question is of such importance that the eventual success of some such scheme must not be endangered by premature action, more especially at a moment when they [HMG] are unable to give a guarantee of any support. No scheme could,

however, command the support of HMG which involved the doing of any violence whatever to the Regent.[51]

In mid-October, amidst concern arising out of the Germans' occupation of Romania, Campbell again reported the possibility of a coup d'état. Rumour had it that the army, or perhaps even Prince Paul himself, might be planning an anti-Axis putsch. The popular mood, Campbell believed, was now far more favourable to such a move. He asked if Britain would now welcome a change in regime. While at least one junior member of the Southern Department relished the prospect, the deciding majority agreed with Campbell that Prince Paul and his government remained their best bet. Campbell was instructed on 24 October that a coup d'état seemed unlikely at present to serve Britain's interests. These were that the Yugoslavs should resist if attacked, that they should refuse any territorial concessions and, most of all, that they should deny passage to Axis troops en route to Greece. The Chiefs of Staff concurred in these desiderata.[52]

The Yugoslav attitude on these points was more important than ever to the British as 1940 faded into 1941. A German operation designed to resuce Mussolini in Greece, an eventuality foreseen two months earlier, was now obviously in preparation. Churchill became convinced that this was the case in late December, apparently on the basis of intercepted German radio messages. He ordered Dalton to reinforce SOE's operations in Yugoslavia. Dalton did so by despatching George Taylor, then serving as chief of staff to SOE's director, Sir Frank Nelson, to Belgrade. Taylor, who left for Yugoslavia in mid-January, was briefed before his departure by both Dalton and Eden. He was directed to intensify efforts to halt the spread of German influence in the Balkan states, to organize post-occupational resistance and sabotage should these efforts fail, and to work to disrupt the Danube traffic in Romanian oil bound for the Reich.[53]

In early January the British grew apprehensive that Prince Paul and his government were proving "unsound". Cincar-Marković was reported to have waffled in answer to a Greek request for assurance that Yugoslavia would not allow

German troops free passage through the country. London immediately demanded a clarification from the Yugoslavs on this score.[54] Meanwhile Prince Paul had reacted with alarm to Campbell's news on 11 January that Britain intended to enlarge on its commitment of forces to Greece, adding machanized troops to the RAF squadrons already there. The Prince accused the British of attempting to drag Yugoslavia into the war by creating a Salonika front, a front which would merely provoke an otherwise unlikely German move to overrun the peninsula. He nonetheless repeated to Campbell that Yugoslavia would never allow free passage to either German or Italian troops.[55]

Certain that the Germans were planning a descent into Greece, Churchill and the War Cabinet agreed on 14 January that Prince Paul's protestations should be ignored. It was for the Greek government, not for Prince Paul, to decide whether or not British land forces should fight in Greece.[56] As reports arrived in subsequent days indicating renewed equivocation in Belgrade on the issue of passage, the suspicion grew in Churchill's mind that Prince Paul was attempting to use the transit rights question as a lever with which to compel the Greeks to decline Britain's offer of troops. He surmised, too, that the Prince might be trying to curry favour with the Germans by creating conditions in which he could claim credit for keeping the British out of Greece.[57] When the Greeks did cite Yugoslavia's unhelpful attitude in turning down the British offer at thsi time, Prince Paul's stock slumped further in British eyes, despite the likelihood that the Greek excuse was as convenient as it was ingenuous.[58] Britain might now know that Hitler intended to consolidate his hold on South-Eastern Europe, but Athens, no less than Belgrade, still sought reasons to believe otherwise. Despite numerous instances of tergiversation, neither the Greeks nor the Turks ever completely forfeited Britain's confidence and esteem; Prince Paul, on the other hand, was beginning to lose both.

With signs multiplying in January that German troops were infiltrating Bulgaria in significant numbers, the British attempted to persuade the Turks and Yugoslavs to issue a joint warning that they would not tolerate an outright occupation. Even had such a warning been likely to give the Germans pause, Belgrade and Ankara dared not take the chance and evaded British promptings. Although Cvetković declared ostentatiously to Campbell in late January that his government knew its duty and would fight rather than see Bulgaria occupied and Yugoslavia surrounded, Prince Paul was less forthcoming. Pleading Croat opposition to a firm line over Bulgaria and pointing to the Turks' lack of interest in a joint demarche, the Prince Regent explained that he must reserve his options.[59] Consulted by Eden on 29 January, the Soviet Ambassador, Ivan Maisky, was no more helpful. Although the Soviet Union would not make difficulties for the Turks, neither would it oppose German advances in the Balkans.[60]

Casting about for some means of stiffening the Yugoslavs' resolve, and bearing in mind Prince Paul's comments about Croat opinion, the Foreign Office sought from the military some crumbs in arms and equipment that might be offered to the Serb generals and, from the Cabinet, some territorial crumbs that might be promised to the Croats in order to stanch their defeatism. Not surprisingly it proved easier to promise territorial compensation in the future than to deliver arms in the present.

Campbell and the Foreign Office proposed to the Chiefs of Staff in mid-January that war matériel captured from the Italians in North Africa be offered to the Yugoslavs. Not only would such an overture make a good impression, they argued, but it would also facilitate the opening of staff talks and thus the opportunity for Britain to get close to General Pešić and his subordinates.[61] This request was rejected out of hand.[62] The Foreign Office then asked in early February that at least some token military assistance, perhaps a few Bren gun carriers, be offered to Belgrade. This, they maintained, would have "political effects out of all proportion to its military significance". Colonel William ("Wild Bill") Donovan, Roosevelt's future director of OSS then on a Balkan fact-finding tour for the President, was reported to concur.[63] Yet this request, too, the Chiefs of Staff refused. There were no military supplies to spare.[64]

The suggestion that the Croats might be induced to support a firmer stand against Germany by promises of territorial revisions in Istria and Dalmatia came from Milan Gavrilović in the USSR in late January. Although expressing itself strongly adverse to "territorial bribery in advance of events", the Foreign Office did go so far as to ask Arnold Toynbee of the Foreign Office Research and Press Service for a paper on the subject, explaining that "it would be useful to know what sort of case the Yugoslavs could produce in support of frontier rectifications on these lines".[65] When Sir Stafford Cripps repeated Gavrilović's suggestion on 23 February, the Foreign Office reaction was less fastidious.[66]

German pressure on Yugoslavia had increased sharply. Cvetković and Cincar-Marković had been summoned to meet Hitler and Ribbentrop in Salzburg on 14 February. As Prince Paul revealed to Campbell two days later, they had been offered accession to the Tripartite Pact on persuasive terms: no passage of troops or use of Yugoslav railways would be required by Germany in its forthcoming moves into Bulgaria and Greece. Prince Paul told Campbell that he intended to play for time.[67]

The strength of Yugoslavia's ethnographic claim on all but the west coast of Istria was affirmed by the FRPS.[68] But it was not this that produced the War Cabinet's sudden decision on 27 February to authorize Eden (then shuttling about the Eastern Mediterranean with General Sir John Dill, the CIGS) to offer the Yugoslavs frontier rectifications in any talks he might have with them. Rather, it was testimony to the vital importance now lent to the disposition of Yugoslavia and its million-man army by the agreement reached in Athens on 23 February (and confirmed by the War Cabinet the next day) to send British and Empire troops to Greece.[69]

Despite Britain's (and America's) express policy of not discussing postwar territorial settlements, the War Cabinet considered that "the decision of the Yugoslav government at the present juncture is of such importance that it would be worthwhile to disregard this rule on this occasion if by so doing we could induce Yugoslavia to intervene forcibly on behalf of Greece".[70] The Foreign Secretary was authorized on 3 March to open to the Yugoslavs the prospect of territorial revisions if this appeared likely to encourage them "to throw in their lot with us".[71]

This then was the context in which the British determined to offer the Yugoslavs territory: land was to serve as future compensation for immediate entry into the war against Germany. For as the Chiefs of Staff had warned the War Cabinet on 24 February:

> We wish to emphasize that if we are to undertake this commitment [to Greece], every possible effort should be made to get the Turks and Yugoslavs to join the struggle on our side. Without the support of one or the other our help to Greece is unlikely in the long run to have a favourable effect on the war situation as a whole. If both came in, however, the Germans would be seriously embarrassed, at least temporarily, and we should have a good chance of successfully building up a Balkan front.[72]

Whether anyone recognized it or not, this analysis put paid to the long-held illusion that the presence of British troops in Greece might somehow embolden the Turks or the Yugoslavs to enter the war. British troops in Greece now signified not support for Yugoslavia and Turkey, but Britain's own immediate need for military deliverance by one or both of these states. The point was underlined by Eden's and Wavell's reports from Athens on 21 and 22 February. Because Britain could send but three divisions to Greece, only Yugoslav participation would enable the Anglo-Greek forces to make a stand north of Salonika.[73] What was worse - and what Eden was to discover to his horror upon returning to Athens a week later - was that the Greeks took this Yugoslav help for granted in the initial disposition of their troops.

(iii)

Eden, Dill and Wavell discussed with the Greeks on 22 February the best means of informing Prince Paul of the results of their talks. It was first decided to despatch a staff officer to Belgrade to brief the Prince Regent, but this idea was discarded for fear that one of the "unreliable" Yugoslav ministers might be informed. Instead it was agreed that Eden would send a message to Prince Paul drawing his attention to the imminent German threat, hinting that the defence of Salonika rested in his hands and asking what he proposed to do. Eden, who planned to arrive in Ankara for talks with the Turkish government on 26 February, requested Campbell to secure an answer from the Prince before then.[74] At the same time, on 24 February, London responded to a plea from Campbell for another personal message from the King. This also pressed Prince Paul to declare himself.[75]

Prince Paul's answers, sent to Ankara for Eden and given orally to Campbell for the King, were considered unsatisfactory. He reaffirmed that he would never willingly permit Axis troops to use Yugoslav territory to launch an attack on Greece, but he refused to say what he would do were an invasion to be mounted from Bulgaria alone. Since it was Yugoslav intervention in just this circumstance that the British now sought to secure, the situation remained unclear. What was obvious, Campbell reported to London on 24 February, was that both the General Staff, thought hitherto be more bellicose than the government, and the Croat leader Maček were increasingly defeatist. In the event of a decision to intervene in favour of Greece, the generals envisaged an Axis attack from the north which would overrun half the country and condemn an army of 250,000 to fight in the extreme south for a government that might be forced to flee the country. Campbell asked if in view of this defeatism he should seek to mobilize the opposition parties subsidized by Britain in support of intervention. Sargent agreed that the time had certainly come for this and minuted that he would speak to SOE.[76]

If Eden was dissatisfied with Prince Paul's refusal to commit himself, the Prince was grieved by the Foreign Secretary's reaction. Eden apparently told the Yugoslav Ambassador in Ankara, Ilija Šumenković, that unless Yugoslavia defended Salonika the country stood to lose all it had gained from the First World War. Prince Paul complained to Campbell of this bullying approach on 28 February, saying that although his regime "might be in a sense a dictatorship, he could not do entirely as he liked". Campbell countered with the contention - to be heard frequently in the next few weeks - that resistance and early defeat would nonetheless be a better and more honourable fate than slow death by encirclement.[77]

In a virtual hail of messages Eden now sought Prince Paul's agreement to a meeting between them, arguing that only in person could he reveal the extent of Britain's commitment to Greece and that this knowledge would be vital to him in determining Yugoslavia's own stand. Pressing such a meeting upon Prince Paul in a letter sent on the morning of 2 March, Campbell alluded again to the "inestimable value which a definite attitude on the part of Yugoslavia would have for the future in giving her the moral force of having been true to her traditions". Admitting that Prince Paul faced a choice between two evils, "both of which involve suffering, loss and territorial division", Campbell contended that defeat in resistance "would provide the foundations for the future rebuilding and . . . might well forge a new Yugoslav unity greater than exists today". But Prince Paul declined to give testimony to his faith in this heavenly kingdom and refused to meet the Foreign Secretary. Thus it was Campbell who flew to Athens to see Eden on the afternoon of 2 March.[78]

Campbell reported to Eden and the Greek government that despite heavy German pressure and uncertainty about the Croats, "Prince Paul in his heart of hearts might already have made up his mind to act." The Foreign Secretary concluded that "we need not despair of Prince Paul, but could not count on him". Yet the revelation by General Papagos at this same meeting that the Greek forces in Thrace and Macedonia had not been withdrawn behind the Aliakmon line made Yugoslavia's intervention more vital than ever.[79]

Still fearful of entrusting to Prince Paul the details of Britain's military strategy in Greece - the source of apprehension being security and not the effect the disclosure of how few troops were actually being sent was likely to have upon the Prince - it was decided that Campbell should return to Belgrade with an exhortatory letter from Eden and a proposal of staff talks in Greece. Making a virtue of necessity, Campbell was to tell Prince Paul that the Greeks intended to defend Salonika, but that Yugoslavia ought really to assume this responsibility. He was also authorized to raise the possibility of territorial compensation in Istria.[80]

Churchill and the War Cabinet were seriously disturbed by Eden's reports from Athens and despaired briefly of the chances of successfully defending Greece unless Yugoslavia and/or Turkey were to "come in" - a prospect that seemed increasingly unlikely to London. Churchill even cabled Eden that he should "liberate" the Greeks from their commitment to reject any German ultimatum.[81] As far as the Prime Minister was concerned, Britain's main hope now lay in inducing the Yugoslavs to fall upon the Italian rear in Albania.[82] Dill's and Wavell's continued faith in the viability of Greece's defence reassured London;[83] but the gloom might have returned had the British known that Prince Paul travelled secretly to meet Hitler at Berchtesgaden on 4 March. There Hitler pressed the Prince Regent to sign the Tripartite Pact, shorn if need be of its military clauses. Prince Paul temporized, replying that he must first consult his advisers and the cabinet.[84]

Campbell and Prince Paul, who both returned to Belgrade on 5 March, met late that night. Listening to Campbell's account of Britain's determination to defend Greece, Prince Paul gave no hint that he had just endured a five hour monologue in which the Führer made plain his own resolve to prohibit the reestablishment of British forces on the continent. The Prince did urge, however, that the British make haste to complete their disposition of troops in Greece. He also promised a formal answer to Eden's letter the next day.[85] When offered British advocacy of Yugoslavia's territorial claims in Istria the Prince's only response, according to Campbell, was "a rather sickly smile".[86]

The Regency Council met on 6 March to consider Hitler's demand that the country accede to the Tripartite Pact. Although split at the outset, the ministers and regents were convinced by Cincar-Marković's assertion that to refuse must mean war, and by General Pešić's estimate of such a war's outcome. The frontiers and principal cities would be overrun almost immediately; resistance in the mountains of Bosnia and Hercegovina might be prolonged for up to six weeks, but after that there would be neither food nor ammunition. Pešić discounted the possibility of help from Britain. Prince Paul standing aside, the Council voted unanimously in favour of signing, provided that the concessions outlined by Cincar-Marković as achievable were obtained. These were that no Axis soldiers enter the country, that Yugoslavia not be required to transship war matériel or wounded men, that no demand to enter the war be made, and that Hitler remember Yugoslavia's special interest in Salonika after the war.[87] Given Hitler's previous assurances on these points, it did not appear likely that he would refuse them now; but by deciding to raise them in a formal way the moment of signature would at least be postponed.

The British decision to mobilize the political parties and nationalist organizations receiving their support was meanwhile being felt, although not in the way intended. A petition inspired by the British was presented to Prince Paul, but instead of demanding resistance to the Axis in the name of the entire country, the Serbs concentrated on accusing the Croats of disloyalty. Their demarche was further vitiated by a private assurance to the German Legation that they meant no offence to the Reich.[88] Britain's Serb friends were obviously more intent upon pursuing their own interests than on going to war for the sake of Great Britain.

Amidst news agency reports breaking the lid of secrecy on Prince Paul's meeting with Hitler, Campbell met twice with Cvetković on 7 March.[89] He was told that Yugoslavia had indeed been asked to sign "what amounted to" the Tripartite Pact. Although a decision would soon be required, none had yet been taken. Cvetković asserted that he personally was against accession. Whether hoping to receive proofs from the British that they were more powerful than they seemed, or simply interested in spinning out events, Cvetković told Campbell that Prince Paul had agreed that a Yugoslav staff officer, Major Milisav Perišić, should fly to Greece the next day for talks. He would be charged with discovering what military aid - especially what naval support in the Adriatic - the British could provide. Reporting to Eden in Cairo that Perišić would travel under a British passport in the name L. R. (Last Ray) Hope, Campbell wrote that, "Much will depend on our being able to give encouraging replies and I most earnestly beg that special effort should be made to meet Yugoslav requests for assistance."[90] Campbell did not yet appreciate who it was that needed help.

Eden responded immediately with a message for Prince Paul assuring him that "if Yugoslavia joins Great Britain and Greece against Germany, the Yugoslav forces will have a call on the common pool of British supplies." Although Britain's resources were "not unlimited" and past uncertainty over Yugoslavia's attitude had prevented Britain from contributing to the country's "warlike requirements", "if she becomes our ally the position will be changed and everything possible will be done to supply her deficiencies . . ." . The Yugoslavs would have not only "the support of British land forces who will be fighting in Greece, but also the covering protection of the British air and naval forces". Eden also pleaded again for a meeting with the Prince, public or private, in Belgrade or elsewhere.[91]

Neither the information supplied to Perišić in Athens nor the decisions of the Chiefs of Staff in London confirmed Eden's intimations of British munificence or offered the Yugoslavs much hope of tactical support. Perišić arrived in Athens with a seven-point questionnaire designed to elicit assurances that the Anglo-Greek forces intended to hold Salonika long enough to cover a Yugoslav withdrawal into Greece, that a naval presence could be established in the Adriatic in order to evacuate troops reaching the coast and that the Yugoslav army would be fully supplied during its withdrawal. Since the British and Greeks could do none of these things, especially in the absence of details regarding Yugoslavia's own order of battle, their replies were confined to urging the Yugoslavs to be more bellicose: to think less of retreat and more of offence, to look less to Britain and more to the Italians in Albania for the military supplies they needed. Perišić was not told about plans to abandon Salonika, to demolish its harbour installations and to make a stand on the Aliakmon River.[92] Meanwhile in London the Chiefs of Staff had concluded that it was "out of the question" to imagine that the tonnage existed either to supply the Yugoslavs through the Adriatic ports or to evacuate an army of up to 300,000 from Salonika or Kavalla.[93]

The British were unacountably encouraged by what they chose to regard as Perišić's satisfaction with the answers he received in Athens.[94] Eden continued to press from Cairo for a meeting with the Prince Regent or for the inauguration of full-scale staff talks - in fact for anything that would draw the Yugoslavs into the Anglo-Greek camp - while Churchill waxed ever more enthusiastic about the benefits that would accrue from a Yugoslav descent into Albania.[95] As he explained to Roosevelt on 10 March, "At this juncture the action of Yugoslavia is cardinal. *No country ever had such a military chance. If they will fall on the Italian rear in Albania there is no measuring what might happen in a few weeks.*"[96]

That Prince Paul might be on the verge of taking this chance seemed possible to the War Cabinet when they considered Campbell's report of a conversation with the Prince on 9 March. But Prince Paul's sentiments, in any case erratic in these days, were susceptible to two interpretations. The British took heart from his emotional expression of opposition to the Tripartite Pact and his affirmation that the majority of Yugoslavs also opposed it; they paid less attention to his disavowal of responsibility for the ultimate decision, his emphasis on his position as a mere trustee for the boy-King Peter II, his determination to explore every possible "way out" by which his country might escape the sufferings of war and his pessimistic prognosis that neither Yugoslavia nor Greece (even with British help) could withstand a German onslaught for much more than a week.[97] In what bore the marks of being a hint as to his future course, he swore to Campbell that he had never lied to the British and would not do so now. He had told them things he had told no one else, but "for this reason he would not tell us he would take action he might find impossible in the end".[98]

Prince Paul's repeated refusals to meet Eden or to agree to staff talks in view of the scant results of Perišić's mission (and the worrying fact that the Germans had found out about it)[99] compelled the British to seek some other means of committing the Yugoslavs. Campbell believed that Salonika offered the last best hope of doing so. Despite Cvetkovic's revelation to him on 15 March that Germany was well aware of Yugoslav feelings about Salonika and had, in fact, already attempted to induce them to seize it, the British Minister pursued his idea of forcing a Yugoslav break with Germany over the Greek port.[100] He sought and received Eden's authorization to insist to the Yugoslavs that they demand inclusion of a German promise not to attack Salonika in any pact signed between them. If Germany refused, the Yugoslav government could have no illusions that its vital interests were not in jeopardy; if the Germans accepted, military necessity would soon require them to break their promise. Either way Yugoslavia would be provided "with a clear justification for going outside her frontiers".[101]

This reasoning reflected the emphasis which Cvetković and Prince Paul put on their personal recognition that Yugoslavia must fight, and on their frustration that the Germans cunningly refused to make the one impossible demand that would enable them to convince their generals, ministers and countrymen of the fact.[102] But the British plan also rested upon the dubious supposition that such warlike sentiments were meant quite literally. Prince Paul and his Premier may have found it convenient to give Campbell the impression that they sought only a salable justification for war; they may even have believed it of themselves, but in practice (and with German help) they proved adept at finding ample justifications for peace. Salonika, in any case, they did not see as meeting their requirements for a *casus belli* acceptable to the Croats.[103]

Cvetković had also admitted to Campbell on 15 March that an agreement with Germany was near. Although he denied that a final decision had been taken, he hinted that there was to be a non-aggression pact. Yugoslavia, he declared, would never allow passage to Axis troops, or flag in its determination to resist attack, or subscribe to the Tripartite Pact *with* its military clauses.[104] Eden either did not appreciate this last qualification or decided to ignore it. He continued to act for several days as though signature of the Tripartite Pact had been excluded. Not only that, he stepped-up his demands. When it did become clear that Yugoslavia would sign the Tripartite Pact *without* its military clauses he felt betrayed.[105]

For the Foreign Secretary had come to the conclusion that Yugoslavia must sign no pact with Germany, however innocuous its terms. As he wired Campbell on 17 March, "It is practically certain that the moment Yugoslavia has signed any agreement Germany, I gather, will regard the event as giving her a free-hand". The Yugoslavs need not declare war "now", but they must not give Germany licence to invade Greece by signing anything. Rather, Prince Paul must be convinced of the strength of his position: that having refused to sign the Tripartite Pact *(sic)* or to renounce an interest in Salonika he had put the Germans in a quandary which they could resolve only by taking aggressive action; that this in turn would unite his country behind him; and that if war came his military position was far from hopeless, since the Italians and their rich booty in Albania would be at his mercy. In order to help proselytize this faith Eden proposed to send Terence Shone, Acting Counsellor and Minister in the Cairo Embassy and an old friend of Prince Paul's, to Belgrade the following day. Eden asked Campbell to ensure that the Yugoslav government made "no irrevocable decision" before studying the letter that Shone would bring with him and which elaborated on the newly encouraging political and military prospects as seen by the British.[106] These did not include, however, any pledge of large-scale military support for the Yugoslavs.[107]

Shone having been delegated to tackle Prince Paul, Campbell decided on 18 March to put Eden's arguments to Cvetković. The Premier agreed that the Germans would regard any treaty signed with Yugoslavia as giving them a green light to invade Greece, but he did not think that the conditions on which he was insisting for accession to the Tripartite pact - including publication of the terms - could possibly be accepted by them. The Germans could not afford to agree publicly to conditions which vitiated everything the Pact stood for. Yugoslavia, he was certain, could not avoid war. But what, pressed Campbell, would happen if the Germans nonetheless accepted Yugoslav terms? Cvetković could only suggest that he would spin things out in the hope that some incident would occur; perhaps Hitler and Göring would be incensed by Stojadinović's deportation, which he intended they should discover.[108]

Besides essaying to revive old friendships, the Foreign Secretary sought to resuscitate a Balkan bloc. When he met the Turkish Foreign Minister in Nicosia on 18 March he extracted from Sarajoglu a promise to initiate talks in Belgrade on joint measures that could be taken in the event of a German attack on Salonika through Bulgaria. He had wanted much more, namely a Turkish declaration that they would regard an attack on the Greek port as a *casus belli* if the Yugoslavs would;[109] but seemed satisfied that his limited success with Sarajoglu had reopened the possibility of coordinated Balkan belligerency. The next day Eden proposed to Ankara, Athens and Belgrade that a secret summit meeting be held in his presence on Cyprus to devise a common front for keeping war from the Balkans(!).[110] As it happened, the Turks failed to carry out their undertaking to raise the Salonika question with the Yugoslavs and Eden backed off his proposal of quadripartite talks for fear of undermining his or Dill's chances of being received in Belgrade - a more important objective.[111]

Such expectations were dashed by the news, given to Campbell by Cvetković late on the night of 19 March, that Germany had agreed to all the Yugoslav conditions. Campbell and Shone each tried again to throw the imagined spanner of Salonika into the works, but these now ground on regardless.[112] Having accepted the Yugoslavs' terms - that passage for Axis armies would not be requested, that Yugoslavia's territorial integrity would be guaranteed, that the country would be exempt from any requirement to participate in hostilities and that a land-link with Salonika would be provided after the war - as well as the scheme for publicizing the first two of them that Cvetković had thought unacceptable, the Germans demanded signature of the Tripartite Pact by 23 or 24 March.[113]

When the Regency Council met on the morning of 20 March it took the inevitable decision to sign. This decision was confirmed by the full Cabinet meeting late that night. Of the seventeen ministers, three opposed the Pact and resigned: Srdjan Budisavljević (Social Welfare), Branko Čubrilović (Agriculture) and Mihailo Konstantinović (Justice).[114] Budisavljević (of the Independent Democrats) and Čubrilović (of the Serb Agrarians) represented parties in receipt of British subsidies and cooperating closely with SOE; while Konstantinović, a non-party appointee, was regarded as being under the influence of both Budisavljević and Tupanjanin. Their resignation had been coordinated in advance with SOE.[115]

(iv)

Shone informed Eden in Cairo of the Yugoslav decision on 21 March, as well as of the agreed conditions and the three resignations. Shone also reported that Britain's policy of evangelism had reached the end of the line.[116] This had become apparent to SOE in Belgrade several days earlier. According to an SOE report prepared for Dalton by Taylor and Masterson in June 1941, any hope that Prince Paul's government would stand firm had been abandoned on 18 March; from which date SOE's objective "inevitably changed from that of endeavouring to influence the government to that of endeavouring to bring down the government".[117]

This new policy was confirmed and a basic stategy agreed at a meeting held in the Legation on 19 March. For SOE's operatives both the policy and the strategy meant continued reliance upon their friends and contacts in the Serb political parties and nationalist associations. SOE hoped that resignations from the Cabinet would suffice to deter signature of the Pact.[118] In fact the three resignations that occurred caused only a slight postponement (to 25 March) in the projected signing date while the vacancies were filled.[119] A coup d'état seemed the only alternative, but whether or not SOE's friends were capable of producing one was open to question.[120]

Campbell explained the situation to Eden in a telegram dated 21 March. Since no agreement between Yugoslavia and Germany could now be tolerated and since all the arguments against one had already been mustered, it remained for Britain either to threaten to break diplomatic relations or to take more drastic action: to encourage a revolt or coup d'etat that would delay or defeat the Pact. The Minister believed that public feeling, at least in Serbia, might now be ready "to burst out". But he had been told that "a revolt could only be produced at the moment of greatest effervescence, i.e. at or *after* the moment of signature". Would this, he asked, be too late, or would the military authorities prefer to minimize the risk of a precipitate German invasion of Greece until defensive preparations were more advanced? It would be necessary in any case to prepare the ground: to assure the leaders of a potential revolt that they would have Britain's support and to be assured, in turn, that their action was likely to succeed. The probable attitude of the Croats would also have to be taken into account. "Enquiries", Campbell wrote, "are being made of persons who have made approaches, in order to judge possibilities and seriousness of the potential movement." Given that the question of encouraging a coup d'etat depended largely upon Britain's strategic requirements, Campbell asked if Eden agreed in principle to such an action.[121]

Campbell and the Foreign Secretary were at the same time making their final efforts to bring Prince Paul's government back from the brink: the Minister by the tried (if not true) method of appealing to Prince Paul through King George VI; Eden by the more novel means of asking Moscow to exert whatever influence it possessed in Yugoslavia. Their concern now, though, was as much with arousing the Yugoslav people as it was with causing their government to think again. Campbell suggested that besides a private message for the Prince Regent from the King, Churchill might send an appeal to Cvetković which could be broadcast after delivery.[122] Churchill's message, despatched on 22 March, not only implored Cvetković to bear in mind Britain's (and America's) certain victory, but also threatened that, "If Yugoslavia were at this time to stoop to the fate of Romania, or commit the crime of Bulgaria, and become an accomplice in an attempted assassination of Greece, her ruin will be certain and irreparable." Salvation was, however, close at hand: "the history of war has seldom shown a finer opportunity than is open to Yugoslav armies if they seize it while time remains."[123] That opportunity lay in Albania.

In Moscow Cripps conveyed to the Soviet government on 23 March Eden's appeal that it press the Yugoslav government and people to stand firm. He was told by Andrei Vyshinski that the Soviet government did not consider it proper to discuss with the British matters extraneous to their bilateral relations. Vyshinski nonetheless summoned Gavrilović to see him, giving the latter an opportunity to ask if the Soviet government would aid his country in the event of its refusing to sign the Tripartite Pact. The Assistant Commissar indicated that he would consult Stalin and Molotov, but the answer soon came back that the Soviet government considered that it was now too late to take any initiative.[124]

Eden's reply on 22 March to Campbell's query as to the desirability of a coup d'état was tentatively affirmative. He dismissed the effectiveness of a mere threat to break relations, but wanted to know much more about the possible leaders of a coup, Campbell's relations with them and their chances of success:

> Are preparations sufficiently far advanced? Such events can hardly be improvised. How do you assess possibilities of success as a result of your soundings? I agree that upon present information suggested coup would have to be staged at the moment of reaction caused by the signature and this may be very soon.

The Foreign Secretary also wanted to know what the fate of Prince Paul and his military chiefs was likely to be at the hands of the putschists.

Then, in a statement of Britain's priorities that seemed to obviate any need for a coup d'état at all given the concessions that the Yugoslavs had secured from the Germans, Eden noted that from the military point of view, "It is more important that Yugoslavia should deny passage, if necessary by force, to German troops than that she should declare war if Greece is invaded through Bulgaria." While there was certainly no reason for Eden to trust the Germans to observe their promises to Yugoslavia, he was overestimating the Anglo-Greek forces' powers of resistance and underestimating the confidence of the Germans that the less convenient route through Bulgaria would suffice. Eden most feared a German advance through the Monastir (Bitola) Gap, for this would round the Anglo-Greek defences on the Aliakmon River: "So long as Yugoslavia is resolute to refuse passage it should now be difficult for the Germans to direct their attack on Greece with good prospects of success." But much would depend on the attitude of the commander of Yugoslavia's southern army. Did Campbell, he asked, have contacts with him and know his attitude? "While I would stop at nothing to ensure that Yugoslavs fight to deny passage to Monastir Gap, I do not yet know enough to estimate the effect of a coup or chance of assuring this."[125]

In a second telegram on 22 March Eden authorized Campbell to spread more widely the agruments which had failed to move Prince Paul:

> You are no doubt in touch with ministers who have resigned and will judge what are the opportunities for creating firmer alternative government which includes those friendly to our cause. If there is anything we can do to help please let me know. Meanwhile you have authority to give assurances at your discretion to their military leaders and others, (a) that Yugoslavia if involved in the war on our side will have the fullest possible British military support and share in the common pool of supplies, and (b) that we will advocate Yugoslav claim to Istria at peace settlement.[126]

Interviews which Campbell had with Cvetković and Shone with Prince Paul on 22 March left the two diplomats with the impression that both men continued to regard the Tripartite Pact with abhorrence, that they still hoped that something might turn up that would spare them from signing it and that Cvetković at least welcomed the prospect that outraged public opinion in Serbia might force his government's resignation and the shelving of the Pact. Yet they also believed it was their duty to sign; otherwise the government and the country would fracture and a war ensue in which they could have no hope of acquitting themselves honourably, let alone of winning.[127] The Prince and his Premier were aware of the insurrectionary current that abetted by the British was welling up against them, but in their tortured position they proved strangely indulgent towards those who, like General Dušan Simović, Commander of the Air Force, bluntly told them that to sign the Pact would mean their overthrow.[128]

Shone, who had only the day before announced the end of missionary diplomacy, was unable to resist the opportunity of his leave-taking from Prince Paul to show him the particularly apposite Biblical lesson from that day's *Daily Sketch* (Second Corinthians, chapter 6, verses 14 and 17):

> Be ye not unequally yoked together with unbelievers: for what fellowship hath righteousness with unrighteousness? and what communion hath light with darkness?
>
> Wherefore come out from among them, and be ye separate, saith the Lord, and touch not the unclean thing; and I will receive you.

The Prince, deeply moved, replied, "I know."[129] Yet when the final German ultimatum arrived the next day, 23 March, the Yugoslav government complied. Ministers would travel to Vienna to sign the Pact on 25 March.[130]

Eden was unmoved by the soul-searching reported from Belgrade. He might have been expected to take heart however from Prince Paul's emphatic declaration to Shone that he would fight if the Germans broke their promise and demanded passage through Macedonia. He did not. For he had now received the Prime Minister's observations (sent on 22 March) on the issues raised by Campbell's telegram of 21 March:

> You must settle this in Cairo. To me it seems more important to get Yugoslavia into the war anyhow than to gain a few days on the Salonika front. Play the hand as you think best.[131]

Now echoing Churchill, Eden advised Campbell on 23 March to go ahead with whatever action he might judge necessary if the need grew urgent and to "bear in mind that rather than allow Yugoslavia to slip by stages into German orbit, we are prepared to risk precipitating German attack".[132]

The next day the Foreign Secretary gave Campbell even wider latitude. Declaring that "Prince Paul's attitude shows such a hopeless sense of unreality that there is nothing to be expected of him," he empowered the Minister,

> now to proceed at your discretion by any means at your disposal to move leaders and public opinion to understanding realities and to action to meet the situation . . . You have my full authority for any such measures that you think it right to take to further change of government or regime, even by coup d'état.[133]

The bare reality that the Yugoslavs, and particularly the Serbs, were to be brought to appreciate was that they must now sacrifice themselves for the sake of their honour (as assayed by Britain), their independence (as defined by Britain) and their future place in Europe (as otherwise menaced by Britain) by coming to Britain's rescue in Greece.

Dalton in London had already taken steps in this direction. He noted in his diary on 21 March: "Bad news from Juggery . . .

Wire sent to use all means to raise revolution. G. screws this through the F.O."[134] There is no reason to suppose that the Foreign Office was unwilling. Sargent initiated consultations with SOE on 23 March regarding the instructions to be sent to Belgrade.[135] The result was a telegram sent on Monday morning, 24 March, which ordered SOE "to put full steam on to assist after consulting the Minister".[136] Cadogan even asked Jebb the same day whether SOE could arrange to blow up the train then carrying Cvetković and Cincar-Marković to Vienna to sign the Tripartite Pact.[137] The Foreign Office also moved to bring all possible propaganda pressure to bear in the BBC's Serbo-Croat broadcasts.[138]

Both Campbell's telegrams during these days and subsequent (and often self-serving) analyses of Britain's role in the coup d'état of 27 March make it plain that however active SOE's agents may have been in arousing and coordinating Serb hostility to the Tripartite Pact, their contacts and influence played an insignificant part in the actual preparation and execution of the putsch. Rather it was the air attachés, Macdonald and Mapplebeck, who maintained liaison with the makers of the coup, gave them encouragement and presumably kept Campbell informed concerning their plans. Yet even the two air attaches, although privy to the existence of a conspiracy, were by no means a party to it.[139]

The fact that it was a "military movement" - and not the politicians or nationalists with whom SOE was working - that held the keys to a successful coup d'état was reported to Eden by Campbell on 24 March. The Minister was not confident that such a movement would be brought to fruition, "specially since Yugoslavia's accession to the Tripartite Pact is susceptible of presentation in a fairly harmless form". This the government was making every effort to do. Moreover, all the military chiefs with the exception of General Simović were in favour of the Pact. But if the leaders could be identified it would be essential for him to be able to approach them with a definite offer of military help, so steeling their resolve to maintain a firm attitude towards Germany even at the cost of war: "The mere promise of a share in the common pool is far too vague and would get us nowhere." Campbell begged to know what he could offer and when it might arrive. He also stressed that a British naval demonstration in the Adriatic would have considerable impact.[140]

Marking specifically Campbell's suggestion that some military supplies might be furnished now by the Greeks against future British replacement, Churchill minuted to Cadogan on 25 March, "I am very doubtful about all this". So was the Foreign Office. Nichols observed that "if a coup d'état is really dependent upon immediate military supplies, the outlook is very gloomy".[141] Eden from Cairo could only tell Campbell to make the best use possible of the information that British forces in Greece possessed the sort of equipment the Yugoslavs lacked. None of it could be transferred to them, but "if they fight with us [they] will thus be fighting side by side with British forces armed with equipment mentioned in your telegram . . .". They should not forget, either, the loot available in Albania.[142]

At 3:30 on the afternoon of 25 March Cvetković and Cincar-Marković signed the Tripartite Pact in the evocative setting of Prince Eugene of Savoy's Belvedere Palace. At the same time Campbell was explaining to Eden from Belgrade on whom it was that Britain must rely to undo their act. Whether an alternative civilian government backed by the army or an outright military dictatorship were to be established, either would necessarily be an exclusively Serb affair. Among the Croats the *Frankovci* (or Ustaše) were already becoming "uppish"; whilst the supporters of the Peasant party, whose loyalty to the Yugoslav state rested primarily upon the maintenance of Croatia's autonomy within it, would not countenance any attempt to defy Germany and plunge the country into war. Campbell felt that the Slovenes were more resolute, but they were too few and too isolated to matter. But since for Britain the attitude of the Serb-commanded forces in the south was paramount, the possible defection of the Croats was no great disadvantage. It was the Serb officers, moreover, who were most likely to succeed in carrying out an early coup d'état, not the political "promoters" (e.g. Tupanjanin) with whom SOE was in touch. Campbell admitted in reply to Eden's earlier questions that he had no contact with the commander of Yugoslav troops in Macedonia. He also advised the Foreign Secretary that although the potential putschists would probably remain loyal to the King and dynasty, Prince Paul would certainly be deposed.[143]

Wing Commander Macdonald met secretly on the morning of 26 March with General Simović, whom he described to London as "head of an organization intending to carry out a coup d'état".[144] This was true in the sense that Simović's deputy, Brigadier Bora Mirković, had secured his chief's permission to act in his name. The actual planning, timing and direction of the putsch - though still a subject of intense dispute-was almost certainly Mirković's alone.[145] This explains the fact that although Simović assured Macdonald that there would be a coup, he gave no hint that it was to take place that night. He did not know that himself.[146] Simović did however manifest a bellicose intent that he would lack once in power. He sought from Macdonald information about Britain's forces in Greece, their plans for Salonika and details of what aid they could render Yugoslavia. He was disappointed by Macdonald's inability to make precise commitments, but "seemed impressed by the conception of a common pool for materials ...". Best of all, he declared that Yugoslav troops would move against the Italians in Albania as soon as the success of the revolution was assured, and that they would enter the war against Germany and Bulgaria a few days later.[147] According to subsequent tesitmony by Mirković, he too had a British visitor that day. Squadron Leader Mapplebeck, Macdonald's assistant and putative SIS agent, told him during the afternoon that a coup d'état must take place within forty-eight hours. Mirković assured him that the coup would occur on time, but not that he intended to act that night.[148]

On the face of it the final and well-known injunctions addressed by Churchill to Campbell on 26 March, and by Leo Amery to the Serbs in general over the BBC that evening, seem inconsistent with the orders supposedly given to Mirković, and certainly with the extreme resolve evidenced in Eden's previous exchanges with Campbell. Churchill charged Campbell to allow no breach to grow between himself and Prince Paul: "Continue to pester, nag and bite. Demand audiences . . . This is no time for reproaches or dignified farewells." Though he was to neglect no opportunity for replacing the government were it to go "beyond recall", the suggestion that it had not already done so was a retreat.[149] Amery, Secretary of State for India and the Cabinet's one speaker of Serbo-Croat, also made it clear that London was not necessarily counting on a coup d'état. He implored the Serbs to remain true to the heroic (if sacrificial) traditions of Kosovo Polje, but he also reminded them that it was not too late for an aroused public opinion to compel the government to refuse to ratify the Tripartite Pact.[150]

Churchill's and Amery's messages have usually been viewed as part and parcel of Britain's attempt to engineer a coup d'état. Actually they show that on the eve of 27 March the British were both uncertain that one would take place and prepared to accommodate themselves to less. It had already been resolved that Britain would not break diplomatic relations with Prince Paul's government unless and until such action was necessary to provoke a coup. It was now accepted that, failing a coup d'état, a determination on the part of the government to resist any German demands in excess of the terms of the Tripartite Pact would also serve Britain's interests.[151] Moreover, it appeared during these hectic days that as much effort was being invested in wooing the commander of Yugoslavia's Third Army in Skopje as was being made in promoting a putsch in Belgrade.[152] The British badly wanted a coup, a coup that would bring Yugoslavia into the war. But they realized that they were in no position to make one. Their closest and most trusting relations were with Serb politicians and professional nationalists who were no better placed than they were. And while the Serb army and air force officers who could (and did lead a revolt were willing to reveal their general intentions, they needed no lessons in conspiracy from Britain's amateur secret agents. What the British imagined they did need as a spur to immediate action - and as a tie to bind them to the British cause - was a specific promise of arms; and this it was impossible to provide.

The British were thus caught off balance by the almost bloodless coup d'état carried out during the early hours of 27 March.[153] The Belgrade agents of SOE were at first alarmed, suspecting until they restored contact with some of their more informed friends that what was afoot was a countercoup on the part of Prince Paul.[154] Eden and Dill, meanwhile, had given up their vigil in Cairo and were en route home when they learned of the putsch upon reaching Malta. Churchill immediately ordered them to return to Cairo, but they went instead to Athens in the hope of going on to Belgrade.[155] London was however quick to apportion credit for the welcome surprise. The War Cabinet Defence Committee agreed on 27 March to send an "expression of appreciation" to Dalton "for the part played by his Organization in bringing about the coup d'état in Yugoslavia".[156]

Having miscalculated the possibilities of a coup, the British now miscalculated the possibilities arising from it. Churchill spoke with understandable relish to a Conservative Party gathering of how "early this morning the Yugoslav nation found its soul";[157] but he was not yet ready to promote it any higher than purgatory. He ordered Campbell to inform the new ministers that Britain was prepared to *recognize* them "on the basis that they were determined to denounce the Pact with Germany and to help in the defence of Greece".[158] The Turks too were pressed to join ranks in "a common front which Germany will hardly dare assail".[159] The despatches of Macdonald from Belgrade encouraged such delusions. He reported Simović as telling him on 27 March that the army would be mobilized fully and concentrated in the south. Meanwhile their attack on Albania would begin that night.[160] The next day Macdonald reported that two Yugoslav divirsions (armed with Italian weapons and dressed in Albanian uniforms) had crossed the frontier. Simović expected to be at war with Germany in 12-15 days.[161] Only the last was not pure fantasy. Within twelve hours of the coup d'état Hitler had issued Directive No. 25 ordering the annihilation of

Yugoslavia. He would not now bypass the country on his way to Mussolini's resuce in Greece.

(v)

Sentence had been passed. It only awaited execution. This lent an aura of unreality to the ten days of peace that remained before German bombers swept in over Belgrade, devastated the city and inaugurated Germany's parade ground exercise in conquest. However genuine the warlike intent of the Serb officers who made the coup, and however heartfelt the cries of the Serb populace that greeted it (*"bolje rat nego pakt, bolje grob nego rob!"* and *nema rata bez Srba!"**), a more sober - if no more realistic - mood soon prevailed. National pride assuaged, the sad spectacle unfolded of a government called into existence on a wave of revulsion towards the foreign and domestic policies of Prince Paul embracing those selfsame policies as its own. For the politicians whom the officers immediately brought in to stitch together the fragile fabric of Yugoslav unity and to buy time from the Germans could find no alternative. It appeared that the only way to appease the Germans was to accept the Pact, portraying the coup as motivated wholly by domestic issues. Yet the only way to secure the participation of Maček and the Croats in the new government was to accept both the Pact and the *Sporazum*. Thus to the negation of the Serb officers' hostility to the Tripartite Pact was added a denial of the Serb politicians' equally virulent hostility to Croatia's favoured status. Serb self-esteem had undoubtedly been rescued by the coup and the anti-German demonstrations that accompanied it, but it is difficult to see what else it achieved. Its consequences, on the other hand, were to be far-reaching.[162]

The British naturally regarded the government formed by General Simović as their friend and ally. The early disappointment of their hopes that the Yugoslavs would move

*Better war than the Pact, better a grave than a slave; There can be no war without the Serbs.

promptly into Albania redounded to the discredit of their Air Attaché, not the Simović government.[163] While Campbell's complaint on 28 March that there were "rather too many old party hacks in the new government", men whom had been "out of office for many years and have in several cases acquired bitterness and personal prejudice", was countered by Sargent's observation that, "It won't much matter if as we hope the generals are really in charge".[164] The British were disposed to view charitably too the new government's immediate assurances to the Axis powers that it stood by Yugoslavia's treaty obligations, as well as its panicky pleas that the Foreign Office rein in the BBC's references to the coup as a British victory.[165] What did matter to the Foreign Office was that Maček should be included in the government and the *Sporazum* reaffirmed. Although British advocacy of the pro-Pact Maček might appear curious (and it certainly did to Greece's King George II), it reflected their appreciation of an essential fact - and one that the new government struggled to escape: that Hitler would soon take his revenge.[166] The British doubtless overestimated Maček's ability to lead his Croats into battle on behalf of Yugoslavia, but their concern for Yugoslav unity at such a critical juncture was understandable.

Seeking to consolidate what he trusted was Britain's new influence in Yugoslavia and to coordinate plans for war, Eden again pressed to be received in Belgrade.[167] Simović seemed enthusiastic at first, but his colleagues, fearful that such a visit would provoke the Germans and upset the Croats, were not.[168] He agreed, however, that Dill might travel secretly (in mufti) to Belgrade for military talks. It was decided in Athens that the CIGS would take with him proposals for staff discussions on the following terms: Anglo-Greek forces would undertake to defend Salonika if Yugoslavia protected the upper Struma valley, cleared the Belasica massif west of the Rupel Pass and attacked the Italians in northern Albania.[169] This plan reflected the high hopes engendered by the coup, not the reality that Dill was to encounter in Belgrade.[170]

The British had other ambitious schemes. They planned to attach a high-ranking liaison officer to Simović and an adviser to King Peter II. The presence of a liaison officer with Simović would, it was thought, obviate the need to deal with the weaklings in his government, while an advisor with the immature King would influence him in the right direction and protect him from intrigues.[171]

British perceptions of the susceptibility of both Simović and King Peter to their influence may have been justified, but they were inspired by a sanguine estimation of Yugoslavia's military strength and Simović's own strength within his government that was not. A Joint Intelligence Committee report to the Chiefs of Staff on 31 March posited a Yugoslav army of over a million men (800,000 of whom were already mobilized) inspired by the sturdy fighting spirit of the Serbs who formed its core, supported by the best air force in the Balkans and committed to the sound strategy of falling back from the north in order to defend the south and attack Albania. The army's principal weakness was in supplies, but the expected rout of the Italians in Albania would remedy this deficiency.[172]

Dill, accompanied by Dixon of the Foreign Office and Brigadier A. W. S. Mallaby of the War Office, arrived in Belgrade on 31 March. In their first meeting with the Yugoslavs that night an indecisive and ill-briefed Simović (the Yugoslav side did not realize with whom they were negotiating, thinking Dill a mere divisional commander from Greece) agreed to sign a note which would form the basis for detailed staff talks at Florina in Greek Macedonia on 2 April. Yugoslavia to war even if not attacked, backed out the next attacked by Germany and would render all possible help to Greece if the Germans' first blow fell there. (It was understood that this would include a descent into Albania.) But Simović, imagining that he had months and not days before such questions became actual and terrified lest the Germans or his own fragile government discover that he was committing Yugoslavia to war even it not attacked, backed out the next morning. After failing to get the British to accept amendments strictly limiting the conditions under which Yugoslavia would be obligated to come to the aid of Greece, Simović simply refused to sign anything at all. Dill was left only with a Yugoslav commitment to send a second-ranking officer to staff talks with Generals Wilson and Papagos at Florina on 3 April.[173]

The British came away from Belgrade disappointed by Simović's refusal to commit himself and depressed by his failure to appreciate the immediacy of his country's peril.[174] The Yugoslavs, on the other hand, seem to have emerged from the talks with exaggerated notions of Britain's strength in Greece (Dill unaccountably told Simović that almost half of a projected force of 150,000 was already in place) and of Anglo-Greek eagerness to help them defend Salonika. They thus prepared a plan for its concerted defence that was to prove unwelcome to Wilson and Papagos.

It was inauspicious that the Yugoslav train bearing General Janković to Florina broke down en route, arriving 10 hours late, at 10 PM on 3 April. The plan he brought with him proposed combined operations in the region west of the River Struma, but Janković had no authority to commit his government even to its own plan, nor to discuss options. Under the impression that the British disposed of one armoured division and four motorized divisions on the Aliakmon line, the Yugoslavs proposed that these forces proceed to the area between Lake Dojran and Strumica where they would join the two Yugoslav front-line and two reserve divisions already committed to the defence of south-eastern Macedonia. The Yugoslavs also expected the RAF to take part in the aerial defence of the entire country.

General Wilson immediately put Jankovic straight regarding Britain's troop strength. He did not have an armoured division, but an armoured brigade; he did not have four motorized divisions, but one infantry division with mechanized transport and the prospect of a second arriving in three weeks and a third in six weeks' time. Wilson did not reject the Yugoslav plan out of hand, but emphasized the difficulties involved in moving his forces forward more than 100 km. into an unreconnoitered and perhaps unsuitable area. He tried also to convince Janković that Yugoslav forces could defend this sector themselves. General Papagos was more blunt. The

Simović government might for political reasons be unwilling to commit more than four of its 24 divisions (his estimate since Janković refused to divulge Yugoslavia's order of battle*) to this vital area, but it should not expect the British and Greeks to make good its inadequacies. Each side having overestimated the capacity of the other to pull its chestnuts out of the fire, there was nothing to agree when the meeting broke up at 2 AM but that Janković would seek his government's approval for further talks in Athens on less restricted terms of reference.[175]

The failure of the Florina talks marked a serious deterioration in the mutual confidence of the Yugoslav and British governments. For the British the revelations emanating from Belgrade concerning attempts to invoke Mussolini's intercession with Hitler, to send Foreign Minister Ninčić to Berlin and to negotiate a mutual assistance pact with the Soviets - as well as allegations of past plots on the part of Prince Paul to poison King Peter and assume the Yugoslav throne - all served to confirm their developing view that the Yugoslav government inhabited some cloud-cuckooland.[176] Churchill attempted on 4 April to bring Simović to his senses. He could not understand, he wired, the argument that Yugoslavia was attempting to gain time. There was none to be gained, only lost: "From every quarter my information shows rapid heavy concentration and advance towards your country by German ground and air forces." Alpine divisions would soon be lodged even in Albania, cutting off Yugoslavia from its one hope for "victory and safety".[177] Simović refused to be warned. He told Campbell on the morning of 5 April that he saw no need to send an officer to Athens for more talks. The Germans' plans had been thrown out of gear by the coup and they were still unprepared to launch an attack. Yugoslavia, on the other hand, would be fully prepared to meet an invasion by 22 April.[178] Simović imagined he had the time. He was wrong. The German war against Yugoslavia began less than 20 hours later.

*In fact the Yugoslavs had almost 30 divisions.

Simović and his colleagues may have been criminally irresponsible in discounting the signs of war; they were probably justified in dismissing Britain's continuing pleas that they concert their military plans with those of the Anglo-Greek forces. As Simović had gone on to make plain to Campbell on 5 April, the Florina talks had convinced them that Britain's forces in Greece were so small that it was not worth Yugoslavia's while to make plans based on cooperation with them.[179] (Or, as Mirković had sniffed to Macdonald the same day, *"Ce n'est pas serieux".*)[180] Campbell could not believe that Janković had heard correctly, that Britain's strength in Greece amounted to just one armoured brigade and one infantry division. He begged Eden to correct this "misapprehension".[181] Yet there was no mistake and it is understandable that Simović, presiding over a country that mobilized at the pace of an ox cart and that risked fracture if the Croats gained the impression that warlike adventures were contemplated, should have refused Britain's summons to action in Albania or Bulgaria without the prospect of substantive support.

The Germans' conquest of Yugoslavia began at dawn on Sunday, 6 April, with a massive bombing raid on Belgrade. This set the government and high command in flight and produced a total breakdown in military communications. The *blitzkrieg* then proceeded without let or hindrance. Units of the Yugoslav army, unready and under strength, were left to meet the overwhelming power of the onrushing Germans without overall coordination. They resisted (occasionally), dispersed or mutinied (more frequently) and surrendered (eventually) on an *ad hoc* basis. The April War was, of course, over before it began, but by 10 April the Germans were already looking for someone capable of signing an instrument of surrender. On 17 April they succeeded. The King and government meanwhile had continued their peregrinations through rural Serbia, Bosnia and Hercegovina until, on 14 and 15 April from Nikšić aerodrome in Montenegro, they flew into exile.

The "Independent State of Croatia" (NDH) had already been proclaimed by the Ustaše on 10 April. The Italians and Hungarians entered the war the next day, thereby guaranteeing their piece of the carcass. The Bulgarians did not enter the war at all. They simply marched in to take their allotted share after the shooting stopped. Though Hitler's improvised division of the spoils (see map) left most everyone more or less unsatisfied - and produced one of the essential preconditions for the resistance and civil wars that followed - Yugoslavia, symbol of the infamy of Versailles (or Trianon, or Saint-Germain, or Neuilly), was no more.[182]

The British response to Yugoslavia's April War tended to recrimination, though such feelings were no doubt tempered by Britain's own disaster-in-the-making in Greece and Crete.[183] On 12 April Campbell relayed from the Serbian spa of Vrnjačka Banja Simović's urgent request for the despatch of two armoured divisions and complement of RAF aircraft. The situation was not desperate, the country might hold out for another 15 days. The request was as ludicrous as the premise on which it was based. Campbell was told as much, though it is unlikely that the message reached him. His next plea was taken more seriously. He asked whether it would be possible for ships or planes to be sent to Kotor to take off the King, government and various Yugoslavs compromised by their services to the British. This provoked on 13 April a typically Churchillian reply:

> We do not see why the King or government should leave the country, which is vast, mountainous and full of armed men. German tanks can no doubt move along the roads and tracks, but to conquer the *Serbian* armies they must bring up infantry. Then will be the chance to kill them. Surely the young King and the Ministers should play their part in this.

The Prime Minister relented to the extent of admitting that a submarine might be sent to Kotor for the King and a small party if absolutely necessary.[184] But the King and his government did not wait.

On 15 April Campbell, now in Kotor (where he and about 100 other Britons wre about to be interned by the Italians), begged that ships be sent to evacuate some small part of the Yugoslav army. Even such a gesture was impossible and Sargent minuted on the telegram: "Mr. Campbell's conception of the extent of our resources in the Mediterranean has throughout been grandiose to say the least of it."[185] This was true, but unfair; for Campbell's persuasiveness as an evangelist of Britain's cause had been in inverse relation to his possession of the facts. London had been well served by keeping him in ignorance.

On only one front had the British remained optimistic about the warlike intent of the Simović government. This was SOE's belief that the government accepted its plans for sabotage, clandestine radio stations and guerrilla operations to follow upon the country's invasion and occupation. SOE had every confidence that its close relations with men like Tupanjanin and Trifunović-Birčanin would ensure that the government undertook the demolitions required by MEW and the Commanders-in-Chief, Middle East, and that its own work in establishing a nationwide system of W/T stations and in fomenting guerrilla uprisings in western Bulgaria and northern Albania would be assisted.[186] On 3 and 4 April Simović and Ninčić assured Campbell that all was in readiness for the demolition of the Danube locks below the Iron Gates.[187]

Yet in this respect too the outcome of the April War was disappointing. An attempt was made to block the Danube locks, but it was only partially (and temporarily) successful. No other significant acts of sabotage were carrid out during the war's brief course. Nor did the anticipated risings in Albania and Bulgaria take place. SOE's agents either fled the country or were interned along the genuine diplomats and other civilians by the Italians. What was worse, the W/T sets left behind with putative leaders of resistance remained silent. As the Axis powers consolodated their hold on the former Yugoslavia during the spring of 1941 it became apparent to the British that they had lost direct contact with the country.

CHAPTER III

A FIGHT FOR YUGOSLAVIA: TITO, MIHAILOVIĆ AND THE BEGINNINGS OF RESISTANCE

(i)

Hitler had put an end to the Kingdom of Yugoslavia, but not to the hope - alive both in the conquered country and abroad - that at least some Yugoslavs might rise in resistance to the newly imposed Axis order. In those parts of the country which had endured 400 years or more of Ottoman rule the traditions and mythology of resistance to foreign dominion were still strong. It was this tradition which the British had since 1940 sought to enlist: first in encouraging Prince Paul's government to fight to maintain Yugoslavia's honour and independence and then, when that seemed unlikely, in pursuing contacts with groups and individuals who might be relied upon to overthrow the Prince Regent and lead the nation to war. In the event the country was not led into war; it shambled into it, a victim of its own pride, backwardness and internal division, as well as of its friends' and enemies' shared determination that it should not escape. The factors that had brought Yugoslavia to this pass now ensured that it should become the locus of a resistance struggle - and a fratricidal bloodletting - unparalleled anywhere else in Europe.

The debacle in Yugoslavia, Greece and Crete in the spring of 1941 did not lessen British interest in organizing resistance in the Balkan Peninsula. The region continued to represent, especially for the Middle East Command in Cairo, what Michael Howard has described as "an area so tantalizingly close and where so much damage could, with comparatively small expenditure of effort, be done".[1] The desire to encourage sabotage and guerrilla warfare in the Balkans was part and parcel of British stratgy at a time when, as Harold Nicolson reflected in his diary, fear of losing the war had receded, but the means of winning it remained to be found. Subversion instigated by the Special Operations Executive, that new and unprecedented organ of ungentlemanly warfare, was ranked by the Joint Planning Staff with strategic bombing and naval blockade as one of the principal weapons in Britain's arsenal.[2] It was anticipated that when the British Army returned to the continent it would do so more as the guarantor of the great popular uprisings expected of the captive peoples of Europe than as an overwhelming invasion force. The British looked to the Balkans for an early implementation of this optimistic and economical strategy.

Churchill, always the romantic enthusiast, had in April urged continued resistance in the Serbian mountains upon the Yugoslavs and their young King. Failing that he accepted the Yugoslav government's evacuation without enthusiasm. By June, when the Simovic government was installed in London, the problem was no longer one of keeping resistance going in Yugoslavia, but of determining the desirability and possibility of restarting it. Although the Yugoslav ministers were inclined to view their country's contribution to the Allied war effort as finished, there appeared to be a considerable measure of agreement between them and SOE on the question of resistance.[3] That this was possible reflected both the ambiguity of SOE's intentions and the close identification of interest which had quickly developed between the Yugoslav government of 27 March and the organization which arrogated to itself much of the credit for the Yugoslavs' heroic defiance of Hitler.

SOE remained fascinated by the prospect of stimulating guerrilla warfare in Yugoslavia. It was even believed that such warfare might itself bring about a German military collapse in the country. Yet immediate action was not desired. The aim, rather, was to create a "fifth column" of secret guerrilla leaders which would proclaim a national uprising on the largest possible scale to coincide with the return of British troops to the continent. SOE assumed that its friends in the Serbian Agrarian Party and the *Narodna Obdrana* constituted such a cadre. First of all, however, communications with occupied Yugoslavia would have to be restored. This would enable SOE to gauge the viability of its pre-occupation network, the possibilities for building up a new one if need be and, eventually, as SOE informed the Yugoslav government and the Foreign Office in June, "to control activities in the country as to ensure their co-ordination with similar work in other occupied countries and to avoid any possibility of premature action which would only lead to useless sacrifice".[4]

Although loath to abandon all hope that one or more of the W/T sets left behind might come on the air, SOE proceeded with plans to introduce new sets and operators. It was envisaged that Istanbul would serve both SOE and the Yugoslav government as the principal listening post for the assemblage of information coming out of the country. To that end the Simović government, while in Palestine, had appointed Jovan Djonović as its delegate in the Near East. Djonović, who had come to enjoy the confidence of the British in Belgrade, was charged with organizing a base for the maintenance of contacts with the homeland and with managing the Yugoslav propaganda effort in the Near East - all in close co-operation with the British secret services.[5]

The first reports of sabotage and diversionary activity in Yugoslavia reached Istanbul during the first half of June. These were followed by vague intimations of an uprising in Hercegovina and predictions of communist action should Germany attack the Soviet Union. Djonović had not yet set up shop in Istanbul, but this information was forwarded to London by the Yugoslav consulate in the city.[6] Although given some play in the press by mid-July, these early reports remained unsubstantiated.

Once established in Istanbul in August, Djonović and his British counterparts began to receive more precise reports of events in the country from Yugoslav travellers. The two most important of these were a Slovene reserve officer, Lt. Stanislav Rapotec, and Dragomir Rakić, a Serbian businessman who had allegedly come to Turkey to buy cotton. Djonović received confirmation from Rapotec that uprisings were taking place in Serbian-inhabited regions, especially Montenegro. He also heard the chilling news that approximately 100,000 Serbs had been massacred by the new Ustaše regime in Croatia. Rakić, meanwhile, brought out the first word of an organization headed by Colonel Draža Mihailović and based in western Serbia. Rakić, claiming to represent Mihailović, reported that his was the largest and best organized force in the field. Although he was being assisted by monied interests in Belgrade, he was in dire need of funds with which to buy food for his men from the peasants. Rakić also confirmed the existence of a communist-led resistance movement which had taken up arms following Hitler's invasion of Russia. Contrasting the two movements, Rakić told Djonović that, "Mihailović and his men defend themselves and the people when attacked", while the communists "set out to kill Germans and consequently provoke punitive expeditions by them which burn villages and mercilessly kill men, women and children." They thus forced those who remained alive to join them. The Germans had decreed in response that 100 Serbs were to be executed for every German soldier killed by the guerrillas. Therefore, Rakić maintained, "Mihailović is only defending himself, because for him the protection of the people is uppermost; while for the communists the most important thing is the defence of the Soviet regime imperilled by German Panzer divisions".[7]

Reporting on 22 August to Vice Premier Slobodan Jovanović in London, Djonović emphasized that Rakić had sought to make contact not with him and the Yugoslav government, but with the British. Consequently, Djonović complained, he had been relegated to the role of intermediary between Rakić and SOE. Although perturbed by this apparent demonstration of Mihailović's lack of confidence in the exile government, the instructions which SOE had ready for Rakić to take back to Mihailović were to his liking:

> I ordered them on behalf of the English to be peaceful, not to attack the Germans and not to provoke reprisals - that they would be told when it was necessary to begin action. Then, when they are advised to begin action, they will be helped with air support and much else. If they do not listen, they cannot hope for aid of any kind.

For, as Djonović continued to Jovanović,

> It is too early in any case for us to start anything, because that would provoke horrible reprisals and the extermination of our people. The English here all agree with this. That being the case, all we can do now is to ease somehow the people's lives and advise them to remain calm and to organize.[8]

Rakić was provided with the equivalent of £20,000 (5 million dinars) by SOE to take back to Mihailović. Djonović, for his part, wrote to his old friend among SOE agents, Captain Julian Amery. Amery, who had met Mihailović on several occasions in Belgrade, was now stationed in Cairo. Djonović asked in Mihailović's name that SOE despatch an aircraft with liaison officers and wireless transmitters to the guerrillas' headquarters on the mountain of Suvobor in western Serbia. He claimed that Mihailović already had some 100,000 men under arms.[9]

Thus by the end of August 1941 not only had the principal issues which were to vex Anglo-Yugoslav relations for much of the war made their appearance, but a choice of sorts had been made: Mihailović and his conception of resistance were offered support, both moral and financial. This was offered on the basis of a consensus which had already emerged regarding the sort of resistance felt to be desirable in occupied Europe. Dalton described that consensus in August:

> The Yugoslavs [i.e. the exiled Royal Yugoslav Government], the War Office, and we are all agreed that the guerrilla and

sabotage bands now active in Yugoslavia should show sufficient active resistance to cause constant embarrassment to the occupying forces, and prevent any reduction in their numbers. But they should keep their main organization underground and avoid any attempt at large scale risings or ambitious military operations, which could only result at present in severe repression and the loss of our key men. They should now do all they can to prepare a widespread underground organization ready to strike hard later on, when we give the signal.[10]

The test during the next few months would be whether this strategy, apparently shared by the British and Mihailović, could coexist with any other.

(ii)

By mid-August the revolt in Yugoslavia was taken sufficiently seriously in London to have become the subject of discussions within the British government and between it and the Yugoslavs. Reuters estimated the guerrillas' strength at 50,000 men, spread over Serbia, Montenegro, Bosnia-Hercegovina, Lika and Sandžak.[11] Within the Foreign Office interest at first centred upon the question of publicity for the resistance. In the face of appeals from various sides that the retailing of resistance news be curtailed lest it provoke the Germans to more horrible reprisals than were already thought to be taking place, the Foreign Office and Ministry of Information determined to abide by the wishes of the Yugoslav government, although both thought that the public's appetite for such news was understandable and justified.[12] The Yugoslav government, however, was of two or more minds. Desirous of maintaining Yugoslav prestige at the rarefied heights to which it had been catapulted by the anti-Hitler coup d'état, the government had provided the press with a great deal of its information on guerrilla activities in Yugoslavia. Some members of the government, on the other hand, felt the strength of the argument that glorification was essentially incitement and would cause the Germans to exact an even more savage revenge were the revolt to continue. Neither at this time nor later did the Yugoslav exiles find a solution to this dilemma. Ministers made speeches to their countrymen over the Serbo-Croat service of the BBC during the summer of 1941 which echoed the advice that SOE and Djonović had already given from Istanbul: remain quiet and await the sign from London, it is still too early.[13] Yet they also continued to fuel the panegyrics to the revolt (and by autumn to Mihailović as its leader) in the British and, especially, in the American press.

The debate on propaganda support for Yugoslav resistance provided another indication of the attitudes being adopted towards the question of the uprising itself. This was necessarily an uncertain process given the scantiness of information on what exactly was happening in the mountains of Yugoslavia. General Simović, who had appealed to his countrymen on 12 August to "remain patient and to await peacefully await the decisive moment of victory which is already in sight", addressed Churchill for the first time on the subject of the revolt two days later.[14] Enclosing two notes - one on the reign of terror in Croatia, the other describing what was known about the revolt - the Yugoslav Minister President asked that a British submarine be detailed to make contact with the resistance committee known to be active in the city of Split and which was in urgent need of funds. The immediate question of submarine was referred to the Admiralty and SOE (where nothing came of it);[15] but on 28 August the Prime Minister, his interest aroused, wrote to Dalton on the general issue of support for Yugoslav resistance:

> I understand from General Simović that there is widespread guerrilla activity in Yugoslavia. It needs cohesion, support and direction from outside. Please report briefly what contacts you have with these bands and what you can do to help them.[16]

Dalton reported back two days later that preparations were in hand: Mihailović was being sent £20,000 by courier from Istanbul and a mission was soon to be despatched to investigate conditions within the country.[17]

Thus is happened that the first Anglo-Yugoslav mission to return to occupied Yugoslavia landed from the Royal Navy submarine Triumph on the Montenegrin coast near Petrovac during the night of 20 September. The mission, codenamed "Bullseye", was composed of three Yugoslavs selected at short notice by the Yugoslav High Command in Cairo and of one representative of SOE, Captain D. T. ("Bill") Hudson. The Yugoslavs were all Montenegrins - Air Force Majors Zaharije Ostojić and Mirko Lalatović and W/T operator Sergeant Veljko Dragičević - who had been selected when it became clear that distance precluded the despatch of a mission by air direct to Mihailović. The Montenegrins' local connections and knowledge of the area influenced their selection.[18]

Bill Hudson, a mining engineer long resident in Yugoslavia and fluent in Serbo-Croat, had joined "D" Section shortly after the start of the war. His brief in returning to the country was a broad one. It was, in Deakin's words, "to contact, investigate and report on all groups offering resistance to the enemy, regardless of race, creed or political persuasion".[19] The instructions of General Ilić, the Yugoslav War Minister, to Ostojić and Lalatović had apparently been quite different. They were to make contact in Montenegro with nationalist bands and groups of officers loyal to King Peter and to proceed via these channels to Mihailović's headquarters. They were not to reveal the existence of any forces disloyal to the King.[20] The intention of the Yugoslav High Command was to re-establish in Yugoslavia a professionally commanded military force loyal to the government of 27 March and to no one else.[21]

The first two messages received from the "Bullseye" mission were dated 26 September. They reached London via Malta on 3 October. Hudson and his colleagues reported that they had contacted a force of approximately 100 "Comitadji" soon after leaving the coast on 21-22 September. They expected, however, that work would be difficult. Montenegro had been fully reoccupied by the Italians following their suppression of the July uprising led by Captain Arso Jovanović and Professor *(sic)* Milovan Djilas. In a message received in London on 7 October the "Bullseye" team recommended that a Yugoslav plane be sent to drop leaflets over Montenegro in order "to counter strong Axis propaganda and assist moral[e]". Subsequent "Bullseye" telegrams, which reached London between 9 and 11 October, reported that the mission was "with staff of Montenegrin National Freedom troops in Radovac [*sic*, Radovče], 17 kilometres from Podgorica". Despite the Italians' success in quelling the uprising and retaking the towns, the warfare "has taken on character of a revolution in practically the whole of Montenegro":

7. The warfare has a national Freedom aspect and is connected with all the warfare in the whole of Yugoslavia. This movement is the only organized anti-occupation force and has a strength of 5,000 whose numbers will rise to 30,000 in revolution. The organization of Montenegrin Army is well carried out. They are also carrying on guerrilla warfare.
8. There are plans in preparation for renewed action on a larger scale: therefore it is necessary to send rifles, machine guns, hand-grenades, explosives and greatest necessity rainproof clothing, money in lira and dollars for maintenance and propaganda. Montenegro serves as a base supply for action in Hercegovina and Sandžak which have no arms at all.
9. Speedy help would have great political and military importance and would achieve results much quicker; for this Montenegro would be a secure base. This help should be dropped by parachute in Radovče area which is in our hands. Later we should secure also the aerodromes which are to be found beside the sea harbour.
10. . . . A great deficiency in armament, ammunition, clothes and food is beginning to be felt. Numbers fighting and action will increase. As soon as your answer is received Hudson is going to Serbia to make contact with the headquarters of the movement.

Telegrams reaching London from Montenegro in the subsequent week reiterated the request for help, provided lists of prominent collaborators with the Italians, reported several engagements with the enemy, detailed the trials of the local population and repeated Hudson's intention to travel to Serbia, where major battles were said to be taking place. Now, however, (in a message received on 16 October) it was reported that Hudson proposed to depart on 13 October in order to establish liaison with Mihailović, and not with the "headquarters of the movement" referred to previously.[22] In the interim (apparently on 9 October) Hudson had been informed that Mihailović was still broadcasting to the British *en clair.* SOE considered it essential that Hudson provide him with safe ciphers as soon as possible.[23] It had also become apparent, at least to the Yugoslav component of the "Bullseye" mission, who it was that led the "Montenegrin National Freedom" troops:

> The Communists who are well organized are now leading an action in Montenegro. Nowadays [they] want everybody to unite in fight against the occupying authorities. Numerous national elements are standing to our side and are waiting. Must urge on Nationalists to organize for the struggle.

This message reached London on 18 or 19 October. It was probably sent by Lalatović, who remained behind to receive the expected supply drops, after Hudson and Ostojić had departed for Serbia.[24]

(iii)

The German invasion on 6 April found Colonel Dragoljub (Draža) Mihailović serving as Assistant Chief of Staff to the Sixth Coastal Army Region based in Mostar. A professional staff officer with a somewhat chequered career behind him, Mihailović was then 48 years of age.[25] In the midst of the Yugoslav military collapse he assumed the duties of Chief of Staff to the Second Army based near Doboj in Bosnia. In the chaotic few days before the proclamation of an armistice Mihailović organized a motorized "Rapid Unit" which operated north and south along the River Bosna from Doboj. After a disastrous engagement with a German armoured column and the announcement of the armistice on 15 April,

Mihailović resolved to take to the forests with the remnants of his force, a total of several dozen men. He apparently hoped to find and join other remnants of the army still offering resistance to the Germans.

The small group found it necessary to fight off attacks by both the Moslem peasantry and the occasional German patrol before crossing the Drina into Serbia on 29 April. On 6 May Mihailović asked his followers - then numbering about 80 after the recruitment of several small groups of soldiers and gendarmes also left at loose ends by the German *blitzkrieg* - whether or not they wanted to continue resistance. Some did not. Mihailović split the remainder into two groups of about 30 and headed with his group for the ridge of Ravna Gora on the slopes of Mount Suvobor, about 10 miles southeast of Valjevo.[26]

Mihailović and his followers, seven officers and 24 men, arrived on Ravna Gora on 13 May. Mihailović probably chose the area because of his friendship with two families prominent in the vicinity: that of Major Aleksandar Mišić, son of the illustrious First World War *Vojvoda,* and that of General Miodrag Damjanović, owners of large parts of the Ravna Gora ridge. Mišić, with whom Mihailović consulted about his plans, was credited with co-leadership of the movement in some of the early reports received abroad. The Damjanović family, whose head was already a prisoner of war in Germany, provided Mihailović and his band with refuge and sustenance on their remote property. Whether or not their appearance on Ravna Gora was in any way planned in advance is not known, despite Mihailović's reputation as a champion of guerrilla warfare and his acquaintance with SOE operatives. In any case his prospects were hardly bright. His handful of men disposed of few arms and virtually no funds. The shock of their crushing defeat by the German war machine was strong. The nature and strength of the occupation regime were still uncertain. On the other hand, Mihailović had no intention of entering upon early action. According to one of his early followers, "The original and primary aim was to remain hidden, to organize and to raise the faith of the people in the ultimate victory of the Allies".[27] Mihailović determined also to assert his control over the various bands, similar to his own, which had escaped capture by the Germans and from which he hoped to construct his organization. In order to have the opportunity to do so, he lost no time in passing assurances to the German-established authorities in Belgrade that his movement on Ravna Gora was "loyal and harmless".[28]

News of Mihailović's "army" spread quickly amongst the neighbouring villages and beyond: "in a short time throughout the whole of Serbia the news had spread that the Royal Yugoslav Army remained on Ravna Gora and that it was continuing to fight the enemy."[29] Besides the officers and other recruits who now made their appearance on Ravna Gora, there were also politicians. They included representatives of the Republican, Agrarian, and Democratic Parties. By August Mihailović was sufficiently alramed at the political dimension of the Partisans' National Liberation Movement (NOP) to form a political advisory group of his own. This was christened the Central National Committee. It was headed by Mihailović's principal political adviser, Dragiša Vasić, a Belgrade lawyer of violently pan-Serb views. The common goal of the politicians gathered around Mihailović was the creation after the war of a greater and nationally homogeneous Serbia embracing all Serbian-inhabited lands.[30]

Mihailovic's followers assumed - both actively and in the popular imagination - the name and role of *četnici* (members of a *četa* or regiment). This was an evocation of the irregulars who had fought for the Serb cause in Macedonia in the late 19th century and in the Balkan Wars. It was not, however, an appellation which commended itself to Mihailović, despite its aura of traditional heroism. For its use denied his contention that his movement represented a continuation of the Royal Yugoslav Army and confused it with the semi-official Četnik Association headed by the aged First World War hero Kosta Pećanac. Pećanac appeared in the early days to be Mihailovic's chief rival for the leadership of the Serb nationalist cause. Although apparently the recipient, prior to the invasion, of a War Ministry directive on the initiation of guerrilla activity, and thus a man of whom something was expected, Pećanac and his Četnik militia entered the service of the occupation regime in the course of the summer.[31] Despite this, Mihailović's forces were almost always known as Četniks.[32]

Mihailović had refused to accept the formal capitulation of the Yugoslav army or, as Serb officers were required, to surrender himself for probable deportation to a prisoner of war camp in Germany. So too did he maintain his belief in the eventual victory of Great Britain and the return of his King. But he was in no position, and in no mind, to continue fighting - beyond offering support for the organization of self-defence units in eastern Bosnia and other areas where the Serb population was threatened by Ustaše terror. In Serbia his aim, rather, was to consolidate his hold over a military and political organization which would escape German notice and yet be ready to seize and hold power once the Germans departed.[33]

(iv)

If history is the propaganda of the victors, then it is natural that the story of Tito and the Partisans has been more widely propagated than that of the loser Mihailović. At the time, of course, the communists enjoyed no such advantage. The Yugoslav Communist Party (KPJ) had been proscribed in the country ever since scoring threatening successes in the only completely free elections held in the inter-war years - those of 1920. The Party's general secretary was a shadowy figure, unheard of before the war, and thought at one time or another during it to be a Russian diplomat, a beautiful woman, a committee, or an acronym for Third International Terrorist Organization. The British had maintained no links with the KPJ before the war and in 1941 had little idea as to its numbers, leaders, or degree of influence.[34] Even less did they expect it to become the principal organizer of anti-Axis resistance in Yugoslavia. The process of coming to grips with this unpleasant truth was to underlie much that was to follow.

On the eve of the German invasion the KPJ could claim perhaps 12,000 full-fledged members and about double that number in their youth organization. This was not a particularly large membership, but it represented a considerable increase since the assumption of leadership by Josip Broz (alias Walter, alias Tito) in 1937 and his formal appointment by the Comintern as general secretary in early 1939. Before his coming the Party had fallen upon parlous times. Burdened with a Moscow-dereed line which compelled it to advocate the break-up of Yugoslavia, directed from abroad by a notoriously faction-ridden leadership, hunted down and penetrated by the royalist police at home, the Party stood so low in the estimation of the Comintern that it seemed likely to be wound up altogether. Tito, 49 years of age in 1941 and a Croat, had moved the Central Committee back to Yugoslavia, tightened discipline, purged the unreliable and factious, and stepped-up activity in the unions and universities.[35] The Party had again become a factor of considerable - if undertermined - importance. In this achievement Tito had been assisted by a new and young Party leadership, loyal to him personally, as well as by Moscow's previous embrace of the slogan of the popular front. This enabled the KPJ to espouse a more patriotic and Yugoslav line.[36]

Controversy has surrounded the role played by the KPJ before, during, and immediately after the April War. Since the Tito-Stalin split Yugoslav historians have been at pains to emphasize the Party's determination in 1941 to fight for Yugoslav independence regardless of the demands of its very real loyalty to the Soviet Union. They cite the formation of military committees to collect arms and train men, the role of the Party in provoking demonstrations against Yugoslav adherence to the Tripartite Pact, the Party's patriotic stance during the April War and the resolutions passed by the May conference of the Central Committee in Zagreb - all well before the German attack on the USSR brought forth Moscow's call for immediate risings in occupied Europe. The Party's critics have discounted this activity, maintained that its behaviour was certainly passive if not actually treacherous up until the Nazi invasion of Russia and emphasized its abject subservience to the twists and turns of the Stalinist party line. While it is undeniable that the KPJ made extensive preparations for launching a guerrilla war before 22 June, it is also true that the communists themselves initiated no anti-Axis operations prior to that date. In fact, before Moscow decreed the inauguration of armed struggle the aims of the KPJ were remarkably similar to those of Mihailović: preparation for action against the occupiers, "but only," in the words of Milovan Djilas, "after the Germans had been spent and demoralized by the war."[37]

At the Central Committee conference held in Zagreb in early May the Party had affirmed its intention to lead an all-Yugoslav liberation struggle against the occupier. The conference further asserted that there could be no return to the past, that the war would necessarily be waged for both national and social liberation, following which the leaders of the Yugoslav bourgeoisie could expect to be called to account. These decisions gave to the projected struggle a revolutionary dimension which Moscow could not approve. The Comintern countered after 22 June with the instruction that "at the current stage the concern must be liberation from fascist enslavement and not socialist revolution".[38]

The KPJ possessed important advantages over other potential leaders of resistance. Unlike the bourgeois parties, the communists were well-practised in the ways of conspiracy and underground organization. And although in this respect the Serbian officer corps could perhaps have claimed an equal expertise, it was shattered by the April War and the German round-up which followed. The Communist Party was less affected by the war and remained less affected by the strictures of the occupation regime. Most importantly, the KPJ was the one all-Yugoslav party in a state where the other parties had been almost exclusively confessional or narrowly national in composition. The Party's relative cohesiveness in a country that had otherwise ceased to exist gave expression to a faith in Yugoslav unity which, for the majority of Serb and Croat party leaders, had died with the Yugoslav state. While the regular political parties fragmented, the communists maintained their unity, discipline and activity.[39]

(v)

The Yugoslav Communist Party did not initiate resistance in Yugoslavia. Rather it sought to take organizational and strategic control of a spontaneous uprising which gained its impetus from people threatened with imminent physical annihilation. The revolt began among the Serbs of eastern Hercegovina in June and proceeded at differing rates of intensity throughout those parts of the Independent State of Croatia which contained a significant Serb population: Lika, Banija, Kordun, Bosanska Krajina and other parts of Bosnia. This was, as Vladimir Dedijer has pointed out, "the homeland of guerrilla warfare in Europe in our age".[40] Whole villages rose to defend themselves or fled to the hills from the Ustaše effort to implement their policy of racial "purification": forced conversions to Roman Catholicism, expulsions to rump Serbia, and mass murder. Whole villages fixed also upon taking revenge on the oftentimes innocent Moslems and Croats in their midst. Long simmering inter-communal tensions over land, religion and nationality were given fierce and bloody rein alongside the basic motive of self-preservation. At first this upsurge in violence caused the occupiers more satisfaction than trepidation. After such a bloodletting Yugoslavia could never be reconstructed.

Communists were sparse on the ground in the rugged Dinaric regions which first rose in revolt. Yet once Hitler attacked the Soviet Union, the KPJ set out to harness the revolt, eliminate its fratricidal aspects, and convert the uprising into a struggle against the Axis occupiers. It seemed to most Party members, and to many traditionally Russophile peasants as well, that with Russia at their side victory was both inevitable and imminent. In May Tito and the Central Committee had moved from Zagreb to Belgrade. There they met on the afternoon of 22 June to consider the news of Germany's invasion of the USSR. It was decided to mobilize the entire Party organization and to issue a proclamation to the people calling upon them to make ready to resist the occupiers.[41]

Acting on its instructions from the Comintern, the Central Committee met again on 4 July to proclaim the armed struggle. There was to be no general uprising as yet. The Party's intention, rather, was to initiate small-scale guerrilla and diversionary actions.[42] The use of terror was also envisaged. As the Serbian Party Committee put it in a circular to their followers later in July: "The terror and atrocities [of the occupier] must be answered with large-scale actions and a massive national terror. We cannot dare to wait one day or one hour: the question is one of life itself - to be or not to be - and is being put to us and to the entire Serbian people each and every minute."[43] Groups headed by seasoned communists, some veterans of the Spanish Civil War, were sent from the cities into the villages to organize detachments. To each of these a political commissar was soon attached. Specially empowered Central Committee members were also despatched to regions of the country already in revolt in an attempt to transform the spontaneous risings into a coherent and centrally directed struggle against the occupier. Tito himself was named to head the newly-formed Chief Command.[44]

The revolt meanwhile was spreading and changing. On 13 July full-scale national uprising erupted in Montenegro. With the exception of the garrison cities of Cetinje, Nikšić, and Podgorica, the Montenegrins succeeded in evicting the Italians from a country whose "independence" and dynastic union with the House of Savoy had been proclaimed the day before. "Wounded self-esteem and bitterness over an unjustly lost but unfinished war" were, according to Djilas, the motivating factors. He soon found it necessary to abandon Tito's instructions to foment only small-scale actions and to align the Party with the people's war.[45] The communists thus shared the leadership of the revolt with all manner of anti-Axis elements. There was little delineation of responsibility, no long term strategy and much extremism. To both communists and nationalists alike it seemed that the entry of the Soviet Union into the war guaranteed the permanence of their early success. For the communists this also meant that their revolutionary ambitions could be furthered without restraint. The peasants in some regions began to mow their meadows so as to afford the descending Russian parachutists an easier landing.[46] The Red Army did not arrive, but the Italians came back in force. By mid-August the uprising had been quelled and the communists were left bearing the brunt of responsibility for the seemingly useless suffering that the population had endured. For many disillusionment, lethargy and an inclination towards accommodation with the Italians succeeded the dizzy expectations of the previous month. The communists too were chastened and disheartened, especially by the continuing German advance into the Soviet Union. Tito was forced to plead to Party members that sterile discussion of the Russian front be terminated.[47]

A more durable uprising was already reaching full tide in Serbia. Expectations here were equally unrealistic at the outset: the skies were scanned for Russian paratroops and the KPJ issued orders that preparations be undertaken to seize power in Belgrade.[48] But the rebels were better led and better prepared for the course they had undertaken. Unlike the Montenegrin revolt, which flared suddenly, the Serbian uprising smoldered slowly before taking flame in August. The German occupation garrison, in any case light, had been further reduced prior to the invasion of the USSR. This facilitated the Serb revolt at the same time as the example of what Serbs outside Serbia were suffering and accomplishing, the exhortations and provocations of the communists, and the rumoured presence of thousands of soldiers in the woods (Mihailović included) provided the impetus for hostilities. After the ignominy of the April War, a second round seemed vital. Honour and tradition demanded it.

The communists had by mid-August succeeded in organizing 21 Partisan detachments in Serbia with approximately 8,000 armed men.[49] The principal centres of activity were in western Serbia, where Mihailović was also located, and in Šumadija. The Partisans' first attacks were mounted on gendarme stations and patrols, on railways and other lines of communication, on town halls (where tax and land-holding records were stored) and, finally, on German soldiers and patrols. In the areas of greatest Partisan activity free zones came to be created where the rule of the KPJ held sway. It was such an area, near Valjevo, that Tito came on 18 September, forsaking his underground existence in Belgrade to assume personal command of the growing Partisan forces.

Seriously alarmed by the dimensions of the revolt after initially underestimating it, the Germans sought to contain and eradicate it in two distinct ways. First, they sought reinforcements from Berlin for the three rear-guard divisions and various police units at their disposal in Serbia. Secondly, they replaced the Commissariat administration of Milan Aćimović with one bearing more of the trappings of a Serbian national government. This "government of national salvation" was headed by General Milan Nedić, the former Minister of War. The Nedić administration was intended to provide a rallying point for anti-communist Serbs and, it was hoped, assume part of the burden of fighting the rebels. This represented a further refinement in the Germans' well developed policy of setting the Yugoslavs against one another. In late August Felix Benzler, the representative of the German Foreign Ministry with the military commander in Serbia, reported to Berlin that "the situation has become more acute. The Communist movement is spreading and is operating with nationalist slogans which begin to meet with a response . . . German troops can move about in the country either by car or by train practically only in convoys."[50] The requested reinforcements were approved only in September, when Hitler ordered that the revolt be crushed with the most energetic measures, including reprisals against the civilian population. An infantry division and a tank battalion were ordered to Serbia from France, an infantry regiment and two further battalions were sent from Greece and, later in the autumn, an infantry division was withdrawn from the Eastern Front.[51]

(vi)

The first contacts between the communists and Mihailović were made by Partisan leaders in western Serbia in late June or early July. The Partisan representatives suggested joint operations against the Axis, but Mihailović demurred, citing the need to avoid falling into the error of Kosta Pećanac at Toplica in 1917: raising the standard of revolt prematurely.[52] Talks between the two sides were renewed in August, but Mihailović continued to maintain that the hour for revolt had not yet struck. Nonetheless a non-aggression pact was achieved. By September the success of the Communist Party in raising a force which threatened to eclipse his own compelled Mihailović to enter the fray - albeit cautiously, partially and against his better judgment. As a professional soldier with recent experience of the *Wehrmacht,* he could scarcely share the vision of immediate success which animated many of his fellow Serbs. Nor could he be unaware that the price of failure would be high.

Yet the exigencies of the situation supervened. Mihailović's strategy depended upon his being in a position to call the tune when the inevitable German withdrawal from the Balkans began, however many years distant that might be. He simply could not allow the communist-led Partisans to supplant him as leader of resistance and, hence, as arbiter of the post-war order - a role he coveted as much as did the Communist Party. If activism were required, he too could don the mask of the activist. That guise would in any case be the one most likely to bring him advantages abroad.[53]

Mihailović began to allow some of his commanders to participate with the Partisans in combined operations against the Germans. To have done otherwise would have risked alienating certain of them from his command. Given that his movement was rarely more than a grouping of local chieftains, whose allegiance to him was often tenuous, this was always a possibility. He also initiated a wider enlistment of peasant conscripts. By September agreements on collaboration had been reached between several individual Partisan and Četnik commanders. As one student of the Četnik movement has observed, "In collaborating with Tito, Mihailović was seeking a 'guarantee' against the Communists and trying to reassert his own authority over a badly split Četnik movement."[54]

The Partisans, already dedicated to relentless war and a harsh and ascetic discipline, looked with scorn upon the sloth, drunkenness and - so they felt - cowardly disinclination of the traditionally dressed and bearded Četniks to fight the Germans. They were also profoundly suspicious of the Četnik's easy relations with the authorities; not only with the local gendarmes and municipal leaders, but also with the Belgrade regime, and perhaps with the occupiers as well. Mihailović, for his part, already considered the Partisans little better than criminals. The catalogue of sins he ascribed to them was lengthy: they looted and robbed the people, they murdered the best and most nationalist-minded Serbs, they raped, they set fire to tax and land-holding records, they replaced village headmen with revolutionary councils, they disturbed the proper relations of society - the deference of poor to rich and of women to men, they provoked the wrath of the occupier and, most of all, they refused to accept his legitimate claim to supreme command.

Despite these mutually felt antagonisms, the KPJ continued its effort to establish and maintain effective military co-operation with the Mihailović forces. From the communists' point of view a model agreement had already been achieved with the small People's Peasant Party of Dr. Dragoljub Jovanović. Jovanović had accepted the Communist Party's claim to leadership of the Serbian revolt; his Party would participate as junior partners in those areas in which it was represented.[55] Mihailović, however, remained the principal imponderable. The Comintern insisted on the formation of a united front. Meanwhile the officers on Ravna Gora had begun to proclaim their close links with the British. If the Comintern's emphasis on the solidity of the Anglo-Soviet alliance were to have its logical concomitant in Yugoslavia, then agreement must be reached with Mihailović. The Četnik leader in any case enjoyed a popularity in Serbia which the communists dared not ignore; and his movement embraced activist-inclined officers needed by the Partisans - officers who might be weaned away if a united front were created.[56]

Suspicious of contacts between Mihailović and the Nedić rgime, the Partisan command also feared that if the Ravna Gora movement were not enlisted on the side of the revolt, then it might be successfully brought to bear against it. As the Regional Committee of the KPJ for Serbia informed the Valjevo Partisan Detachment in August, "We must win them over to common action and do so immediately, or else neutralize them at the proper moment. We must, in any case, protect our rear."[57] The seeds of future conflict were implicit in the Partisan effort at accommodation with Mihailović.

Arriving on liberated territory in western Serbia on 18 September, Tito immediately sought an interview with Mihailović. His intentions were, according to Marjanović, "to see for himself what the position of the command on Ravna Gora was and to try to win that group of officers over to active struggle against the occupier, whatever their connections with the English might be - in fact just because of those connections".[58] A meeting was arranged for the following day at the village of Struganik near Ravna Gora. The views of the two men on the proper form which resistance should take proved to be as irreconcilable as were their mutual pretensions to sole leadership of the anti-Axis movement. Tito upheld his established position that unrelenting struggle was the only possible course of action; Mihailović pointed to the Germans' military strength and to the likelihood that brutal reprisals would follow were anything other than "intelligent sabotage" undertaken at present. The only achievement of the meeting was a reaffirmation of the non-aggression agreement between the two sides, an agreement already being subjected to the strain of open clashes in some areas.[59]

Although neither side changed its strategic outlook in the month intervening between the first and second Tito-Mihailović meeting, the situation was altered significantly in other ways. The Partisans grew relatively stronger, the Mihailović Cetniks weaker. At a conference of military commanders from all regions of Yugoslavia, held in the west Serbian village of Stolice in late September, the Partisans reorganized their command structure and further elaborated their ideas about how their combined military and political struggle ought to proceed. The Partisans' Chief Command was transformed into a Supreme Command - headed still by Tito - and regional commands were established for each of the country's national units except Serbia. There it was intended that the Supreme Command would remain to direct the struggle. The regional commands were to prosecute the war in their own areas with only general directives from the Supreme Command. The political dimension of the National Liberation Movement was confirmed by the decision to proceed with the formation of National Liberation Councils in each liberated village or town. These would serve both as local supports for the Partisan military detachments and as instruments of revolutionary self-government. It was further envisaged that these councils would remain behind, underground, if and when enemy pressure forced a Partisan unit to abandon its native area. They would thus maintain the presence of the National Liberation Movement behind ever-fluctuating lines and provide the organizational framework for the formation of new Partisan detachments should that again become possible. Meanwhile the Partisans found themselves administering most of west central Serbia, an area now dubbed the "Užice Republic" after the town on which it was centred.[60]

Mihailović, who still viewed his interests as being best served by a show of unity, continued to permit some of his commanders to co-operate in operations with the Partisans, although he refused to commit his own small force to the anti-Axis struggle. In his messages to his government he sought nonetheless to ascribe any resulting successes to himself. He also allowed his followers to participate in the National Liberation Councils established in the towns and villages of the Užice Republic so as to share in the division of the spoils.[61] This collaboration was strained by disputes over the administration of these areas, over access to new recruits and over the advisability of further joint operations. The Partisans suspected that not only did Mihailović maintain links with Nedić, but also that he was seeking to reinsure himself with the

Germans by bailing their troops out of difficult situations and by treating their captives with unusual generosity. This, the Partisans felt, was the precursor of out and out collaboration between his movement and the occupiers. "Undoubtedly", according to Milazzo, "the only ones who took seriously Mihailović's collaboration with the Communists in September and October 1941 were the German authorities."[62]

(vii)

This was the situation in which Hudson and the British were now to become enmeshed. Accompanied on the long trek from Montenegro by several senior Partisan leaders whose function they did not yet realise, Hudson and Ostojić reached the Partisans' headquarters at Užice on 23 October. Three days before Tito had sent Mihailović a letter proposing more joint operations and a second meeting between the two men was in prospect. The presence of a British liaison officer at such a juncture might have been expected to have important consequences. And such was the case; though the ways were various and unexpected.

Lalatović, the radio operator Dragićević and the one functioning W/T set had been left behind by Hudson and Ostojić when they set out for Serbia. Lalatović's apparent object in remaining in Montenegro was to create an organization which would serve exclusively the interests of the Yugoslav government and its nominee, Mihailović, principally as a funnel for British arms and money. While Lalatović was thus endeavouring to secure the future, Hudson was forming a positive impression of the Partisans' strength, organization and activity in the territories through which he passed. He was shown no signs of Mihailović's organization. These observations could not, however, be reported to Malta, Cairo or London. Lalatović, suffering no such constraint, was meanwhile sending messages confirming that the Montenegrin nationalists had been instructed to co-operate only with elements recognizing the Yugoslav government and that Mihailović was being advised to refrain from warlike activity and to confine himself to the organization of such sabotage as would be unlikely to bring down the wrath of the occupiers on the civilian population.[63]

Hudson met Tito soon after arriving in Užice. According to Deakin, in the course of their cordial but non-commital conversation Hudson offered Tito the technical information necessary for him to make radio contact with British Middle East Headquarters in Cairo using his own equipment. The British, he said, would welcome the establishment of such a link. Hudson felt that Tito was not really interested in his proposal, that he would prefer to maintain what communication was necessary with the Allies through the Russians. The Partisans, he sensed, continued to believe in an imminent Russian breakthrough on the Eastern Front. Tito appears not to have asked Hudson for aid. He was, however, very interested in determining the nature of the British commitment to Mihailović. Hudson had made it clear that his orders were to proceed from Užice to Ravna Gora - where, in fact, Ostojić had already gone.[64] Tito gave the impression that he continued to hope that an accommodation with Mihailović would be possible, but he desired to know how it was that the Colonel had come to be regarded as a hero abroad when in fact "he was not fighting the occupiers at all". Hudson replied that the British government knew nothing about Mihailović: "That the whole thing has its source in some American newspapers for which an American journalist, who had been in Turkey, wrote a long article describing the heroic resistance of Draža Mihailović to the invaders."[65]

Hudson's stay in Užice was brief. On or about 25 October Ostojić returned there from Ravna Gora bearing a message from Mihailović requiring Hudson's immediate presence at his headquarters. Ostojić having, it seems, warned him in advance of Hudson's dangerously favourable attitude towards the Partisans, Mihailović greeted the new arrival with a reprimand for having been with the "communist rabble". When Hudson explained that his orders were to report on all resistance elements and that he therefore intended to visit Tito in Užice from time to time, Mihailović retorted that in that case he would be forced to sever all relations with him.[66] Contacts between his movement and the Partisans were an internal Yugoslav affair. It was Hudson's job to maintain liaison between the Yugoslav Army in the Fatherland and British Middle East Headquarters; it was not to meddle in his relations with the Partisans.[67] Mihailović subsequently added regarding Hudson, "He was to me a boy and I take no orders from boys!"[68]

Aside from the offence to Mihailović's *amour propre* evidently caused by Hudson's age and modest rank - and the more serious threat posed by his desire to maintain contact with the communists - there is no evidence that Hudson indicated anything but approval on the part of his superiors for Mihailović's movement and its aims. Indeed Mihailović later claimed that Hudson brought orders with him which confirmed British acceptance of both his passive strategy and his claim to sole leadership of the anti-Axis cause in Yugoslavia.[69] However that may be, Hudson's presence on Ravna Gora certainly signified for Mihailović the confirmation of what Ostojić had lately told him and what General Simović had promised in telegrams from London in mid-October: that he was henceforth to be regarded as the leader of Yugoslav resistance, that any co-operation with the communists would be on his terms, and that he could expect material aid to arrive shortly.[70] Mihailović could now meet Tito with a stronger claim to over-all command than his military strength or activity had heretofore afforded him.

Mihailović met with Tito in the village of Brajići near Ravna Gora late on the afternoon of 26 October. Tito suggested that Hudson participate, but Mihailović refused. In agreeing to a meeting which he had several times put off in recent weeks Mihailović appears to have aimed at impressing Hudson with his commitment to the achievement of a unified resistance. But he may not have wished to lay himself open to the risks which Hudson's participation in the negotiations might entail.[71] The atmosphere at the meeting was cold and unfriendly. Mihailović, supported in the discussion by Dragiša Vasić and

Colonel Dragoslav Pavlović, launched into a tirade against the Croats, accusing them of having betrayed Yugoslavia and holding them generally responsible for the outrages of the Ustaše. It would be necessary, he claimed, to settle accounts after the war; they could have no place in a renewed Yugoslav state. The Moslems would have to be "slaughtered". The political goal of the resistance must be to bring all Serb-inhabited lands inside Serbia's frontiers.

Mihailović's negotiation consisted of putting forward his demand that his headquarters assume command over all of Serbia. It was he who had the necessary officers and expertise. Tito said little and allowed his more detailed proposals to be argued by his lieutenants, Sreten Žujović and Mitar Bakić. They tabled a twelve-point plan for ensuring the continuation of combined operations against the Germans and Nedić. No doubt attempting to push Mihailović off his fence, the Partisans proposed the formation of a united headquarters to direct joint operations and a common quartermaster corps to oversee the equipping and feeding of troops from both movements. Titular command would in many cases have fallen to Mihailović's officers under such an arrangement, but the Partisans intended that their political support structure should be grafted on; political commissars and National Liberation Councils would make their appearance in Četnik areas as well.[72] Mihailović rejected these proposals out of hand, as well as the Partisans' suggestion that he abandon his claim to compulsory enlistment in the name of the King of Yugoslavs liable to conscription.

Limited agreements were reached however on the establishment of joint commands in areas already liberated, the sharing out of the production of the small arms factory in Užice and the vast quantity of Yugoslav bank notes found in vaults in the town, the creation of mixed commissions to examine the causes of disputes between the two sides, the establishment of war courts and, finally, on a pious declaration by both sides of their desire to avoid future conflicts and to co-ordinate activity. Neither had achieved what it wanted, but Mihailović least of all. It was immediately after this meeting that he determined to approach the Germans for help in his now firm resolve to destroy the Partisans.[73]

Hudson was very clearly worried by what was developing. Either just before or after the Brajići meeting Mihailović told him that he intended to launch an attack on the Partisans, but that this was an internal Yugoslav affair and no business of the British.[74] In his first message from Serbia on 27 October Hudson reported that Četnik-Partisan relations were "very delicate":

> Impossible maintain further contact with both parties. Necessary I return Cairo. Emissary [corrupt group] Mihailović has to acompany me. Safe aerodromes Čačak and Požega. [corrupt group] awaiting British planes . . . Five escaped British officers could accompany. Bring A.C. and accumulator W/T sets . . .[75]

There is no trace of any reply by SOE to this appeal. Hudson was on his own.

Mihailović had apparently regarded Tito's proposals as an ultimatum which he could not possibly accept.[76] He would cooperate with the Partisans only on condition that they accept his command unreservedly. This Tito was unwilling to do. The two movements' conceptions of resistance remained antithetical. Mihailović had made a show of entering the fray, but he had done so convinced that no struggle the Yugoslavs themselves might wage could avail unless and until an Allied landing in the Balkans were imminent. The Germans were now proving his point. Strengthened by reinforcements drawn from other fronts, they were massing for a full-fledged offensive on the rebel-held territory in west and central Serbia. They were also carrying out the sort of reprisals against the civilian population that Mihailović had feared. On 21 October in the industrial city of Kragujevac the Germans executed a large proportion of the male population, including schoolboys marched from their classrooms to the firing squads. Similar punishment was meted out on the city of Kraljevo for rebel activity in the vicinity. Mihailović reported the death toll to his government as being 2,300 in Kragujevac and 2,100 at Kraljevo.[77] More than ever the Partisans' strategy appeared criminal to Mihailović.

Hudson was later to feel that his own presence and, more especially, the promises made to Mihailović prior to his arrival on Ravna Gora encouraged him to feel that he could seek to eliminate the Partisans with impunity. As Hudson wrote in 1944:

> [The] British promise of support had the effect of worsening Četnik-Partisan relations. When I first arrived at Ravna Gora and Uzice at the end of October 1941, before Četnik-Partisan hostilities, Mihailović already knew by telegram that he would get British suport. He felt rightly that no one outside the country knew about the Partisans or that he alone was not responsible for the revolt.[78]

On 9 November, when the Četniks and Partisans had already clashed openly, the first British plane-load of arms and supplies was parachuted to Mihailović on Ravna Gora. The arrival of this first "symbolic airplane" strengthened Mihailović in the belief that he could disregard Hudson's warnings that something must be done to avert civil war. Hudson's position was rendered even weaker in subsequent days by his recommendation to Cairo, about which he informed Mihailović, that sorties be suspended while he tried to make peace between the two sides. No more arms were sent, but for technical reasons, and not because Cairo consciously adopted Hudson's advice. Hudson, however, now found himself regarded by Mihailović as a saboteur.[79] The Četniks, meanwhile, reaped the reward of their efforts to ensure that the population saw that the British plane had been intended for them. In real terms the aid rendered by one British airplane was insignificant; but, as Djelević observed, "the arrival of the airplane had a strong moral effect among the people. The news spread over the country that 'more than 100 airplanes' had brought us arms."[80]

(viii)

Hudson's was a unique perspective. He had been with both the Partisans and the Četniks. He was now to share with them the experience of a German offensive and the outbreak of civil war. The difficulties of interpreting this experience for decision-makers living in circumstances far removed from those prevailing in Yugoslavia in the autumn of 1941 were certainly formidable. In Hudson's case they were nearly insuperable. His access to Mihailović's radio apparatus, limited at best, was to cease altogether in the course of the German offensive. What few messages he did send were necessarily interpreted on the basis of a knowledge and understanding less complete than his own. This produced a clarity of thought and sharpness of analysis exceeding that evidenced by Hudson's surviving despatches, but which often also bore little relation to the complex reality of Yugoslav events.

Only in October did the question of resistance in Yugoslavia begin to press upon British policy-makers. It was then that it became apparent that a large-scale uprising was in progress and that previous, abstract considerations about the desirability of resistance might no longer apply.[81] On 3 October General Simović called upon Eden at the Foreign Office. He brought with him French translations of messages received from Djonović in the Near East. These described the resistance struggle and asked that arms be sent to those fighting in the mountain regions of Suvobor and Rudnik. They also provided more news of the massacres of Serbs being perpetrated in Pavelić's Croatia and asked that the British mount a bombing raid on Zagreb in retaliation. Simović lent his support to both requests.[82] The Foreign Office was more startled by the fact that Simović should have raised such topics with Eden than it was by the contents of the messages. Heretofore MEW had dealt with the Yugoslav government on resistance matters. From now on, however, the Foreign Office was to assume a far more active role in all Yugoslav affairs.

In his message asking for material support for the rebels Djonović distinguished three groups offering resistance: the regular army, the cetniks and the communists. Of these, according to Djonović, the regular army under Mihailović was the most prominent and exercised the greatest authority. In recent negotiations the communists had offered him the leading role in the uprising - *"le rôle de conduire"*.[83] Djonović did not say whether or not Mihailović had accepted, but went on to disparage the communists as *"vagabonds"* whose activity *"souvent se reduit au pillage"*. The impression created was that securing the collaboration of such elements was not really important. It was equally apparent that the Yugoslav ministers had chosen to regard Mihailović as their own.[84]

In its own councils the Yugoslav government took the appearance of the communist-led Partisans more seriously. On 2 October Ilic reported to Simović from Cairo that Mihailović was distressed by the activity of the Partisans:

> Colonel Mihailović complains that the communists are waging an ill-advised struggle and threatening by their premature action to compromise the entire affiar. They are courageous, brave and self-sacrificing - and are worthy of every attention. I have had to warn Mihailović, making him aware that the communist groups (or bands) are a dangerous and treacherous enemy. Today they are fighting against the Germans, but tomorrow they will be against the King and dynasty. In the mantime, I consider it necessary to emphasize that measures must be undertaken so that the communists defer to the command of Colonel Mihailović, because under control and skilful management their enthusiasm will be beneficial to our interests.[85]

The government stepped-up its efforts to bring the revolt to the attention of the British and to secure assistance for Mihailović. On 13 October King Peter visited the Prime Minsiter, bringing with him an aid memoire on the resistance. The Yugoslav note asked that a squadron of aircraft be established to supply the patriot forces, that tactical air support be afforded, that supplies and arms also be sent by submarine and that an immediate decision be reached on the creation of a Balkan front. The Yugoslavs wanted British troops to be landed as quickly as possible on the Montenegrin coast "to reinforce the action or at least safeguard the rear and bases of the rebels."[86] Notwithstanding the unreality of the specific requests, Churchill referred the King's note to the

Chiefs of Staff Committee with the admonition that urgent consideration be given what immediate help might be sent to the rebels. General Sir Hastings Ismay, architet of Churchill's high command structure and Deputy Secretary of the War Cabinet, circulated the paper to the Chiefs of Staff Committee on 14 October. They expressed doubts about both the timelessness of the Yugoslav revolt and their own competence to decide the matter, but also asked for information on what sort of aid the rebels required and what it was in Britain's power to provide.[87]

Reports by SOE and the Joint Planning Staff were put before the Chiefs of Staff the next day. These again raised the essential question of whether or not a revolt was wanted in Yugoslavia. Gladwyn Jebb explained what SOE knew, as well as what had already been done to establish contact with the patriot forces. According to SOE's information, Mihailović was the principal leader, though there were other bands of *komitadji* and a group of communists was operating in eastern (*sic*) Serbia. Mihailović had been sent £20,000 and advised to expect drops of supplies in the near future. Jebb also furnished a list of the rebels' most immediate needs and indicated that SOE and the Commanders-in-Chief, Middle East, were working closely on the matter. The Joint Planners' report emphasized that SOE's close involvement with the Yugoslavs in fostering and spreading the revolt perhaps rendered inapplicable the general rule that premature uprisings in occupied countries not be encouraged. This of course was disingenuous, but was apparently thought to provide the necessary rationale for the Joint Planners' conclusion that the "guerrillas should be supported and encouraged to cause the maximum trouble to the Axis now".[88]

These reports, plus a minute from Dalton to the Prime Minister, induced the Chiefs of Staff Committee to approve a telegram for the Commanders-in-Chief, Middle East, which attempted to reconcile their own continuing lack of enthusiasm for the revolt with the favourable views of SOE and the Joint Planning Staff: "From our point of view revolt is premature, but patriots have thrown their caps over the fence and must be supported by all possible means." The Commanders-in-Chief were asked to report on what they were doing to help the rebels and what they could do in future without prejudicing their own operations.[89] No reply had been received from General Sir Claude Auchinleck when the Chiefs of Staff next discussed the Yugoslav uprising on 22 October. Faced with another appeal by the Yugoslav government that all possible help be sent to the 80-100,000 men claimed to be fighting, the Chiefs of Staff despatched a second telegram to Cairo: "Transportation difficulties are realized but we urge the importance of doing anything which is in any way possible for these people who are fighting for their lives."[90]

The importance of the Yugoslav revolt was now accentuated by the intervention of the Soviet Ambassador, Ivan Maisky. He called upon Eden on 22 October to testify to his government's concern, and to propose joint action in support of the uprising. Policy towards the revolt, he said, was too important a matter to be left to the military authorities: "he himself had some experience as a guerrilla and had a number of suggestions that he would like to make". Armed with a list of the rebels' requirements provided him by the Yugoslav government, Maisky asked Eden to secure authority to concert plans for aiding the uprising. The Foreign Secretary assured Maisky that the British shared his view of the importance of Yugoslav resistance and already had action in hand. He promised to seek approval from the Prime Minister for an exchange of ideas between the two governments on joint measures that might be taken to aid the Yugoslav insurgents.[91]

Churchill agreed and Eden scheduled a meeting with Maisky for the following week. The Foreign Office prepared a report on what was known about events in Yugoslavia and what had been done to restore contact with the country. It was the intention of the Foreign Office to pass this information on to the Soviet Ambassador. The Chiefs of Staff approved the plan, but Jebb expressed reservations on behalf of SOE. In a letter to Sargent he explained that SOE already maintained liaison with OGPU (The Soviet secret service) and would prefer that details of "joint help" being given to the insurgents not be discussed with Maisky. The Foreign Office draft was suitably amended. Maisky would be given an oral account of what the British knew about the uprising, and what they were doing to aid it, but there would be no discussion of Anglo-Soviet operations - past, present or future.[92]

Jebb's reference to joint help for the rebels by SOE and the Soviet secret service remains as obscure as his reasons for asking that Maisky be excluded from any discussion of the subject. The only recorded attempt to co-ordinate SOE and OGPU policy towards the uprising had already fallen through, although it is possible that there was talk of reviving it. This effort had taken place in Turkey and the Middle East during the summer. Disturbed by Rakić's account of the division of the Yugoslav resistance into communist and nationalist factions, Djonović had advised his government that co-ordinated action by the British, Soviet and Yugoslav governments was necessary to heal the breach. He proposed that a mission composed of officers from all three countries be sent to Yugoslavia with instructions to promote a united resistance. His hope was that the Soviets might thereby be committed to the support of Mihailović and would call the Partisans to heel.

Djonović approached Colonel S.W. Bailey, SOE station chief in Istanbul, and his Soviet counterpart, Colonel Nikolajev, with his proposition. Nikolajev replied that his government endorsed the idea and stood ready to provide an aircraft for the despatch of a mixed mission to Mihailović's headquarters on Suvobor, crash landing there if need be. This offer was accepted by SOE and the operation was scheduled to take place during September, in fact at about the same time as Hudson was being landed on the Montenegrin coast. A second Anglo-Yugoslav mission was to be formed and sent to join its Soviet component and the aircraft at an airbase in Armenia, whence the joint mission was to be flown to Serbia. This flight never took place.

According to Djonović, last minute orders came from both the British and Simovic torpedoing the plan. Julian Amery, who was also involved in planning the operation, places the responsibility for the cancellation on the Yugoslav government. Suspicious of Soviet intentions and desiring to exclude them from contact with the resistance, the Yugoslav government, according to Amery, sent orders to Ilić that he should advise the British against the Soviet scheme. The SOE Balkan section chief in Cairo, Tom Masterson, accepted Ilić's advice and the mission was scrapped. The Russians, for their part, discovered the reasons for the cancellation and withdrew their agent from Istanbul. His successor appeared to be under orders to be less forthcoming.[93]

Amery regards this incident as the great missed opportunity to have insured cooperation between the Partisans and the Četniks - and on terms favourable to Mihailović - before hostilities between them began. It is arguable, however, that with immediate experience of Mihailović and his organization the Soviets might have been even quicker to consign him to the obloquy which they later proclaimed his. Maisky's approach to Eden in October indicates in any case that the Soviets had not yet given up the idea of cooperation; they had simply changed the line of approach and the venue. It is likely that the Russians would have considered it both physically impossible and politically risky to have attempted to aid the Partisans at this time. On the other hand they were being subjected to the same desperate appeals for help from Tito as Mihailović was now making to the British and Yugoslav governments. Asking the British to lead the way in providing aid to the insurgents may have seemed the only way forward.[94] The British, however, still appeared unconcerned. In the absence of actual fighting between the two movements in Yugoslavia, and possessing little information about the Partisans, London did not seem to attach any great significance to the Soviet approach. SOE and the Foreign Office determined to share information, but they did not yet feel the need to propose to the Soviet government positive action to assist or unite the rebels. When they did they were to find both the problems and the Soviets far more intractable.

Eden met with Maisky on 29 October. As agreed with Jebb, the Soviet Ambassador was given an oral summary of British aid to the insurgents and an appreciation of events in the country as seen from London. According to the brief prepared for the meeting by SOE, events had compelled the British to amend their policy on resistance. The development of what was now seen as a national uprising had eclipsed the former goal of reintroducing agents to stimulate passive resistance and economic dislocation: "realising the great importance of assisting such a revolt, particularly to draw off pressure from the Russian front, it was decided to give the insurgents every aid in our power." So far that aid had consisted only of 5 million dinars,[95] sent to Colonel Mihailović to finance his operations until further assistance could be provided. For, as Maisky was told, it had been impossible to make arrangements with Mihailović for the receipt of air sorties at his headquarters whilst his communications remained insecure. Now that the agents landed in Montenegro had made their way to Ravna Gora and provided Mihailović with safe ciphers, it was expected that the first direct supply flights from Egypt would soon take place. In future a squadron of specially adapted long-range aircraft would be established on Malta which, in combination with the occasional submarine, would meet the needs of the resistance: "It is confidently expected that the revolt can not only be maintained, but that it will be progressively successful." Maisky pronounced himself well-satisfied with this over-sanguine analysis. He did not, it seems, take exception either to SOE's attribution to Mihailović of national leadership or to the information that a communist group operating near Šabac was led by a Russian named Lebedev. Rather, he devoted his energies to endorsing another list of Mihailović's requirements provided by the Yugoslav government.[96]

Having set the seal with Maisky upon their common commitment to an active and politically undifferentiated resistance in Yugoslavia, Eden had something of a surprise later the same day when he met with General Simović. In the course of the conversation Simović remarked that he had just sent orders to Mihailović "to go slow for the present in order to avoid provoking German retaliation on a large scale".[97] Eden asked Simović if he had consulted SOE before sending such instructions. He had not. This was disturbing to the Foreign Office on two counts. First, it seemed that Simović did not have "the right ideas" about the uprising (it was now mentioned that he had lately been heard to enquire what provisions the British might be able to make for evacuating the rebels should Axis pressure become intolerable) and, secondly, it revealed that there was no effective policy coordination between SOE and the Yugoslav Premier. The latter, the Foreign Office feared, would not feel obliged to consult the junior emissaries of SOE before sending off orders to Mihailović.

Eden delegated the Minister to the Yugoslav government, George Rendel, to tackle Simović on the current issue and to serve in future as policy coordinator between the Foreign Office, SOE and the military chiefs on the one hand, and the exile government on the other. Rendel was to urge upon Simović the necessity for full consultation and to point out the importance of not sending defeatist instructions to the men in the field. It was typical of Simović that by the time Rendel met with him on 3 November he had waxed enthusiastic about the revolt, urging that it be expanded lest the Germans crush it before it assumed really formidable proportions. Anything less, he opined, would be to play the hand of the quisling Nedić.[98]

The Foreign Office had meanwhile set out to proselytise the military establishment as well. No reply having yet been received from Cairo to the Chiefs' various inquiries about what the Commanders-in-Chief proposed to do, the Chiefs of Staff had themselves offered to send two long-range aircraft out from England for use in supplying the Yugoslavs from Malta. Even this would not permit, however, the sort of large scale assistance that the Foreign Office deemed necessary.[99] At a meeting of the War Cabinet on 30 October Eden moved that the entire question of aid for the insurgents be referred to the Defence Committee. This was agreed.[100]

Drawing together the strands of his recent discussions with Maisky and Simović, as well as the telegrams to Cairo by the Chiefs of Staff, Eden placed before the Defence Committee on 31 October a memorandum on the revolt. His purpose was to acquaint his colleagues with the measures that had been taken and were likely to be taken to help the rebels, to emphasize their high importance and to insert the Foreign Office into the role of policy coordinator should the military decline or disparage that task. The revolt, it was pointed out again, had assumed the proportions of a national uprising. In such circumstances the scale of aid being contemplated by the Chiefs of Staff was hardly adequate:

> It seems to me that we should regard this revolt not as a premature incident owing to which we are obliged to give limited help to patriots fighting for their lives, but as at least a minor diversion in the war against Germany which should be treated as part of the operations conducted by the Commanders-in-Chief, Middle East.

Eden called attention to the fact that by helping the Yugoslavs Britain would be able to assure the Soviets that everything possible was being done to create the second front in the Balkans that they desired. Eden also endorsed SOE's view that British staff officers should be sent to help Mihailović in the direction of the uprising. This would make it plain to the Middle East Commanders that Yugoslav resistance fell within their operational sphere. Policy towards the revolt, he concluded, ought in future to be coordinated with General Simović either through the Foreign Office or the CIGS so as to ensure that the Yugoslav government did not again send out undesirable instructions.[101]

While the Foregin Office awaited the reaction of the Defence Committee to the Secretary of State's memorandum, replies were finally received from Cairo on the measures being taken there to assist the revolt. In a telegram dated 31 October the Commanders-in-Chief detailed their plan to send three planeloads of supplies and a Yugoslav officer to Radovče on the night of 3-4 November. (This sortie had apparently been arranged by Lalatović. But as Cairo reported several days later, bad weather over the drop area forced the planes to divert to Malta, where their cargoes were unloaded in expectation of the arrival of the two aircraft being sent out from England.) More generally, however, the Commanders expressed themselves unwilling permanently to allocate aircraft belonging to their command for duty ferrying supplies to Yugoslavia. Sorties such as the abortive effort of 3-4 November would be exceptional occurrences, although Cairo did promise to use to the utmost the two Whitley bombers being sent to Malta. Nor did they exclude the occasional employment of submarines for supply runs. The Foreign Office was disappointed. Dixon minuted that "the scale of help is appropriate to an incident and not to a minor operation". Eden despaired at the "very slow progress'.[102]

Yet worse news was at hand. On 3 November the War Office informed Dixon that the Director of Military Operations had decided against aiding the resistance on an increased scale and was arguing as much in a report to the CIGS. The revolt, the DMO felt, was premature. Nothing would be gained by attempting to implement the proposals made by the Foreign Secretary in his 31 October memorandum. Cadogan and Sargent were at a loss to understand such reasoning. As Sargent minuted, the Germans were now stretched almost to the breaking point on the Russian front: "What better conditions can we expect, short of the actual collapse of the German armies?"[103]

The Defence Committee met on 3 November to consider a draft of instrutions by the Chiefs of Staff for the Commanders-in-Chief, Middle East. This draft, like the Chiefs' orders to Cairo on 15 October, was a compromise - an attempt to split the difference between the aggressive views of SOE and the Foreign Office and the DMO's lack of enthusiasm for the revolt:

> Rebels are located in difficult hill country whence they may well be able to keep movement in being for a long time, but probably only as a nuisance to Axis and not more. For revolt to develop into a nationwide rebellion, the movement would have to spread to the towns where in the absence of British forces it would certainly be quelled by the Germans with extreme ruthlessness. This must be avoided. Our policy should therefore be to provide rebels with supplies necessary to maintain movement in the hills.[104]

The military authorities were proving unwilling to abandon their fixed conception of the type and manner of resistance which was possible and desirable in occupied Europe. The assurances of SOE and the Foreign Office that, at least in Yugoslavia, a full-fledged national uprising was already in progress seemed to count for little. Wedded to the concept of secret armies in countries more developed, ethnically homogeneous and urban than Yugoslavia, the Chiefs of Staff showed little understanding for what was happening in the country. They were thus unwilling to enter into what might prove to be an open-ended commitment of Britain's scant resources for what they considered to be a dubious adventure.

The Foreign Office and SOE returned to the charge the following day. Meeting with Churchill and the Chiefs of Staff, Eden and Dalton urged that more be done, particularly as the other occupied nations of Europe would regard this first revolt as a "test case" of Britain's willingness and ability to lend them assistance. Although the Air Chief Marshal, Sir Charles Portal, pointed out that the number of aircraft available was insufficient for the task and described the manifold difficulties of dropping arms by night to guerrillas on mountain tops, Churchill ordered that everything possible be done to keep the Yugoslav revolt going. His only proviso was that the effort not interfere with any major operations planned in the Middle East theatre. The Admiralty and SOE were also directed to investigate the possibilities of using local shipping, including caiques, to ferry aid to the rebels.[105]

On 7 November the Chiefs of Staff nonetheless approved the draft instructions for Cairo that they had previously placed before the Defence Committee. The Foreign Office was disturbed that such a discouraging brief was to be sent to the Commanders-in-Chief in apparent contravention of the Prime Minister's rulings on 4 November.[106] "If the Cs-in-C receive a telegram in these terms," Dixon minuted, "they will not be disposed to make any special effort to help the revolt." This, he feared, was the real intention of the War Office.[107] Cadogan wrote immediately to Hollis, Secretary to the Chiefs of Staff, proposing amendments designed to make the directive less dampening. These were accepted and the telegram sent off, but the substance remained the same: the revolt was to be regarded as premature and should not be encouraged to spread since "we are not in a position to give the Yugoslavs substantial military aid". Apparently resentful of the Foreign Office's repeated interventions, Hollis now delivered himself of a small lecture on the traditional military precept that a local commander must always be allowed the greatest leeway in deciding how to fight a campaign. To this Sargent confided to his department, "All right. But I wish I felt more sure that the C-in-C, Middle East, did consider the Yugoslav revolt as a 'campaign' in the success of which he was directly concerned."[108]

(ix)

The enthusiasm of the Foreign Office and SOE for sending all possible assistance to the Yugoslav insurgents rested upon premises which were now severely shaken. In the first place, detailed reports were received from the country during November which cast doubt upon the assumption that Mihailović was the principal leader of Yugoslav resistance and offered new information about the role and aims of the communist-led Partisans. Secondly, and more importantly, it became clear in the course of the month that civil war had broken out between the two movements. Exclusive backing for Mihailović was to be reaffirmed, but it could no longer be assumed that the grounds were solely military.

Two reports dealing with the events of the past summer were received in London in November from Yugoslavs lately escaped from their homeland. Apparently the first to reach the Foreign Office was that of Gordana and Gradimir Bajloni, members of a prominent Belgrade family who arrived in Lisbon in late October. Their report asserted that the communists, led by the Russian Lebedev, had been responsible for nearly all guerrilla activity. About Mihailović they reported:

> Up until now the Germans have not pursued the followers of Mihailović (except for one insignificant bombing of the headquarters on Ravna Gora) due to the fact that they have not undertaken any sort of action against the Germans, considering that it is still too early for that and also because they are awaiting instructions from the [Yugoslav] High Command.[109]

Mihailović's purpose, according to the Bajloni report, was to prepare an uprising for the moment of German collapse:

> The aim of action at the given moment will be to expel the enemy from the country, to maintain order and to secure the state's frontiers - and, insofar as possible, also those areas which we claim - and to hand over power to the King as soon as he arrives.

The Serbs would remain peaceful while the work of organization went on.[110]

The other report on the resistance which reached the Foreign Office at this time was the work of Dr. Miloš Sekulić, a prominent member of the Serbian Agrarian Party who arrived in Istanbul in late September claiming to represent Mihailović.[111] Besides information on the military situation, Sekulić brought with him a document originating with the Synod of the Serbian Orthodox Church. It was this which caused the greater stir at the time since it contained the first detailed account of the massacres of Serbs in the NDH and provoked a crisis in the exile government. Amidst the unleashing of passions on this score, the military report, which he compiled in London, appears to have gone largely unnoticed; and there is no indication that anyone in the Foreign Office even read the forty-odd closely typed pages of Serbo-Croat text which the Yugoslav government passed on to them in late November. SOE in the Middle East must, however, have been aware of what Sekulić intended to report upon arrival in London.[112]

Sekulić confirmed and expanded upon much of what the Bajloni report had indicated. Mihailović, he wrote, knew that victory would come on the principal Allied battlefronts and not in Yugoslavia. Therefore, the time for action by his army would come only during the interregnum when the Germans had begun to withdraw from the Balkans. It would be his task then to maintain order, to prevent looting and destruction, to disarm the Germans - inflicting upon them losses sufficient to cause the survivors to dread ever again invading Yugoslavia - and to punish Yugoslavs guilty of collaborating with the occupiers. The eventual accomplishment of these aims required the establishment of a secret army organized along traditional Četnik lines. A small cadre of officers and men would organize the population as a whole for future action. Peasants would be enrolled in Četnik units, but not called upon to abandon their normal pursuits until the edifice of German power began to crack. Meanwhile, activity would be defensive in nature. Only occasionally would sabotage be carried out and the Germans would be fought only when engagements were unavoidable. Sekulić contended that more and more Četnik bands were accepting the overall command of Mihailović and that the movement was thus assuming the shape of a regular army.

The communists, on the other hand, were mounting an offensive campaign. Their detachments covered Serbia, Banat and Montenegro and had lately appeared in Croatia and Dalmatia as well. In Backa, Macedonia and Slovenia they were reported to be in the organizational phase. "These detachments," Sekulić wrote, "are linked to one another and to a central leadership by orders issued by it." Their ranks were filled not only by communists, but by all those who demanded an immediate offensive against the Axis: "One could say that often there are only communists at the head, but that their detachments haven't a clue about communism."

> Their morale is exceptional and their disposition is for direct action and sabotage. Their desire is that this action spread not only over the territory of Yugoslavia, but over all of Europe with the aim of easing the Soviet front by breaking-up Hitler's rear. As we are seeing, they are not thinking about the situation during the interregnum, but are acting . . . to help the Soviet army and to hasten the end of the war.

As part of that effort the communists had continually pressed Mihailović to join them in a common front.[113]

That the Yugoslavs passed this report on to the British with apparent approval was a measure of their continuing confidence that British policy remained identical to theirs. The principal reason why this could be taken for granted was the outbreak of civil war. As we have seen, in late October Mihailović concluded that further resistance to the Germans could only have catastrophic consequences both for his movement and for the Serbian people with whom he equated it. Despite his frantic pleas and Simović's frequent promises, aid in arms had not yet arrived from abroad. His only alternative seemed to be to suggest cooperation to the Germans and to seek arms from them for the necessary reckoning with the Partisans. As one of Mihailović's intermediaries in the imminent talks with the Germans, Colonel Branislav Pantić, testified, "Because of the stand of the communists there was no other way but to use force to put an end to their destructive campaign; for discussions with them had not led to their abandonment of their military action." At a meeting of his top advisers, held in Struganik on 27 or 28 October, Mihailović decided to approach the Germans and drew up a list of demands.[114]

On 28 October two of Mihailović's liaison officers in Belgrade, Colonel Pantić and Captain Nenad Mitrović, met with Nedić. They declared that Mihailović was ready to offer his services to the Axis in the struggle against the Partisans. A meeting was arranged later that day with a representative of the *Abwehr*, Captain Josef Matl, to repeat Mihailović's offer. In return for 5000 rifles, 375 machine guns and a free zone for operations against the communists, the Četniks pledged to recognize that the country was defeated and that the Germans possessed rights of occupation. Matl, after referring the offer to his superiors, replied the next day that Mihailović should come to Belgrade for negotiations. It was agreed that Matl would meet Mihailović on 3 November in the town of Lajkovać (just north of Ravna Gora) and escort him to Belgrade.

Mihailović, meanwhile, overestimating his ability to deal the Partisans a knock-out blow, had launched an attack on Užice during the night of 1-2 November. The Partisans anticipated his intentions and counter-attacked on a broad front. Because of the raging battle Mihailović failed to appear at the appointed spot on 3 November. His representatives, Pantić and Mitrović, arrived late bearing his excuses and a letter explaining his need to remain with units fighting the Partisans in the Užice - Požega - Kosjerić and Ivanjica regions. He proposed that the meeting be postponed until at least 9 November.

After suffering serious reverses at the hands of the Partisans at Užice and Čačak in the intervening week, Mihailović renewed his approach to the Germans. He did so despite the arrival on 9 November of the first British airplane bearing arms and money for his movement. Compared to his needs the aid rendered by one British sortie was insignificant;[115] while Hudson's attitude boded ill for further shipments. Mihailović proposed a meeting closer to his base of operations. The Germans agreed. Thus Mihailović met Matl and two senior German officials at an inn near the village of Divci (five miles east of Valjevo) on the evening of 11 November.

As in his hopes of scoring a quick and decisive victory over the Partisans, Mihailović was likewise deceived in expecting the Germans to provide him with both the wherewithal and the licence to continue the struggle. The German command had authorized the meeting not to negotiate an alliance with Mihailović, but to present an ultimatum requiring his unconditional surrender. Not only did the Germans fully intend in the near future to rid Serbia of the communist menace themselves, Mihailović was told, but they had no faith in him as an ally. He had refused past overtures from Nedić seeking close cooperation and had participated in attacks on German forces. Mihailović essayed to convince the Germans of his good faith. He claimed that he was not London's representative, he dismissed Četnik attacks on German soldiers as the work of "disobedient elements" and he discounted his agreements with the Partisans as not being serious. He asked for large quantities of arms and munitions at least five times in the course of the 90 minute meeting, expressing the hope that they might be delivered that very night. When the Germans replied that they had no instructions save to demand his surrender. Mihailović terminated the discussion. He had not, he said, ridden all day on horseback while his units fought a heavy engagement with the Partisans around Čačak in order to hear this. Such a message could have been passed through intermediaries. He would discuss his eventual answer with his commanders. Despite the manner of Mihailović's leavetaking, his representatives continued to urge an alliance on the Germans during their journey together back to Belgrade.[116]

On 13 November Simovic addressed a letter to Eden which contained the text of a telegram just received from Mihailović:

> The communists have attacked us, and forced us to fight at the same time against Germans, communists, Ustaše and other factions. In spite of this the whole nation is for the King. Hundreds of thousands of our men are without arms, and those who have arms lack ammunition. The communists have established themselves in the valley of the [Western] Morava, with their chief centres of resistance at Čačak, Požega and Užice.
>
> The impressions of an English officer are that the communists at the head of the 'Partisans' are also against the forces of the Axis. Montenegro is organized by the 'Partisans'. The Četnik leaders say openly that they prefer to collaborate with Nedić (*sic*) rather than with the communists. Colonel Mihailović and his officers are loyal to the King. Both parties are engaging important German forces. Many of the fighters now working with the communists would go over to the Četniks at once on the latters' receiving the promised help from England. A civil war would last long, and in the meantime, nothing would be undertaken against the Germans.

Simović reported that he had already ordered the Yugoslav Minister in the USSR to ask the Soviet government to warn the communists in Yugoslavia that they must help Mihailović and collaborate with him against the Germans. He had also put the same request to Maisky. Now he asked that the British support his initiative.[117]

Mihailović's message - though contradictory in parts - was a skilful appeal. It raised the spectre of his forces being compelled to collaborate with the Axis against the communists were significant aid not forthcoming and were the Partisans not forced to submit to his command. The onus of responsibility was thus placed squarely on the British and Yugoslav governments. Meanwhile, the action of the Partisans was reduced to the "impressions of an English officer" that they too were opposed to the Axis.

Hudson's own proposals in light of the civil war were embodied in a radiogram sent out by him on 13 November. He too assumed that Mihailović was the man around whom all elements must unite. He urged, however, that Mihailović be denied help unless and until he permitted an attempt "to incorporate all anti-fascist elements under his command". Hudson asked Cairo for permission to travel to Partisan headquarters to mediate the dispute and suggested that his effort be preceded by a broadcast appeal for unity from Moscow to the Partisans.[118]

But in a previous telegram, dated 5 November, Mihailovith revealed the depth of his own dread of Tito's movement and offered his answer to Hudson's efforts to reconcile the two sides:

> The leader of the communists in Serbia under the false name Tito cannot be considered a leader of resistance. The fight of the communists is illusory. They are supplied with arms from the factory in Užice. They have attacked my troops in Ivanjica, Požega, Arilje, Užice, Gorjevnica, Ražana, Kosjerić and other places. I have accepted the battle and believe that its outcome will be favourable to me. I repeat, the communists have no leaders of resistance against the Germans. If they are aided by England, then I will refuse [English] aid. The Partisans seized their arms from the people. I could not follow the same

> course. They have the arms factory at Uzice from which they give us nothing, and if it is still necessary for you to supply them with English arms, then we are finished for good.[119]

This last comment no doubt reflected Mihailović's fear lest the British approve Hudson's idea, dating from before his arrival at Ravna Gora, that the Partisans should also receive British help. Such a suggestion in the circumstances in which Mihailović now found himself was simply unthinkable.

In London, where consideration was being given the question of how best to deal with the outbreak of civil war, it seems that nothing was known about Mihailović's talks with the Germans. On the other hand, SIS was aware that his forces were now working with those of Nedić. An intelligence summary based on information received on 13 and 14 November from "Most Secret Sources" reported that, "Government irregulars have been cooperating with the (Nedić) Serb Gendarmerie in fighting the 'communists'."[120] It was also apparent that Mihailović expected to be provided with British arms for this purpose. On 12 November he telegraphed that as soon as the requested quantity of arms was received he would "be able to liquidate the communists immediately".[121] Although some officials at SOE and the Foreign Office were later to regret that he did not succeed, at the time all attention was focused on finding a means by which the conflict might be resolved. Hudson had been preaching resistance unity for some time past. Now London sought to find a formula to revivify this message in far more inauspicious circumstances.

The Commanders-in-Chief, Middle East, had, like Simović, weighted in on 13 November with news of the civil war and with the same prescription: an appeal to the Russians. Cairo reported that the Adriatic coast was no longer in rebel hands and that the onset of winter weather would severely limit their ability to send Mihailović support by air.[122] Thus it seems that despite the realization that Mihailović intended to use any arms sent to him against the Patisans - and Hudson's explicit recommendation that the denial of arms be used to force a reconciliation between the two sides - it was the weather and not a policy decision which precluded the shipment of aid at this time.[123]

On 15 November SOE provided the Foreign Office with its considered opinion. Elaborating on the telegrams received from the country, Lord Glenconner wrote to Douglas Howard, head of the Southern Department, that the communists provided the leadership in Montenegro, but that Mihailović dominated events in Serbia. This neat analysis was understandable given the inadequate mention by Hudson of the Partisans' organized existence in Serbia, but it resulted in an underestimation of the problems involved in restoring peace between the two factions. Nonetheless, as far as SOE was concerned, two points stood uppermost:

> (i) To back up the Partisans would be tantamount to the repudiation of the Yugoslav government, who have naturally designated Mihailović as the leader of all Yugoslav forces in Yugoslavia.
>
> (ii) If the revolt is to prosper, its inspiration must be that it is a fight taken up by all Yugoslavs for Yugoslavia, and not a revolt against the occupying forces, engineered by Moscow and led by communists who are fighting for Russia.

Glenconner continued that the Mihailović forces, if supported by both the Yugoslav and British governments with arms and money, would be far more likely to establish "their undisputed authority" than would the Partisans. It was therefore not a question of whom to support, but of how to manifest that support. It was proving difficult to send aid to Mihailović by air; anything sent by sea to Montenegro might fall into the hands of the communists. Thus the best means available of expressing support for Mihailović would be to allow the Yugoslav government to designate him officially as the leader of the anti-Axis rebellion and to point out to the Russians that it was in their own interest to support this decision. They should be aksed to broadcast orders to the Partisans "to put themselves unreservedly at the disposal of Mihailović, the national leader".[124] Thus SOE remained firm in the belief that it was possible to anoint from outside the leader of Yugoslav resistance.

The Foreign Office, agreeing completely with Lord Gelnconner's analysis, went into action. Howard wrote to Hollis on 16 November that "it is essential if the revolt is to prosper that we should continue our support to Colonel Mihailović and endeavour to rally the communists to him".[125] Messages were sent to the Commanders-in-Chief, Middle East, and to Hudson advising them of the new policy of unity under Mihailović and of the steps being taken to secure it.[126] What these steps should be had already been suggested by Simović in his letter to Eden of 13 November, as well as by Mihailović in his all too apparent haste to liquidate the Partisans. Cripps was instructed on 16 November to lend support to the representations of his Yugoslav colleague in Kuibyshev; while on the same day in London (a Sunday) Maisky was summoned to the Foreign Office by Cadogan. The Soviet Ambassador assured Cadogan that he had already acted upon Simović's request and would now repeat to his government how important London considered the matter to be. Cadogan urged that both sides in the Yugoslav conflict be warned to abstain from retailiatory acts. All elements must rally round Mihailović if the revolt were to succeed.

In the USSR the Yugoslav Charge d'Affaires, Dragomir Bogić, and Cripps saw Vyshinski on 17 and 18 November respectively. Cripps reported later that Bogić had attempted to strengthen his case by concealing from the Russian that fighting was already going on between the two sides. He hoped thereby to avoid making the Soviets feel obligated to come to the aid of their Yugoslav followers. He also tried to convince Vyshinski that the Partisans were not real communists and that Mihailović's politics were far to the left. Cripps took a different tack in urging Mihailović's case as national leader. He did not attempt to hide the fact that the two sides were fighting. When Vyshinski inquired how it had happened that they had fallen out, Cripps replied that Simović's earlier discouragement of active resistance had led Mihailović to seek contacts with Nedić. This may have led the "other groups" to turn against him. Vyshinski asked if this had not compromised Mihailović, but Cripps assured him that it had not; for nothing had come of the contacts and the Yugoslav government had since changed its attitude. Vyshinski affirmed that his government desired to see a unified resistance movement, but would not be inclined to intervene unless there appeared to be some prospect of success. Cripps gathered that the Soviets had no direct communications with Yugoslavia.[127]

When he met with Eden on 19 November Simović naturally expressed full agreement with the British effort to rally the communists to Mihailović. He showed Eden a telegram he had already sent to Mihailović urging him to "smooth out differences and refrain from any kind of vindictive action". Less satisfactory from the British point of view, however, was the assurance offered to the Colonel in the same telegram that the government had "taken measures for the Partisans to cease unnecessary action and place themselves under your command in the sense of my speech of the 15th [November]". In that broadcast speech Simović had ordered an end to sabotage in Yugoslavia. He now told Eden that not only did the communists' campaign of sabotage provoke cruel reprisals by the Germans against the civilian population of Serbia, but it also handicapped Mihailović. He asked the Foreign Secretary to raise this issue with Maisky as well. Uneasy about this recrudescence of defeatism, which threatened besides to undermine the possibility of securing Russian cooperation in managing the Partisans, the Foreign Secretary determined to canvass SOE and the military for their views on what was and was not appropriate resistance activity.[128]

The views of the War Office and SOE matched those of the Foreign Office. Brigadier Mallaby, replying for the former on 22 November, wondered what the insurgents, "whether they be communists or followers of Mihailović, would find to do if they gave up sabotage".[129] While Jebb, whose opinion the Foreign Office especially valued, wrote on 2 December also to dispute Simović's line. Not only was sabotage the basic means by which resitance should be carried out, but:

> Finally, reprisals are a double-edged weapon in the hands of the German authorities, since the more savage the measures they adopt, the more do they rouse the people and make them ready to accept any sacrifice. This principle, it is true, does *not* apply to countries where we are endeavouring to form subversive organizations on a large scale and where no revolt has, up to now, actually broken out; but it certainly does apply to a country where operations of war are actually being conducted against the occupying forces; for in such circumstances it is only by hotting up the nation to murder Germans and Italians wherever they may see them that the revolt has any prospect of maintaining itself in being at all.

Jebb qualified his conclusion that sabotage could not handicap Mihailović by observing that he was the leader on the spot and therefore in the best position to judge.[130] This inclination to give Mihailović the benefit of the doubt was influenced by a combination of distance, ignorance, and impotence; and now, most of all, by the news from Mihailović that he had settled his quarrel with the Partisans.

(x)

On 22 November Mihailović sent the following telegram to his government:

> I have done everything and succeeded in stopping this fratricidal war declared by the other side. In this fight against one side and the other [i.e. against the Partisans and the Germans] I have nearly used up all my munitions. I am doing my very best to unite all the national forces and to reorganize them for the decisive battle against the Germans. I urgently need to receive arms, munitions, money, uniforms, clothing and other necessary things.[131]

Simović passed this message on to Eden on 26 November, adding his own dramatic appeal for help. If Mihailović did not now receive significant assistance, Simović warned, he would be forced to capitulate. Dalton confirmed both points in a letter to Eden the same day.[132]

Refused arms by the Germans and doubtful of receiving them from the British, conscious after recent battles of his movement's weakness yet hopeful of Russian intervention with the Partisans and perhaps even influenced by Hudson's arguments, Mihailović agreed to break off hostilities with the communists. That Tito proposed an armistice is perhaps more surprising. According to Partisan legend the reason lay in Moscow Radio's sudden lauding of Mihailović on 16 or 17 November as the leader of Yugoslav resistance. Dedijer quotes Tito as explaining at the time, "We must be careful not to cause difficulties in the foreign relations of the Soviet Union."[133] In fact it seems that the first Soviet broadcasts in this vein did not take place until 23 or 24 November. (This is also in closer accord with the timing of Yugoslav and British appeals to the Russians to broadcast instructions to the Partisans - and with Tito's protests to the Comintern because of them.[134]) The more likely explanation for Tito's decision to propose an armistice to Mihailović on 17 November lay in the difficult military situation he then faced: although surrounded, Mihailović was proving difficult to defeat, while the German onslaught made it imperative that the Četniks be neutralized one way or another.[135]

Negotiations began immediately, but not again between Tito and Mihailovic personally. Neither side believed in the possibility of achieving a permanent alliance, but each desired a respite from the internecine struggle. Tito wrote to the Croatian Partisan Command on 17 November that the prospects for a negotiated settlement were dim. Mihailović continued to demand nothing less than the disbanding of the Partisans' units and their subordination to his command: "Clearly the Supreme Command dare not and will not accept such proposals."[136] As a consequence the first meeting, held in Čačak on 18 November, was a failure.[137] On 20 November, however, a limited agreement was reached. The previous day Mihailović received the telegram that Simović had shown to Eden on 19 November. This not only pressed him to make peace with the communists and offered assurances that they would be compelled to abandon their campaign of sabotage, but also notified him of his impending promotion to general. Mihailović sent word to his delegates at Čačak that they must sign some sort of accord immediately. In the resulting document both sides pledged themselves to refrain from mutual hostilities, to throw all their strength against the occupiers, to exchange prisoners, to form a mixed commission charged with examining the causes of their recent conflicts and punishing those guilty, to cooperate in future against the Axis and, finally, to resolve all other issues through a joint representative body.[138]

News of this agreement revitalized SOE and the Foreign Office in their efforts to ensure that Mihailović now received significant material aid. These efforts were now aimed less at affording assistance to patriots fighting for their lives than at increasing Mihailović's prestige. This, it was thought, would cause the Partisans to rally to him.[139] Neither the fragility of the Čačak agreement nor its irrelevance in the face of increasing German pressure on what was left of liberated Serbia was appreciated in London.

Eden reported news of the agreement to the War Cabinet on 27 November. Its achievement, he said, made it more necessary than ever to send aid. The cabinet invited him to arrange for the Chiefs of Staff to discuss the matter.[140] This discussion took place the next day. A memorandum setting out Mihailović's needs and stressing that they must be satisfied now that he had "disposed" his difficulties with the communists was put before the Chiefs:

> There can be little doubt that provided that the Partisans realize that Colonel Mihailović is the person whom we are supporting, they will tend to turn to him. On these grounds alone it seems, therefore, of the highest importance to give Colonel Mihailović the assistance for which he was asked.[141]

The Chiefs of Staff could not comply. As Portal informed them, the battle then raging in Libya required every available aircraft. It was impossible to do anything for Yugoslavia.[142]

This put Eden and SOE in an embarrassing position. They had already sent a message congratulating Mihailović in the name of the British government for having reached a settlement with the communists and promising that aid would arrive within the week. Assistance would continue so long as a united front were maintained under his command. Eden had also requested Simović on 28 November to reinforce this condition with Mihailović.[143] When informed of the Chiefs' decision the Foreign Office immediately asked that it be reconsidered in view of the promises made to Simovic and Mihailović. This request was supported by the Prime Minister, who had by now also received a copy of Mihailović's latest appeal for help. Churchill minuted to the Chiefs of Staff, "Everything in human power must be done to help the guerrilla fighters in Yugoslavia. Please report what is possible."[144]

The Chiefs considered the issue again on 29 November. Portal continued to insist that no aircraft could be spared in the Middle East, but he offered to send two bombers out to Malta from England - one Whitley and one Halifax. The two aircraft sent earlier in the month had apparently been diverted to other duties by the Middle East command; it was thus a question of starting all over again. Meanwhile seaborne supply runs were impossible so long as the rebels did not control some part of the coast.[145] During the next few days the Foreign Office learned that a scheduled attempt to investigate conditions along the Montenegrin littoral had been scrapped when the submarine involved was diverted to another mission. It was also discovered that one of the aircraft now promised by Portal was being taken away from SOE's meagre complement of planes in Britain. SOE and the Foreign Office were understandably depressed that Yugoslav operations always took second place to anything else going on at the moment.[146]

The problems of supplying Mihailović continued until year's end to preoccupy those in London concerned with the revolt. Not only were long-range aircraft at a premium, but so too were such vital ancillaries as parachutes and parachute containers. The Foreign Office and SOE pressed for the creation of a flight of aircraft for exclusive service with SOE. Eden proposed this to the Prime Minister on 7 December. Dalton joined in on 14 December - again pointing out that the Yugoslav revolt was no mere "sideshow", but an extension of the Libyan front. Churchill needed no convincing and had already urged the Chief of Air Staff to take action. The latter replied on 15 December that weather conditions had so far frustrated attempts to send supplies by air from Malta. The difficulties were enormous. Malta could not cope with a special flight of bombers on a regular basis; planes would instead have to be sent out from England during each suitable moon period. He hoped, however, that SOE's total complement of aircraft (for operations all over the continent) might shortly be increased from eight to twelve.[147] Aside from such frustrations, the task of rendering aid to Mihailović was now made impossible by the Germans' liquidation of the uprising in Serbia and by the near breakdown in communications with the country that followed.

More talks between the Četniks and Partisans (with Hudson participating) had taken place during the week following the 20 November agreement at Čačak. Another round of discussions was held there on 27 November. But as the town was now coming under German fire, the talks had to be transferred to Pranjani the next day. In the course of these fruitless negotations Hudson offered his government's congratulations to the Yugoslav leaders for their agreement and assured them that Britain had consulted with the USSR on the Yugoslav question and had agreed that the country did not fall within the sphere of interest of either power. Vladimir Dedijer, who attended as one of the Partisan delegates, recorded in his diary his suspicions of Hudson and the British. He saw in Hudson's words evidence of some deep and typically English deceit.[148]

With the headquarters of both movements under direct German threat, Tito telephoned Mihailović on 28 November to ask what his intentions were. Mihailović replied that he would revert to his original plan: each of his units would return to "its own territory and carry out appropriate guerrilla actions until the conditions are created for a general uprising".[149] This was the last direct contact between the two men. On 29 November the Germans entered Užice, minutes after Tito and the main column of Partisans had fled the city. The Partisans made their way southwards, first towards the mountain of Zlatibor in what Hudson characterized as a "rout", and eventually into the relative safety of Sandžak. Hudson, who had returned to Užice with the Partisan negotiators on 28 November in search of his long lost W/T set, was obliged to join the Partisans fleeing south the next day.[150] He decided on 1 December, however, to return to Mihailović, with whom he obviously felt his duty lay. He joined a small Partisan unit travelling north. This group was attacked by independent Četniks and Hudson (along with his now recovered radio) was taken prisoner. He escaped in the course of the night and set out alone for Ravna Gora, but apparently without the heavy W/T set.[151]

Mihailović, meantime, had called a meeting of his commanders for 30 November on Ravna Gora. Desirous at all costs of avoiding the fate which had just befallen the Partisans, he decided to "legalize" his Četnik units in agreement with Nedić, and thus to preserve as much as possible of his organization. Although in fact merely sanctioning what some of his commanders were already doing, Mihailović's decision meant that his followers would now be enrolled in the Serbian State Guard.[152] Such a stratagem had the advantages of assuring the Četniks arms and munitions, of providing a cover under which they could renew the struggle against the communists and of offering some guarantee that their movement might remain in existence when the long-heralded hour for revolt finally struck. For Nedić, on the other hand, this arrangement offered a measure of reinsurance should the Germans ultimately lose the war. He could then claim to have been supporting the resistance all along. The disadvantages for both were those inherent in a policy based on deception.

Mihailović immediately passed on to his government the glad tidings of the collapse of the Partisans in Serbia, commenting that those communists who remained were insignificant in number and badly led. He assured London on 1 December that he was continuing the struggle: "I am passing into complete guerrilla warfare."[153] The next day, with the Germans still threatening Ravna Gora itself, he ordered a general attack on the Partisans. The timing of this bald repudiation of the 20 November agreement may indicate that Mihailović hoped to influence the Germans to break off their offensive against him. If so, the Germans were unmoved. On 5 December Mihailović signalled Cairo that he could no longer maintain radio contact and that the aid he still expected should not be sent until he restored communications. During the next two days his headquarters was overrun, the Germans killing 12 and capturing 480 of his men.[154]

When Hudson arrived back on Ravna Gora during the night of 7-8 December he found no remnant of Mihailović's force, save for the Colonel himself (or rather General since 7 December) and a few followers who had managed to remain hidden while the Germans combed the area. As Hudson reported later, "Everyone else converted themselves into Nedić men and departed to the complete frustration of the Boche."[155] Mihailović refused to see Hudson and, in fact, effectively banished him from what remained of his headquarters.[156] The last the British were to hear of their liaison officer for some five months was Mihailović's signal of 1 December telling them that Hudson had not returned from Užice and was now cut off.[157] Mihailović and his tiny band first fled east and then south towards Sandžak. Their hide and seek existence was to last approximately three months, until Mihailović decided to enter Montenegro in an attempt to assert his command over the indigenous Četniks there. Hudson, meanwhile, began a wandering and solitary exile that was to continue into the spring of 1942.[158]

The Serbian uprising had been extinguished. Insofar as the British knew the Partisans had been eliminated as a force of any significance. Only several months later would it become apparent that they had again raised the standard of revolt, first in Sandžak and later in western Bosnia. Mihailović, in contrast, enjoyed an apparently complete monopoly of international recognition and support. Where he had failed in destroying the Partisans, it seemed that the Germans had succeeded. He no longer possessed a fighting force of his own, but appeared - through Nedić and the Serb bands outside Serbia whose recognition he continued to gain - to have found the next best solution: he would allow the Axis to maintain his units for him. A vulnerable and hunted figure, he dared not communicate often or openly with the outside world, but then neither did he need to endure Hudson's interference.

What Mihailović had put in jeopardy was his moral capital as a leader of resistance. He had shown himself to be more concerned with the political balance at war's end than with hastening the end of Axis occupation. The Partisans had become his principal enemies and any resistance to the Axis would necessarily take second place to the war against them. Such a position was inconsistent neither with Serbian history nor with the maintenance of Mihailović's own standing as a traditional hero for many of his countrymen. What remained to be seen was whether or not the ethos and ethics of the Serbs' struggles against the Turks held true in the middle of the twentieth century - not just for Serbs, but for Croats and Slovenes, Britons and Russians. In March Mihailović met with Milan Aćimović (Interior Minister in the Nedić government) to renew his offer to put himself at the quisling government's disposal for the anti-communist struggle. The Germans' eventual response was still negative, but the man making the offer was now Minister of Army, Navy and Air Force in an Allied government.[159] This was the contradiction which was to be put to the test.

During the next several months the itermittent nature of communications with Mihailović, the failure to establish other intelligence missions, the uncooperativeness of the Russians and the absence of any overwhelming military interest caused the British to relegate Yugoslav resistance to a very secondary importance. In such circumstances the politics and personalities of the exile government were to bulk larger in London's perspective of events than did either Mihailović or the Partisans.

CHAPTER IV

IN BAD COMPANY: THE EXILE GOVERNMENT, 1941-1942

(i)

King Peter II and those of his ministers who arrived with him in Great Britain during the summer of 1941 found themselves accorded a welcome and credited with an importance which owed more to the inspiring memory of the anti-Hitler coup d'état than to its denouement. The King, General Simović, Foreign Minister Ninčić and the Minister of Court, Radoje Knežević, reached England by air on 21 June.[1] Met by the Duke of Kent, they were in short order conducted on a round of audiences, receptions and meetings with King George VI, Churchill, Eden, Amery and others. As George Rendel (appointed Minister to the exile government in August) later commented, this constant feting went "a little to their heads".[2] They conceived themselves to be the most popular of the half dozen other exile governments in London, an impression which was only enhanced as reports of resistance in their homeland filtered out during the summer and autumn.

The Times, greeting King Peter in a leading article on the occasion of his eighteenth birthday on 6 September, reflected this feeling when it wrote that, "The fight initiated by King Peter and General Simović last March has in fact never ceased; and, short as was the campaign of the regular army, it may yet be proved to have completely upset Hitler's plans." Churchill agreed. He told the War Cabinet on 8 September that the part played by the Yugoslavs, and particularly by General Simović, in delaying the Germans' plans and making them fight for their successes should not be overlooked by the press.[3] By 16 September, when a splendid service celebrating King Peter's majority was held in St. Paul's Cathedral in the presence of King George VI and the royal family, members of the British government and the various other heads of state and government gathered in London, the Yugoslav ministers could feel that, despite the collapse of their armed forces in April and their own flight, the Yugoslav King and his legitimate government still counted for something in the eyes of the great power most fully committed to their restoration.[4]

The exile government in London in 1941 was composed of eleven ministers: one Slovene, two Croats and eight Serbs.[5] They represented the remnant of the multi-party coalition formed in Belgrade on the morrow of the coup d'etat. The leader of the Croatian Peasant Party, Vladko Maček, a reluctant Vice-Premier in the new government, had refused to leave the country. He designated as his successor Juraj Krnjević, HSS secretary and a man much practised in political exile. Although one minister was killed during the bombing of Belgrade and a few others followed Maček's example and stayed behind, the only party to opt out of the government at the time of the German invasion was the Yugoslav Moslem Organization. Otherwise the party composition, if not the membership and distribution of portfolios, remained the same. Each of the seven parties was represented by one minister in London, with the exception of the HSS (which had two) and the Serbian Agrarians (who added a second when their leader, Milan Gavrilović, was recalled from Moscow later in the year). Two important members of the cabinet stood outside the party system: the Premier, General Simović, and the Serbian Vice-Premier, Slobodan Jovanović; while one of the most influential ministers, Radoje Knežević, was not, as Minister of Court, a member of the cabinet at all. Besides the 11 ministers in London, five ministers and the Ban (Governor) of Croatia, Ivan Šubašić, were resident in North America. The War Minister, General Ilić, remained in Cairo with the skeleton high command and the small contingent of military personnel that had escaped the country.[6]

Although far from blind to the deficiencies of the mainly elderly and disputatious politicians gathered around the young King, and especially of those Serbs who had been in the political wilderness since 1929 - "harbouring old grievances and creating new ones" - the British saw in General Simović the popular symbol of the revolution of 27 March and, hence, of Yugoslavia's resistance to the Axis. His presence would, they hoped, ensure that the government remained closely identified with the continuing struggle of the Yugoslav people. As an extra-political figure, committed to neither the ultra-Serb nor the ultra-Croat camps, Simović appeared to be the person best equipped to bind together the chronically disunited national and party elements which made up the Yugoslav emigration and so keep to a minimum the inevitably divisive effects of exile politics.[7]

If Simović was seen as the best possible guarantor of Yugoslav unity and resistance in the near term, then the young King Peter appeared to be the natural focus of Yugoslav loyalty for the future. His presence in England seemed to hold out the promise that, with the proper care and attention, a sovereign might be created who would be wise, just and responsive to British interests. The Foreign Office and others spent considerable time during the summer of 1941 examining the question of King Peter's education and employment. As Dixon and Nichols wrote to Eden in June, "We feel that there is a great opportunity, which should if possible not be lost, to ensure that the King is thoroughly Anglicized during his stay." His three weeks' training at Sandroyd just prior to his father's assassination in 1934 had been all too brief, for he exhibited now the baleful effects of overmuch "Amerianization". Dixon and Nichols did not consider that residence with his mother,

Queen Marie, offered either a satisfactory or a long-term solution, "as he is at an awkward age". They recommended that King Peter enrol in a British regiment or, as a second best, that a dashing young officer be attached to him as a confidant, model and aide-de-camp.[8] Buckingham Palace was consulted, while others, notably Professor R.W. Seton-Watson and Leo Amery, volunteered their advice on the proper education of a model constitutional monarch.[9] The final decision on the King's future was, however, made by the two royal families: Peter would be sent to Cambridge.[10] Not only was Cambridge convenient to the Queen Mother's house at Little Gransden, but as the Foreign Office noted approvingly, training there "should provide the necessary education while preserving the King's position as an adult sovereign". The Foreign Office continued to hope that a young wounded officer might be attached to him.[11]

Yet even before going up to Clare College, King Peter began to show signs of behaving not as the model constitutional monarch the British desired him to be, but as the authoritarian ruler the octroyed constitution of 1931 permitted him to be. Apparently taking his recent majority to heart, the King suddenly announced to Rendel on 13 September that he intended to dismiss General Simović and replace him with Slobodan Jovanović. Simovic, he maintained, had become a tool of the Croat faction in the government and had generally bungled government affairs, especially the effort to create a Yugoslav army in exile. The Foreign Office suspected an intrigue by Ninčić and determined to oppose any change. As Eden minuted, "This impetuous boy must be warned . . . We must not lose General Simović without a struggle." He also felt that the incident raised questions about the wisdom of sending King Peter to Cambridge: "I like King Peter, but I am not sure that a dose of Sandhurst would not do him more good than the gentle waters of the Cam."[12]

A meeting was hastily arranged on 15 September at which King George VI and Eden counselled King Peter and Queen Marie not to take any action against Simović. They pointed to the danger of removing the man who symbolized Yugoslav resistance and pressed the King to postpone making any changes for as long as possible. King Peter agreed only to hold his fire for at least a month.[13] The Foreign Office determined in the meantime to seek to boost the stature and reputation of General Simović - in the first instance by asking Cambridge to confer an honorary doctorate upon him.[14]

Although Simović continued to symbolize Yugoslav unity and defiance of Hitler in the eyes of the outside world, he had come to symbolize just the opposite in the world of the Serb emigres in London. His management of the April war, and especially the manner in which he had authorized the Army Chief of Staff to seek an armistice from the Germans without consulting the cabinet, were increasingly held against him, particularly as it became clear that some elements of the Yugoslav army had refused to lay down their arms. Thus the outbreak of resistance during the summer not only made Simović's conduct in April appear less excusable than it had at the time to men who had scrambled with him for seats on the planes into exile, but, more importantly, the emergence of Mihailović as an armed exponent of the royalist cause in the homeland made his symbolism increasingly redundant. The explosion of Mihailović and his indomitable Četniks onto the world's front pages by year's end rendered Simović expendable. The General compounded his problems by sheer ineptitude. Given the disposition of the British in his favour, it should have been very difficult to remove him against their wishes. Yet Simović managed to alienate all sides - Serbs, Croats, Slovenes and the court - so completely that in the end the British, too, were compelled to accept his removal as inevitable.

The government crisis took several months to resolve itself. In early October the report of the Serbian Orthodox Church alleging that 180,000 Serbs had perished at the hands of the Ustaše between April and August was received from Istanbul. Ever-increasing estimates of the death toll followed in train. To Serbs - and for that matter to the Foreign Office - it seemed difficult to imagine that the concept of a Yugoslav state could survive such slaughter.[15] The report implied - and some Serbs in London said openly - that the entire Croat people must share the responsibility for the Ustaše massacres. The Croat ministers understandably refused to accept this view. Unfortunately, neither could they bring themselves to condemn the massacres in terms sufficiently strong to mollify the Serbs.[16] The most chauvinistic Serbs, led by Ninčić and Milan Grol, clamoured for government publication of the Church report - in effect for the proclamation to the world that Yugoslavia was irredeemable. Simović sided with the Croats and Yugoslav-minded Serbs in cabinet against any such suicidal act. The Foreign Office, feeling it necessary to make peace between the two sides lest the Croats tread further along the trail blazed by the Slovaks, intervened to point out the obvious: that nothing would please the Axis more than that Serbs and Croats should be at each others' throats.[17] The crisis seemed to pass temporarily, but attitudes hardened on both sides. A full-blown anti-Croat campaign was launched in the Serbian press in America (where the Church report was eventually published) and the far larger Croat community there responded in kind. Ninčić meanwhile began to talk of creating a greater Serbia after the war which would embrace all Serb-inhabited regions and share a common border with Slovenia.[18]

By November the government was again in crisis, as was illustrated by a series of stormy cabinet meetings in the middle of the month. The issues were many, but significantly they did not include the now evident breach between Mihailović and the communists. There were those within the ambit of the exile government who appreciated the portent of this development,[19] but most ministeres remained preoccupied with the proportion of Croats to Serbs in plum diplomatic posts, the reputed desire of Simovic to assume dictatorial 'powers', his supposedly questionable devotion to the dynasty, the Serb ministers' reluctance to reaffirm the *Sporazum* (the cornerstone of Croat cooperation in the government) and the Croats' alleged effort to secure control over the government's fairly impressive financial resources.[20]

Jovanović for the Serbs and Ilija Jukić (Deputy Minister of Foreign Affairs) for the Croats attempted, evidently at Slovene instance, to reconcile the two warring factions and to get them to agree on a statement of basic government policy. Their effort foundered, however, on Ninčić's unwillingness to accept any resolution of the crisis that might ease Simovic's position and endanger his own.[21] For their part, the Croat ministers considered themselves well-served by a situation in which the Serbs were divided; while Simović also believed that his hold on office was secure so long as the ministers continued their bickering. He underestimated, however, the enmity towards him developing in the court and the possibility that his ministers might cease their quarrelling long enough to rid themselves of him.[22]

Matters came to a head when Milan Gavrilović arrived in London from Moscow in December.[23] Simović had intended to replace Ninčić with Gavrilović, despite warnings from General Ilić in Cairo that Gavrilović could be expected to lend his support to the developing cabal against him.[24] Gavrilović was the one Yugoslav politician held in high esteem by the British. His quick realization that Simović was hopeless and must go influenced Rendel in the same direction, as did the fact that he was daily suffering the confidences of all sides regarding the latest examples of Simović's incompetence and/or duplicity. He summarized Simović's situation in a letter to Sargent on 23 December: the Serbs hated him, the Croats distrusted him and the Slovenes no longer believed him. He had in fact accomplished the unique feat of uniting the Yugoslav government - against himself. The Foreign Office, Rendel suggested, ought now to have an alternative candidate in view.[25] Neither Sargent nor Eden agreed that the time had come to acquiesce. Sargent replied to Rendel on 24 December that Simović must stay and that he, Rendel, should speak very plainly to King Peter. The reasoning behind this decision to cling to Simović was somewhat convoluted since it was based, in part, on the Foreign Office's new-found disinclination to part with Ninčić. Although they found him odious personally, he was felt to be "right-minded" on the larger question of postwar confederation in South-Eastern Europe.[26] Most importantly, however, Eden felt that Simović's dismissal would seriously dishearten the resistance forces of Mihailovic.[27]

But British efforts were in vain. Simović had already sealed his own fate. Spurned by Gavrilović and apparently fearful that his alliance with the Croats would not hold, Simović turned on them in a desperate effort to redeem himself with the Serbs. The predictable result of this move was that it united the Serb and Croat ministers in their resolve to be rid of him. Flailing about for a way out, Simović sought to create diversions by reneging on his earlier undertaking not to publish the Orthodox Church report and by denouncing Ninčić and Grol to the British and King Peter for allegedly maintaining links with the Germans and Italians via Lisbon.[28]

Ninčić called on Sargent on 31 December to tell him that Simović would have to go - and soon. He asked that Eden not again intervene on the General's behalf. He was no longer a symbol of Yugoslavia's resistance to the Axis and his role in the coup d'état had been forgotten. All elements within the government were united in pressing for his dismissal.[29] In a well-planned exercise the London ministers submitted their resignations directly to King Peter on 9 January. Simović, absent at his country home at Harpenden and unaware of what his ministers were about, was only informed on 11 January in a letter from the King that he had been relieved of his duties and replaced as President of the Council by the 72 year-old Slobodan Jovanović.[30]

Although by the time it finally took place the Foreign Office permanent officials were reconciled to Simović's departure, Eden was furious and even considered briefly trying to have him reinstated. As he minuted on 9 January:

> This is all thoroughly unsatisfactory. I suspect that part of the feeling against General Simović is that he is the only one of the gang who is *not* a Balkan politician. Anyway he was in the public eye the figurehead who brought about [the] coup d'état and his removal - just reported to me - is a

> misfortune to the Allied cause. The rest of the collection are worth every little anyway. I suspect the Queen in all this.
>
> In any event, the essential minimum is that General Simović should be given an honourable position that will save appearances.
>
> Even so, I fear the effect of the news on Yugoslav resistance which matters a thousand times more than the activities of these miserable political intriguers whom we have unhappily allowed to "get away with it".[31]

Sargent attempted to salve Eden's anger and to reconcile him to the loss of the General, not so much by pointing out that it was Simović the Balkan politician who had been the author of his own downfall, as by accentuating the promise held out by Mihailović's nomination as War Minister. It was, he wrote on 10 January, "a brilliant idea" and Britain should do all in her power to "build him up" as Simović's worthy successor.[32] Eden agreed that Mihailović's inclusion in the government was "good" but wondered - with some prescience - whether there would not be difficulties involved in pushing aside General Ilić and the other senior officers in Cairo. The change must in any case be represented - however fancifully - as an expression of a new-found unity of purpose in the government. As for King Peter, Eden despaired, "This boy hasn't much chance with that mother, but we must consider whether we cannot guide and help him more."[33]

In his fear lest damage be done the Allied cause and in his concern over the public interpretation of the change Eden was certainly exaggerating the importance of the entire affair. Yet the General's removal was not without important consequences. In the first place, as the Foreign Office realized, it represented a setback for the idea of Yugoslav unity.[34] It delivered the exile government more firmly into the hands of the Serbs, especially the Serbs of the court and young officer parties led by Radoje and Živan Knežević. The Croats, Vice-Premier Krnjević and Finance Minister Šutej, were relegated to their historically sanctioned (and probably more comfortable) role of intermittently obstructive observation. While the lone Slovene, Vice-Premier Krek, continued as before to look after the interests of his own people with relatively little regard for wider Yugoslav issues. Jovanović, though Serbia's greatest historian and legal scholar, was too old, too politically inexperienced and too philosophically detached to exert a vigorous control over the government.[35] This was significant because in a chronically divided cabinet almost all real responsibility devolved ultimately upon him. Besides being President of the Council and Minister of the Interior, Jovanović increasingly acted as Foreign Minister as well.[36] But most importantly, the inclusion of Mihailović in the government meant that Jovanović was also saddled with the day to day supervision of military affairs (as Deputy Minister of Army, Navy and Air Force).

To contend with what was now the most significant of the government's activities, Jovanović established a military cabinet within his prime ministerial office. Headed by Major Živan Knežević, the military cabinet became the effective controller of military policy and relations with Mihailović.[37] The creation of the military cabinet marked the beginning of the period of ascendency of the notorious "Majors' League" and its leading lights: Majors Knežević, Roždjalovski and Vohoska.[38] In alliance with the other two Knežević brothers, Radoje and Nikola,[39] the Majors' League was widely suspected of exercising a dominant and pernicious influence over the government in general and over King Peter in particular.[40] Representative of the ambitious younger Serb officers who had participated in the coup d'etat only to see its purpose vitiated and their ambition thwarted, Major Knežević and his allies were convinced that Simović had been insufficiently energetic in his support of Serbia's new hope, Draža Mihailović. They now succeeded in putting the government at his long-distance service. He was designated Commander-in-Chief of the Yugoslav Army in the Fatherland and promoted again (to the rank of Division General) soon after entering the government. At the time this effort to identify the government with Mihailović seemed - as the Foreign Office agreed - a brilliant stroke. Not only did it demonstrate that the Yugoslav exiles were more than nominal participants in the grand alliance against Hitler, but also that their government was more than a mere exile government. With a minister in the homeland leading the struggle against the fascist occupiers and domestic traitors the Serbs in exile could be more confident that they would one day return with their King to a liberated Yugoslavia and impose there a constitutional settlement reflecting both the losses Serbs had suffered and the heroism they had shown. Yet the Knežević brothers and their supporters also tied the future of the government and dynasty to a man about whom they knew little and over whom they could exercise even less control.

(ii)

The first unhappy consequence of the change in government came quickly and from a not unexpected quarter. This was a rebellion by senior officers in the Middle East against the attempt of the Knežević-dominated regime in London to remove them from their positions: a prolonged crisis known as the Cairo Affair (*Kairska afera*). Eden had foreseen that the displacement of General Ilić might pose problems for the Jovanović government, but he could scarcely have imagined the extent to which the Cairo Affair would entangle the British government, divide it against itself and generally poison Anglo-Yugoslav relations during the bulk of 1942. The Foreign Office was to find itself singularly ill-equipped to deal with a crisis which seemed to owe more in its inspiration and development to the conspiratorial traditions of the Black Hand and the Salonika Trial than to any theories of political economy practised in Great Britain - and especially a crisis in which the British in Cairo took part with gusto.

Convinced themselves (and convincing the government as a whole) that the senior officers in Cairo were plotting a rearguard action on behalf of General Simović, the Knežević brothers moved quickly to eliminate their competitors for control of the armed forces and the mantle of responsibility for 27 March. Their long-term objective was apparently to ensure that when the war neared its end they would return to Yugoslavia at the head of a significant body of armed men and share with Mihailović the task of organizing the new Četnik-dominated state.[41] In 1942 there was no such body of men. The Yugoslav armed forces in the Middle East totalled no more than 1200 men, most of whom were Slovenes impressed into the Italian army, captured in North Africa and permitted to volunteer for service with the newly-formed Royal Guards Battalion. The government still hoped, however, that significant numbers of volunteers might be forthcoming from North America. In the meantime the Middle East force had considerable symbolic importance.

One of the first acts of the Jovanović government was to dismiss General Ilić from his remaining post as Chief of Staff of the Supreme Command and to remove General Bora Mirković as Air Force Chief of Staff by abolishing his command and recalling him to London.[42] A relatively junior Air Force officer, Lt. Colonel Miodrag Lozić, was nominated to replace them both as Acting Chief of Staff of the Supreme Command.[43] Ilić, having been advised by Simović that his own dismissal by the King was unconstitutional, professed to regard these orders of the new government as of doubtful authenticity.[44] Ilić refused to yield up his command and Mirković refused to answer the summons to London. They and Colonel Žarko Popović, Chief of Military Intelligence, appealed to King Peter, Queen Marie and Jovanović to set aside this latest example of the vengefulness and vaunting ambition of the brothers Knežević. As a first step they suggested that a delegate be received in London to explain the "true situation" in Cairo. Jovanović replied during January that the orders stood and that no representative would be received. He also escalated the dispute by placing Ilić and Mirković on the retired list. In early February Ilić resigned his command on grounds of ill-health, but rather than hand over to Lozić, he named Mirković as his successor. It was now the turn of the government to issue appeals, asking Eden on 12

February for help in imposing its will in Cairo.[45]

The situation was complicated by the fact that not only did the majority of Yugoslav officers in the Middle East side with Mirković, but so too did their British opposite numbers, those whose ultimate task it would be to enforce a settlement. Auchinleck reported to London on 9 February that he strongly disagreed with the government's decision to impose Lozić on the Yugoslav forces. He was both unpopular and incompetent. The senior officers were united in condemning the appointment of a man who, they were convinced, was nothing but a tool of the Knežević brothers. If Mirković were bypassed Auchinleck feared that his supporters would mutiny.[46] And these men the British in Cairo considered to be the best of the Yugoslav officers in exile. Behind this support for Mirković's claim on command there lay, of course, the credit accorded him as prime-mover in the coup d'état.[47] The Commander-in-Chief was thus defending Mirković in the same terms already used by the Foreign Office on behalf of Simović.

Mirković was in early March prevailed upon to surrender command to Lozić. This formality took place on 4 March; but so too did the predicted mutiny. One hundred officers proclaimed their refusal to serve under Lozić and their continued allegiance to Mirković. Several hundred NCOs and other ranks followed suit.[48] Lozić appealed to the British for help in assuming control by force and in removing all Yugoslav forces to Britain. Mirković asked in turn that the 100 dissident officers be allowed to join the RAF.[49] Fearing bloodshed between the two factions, Auchinleck intervened on 5 March. He despatched the loyal Guards Battalion to active duty near Tobruk, ordered Lozić and his staff to go on leave and installed a British officer, Lt. General R.G.W.H. Stone, as temporary commander of all Yugoslav forces. He also requested that Lozić be recalled to London by the Yugoslav government, threatening to disarm and disband the Guards Battalion if it did not behave: "I have not the time to waste on them."[50]

The Jovanović government appreciated the weight of this rebuke and protested loudly to the Foreign Office at Auchinleck's failure to help it impose its will. Jovanović refused to recall Lozić, but agreed to send out another officer, Colonel Miodrag Rakić (another of King Peter's ADCs), to conduct an inquiry into the dispute. Meanwhile he insisted that Mirković and Ilić be removed to South Africa (where they could do no more mischief) and issued a proclamation in the King's name on 7 March calling upon all Yugoslav troops to obey orders. But the Commander-in-Chief, Middle East, supported by the Minister of State, continued his defiance of the wishes of the Yugoslav government. He cabled the War Office on 10 March to explain that King Peter's proclamation was inflammatory, that it prejudiced the outcome of the proposed inquiry and revealed the extent to which the King had fallen under the influence of the Knežević clique. He would not promulgate the King's decree, nor would he banish Mirković and Ilić before the inquiry had brought in its result. Not only, he wrote, was "every good officer demanding the complete reinstatement of General Bora Mirković", but he doubted that Rakić possessed either sufficient stature or impartiality to carry out an investigation.[51]

The Foregin Office was reluctant to question the authority of the British commander on the spot in a matter so obviously within his province, but feared the repercussions, especially on Mihailović, should the King's orders be defied with impunity by his forces in the Middle East. They thus felt that the King's decree must be published whatever its effect upon the crisis.[52] But Auchinleck maintained his ground. He would not, he telegraphed on 13 March, allow the promulgation of King Peter's proclamation and so provoke a confrontation which might necessitate the use of force against Allied soldiers ready and eager to fight the common enemy just to ease the embarrassment of the Foreign Office. The Chiefs of Staff upheld the Commander-in-Chief's position at their meeting the next day.[53] The Foreign Office was asked to tell the Yugoslavs that the King's proclamation was not to be published and that Rakić was not considered a suitable arbiter. When Rendel broke this news to Jovanović on 15 March the Premier insisted that Rakić's inquiry go ahead. Not only was the government's authority at stake, but so was the government itself.[54]

Following a subsequent suggestion by Jovanović that Rakić might replace Lozić at the same time as he carried out his investigation, Sargent came up with the idea of scrapping the inquiry and simply having Rakić named as Lozić's successor.

This stratagem too was dismissed by Auchinleck. He reported on 24 March that Rakić's appointment would precipitate violence, the likelihood of which had been much increased in recent days by the constant menaces of Lozić against the dissidents. Either Mirković were restored to command or he would expel *all* Yugoslav forces from his theatre. Even an inquiry was now unthinkable. The Chiefs of Staff again upheld the Commander's views. Feeling that Auchinleck's alternatives were "quite impossible", Sargent pleaded with the Chiefs of Staff for some compromise; otherwise the Yugoslav government would be compelled to resign. Perhaps, the Foreign Office suggested, the impartiality of the inquiry might be assured by the participation of the Acting Minister of State.[55] At a meeting of the War Cabinet on 27 March it was agreed to ask Auchinleck whether Henry Hopkinson's participation in the investigation would not meet his objections. He was now told flat out that Mirković's reinstatement was out of the question.[56] Auchinleck however remained obdurate, replying on 30 March that Hopkinson's involvement would not help. The Knežević brothers and not Mirković bore the responsibility for the crisis. There was too great a risk of violence were the inquiry to proceed. He repeated that if Mirković were not reinstalled he would expel the Yugoslav forces from the Middle East. London only succeeded in imposing its will to the extent that Hopkinson now began consultations with the various parties aimed at finding a settlement.[57]

The Foreign Office had become suspicious by early April that Auchinleck was being "led up the garden path" by pro-Mirković officers in the British organizations dealing with the Yugoslavs - presumably SOE and SIS.[58] Rendel, meanwhile, had been indefatigable in his efforts to convince the Foreign Office of the importance of what both he and the Yugoslav government saw as being at stake in the affair: namely, the survival of the government's authority over its armed forces. And these forces, albeit mere tokens, nonetheless embodied, along with the dynasty and Mihailović, the government's claim to exercise the powers of a sovereign state. Auchinleck, on the other hand, regarded the dispute as a tiresome and ridiculous waste of time and effort over a minescule band of men which should either be usefully employed or quickly disbanded. Rendel and the Foreign Office felt that he missed the political point completely.[59]

It was expected in London during April that a compromise would be reached that would allow Colonel Rakić to assume command of the Yugoslav forces. The continued talk on the part of the dissidents about joining the British army or asking to be interned should Rakić take over thus met with little favour. Rakić's authority, the Foreign Office felt, must be backed up - by force if need be. But there was also discussion of whether King Peter (and perhaps the entire government) ought not be sent out to Egypt to reinforce the point, either on a temporary visit or permanently. "It is generally agreed", Dixon wrote on 12 April, "that King Peter (or the dynasty) is the only real focus of Yugoslav loyalty, and King Peter's presence in the M.E. would thus probably have a rallying effect." Reflecting that the popularity of his father, King Alexander, had rested in large measure on his having shared the privations of the retreat through Albania and Salonika Front with his troops, Dixon reasoned that King Peter's proper place was beside General Mihailović. This being impossible, residence with his forces in the Middle East seemed the next best means of guaranteeing his and the dynasty's future. It was also felt that King Peter, having shown a greater interest in the diversions of London than in the academic life of Cambridge, would do well to have a taste of war: "If King Peter is degenerating, a prolonged spell of camping should supply the necessary corrective and would provide him with a larger range from which to choose his companions."[60]

A compromise was in fact worked out in Cairo on 12 April and accepted by the principals during subsequent days. It provided for the transfer of command from General Stone to

Colonel Rakić and for the removal of the three rebel officers most obnoxious to the government: General Mirković, Colonel Popović and Major Stanojlović (the OCAF). However, when it came time to implement the agreement on 20 April, the supporters of Mirković again asserted themselves, forcibly preventing the despatch of their leaders to Luxor and seizing the building housing the Yugoslav Supreme Command. This action, carried out by 40 air force officers, was presumed to have the support of a further 84 officers and 195 other ranks. The Minister of State reported to London that the rebels would be interned, Mirković and Stanojlović along with them. The Foreign Office at once protested to Cairo that the two officers must be separated from their supporters; otherwise the Yugoslav government would justifiably object that the British had failed to keep their part of the bargain, allowing if not actually encouraging the rebellion.[61] Cairo objected that to attempt to separate Mirković and Stanojlović from the rest would be to invite bloodshed. London was not convinced. Yet the Foreign Office, as Douglas Howard minuted desparingly, was at the end of its tether in trying to secure from London a solution acceptable to the Yugoslav government. The whole affair was simply too ludicrous to be allowed to continue. It would have to be left to Auchinleck to pick up the pieces as best he could. To send King Peter to Cairo now would only worsen the situation; he would doubtless take one or more of the Knežević brothers with him. While Rendel, who had volunteered to go, took the government's side so completely that he could hardly be expected to do any good.[62]

The internment of the rebels was accomplished during the course of the next few days. On 7 May Rakić assumed formal command of what remained of the Yugoslav forces: the Guards Battalion (still in the desert with the Eighth Army) and a handful of loyal air force an navy personnel.[63] Yet the internees - whose confinement turned out to be as symbolic as their fighting capacity - continued to agitate against Rakić and the government. This convinced the Yugoslav ministers that the British were bent upon forming a rival Yugoslav force led by Mirković from the 300 who ultimately chose internment rather than service under Rakić.[64] Jovanović therefore refused to enter into negotiations aimed at putting an end to the schism unless and until the British fulfilled their original promise to remove Mirković and the other ringleaders from Egypt. He, King Peter and the officers of the military cabinet contented themselves instead with sending a continuous stream of protest notes to everyone from King George VI on down. The British argued in reply that it was only by treating with Mirković and the other rebel officers that the government could hope to put an end to the dispute.[65] In this impasse Rendel suggested that the conflict be referred to Mihailović - theoretically the responsible minister - for settlement. But this was rejected as being both technically difficult and needlessly depressing for the General and his followers. They would be better off kept in ignorance of the full dimensions of the scandal.[66]

At a series of meetings in late May the Foreign Office decided that the British government must not risk forcing the resignation of the Jovanović cabinet by attempting to impose a settlement. It would therefore be necessary to accept the Yugoslav pre-condition for negotiations: the separation of Mirković and five other ringleaders now named by Jovanović from the bulk of the internees and their removal from Egypt. The Foreign Office trusted that the Yugoslav government could then be persuaded to send the authoritative Gavrilović out to Cairo - with Rendel accompanying - to settle the fate of the remaining dissidents. They feared in light of experience, however, that it would be difficult to secure the assent of the Minister of State and Auchinleck to the essential first step. A telegram outlining the new scheme was sent to Cairo on 30 May. Separation and removal of the ringleaders, it maintained, must not be put off for fear that such an action might require the use of force.[67]

The new Minister of State, Richard Casey, replied on 5 June that the time had long since passed when a solution along such lines might have been practicable. The internees were armed and "in no mood to accept the dispersal"! Auchinleck was determined to allow no Yugoslav forces to remain in the Middle

East unless proposals made by Casey in the interim were accepted. These provided for: (1) an end to internment; (2) the removal to England of the senior dissident officers, Colonel Rakić and the Yugoslav Minister in Cairo, Milan Smiljanić; (3) the closure of the Yugoslav headquarters in Cairo; and (4) the assumption by Colonel Prosen of the Royal Guards Battalion of command over all Yugoslav forces. Any dissidents unwilling to serve under him would also be returned to England. Unless this plan were accepted by London before 15 June, Auchinleck proposed to deport all 1200 Yugoslavs to Britain on the first available ship. Cairo had abandoned its insistence on Mirković's reinstatement, but on that alone. As Howard commented on 6 June, "Our military authorities are, therefore, now in a position, so they say, of not being able to send away the six ringleaders without a pitched battle involving a whole battalion. This is such a ludicrous situation that it is difficult to know how to explain it to the Yugoslav government." Acceptance of Cairo's ultimatum, putting as it did Mirković and the rebels on the same footing as the loyal Rakić and Smiljanić, would be so humilitating to the Yugoslav government that it would have no recourse but to resign. No new government could be expected to be any better and would, in any case, "hate us fervently".[68]

Eden now appealed to the War Cabinet for support against Cairo. On 8 June he requested and received authority to insist to the Minister of State that the Yugoslav government be upheld in its efforts to restore discipline and that the Foreign Office's scheme of 30 May be reconsidered. Cairo was told on 10 June that if it was impossible to separate the six ringleaders from the remainder of the internees without a pitched battle, then all 300 dissidents would have to be removed from Egypt. The loyal Guards Battalion must on no account be treated similarly. It would remain in the Middle East as tangible evidence of Yugoslavia's participation in the war. Any ringleaders sent to England would be received only in order to separate them from their followers, and not to enable them to negotiate as equals with the Yugoslav government. Casey replied on 14 June with counterproposals which sought to ensure for the rebel leaders just such equal status and which lent credence generally to the deepening suspicions of the Yugoslav government that the British were determined to create a rival Yugoslav army. Eden rejected these counter-proposals on 17 June, reminding Casey that his previous message represented a War Cabinet decision and was not subject to discussion. The internees must now be disarmed, Mirković and the other leaders removed from their midst and Rakić allowed access to the rest in order to present his government's case.[69]

Still Cairo refused to comply, pleading on 18 June that the deteriorating situation on the Libyan front (Tobruk was about to fall to Rommel) precluded the use of force to separate Mirković and company from their followers. The Foreign Office threatened Casey with further recourse to the War Cabinet.[70] However the crisis on the battlefield now imposed its own logic on events - and some hope that an end might finally be put to the affair. With the Germans threatening Alexandria in early July, Mirković was prevailed upon to agree that Rakić might appeal to the rebels to join in the defence of Egypt. They were to be given a choice between accepting Rakić's command or serving in the British Army. Jovanović agreed to this plan, telling Rendel that the erring brothers might now depart in peace. He expected, however, that most of them would choose to return to the colours once Rakić had explained that by joining the British army they would be severing all connection with their army and their King. He was wrong. Rakić convinced none of the dissidents to return to the fold and the British were left with the problem of finding places for them in British units.[71]

This proved impossible to do without exacerbating Yugoslav fears that the British were intent upon building up a rival army under Mirković whose ultimate purpose would be to recall Simovic to power - or worse. (Gavrilović, for instance, intimated to Rendel that the Cairo Affair was a British plot to so weaken the Serbs' position in the government that they should be forced to accede to the Croats' political demands.) The Foreign Office interpreted such suspicions - as well as the denial now put forward by Jovanović that he had ever consented to allow any but the ringleaders to enlist in the British army - as a result of mortification that not one rebel had elected to return to the Yugoslav forces. As Howard expressed it on 19 July, "All this talk of a second Yugoslav Army under Mirković seems to me utter rubbish. The second army, after all, would consist of 280 men (a motley crowd of naval, military and air force men) - in fact about two companies all told." Jovanović should be told plainly that Britain had no such intention. It was clear, he continued, "that the Yugoslav government, in their futility, are using the crisis to blame us for all their own failures."[72]

Yet this dismissal of Yugoslav fears was to appear facile in subsequent weeks - as Howard himself admitted - when information reached London that the dissidents were being kept together in one unit (the 244th Provisional Battalion of the King's Own Royal Regiment), that they were continuing to wear Yugoslav uniforms and badges and to fly the Yugoslav flag, and that they had even been given access to the British radio station in Cairo for broadcasts to Yugoslavia.[73] The Foreign Office, having passed on to Jovanović Cairo's assurances that the rebels would be integrated into British units, was understandably embarrassed. "I am afraid we must face the fact," Sargent minuted, "that in this Yugoslav army crisis, the Army authorities in Cairo are prepared to resort to this kind of chicanery in their zeal for the Mirković faction."[74]

The Foreign Office thus leavened its anger with understanding when Jovanović, under pressure from his colleagues, again reneged on his word and began in August to threaten the now-departed dissidents with the loss of their Yugoslav nationality. He was persuaded to let the issue lie, but not before Rakić had enthusiastically taken up the threat in Egypt. Mirković's followers now began to claim that they had not understood that by joining the British army they should be putting their Yugoslav nationality in jeopardy. They accused the British of luring them into the army under false pretences and began to desert to the Yugoslav forces! After nearly eight months of crisis the humour of the situation was lost on nearly everyone. Rendel, all the while continuing his ill-tempered dispute with Jovanović over whether the latter had or had not consented to the enlistment of the dissidents in the British forces without victimization, argued that the Mirković faction had in effect been suborned. He suggested that the choice be put to them once again. The Foreign Office agreed, despite the fact that any failure to explain to the rebels the likely consequences of their actions was Rakić's. The Minister of State was asked to arrange for a second opportunity for the Mirković faction to declare themselves.[75]

Cairo now proved remarkably cooperative. Whether convinced by the Foreign Office's arguments about the deleterious effect the crisis was having on all aspects of Anglo-Yugoslav relations, or simply disenchanted with the Mirković faction, the detailed proposals prepared by Rendel and Howard for the final resolution of the affair were agreed during the balance of September at a series of meetings in Cairo and London.[76] The men of the 244th Provisional Battalion were to be given a second chance. Those who did not agree to rejoin the Yugoslav forces would be dispersed in British units throughout the Middle East. The leaders of the revolt - five in number - would be given employment even farther afield and unrelated to Yugoslavia in any way. (Rendel and Howard noted with heavy irony that this separation could doubtless now be accomplished without bloodshed.) The Yugoslav government would in future have no reason to suspect that the British were seeking to create a rival army. With London and Cairo in the unaccustomed position of agreeing on a course of action, it remained only to secure the consent of the Yugoslav government to withdraw its threat to strip the dissidents of their citizenship and to receive all but the ringleaders back into the fold without reprisals. Jovanović would also be requested to replace Colonel Rakić.[77]

Despite raising some difficulties over the penalties which soldiers not returning to the Yugoslav forces would incur, Jovanović accepted the British proposals in early October.[78] A protocol was signed on 19 October by the two governments. Attached to it were two supplementary agreements: one stipulating that Raković would be replaced by Colonel Dimitrije Putnik as Yugoslav commander in the Middle East;[79] the other regulating the conditions under which the ex-Italian Slovenes in the Guards Battalion might be employed against their former masters.[80] The implementation of the protocol was not without problems, but these were of a minor order in comparison with what had gone before. Besides the five "ringleaders" whom the British agreed to disperse and nine other officers specifically excluded by the Yugoslav government, only four officers and nine other ranks elected to remain in British units. Ironically, Mirković was given a great deal of the credit for persuading the majority to return. Howard judged this result "more satisfactory than I dared hope".[81]

The legacy of the Cairo Affair was not insignificant. The conflict between the Foreign Office and the Middle East Command offered a foretaste of the bitter disagreements to come both between and inside the British agencies dealing with Yugoslav affairs. The Yugoslavs' fissiparous tendencies were proving highly contagious. Early on in the army crisis, when it was first alleged that the old Balkan hands Hatch and Mappleback were responsible for Cairo's enthusiasm for Mirković, Rendel wrote to Howard putting forward the general proposition, based on his experience of the Balkans, that seldom could a Briton who had lived more than ten years in a Balkan country be regarded as impartial and objective where the political and/or national issues of that country were concerned.[82] In the case of Yugoslavia the heightening of experience and the unleashing of passions brought on by war seemed to reduce the ten year term postulated by Rendel to a matter of months if not weeks.

Rendel's assessment of the crisis as a whole - that it so lowered the prestige of the Yugoslav government that "the foundations were laid of the lack of confidence and respect for the exiled Yugoslav politicians which made it possible for us, and for the bulk of the Yugoslav people themselves, some two years later, to abandon them with hardly a qualm, and to acquiesce in Tito's anti-monarchical revolution"[83] - is as exaggerated as it is simplistic. Caught as he was in this frustrating and exhausting affair for nearly a year, a period in which - true to his own dictim - he acted more and more as Yugoslavia's ambassador to Britain, Rendel perhaps lost sight of the main issue. The British, let alone the Yugoslav people, were not to foreswear Mihailović simply because they had little respect for the government of which he was a member. As Eden had already insisted, the Yugoslav resistance mattered "a thousand times more than the activities of these miserable political intriguers". It was precisely because they appreciated this that the Yugoslav exiles sought during 1942 to bind themselves ever more closley to Mihailović and his cause. Thus the public value of their stock, or at least of their King's, remained relatively high at year's end despite the Cairo Affair and the disenchantment of the British with their incessant squabbling and general futility. That the Cairo Affair contributed to this disenchantment is certainly true. Having demonstrated themselves incapable of managing their own affairs with any degree of competence, yet adept at discomfiting the Foreign Office with the legitimacy of their strident complaints, the Yugoslav ministers would in future be treated with little short of contempt. But this was not to be the cause of their downfall.

(iii)

The British had played a variety of roles in the weeks and months preceding Yugoslavia's adherence to the Tripartite Pact. They were zealous missionaries preaching national honour and the cause of Western Civilization to Prince Paul; they were desperate supplicants seeking salvation for their forces newly committed to Greece in the intervention of Yugoslavia's million-man army; and they were generous tempters, putting before the fainthearted Croats the prospect of recovering their national irredenta in Istria after the war. Yet despite the importance lent the country by these several roles, and by the brief triumph of 27 March, the British were convinced that Yugoslavia had been a conspicuous failure on the European stage in the inter-war years. States whose "only" justification had been ethnographical had proved dangerous both to themselves and to the security of Europe. They had attempted to play the part of great powers - strutting at Geneva, constructing and then ignoring elaborate alliance structures, maintaining swollen military establishments - but in the end had proved powerless to counter a resurgent Germany. Hitler's piecemeal conquest of Europe pointed, Sargent wrote in June 1942, to "the mathematical fact that any numbers of zeros only add up to a total of zero."[84] Fearing from the earliest days of the war that the Soviet Union, fortified by its pan-Slav appeal, was likely to fill any vacuum in Eastern Europe created by Germany's eventual defeat, the Foreign Office cast about for an alternative. For as a former British Consul in the Balkans noted in April 1941, "History has shown that the sturdy and gallant individualism of people like the Serbs and the Poles is not capable of finding a solution."[85]

Meanwhile King Peter and his government existed. And their first concern in exile was to secure pledges from Britain and the United States that Yugoslavia would be restored after the war and its territorial integrity guaranteed to its full pre-war extent. In light of the Yugoslav ministers' decision in Athens on 17 April to continue their belligerency until final victory was won, neither Britain nor America proved unwilling to meet the first of the Yugoslavs' requirements. In a personal message to General Simović on 22 April, Eden wrote that Yugoslavia would continue to be recognized by the British as an ally whose independence they fully intended to see restored and whose government they regarded as representing all Yugoslav territory. A statement to this effect was made by the Foreign Secretary in the Commons the next day.[86] Cordell Hull announced in Washington on 25 April that the United States continued to recognize King Peter's government as legitimate; in subsequent weeks he reiterated American nonrecognition of Hitler's and his allies' dismemberment of the country.[87]

Simović was not satisfied with these assurances, desiring from Britain especially a specific territorial guarantee. This the British were unwilling to give. They should not tie their hands, the Southern Department explained, over the restoration of what had proved to be one of the most politically and strategically ineffectual states in the period between the wars.

It might prove necessary to separate Croatia and Serbia, or perhaps to include the entire country in a larger state whose shape could not yet be foreseen. Simović would have to be content with a vague statement that Yugoslavia would not go unrewarded.[88] Given this sombre appraisal of Yugoslavia's past history and future prospects, the Foreign Office looked with approval upon Simović's tendency during the summer of 1941 to speak only to the Serbs in his broadcast speeches to the country. This appeared to indicate a realistic acceptance of the likelihood that the Croats would be cast adrift after the war. The British felt that such realism would make any necessary changes easier to effect.[89]

In practice, however, it was difficult to maintain inner reservations about the viability of Yugoslavia and its future place in Europe while, at the same time, making the necessary public professions that the country was an esteemed ally whose prospects were not in doubt. The reservations and the contemplation of alternatives inevitably took second place to the more pressing wartime need to reaffirm the country's status among the United Nations and, as a consequence, the unity of its peoples. In 1941 it was impossible to foresee the circumstances in which the map of Europe might be redrawn to ensure the maintenance of perpetual peace. It was all too easy, on the other hand, to see that unless a lead were offered, either in the country or from abroad, the Serbs and Croats might destroy the possibility of their ever again sharing a common homeland. Choosing to work to prevent such a forestallment, the British came to interpret their pledge to restore Yugoslav independence as carrying with it a promise to maintain Yugoslav unity, that is the triune Kingdom of the Serbs, Croats and Slovenes.[90] By means of their propaganda to the occupied country and their activity among the personalities of the exile government the British became, almost by default, the principal defenders abroad of the Yugoslav idea against a background of increasing separatism and/or hegemonism on the part of the exiled politicians and the vague hostility of the United States and the Soviet Union.[91] Although the Foreign Office did not cease to debate the relative merits of one long-term solution or another - *Staatenbund* or *Bundestaat,* Balkan confederation or South Slav union, a system of East European confederations or a Danubian federation - it came to concentrate first of all on bolstering the authority of the Yugoslav King and government. This the Foreign Office sought to do by encouraging the Yugoslavs to take political initiatives which would demonstrate both their unity and their relevance to their countrymen. For the sake of clarity and convenience, if at the risk of artificially separating these two intertwined questions, it will be best to consider them in sequence: first the British effort to save the Yugoslav exiles from themselves, then British thinking about the future ordering of the Balkans.

It is remarkable that the British should have imagined that any policy pronouncement which they might persuade the exile government to make would affect the political balance in Yugoslavia. They had, though, few other instruments at hand. Aware that the aspirations of the peoples of occupied Europe were fast outpacing those of their exiled governments, the Foreign Office came to believe that only by making a declaration of basic policy could the Yugoslav government maintain its credibility with its people. As always in Yugoslavia, the key was to find a solution to the vexed problem of relations among the country's nationalities. To the Foreign Office, as to certain elements within the exile government, federalism seemed to offer the best hope for the future. The federal principle also had the advantage of malleability. A Yugoslav federation could be extended to encompass all the Balkan states or divided, its constituent parts joining whatever other system or systems that might emerge.

The idea, first mooted in the autumn of 1941, that the Yugoslav government seek to counter the centrifugal forces at work in both the country and in its own councils by issuing a declaration on domestic policy was renewed in the early months of 1942 by the Political Warfare Executive. Ralph Murray wrote in February to his chief, R. H. Bruce Lockhart, that it was essential for British propaganda to Yugoslavia that the exile government issue a political programme which would assure cooperation between Serbs and Croats for the duration of the war and create conditions favourable to future resistance by Yugoslavs heretofore passive. The Croats especially needed to be offered proof that there would be a place for them in a new Yugoslavia. Unless the Yugoslav government could be persuaded to issue such a declaration, it would become increasingly difficult for Britain to maintain its advocacy of Yugoslav unity - an advocacy already weakened by its abstract character and by the actual resentment it aroused among many whose experience had discredited the Yugoslav idea. The alternative - separate and narrow appeals to the Serbs and Croats - would, he warned, carry with it grave implications for political warfare and British post-war interests. The Foreign Office agreed with Murray's analysis. But since any declaration that the Yugoslav ministers might produce would almost certainly include an affirmation of their commitment to embrace all Yugoslavs in the common state (and thus their claims in Istria, the Julian March and Carinthia), the Southern Department recommended caution in associating Britain with whatever programme resulted.[92]

Such quibbles soon proved irrelevant. Rendel pointed out to Howard on 31 March that any declaration would have to be drafted by the Foreign Office if it were to say something significant and still stand a chance of being accepted by all the Yugoslavs. There were few points on which the ministers could agree - and these did not include a reaffirmation of the *Sporazum* (which was anathema to the extreme Serbs Grol and Ninčić), nor the concept of a federal Yugoslavia (which even if acceptable in principle to the Serbs, was bound to provoke endless conflict over the division of Bosnia, Hercegovina and Dalmatia between the Serbian and Croatian units). What Rendel offered instead as being withinthe realm of possibility was a reconfirmation of the principles of the Declaration of Corfu,[93] an expression of loyalty to the Karadjordjević dynasty and a statement of intent to maintain the common capital at Belgrade. The Serbs might, in addition, be persuaded to promise equal access to the public services for Croats and Slovenes. This was hardly stirring stuff, but Rendel urged that work proceed on drafting a declaration which could be put to the Yugoslav government.[94]

The Foreign Office decided in April to go ahead with the

preparation of a policy statement for the Yugoslav government. Its objects would be to quiet fears that the King and government were implacably great-Serb in outlook and aimed to restore Serb hegemony after the war, to convince Croats that the principles of the *Sporazum* would be maintained locally as well as extended to the central administration and to assure Serbs and Slovenes that they too would receive the same measure of self-government. The specific points were left to Rendel offered instead as being within the realm of possibility hoped that such a declaration, if made, would serve to restore the deteriorating reputation of the government and strengthen the voices of moderation within both the cabinet and the quarrelling Yugoslav communities in America. Most importantly, the Croats might be emboldened to throw over the Ustaše regime and make common cause with Mihailovic and the Serbs.[95] The Foreign Office was less sanguine about the chances of getting the Yugoslavs to accept such a programme than it was about its potential effects. Nonetheless, the moment seemed opportune. The British were then considering the elevation of their legations to the smaller Allied governments to embassy rank. The Yugoslavs might be told that if they proved incapable of taking such a policy initiative, then they could not expect to be accorded similar treatment - on the ground that Yugoslavia's continued existence after the war was in doubt. Also auspicious was the dawning realization on the part of men like Grol and Krnjević that some such pronouncement was necessary. Eden agreed to the plan and to the Southern Department's request that he lend it his authority by urging it upon Jovanović.[96]

The Foreign Secretary met with the Yugoslav Premier on 20 May. Jovanović was not hostile to the idea, but neither was he optimistic about the likelihood of gaining the assent of his colleagues. He promised merely to study the matter.[97] Later he told Rendel that, aside from the problem of securing his colleagues' consent, he feared that it would be difficult to tailor a declaration that would both encourage Mihailović's Serb following and offer the Croats something to fight for. It seemed, however, in subsequent days that Rendel was making sufficient progress in his campaign to convert the Yugoslav ministers that it was unnecessary to exact any *quid pro quo* for the elevation of the legation. In fact Jovanović suggested that he make the declaration in the form of a speech at a luncheon he planned to give in honour of Rendel's nomination as Ambassador. The Foreign Office thought this neither the form nor the forum appropriate for such an important pronouncement, but Rendel, aided by Professor R. W. Seton-Watson, went ahead to produce a first draft.[98] This enunciated the principles which would guide the government's activity in future: a commitment to democratic government, the election of a constituent assembly to frame a constitution on federal lines, the reaffirmation of the Corfu Declaration and the Pact of Rome[99] as expressions of the full equality of the Serbs, Croats and Slovenes and, finally, the reconfirmation of the validity of the *Sporazum* pending the establishment of a definitive federal system for the country as a whole.

Not unexpectedly, this formulation did not win the acceptance of the Yugoslav ministers. The most extreme Serbs (now led by Gavrilović) considered it nothing but a "Croat document"; Jovan Banjanin, an integral Yugoslavist, rejected explicit federalism; the Serbs in general objected to mention of the Pact of Rome, the Croats to the Corfu Declaration; many ministers regarded the call for a constituent assembly as implying that their own government was unconstitutional; while Grol was of the opinion that it was premature to consider constitutional questions at all. Confronted with these diverse criticisms, Jovanović produced a redraft which said precisely nothing. The idea of launching the declaration at the luncheon in Rendel's honour was scrapped and the new Ambassador sent back to the drawing board.[100] Subsequent drafts, omitting mention of the Corfu Declaration or the Pact of Rome and substituting woolly talk of "redefined relationships" among the Kingdom's peoples and "unity through diversity" for an explicit espousal of federalism, were put before the Yugoslavs. These foundered on what the Foreign Office was shocked to learn, notwithstanding Rendel's earlier warning, was the fundamental unwillingness of the more extreme Serbs to countenance any reaffirmation of the *Sporazum*. Since a basic purpose of the proposed declaration was to offer the Croats an alternative to Pavelić and/or passivity, the Foreign Office felt that a declaration without mention of the *Sporazum* was worse than no declaration at all. As Dixon put it, "To reject the *Sporazum* is tantamount to refusing to acknowledge the existence of 'Croatia' as an entity in the future Yugoslavia. This, I think, is the first time that the Serb element in the Yugoslav government have so clearly shown their hand."[101]

The Serbs, for their part, now made free with accusations that the British were irrevocably committed to the Croat cause, that they were out to "do the Serbs down", and even - as the Cairo Affair seemed to show - that they hoped to overturn the Jovanović cabinet. His government's slipping prestige, Jovanović told Rendel, was not caused by its failure to settle the constitutional issue, but by the army crisis and Britain's support for the dissident officers.[102] Although another emasculated draft was produced by mid-July which met even Gavrilović's terms (it made no mention of the *Sporazum*), Jovanović called a halt to the entire proceeding on 16 July. He could not agree to any declaration so long as the British continued to suborn Yugoslav troops and - it was "universally believed" - endeavoured to bring down his government. Settlement of the Cairo Affair mattered above all else. In these circumstances the Foreign Office was not unhappy to drop the entire idea. The current draft was in any case useless; it was obvious that the government was using the army crisis as an excuse for its own futility. The idea would not be resurrected unless and until the Yugoslavs did so themselves.[103]

By autumn both sides were ready to try again. Jukić, Šutej, Banjanin and Grol were working to secure a declaration of policy.[104] The British determined to lend a hand. On questioning Jovanović, Rendel found that despite conceding that some sort of federalism was the only long-term solution, the Yugoslav Premier argued that the whole question should be shelved until after the war.[105] It was more important that co-operation be established on the ground between Mihailović and Maček. This he thought possible. Given a last flare-up in Cairo, the Foreign Office decided not to press the Yugoslavs until the army crisis was "decently interred". But the British certainly did not share Jovanović's professed faith that

Mihailović, left to himself, would find an acceptable solution to the problem of Serbo-Croat relations. His hostility to the Croats was by November as obvious to the Foreign Office as was the hopelessness of his government.[106]

Realizing, in Michael Rose's words, "how well-founded are the fears of the Croats and the Slovenes that there is a party aiming at establishing a Serb hegemony after the war," the Foreign Office considered that it was more important than ever "to set these fears to rest by some government declaration".[107] Yet a note of despair had now crept into British discussion of the subject. No longer did they assume either that the Yugoslav ministers could be persuaded to act reasonably or that their pronouncements would carry any weight in Yugoslavia. In a minute occasioned by the debate that fall on whether or not they should seek to unseat Ninčić, Sargent wrote on 12 November that,

> I am beginning to wonder whether it is worth while struggling to make Serbs and Croats work together with the object of recreating a centralized Yugoslavia which the late King Alexander had brought about before the war. The centrifugal forces have grown enormously not merely among exiled politicians in London but I suspect among people in Yugoslavia itself, and I doubt whether any juggling with the exiled government in London would really exercise any influence on the course of events once Yugoslavia has been freed from enemy domination. The London government at that stage, however constituted and with whatever policy, will I fear play a very small part if any at all. The only personality who may be able to make his position felt is General Mihailović, who as far as we know has no love of the Croats and is not likely to work for the recreation of a united Yugoslavia unless it be in the form of a Serb domination of Croatia and Slovenia.[108]

Sargent concluded, however, that it would be better to renew the efforts to secure a political declaration than to try to oust Ninčić, largely for fear of worse succeeding him. Eden agreed, adding, "I am sorry for King Peter; I wish I thought that the boy had better prospects. They seem pretty desperate to me."[109] Not for the last time would the medicine prescribed seem unequal to the affliction - even to those making the diagnosis.

This pessimism reflected London's greater appreciation in late 1942 of the intractability of Yugoslav issues. It was only now, for example, that the Foreign Office really began to apprehend the territorial as opposed to the constitutional difficulties inherent in any Serbo-Croat settlement. Serb and Croat pretensions to Bosnia, Hercegovina and Dalmatia were irreconcilable. The *Sporazum* was anathema to the Serbs not merely because it gave the Croats an autonomy which Serbs did not enjoy, but also because it provided for a Croatian Banovina which embraced much territory inhabited by Serbs. This had been denounced in 1939; since then the slaughter perpetrated by the Ustaše had made Serbs even less willing to tolerate the abandonment of their brethren to Croat dominion. The Croats, meanwhile clung to their conception of Croatia's historical frontiers. As Rendel noted about Krnjević, "At best he can only think of Croat rights and never of Croat obligations."[110] The enormity of the more extreme Serbs' appetites only hardened the Croats in their resolve to maintain their own extensive claims.[111] The obvious solution - a Bosnian unit within a Yugoslav federation - was inconceivable to both Serbs and Croats in the exile government, although not to the Yugoslav communists or to the Foreign Office.[112]

After these trials it naturally came as a pleasant surprise to the British when King Peter and Jovanović, speaking to their countrymen over the BBC on 1 December (Yugoslavia's national day), seemed to lay the groundwork for the sort of policy statement that the British had long deemed necessary. Jovanović spoke of the need for Serbs, Croats and Slovenes to remain united, while King Peter promised that "the new Yugoslavia will, by the will of her people, have a constitution which will sufficiently protect the particular interests of narrower communities and also secure the unhindered strengthening of the common foundations."[113] The Foreign Office regarded this statement as a first hesitant step towards a political declaration. As it happened, it was also the last. The government as a whole was never able to give substance to the hints offered by the King's speech; and by the end of 1942 events in Yugoslavia reasserted their claim to the predominant share of the Foreign Office's attention. The British did not again look to the exile government to provide a lead which, it was now realized, could come only from the contending parties in the country itself. Henceforth the Yugoslav government would occupy much the same position in relation to the British as Banjanin claimed most of his fellow ministers did in relation to the crown, Jovanović and the military cabinet: they would be a government on sufferance - legitimate but irrelevant.

(iv)

When Churchill extended the hand of friendship and assistance to the Russian people in June 1941 there was little expectation in Britain that the Red Army's resistance would prove either effective or prolonged. By the end of the year, however, the conviction had grown that the Soviet Union must also emerge from the war triumphant. This change placed the British government in an anomalous position. The Prime Minister, despite his anti-Bolshevik past, may have been able for a time to free his vision of all objectives save the destruction of Hitler and every vestige of Nazism, but the Foreign Office existed to eschew such single-mindedness. Military victory required that Britain strive to make an effective Anglo-Soviet alliance, but political self-interest demanded that some means be found of denying the Soviets the full fruits of that victory. Post-war confederations of the East European states appeared early in the war to offer one of the most promising political solutions to the twin problems of German and Russian expansionism.

In April 1941 the Foreign Office had discerned "sufficient indications to assume that Soviet long-range aims are very much the same as the German, i.e. a number of small federated socialist states under the Pax Sovietica."[114] But after June the British were naturally more inclined to recognize certain of the Russians' territorial claims. For Stalin acceptance by Britain of Soviet title to the lands acquired during his period of association with Hitler was a prerequisite to the negotiation of a meaningful alliance. Eden was told as much during his visit to Moscow in December 1941. The British had hoped to satisfy

Stalin without entering into specific commitments regarding the cession of other peoples' territories, but they eventually found it necessary to meet Stalin's demands in every case but that of Poland - despite American displeasure. On the other hand, Stalin's expressed preference at Moscow for "practical arithmetic" - that is the explicit delimitation of territorial claims - rather than for Eden's higher "algebra" - or subscription by both powers to a self-denying ordinance in line with the Atlantic Charter - at least had the virtue of spelling out what Soviet intentions actually were.[115]

In Central Europe Stalin made plain his view that Poland should "slide" westwards at the expense of Prussia and that the remainder of Germany must be dismembered. He allowed in return that the British might have any bases in France, the Low Countries and Scandinavia they thought necessary. In the Balkans he indicated that he had plans in store for Romania and Yugoslavia. The former would, as the Southern Department later adjudged it, "not unnaturally" be required to yield up Bessarabia and Northern Bukovina. Compensation would come in the form of an alliance with the USSR under which the Russians would guarantee Romania (and evidently its claim to Transylvania) against Hungary, but which would also permit the Russians to maintain naval and military bases in the country. The Foreign Office felt certain tha Romania was destined to become a Soviet dependency. Regarding Yugoslavia, Stalin maintained that the country should be restored and extended at the expense of Italy. This the Foreign Office took to mean the incorporation of islands and cities lost to Italy under the Treaty of Rapallo in 1920. It was further speculated that "the Soviet plan may well be the constitution of a greater Yugoslavia, not only as a counterweight to Italy, but also as a channel for Soviet penetration on to the Adriatic via Romania and Bulgaria."[116]

It was on acount of Bulgaria, in fact, that the Foreign Office was most alarmed. Stalin's only reference to the country in December had been an observation that it should not go unpunished, and that perhaps Turkey might be awarded some Bulgarian territory. This suggested to the Foreign Office that Stalin was serenely confident that Bulgaria would, in

Howard's apposite Balkan simile, "fall to him like a ripe plum". Spurred by the Bulgarian preoccupations of George Rendel and Milan Gavrilović, the Foreign Office regarded it as axiomatic that the combination of traditional Russophilia and despair at having lost yet another war of aggrandizement would spell the end of Tsar Boris and his dynasty. In such circumstances the country would "lapse into communism" and - with or without Soviet connivance - ask for incorporation in the USSR. The near-certainty of Russian predominance in Romania and Bulgaria would make it difficult for Greece and Yugoslavia to resist further Soviet encroachments.[117]

The Southern Department appreciated the unpleasantness of Britain's dilemma. As Dixon minuted on 8 January 1942, "On the one hand it is of vital interest to our present strategical needs that nothing should be said or done to impair Anglo-Soviet relations- on the other hand, it is to our ultimate interest to lay our plans to counter the expansionist moves on the part of the Soviet Union which are to be anticipated at the end of the war."[118] There appeared to be two possible courses of action by which these conflicting imperatives could be reconciled. The first - despatch before the end of the war of an expeditionary force to the Balkans - was the most certain to stabilize the states of the region, particularly Bulgaria, and to drive a wedge between the advancing Russians and the retreating Germans. Stalin himself, by his demand for a second front and by his indication to Eden in Moscow that he considered the Balkans a suitable target, had provided an opening. The need for a Balkan offensive had also been underlined by Simović and other members of the Yugoslav government.[119] The prominence of the communist-led Partisans in the resistance struggle increased their fears of Soviet intervention while, at the same time, it raised the spectre of collaboration on the part of their adherents with the Axis were the Western Allies to "disinterest" themselves in the fate of the country.[120] The Foreign Office could do no more in early 1942, however, than resolve to put such considerations before the military authorities when the time came.[121]

The second course of action - and the one which it lay in the power of the Foreign Office to pursue immediately - was to encourage the planning of post-war confederations by the East European Allies. It was realized that the possibility of erecting barriers against German and Soviet imperialism would depend upon the military balance at war's end and, hence, in part on the decision taken regarding the opening of a Balkan front. But as Sargent minuted on 11 January,

> this is no reason why we should not for our part take time by the forelock and do what we can to meet any tendency on the part of the Soviet government to fish in the troubled waters of the Balkans. At the present moment the only instrument at our disposal is the policy of a Balkan confederation and I feel that we ought to make as much use of this as we can.[122]

The Greek and Yugoslav governments gave every sign of taking the point - and demonstrated it by their willingness to hold open the door to their old enemies, the Bulgarians, in a future confederation.

Talks between the Greeks and Yugoslavs had begun in September on the initiative of the latter, but with strong British encouragement.[123] They followed in the wake of negotiations on post-war confederation between the Polish and Czechoslovak governments; talks which resulted in the signature of an agreement on 3 December.[124] By January 1942 conclusion of a similar Graeco-Yugoslav pact, providing for a Balkan Union, awaited only the resolution of the first Yugoslav government crisis and the need to give prior notice to the American, Russian and Turkish governments. As far as the would-be confederates were concerned, their Union also required explicit British sponsorship. Eden was asked to preside over the signature of the agreement in his room at the Foreign Office. This ceremony took place on 15 January.[125]

The Balkan Union agreement called for the establishment of permanent consultative machinery by the two governments in the political, economic and military spheres. It was envisaged that foreign policy would be coordinated, that plans for a customs and monetary union and a joint economic development programme would be elaborated and that the defence establishments of the two states would be integrated by means of a combined general staff. It was expressly stated that the two governments looked forward to the accession of other Balkan states to the Union.[126]

Although merely a declaration of intent on the part of two exiled governments whose prospects of returning home were far from certain, the Foreign Office was encouraged by this demonstration of their "vision". From Cairo Sir Miles Lampson, Ambassador to Egypt, suggested on behalf of SOE that the British government also declare itself in favour of an all-inclusive Balkan confederation. Such a pronouncement, SOE held, would act as a tonic to pro-Allied sentiment in the Balkans, and particularly in Bulgaria.[127] Some in the Foreign Office agreed, pressing too for a British declaration that the Graeco-Yugoslav Union was but the forerunner to a giant East European confederation system extending from the Baltic to the Aegean. They argued that Britain should not be constrained for fear of arousing Soviet suspicions.[128]

Although the Soviet government refrained initially from either lauding or denouncing the Graeco-Yugoslav pact, it was appreciated by the Foreign Office that the Russians could hardly be expected to welcome the prospect of confederations intended, at least in part, as barriers against the expansion of their influence. Eden seemed to accept this in rejecting the advice of his subordinates that Britain mount a pro-confederation campaign. He ordered, moreover, that the Balkan Union's open invitation to other states, still members of the Axis, should be downplayed. Despite representing the "underlying idea of the agreement", he held that Romania and Bulgaria must not be encouraged to believe "that after the war they will live happily and without punishment on equal terms with Allied Balkan states". Britain should "bless and encourage" the agreement, indicate that it was regarded as "a prelude to the type of arrangement we welcome for [the] post-war settlement", but leave further elaboration of its implications to the exile governments concerned.[129] Several days later the Foreign Office resolved to promote confederation schemes on their own merits - be they economic, national or political - but not as part of a plan to frustrate Soviet ambitions.[130]

Having applied its stamp of approval to the Graeco-Yugoslav agreement, the Foreign Office moved on during the first half of 1942 to consider the replacement models for what Sargent characterized as "the pre-war congeries of weak, irresponsible and jealous national states" in Eastern Europe. He and Eden agreed that the accepted notion of state sovereignty must be modified. They hoped that fear of German revenge and Soviet imperialism would provide the "cement" necessary to work this miracle. They were willing, however, for the sake of European security, to contemplate the use of coercion against any state reluctant to merge its identity with a larger grouping or desirous of secession once inside. "The peace and security of Europe as a whole, as contrasted with the wishes and prejudices of any individual state," Sargent wrote on 29 January, "will justify the use of force in just the same way as the American Civil War was justified in order to preserve the Union in the interests of the future of North America as a whole."[131]

The academic experts at Balliol (the FRPS) maintained in a memorandum submitted on 20 January that in the modern world confederations were expedients only; they dissolved if not quickly transformed into full federations. This the Foreign Office regarded as a counsel of perfection. Whilst Ninčić shared the theoretical preference of the British for an inclusive Balkan federation linked to a similar unit in North Central Europe, neither the Greek government nor all the Yugoslav ministers agreed.[132] Gavrilović, for example, was a strenuous advocate of South Slav federation (between the Yugoslavs and Bulgarians, or perhaps only between the Serbs and Bulgarians) as the basis for a new order in the Balkans. In either case, his point seemed to be that the Serbs and their dynasty should prevail. Far from immunizing the Bulgarians against the pan-Slav bacillus as Gavrilović argued, the Foreign Office was certain that such a unit would prove far more susceptible to Russian influence that would a broad confederation embracing the Greeks and other non-Slavs. For its part the Greek government had already recoiled from the idea of a tight federation and was upset, too, by the loose talk of links between Graeco-Yugoslav and Polish-Czechoslovak units. Gavrilović's plan, Sargent concluded, was sure to frighten the Greeks even more.[133]

The Foreign Office attributed the Greeks' fears to their insufficiently European outlook. Ninčić's ideas, especially his belief in the necessity for ties between confederal units in north and south, were much preferred.[134] Yet in this case the anti-Soviet passions of the Poles soon posed an additional problem, for General Sikorski was all too explicit in his pronouncements on the underlying purpose of confederations. Ninčić, who had no greater wish than the Greeks to get on the wrong side of the Soviets (whom he described as extremely "*susceptible et mefiant*"), began to adopt a more reserved position.[135]

Sargent interpreted the Yugoslav government's positive and European approach to the confederation issue as reflecting its realization that the reconstitution of Yugoslavia was not practical politics; that the alternatives, in fact, were disintegration followed by Soviet intervention in Serbia, or participation in a wider East European system. The Yugoslav ministers naturally preferred the latter.[136] But the Yugoslavs also sought to strike a bargain with the Russians that would improve their chances of survival. This seemed vital in that by March the Soviets had become openly hostile towards the idea of a Graeco-Yugoslav union.[137] Thus in the spring of 1942 the question of Balkan confederation became entangled with Ninčić's desire to conclude an alliance with the Soviet government, as well as with the final negotiations between Eden and Molotov on the terms of the Anglo-Soviet alliance.

Despite continuing Foreign Office devotion to the confederation concept, Soviet suspicions and the presence of more immediate obstacles to agreement compelled the British to drop their proposed confederation plank (and much else besides) from the alliance finally negotiated with Molotov in May.[138] The Foreign Office determined, however, to raise the issue again when Molotov returned to London from Washington in early June. To this end Sargent produced a long and complicated memorandum on 1 June which sought to summarize British thinking on the question.[139] In the event confederation was again lost in the shuffle, largely because it seemed more important to squelch plans for a Soviet-Yugoslav alliance.

The Foreign Office had not been adverse to the original Yugoslav proposal in April to reactivate, update and ratify their non-aggression pact with the Soviets dating from April 1941.[140] But the Soviets' counterproposal - that a five-year mutual assistance treaty be signed - was open to serious objections. In the first place, by extending into what it was assumed would be the post-war period it rendered Yugoslavia liable to being regarded as a Soviet protectorate. Secondly, it would be likely to prejudice the chances of forming confederations after the war.[141] Whether a charter for Soviet interference in the Balkans or Moscow's answer to Britain's confederation schemes, Sargent regarded it as "slightly ominous that the first of the minor Allied governments to be offered such an alliance is the one whose future is the most uncertain."[142]

Eden decided to tackle Molotov on the issue, proposing a self-denying ordinance which would remove the risk of an Anglo-Soviet "treaties race" with the lesser Allies.[143] Molotov was non-committal when Eden broached the subject on 9 June, but acted according to British wishes when he saw Ninčić the next day. He told the Yugoslav Foreign Minister that the Soviet government was ready to guarantee Yugoslavia's territorial integrity, but he did not propose putting this or any other guarantee in treaty form. The unhappy Ninčić was left in ignorance as to why the Soviet line had suddenly changed. That it had was underlined in the next month when the Russians began to attack Mihailović openly in their propaganda.[144]

Although the Greek and Yugoslav governments made one last attempt in September to revivify their Balkan Union and to put into practice certain of its foreign policy provisions while still in exile,[145] Russian opposition and the evermore uncertain prospects of the Yugoslav government and its Minister of War rendered the whole British-sponsored confederation project increasingly unreal in late 1942. The men in the Foreign Office continued, usually at Rendel's instance, to discuss the question, but their thoughts now turned more often towards the possibility of making a deal directly with the Soviets on the post-war settlement in the Balkans. Even Sargent no longer counted confederation among Britain's high cards in meeting the expected Soviet challenge in the area. He listed these in January 1943 as being:

> (1) the possibility that at the end of the war there will be British and American armies in the Balkans; (2) that Turkey may be a belligerent with an army also in the Balkans; and (3) the fact that we and the Americans will control the relief organization which will have to feed the starving populations throughout the Balkans for an indefinite period after the withdrawal of the Axis forces.

Sargent recommended - and Eden agreed - that Sir Archibald Clark-Kerr should approach Stalin upon taking over the Moscow embassy, initiating discussions which would serve to convince the Soviets that it was in the general interest that they make plans to prevent the collapse into chaos of the Balkan states after the Axis armies withdrew.[146]

Nothing came of this or other British soundings of the Russians during 1943,[147] until, at the Moscow conference of foreign ministers in October, Molotov (intentionally) and Hull (accidentally) put paid to the idea of British-sponsored confederations in Central and South-Eastern Europe.[148] When Tito enunciated a confederation policy of his own in 1944, and in the guise of a South Slav union under communist auspices, the British moved decisively against it. In the meantime the decisions of both the Moscow conference and the first Quebec conference (which effectively ruled out the employment of Western Allied armies in the Balkans) caused the British to find new merit in Stalin's preference for "practical arithmetic". The way was cleared for Churchill's percentages deal with Stalin in October 1944.

Planning for post-war confederation had during 1941 and 1942 been the second pillar of Britain's policy of keeping open a non-communist future for Yugoslavia. The first was support for Mihailović. Both proved wanting in 1942 and were abandoned in 1943. It now remains to be seen how Britain's policy towards Mihailović and the Yugoslav resistance changed in these years.

CHAPTER V

THE LEOPARD'S SPOTS: MIHAILOVIĆ AND THE BRITISH IN 1942

(i)

It has frequently been implied that a principal reason for Britain's unwavering commitment to Mihailović and his movement during 1942 was ignorance of the true state of affairs in occupied Yugoslavia. Deakin has given such a view particularly vivid expression:

> The attempts made by SOE Cairo during the course of 1942 to reestablish contact with Bill Hudson by sending further parties, and to obtain a wider picture of resistance elements in other regions of the country outside the immediate areas of western Serbia where Mihailović was assumed to be operating, had been without success. The curtain was impenetrable, the picture dark.[1]

Yet if darkness reigned it was as much because the British made ineffective use of what information they did possess as it was because few shafts of light penetrated the curtain. Inadequate coordination of intelligence, inter and intra-service rivalries, personal antagonisms, exclusive loyalties, divided responsibilities and - through the middle of 1942 - the absence of any overwhelming need to overcome these deficiencies added to the burden of maintaining an accurate appraisal of events while communications with Hudson remained in suspension.[2] But they did not render the task impossible.

Distrusted, disparaged or disregarded by the mandarins of the Foreign Office, the brass hats at the front and in the rear and the spooks of SIS - and failing before late December to reinforce Hudson with a man it trusted - SOE may have remained in comfortable darkness. But these others were not, or need not have been. SIS had at its disposal intelligence derived both from *Sicherheitsdienst* intercepts and from its own agents on the ground in Yugoslavia.[3] (SOE Cairo did not begin to receive intercepts until December 1942 or January 1943, and then only by grace of a bureaucratic oversight. SOE London did not get them at all; though whether or not this made any difference is hard to tell.)[4] The existence of SIS operatives in Yugoslavia has long been obscured. While Deakin examines in detail the fates of the three failed SOE missions in early 1942 - those of Lieutenant Stanislav Rapotec, Major Terence Atherton and Major Cavan Elliot - he makes no mention of nine other Anglo-Yugoslav or wholly Yugoslav teams sent in between April and September.[5] The majority of these missions probably originated with SIS. Seven were successful (i.e. they avoided capture upon arrival) and must be assumed to have provided their controllers with valuable intelligence.[6]

As a principal supervisor of SIS the Foreign Office obviously had access to all intelligence originating with it - including intercepts. What is not so certain is whether or not this information meant very much to those who saw it. Frequent references in the much 'weeded' Foreign Office files to papers coded "RJ" (Red Jacket) indicate that super-secret intelligence of particularly striking importance was seen and discussed at the highest levels.[7] But what of the more routine items on which a continuous assessment might have been based? Elisabeth Barker has suggested that the Foreign Office was ill-equipped in terms of manpower and organization to deal effectively with all the material at its disposal.[8] While necessarily speculative in regard to the expurgated SIS intelligence, this judgment is vindicated by the paucity of minutes on the extant (and often very valuable) reports on events in the country passed on to the Foreign Office by various Yugoslav ministers (especially Krek) and by the press reading bureaux in Stockholm and Istanbul.[9]

Only when Yugoslav resistance pushed its way to centre stage - that is when, propelled by the Russians, it presented explicitly political problems - did the Southern Department seem to make sustained efforts to digest masses of raw intelligence. Thus it was after the Soviets lashed out at Mihailović in July that the Foreign Office made a concerted attempt to keep abreast of what was taking place in Yugoslavia.

(ii)

However perfect or imperfect the state of British knowledge about the Četniks and Partisans during the bulk of 1942, it was a frustrating year. Communications difficulties, departmental infighting, exile government harassment, Četnik fulminations, apparent Russian wrecking, aircraft shortages, military reverses in the North African desert, first doubts about Mihailović and the survival of the Partisans all combined to see to this.

The British appear to have reacted to the quelling of the autumn revolt in Serbia, and to the realization that their military authorities were both unable and unwilling to supply the wherewithal for a large-scale insurgency, by reverting to the view that a national uprising was premature. Throughout the first months of 1942 the propaganda directives of the Political Warfare Executive counselled that "the aim is to encourage resistance and boost Mihailović without instigation to revolt."[10] The "Disclaim" mission of Captain Elliot, parachuted into Eastern Bosnia on 4/5 February and immediately made prisoner, carried with it instructions stating that, "The clandestine organizations must be instructed not to undertake any excesses against the occupying power which would provoke too sharp reprisals, and therefore make all resistance impossible."[11] On 26 April Mihailović was ordered from London, "do not enter unarmed and empty-handed into large actions which cause disproportionate casualties. Continue organizing the whole country and await the decisive hour."[12]

Yet Mihailović still had reason to suspect that the British wanted resistance on a suicidal scale and, worse yet, that they did not share his perception of the Partisans as the principal enemy. The adventurer Atherton had apparently represented his brief in a manner calculated to fuel such primordial Četnik fears. As Ostojić reported to Mihailović in a radio message,

> Yesterday, 10 May, Captain Nedeljković arrived, a member of the mission which landed on 4 February and was in Partisan confinement until 15 April . . . The English Major Atherton is even worse than Marko* and is seeking help for the communists, but he has not been able to make contact with Malta. He wishes to see you and is writing a letter. Now he is somewhere in Bosnia. He has from his command instructions to mix with all forces and to undermine the struggle against the occupier regardless of the losses of our people. Politically, he wishes to form some kind of forest government on which he would exercise influence as an Englishman, as well as in London on our government there. All in all, he desires to put our people in their graves for the sake of England. In a word, he is a trader in human lives. He is the chief of four or five missions in Yugoslavia sent without our knowledge.
> Missions are located in Montenegro, Croatia, Dalmatia, South Serbia and Bosnia. Atherton gave the communists 250,000 lire. It is necessary to prevent this gentleman from wandering about and to explain to him that we do not want his kind and that we are not selling our people, but dying for their good.[13]

Mihailović reported to his government in a telegram dated 24 May that he had received the promised letter from Atherton. He complained not of Atherton's apparent desire to stimulate resistance, but of the presence of so many English missions in the country about which he had not been informed.[14] London

*Hudson's *nom de guerre* with the Četniks.

replied on 30 May that "Atherton is our man, sent to you in January. Help him and heed his advice."[15] By then, however, Atherton was dead and no longer a threat to either Četniks or Partisans.

The British missions of which Mihailović complained were, of course, designed to restore the regular communications which his virtual dismissal of Hudson and his constant harrassment by the Germans rendered impossible. Hudson was incommunicado from late November through April.[16] Mihailović remained silent for weeks at a time between early December and early May.[17] When he did resume fairly regular communication in March he reported that the communists were still hindering his work and that they were being aided by the occupiers and the Ustaše in order to plunge the country into internecine war with the advent of spring. He implored his government, "Do all in your power to put them on the right track." This was to be accomplished by an appeal to the Russians.[18]

Up until this time the Foreign Office, although possessing information about the dire straits through which the Yugoslav resistance was passing, seems to have assumed that Mihailović's differences with the Partisans remained composed, or at least quiescent. Thus the decision of the Soviet government, communicated to Cripps in early January, that it did not "find it expedient to intervene in the partisan affairs of Yugoslavia", was not taken too tragically.[19] Moreover, Soviet propaganda continued to laud Mihailović as a leader of Yugoslav "partisans" and "patriots".[20]

What did move the Foreign Office and SOE to review policy towards the resistance and then to mount a new assault on the Defence Committee and Chiefs of Staff was an omnibus appeal addressed by Jovanović to Eden on 5 February and reinforced by a personal visit a week later. Besides reiterating various long-standing requests for ships and planes to equip Yugoslav naval and air force personnel in Egypt, the Premier complained bitterly of Britain's failure to send aid to Mihailović and pleaded that new efforts be made, especially as he expected another general uprising in the spring. Jovanović also asked that his government be given exclusive control over communications with Mihailović. (And this, it seems, was the principal object of his multifaceted appeal.) Eden, however, focused only on his proposals for assistance to Mihailović. The Foreign Secretary demanded to know of the Department why nothing had been done to assist the rebels.[21]

A joint policy review by the Foreign Office and SOE followed. Although its record has been withheld, the result was a memorandum from Eden to the Defence Committee on 28 February which revived the argument of the previous autumn: the Yugoslav resistance was not a premature incident of little significance, but a serious (if small scale) diversion in the war against the Axis and as such was worthy of all possible support. Eden proposed, in view of the evident failure of SOE's three recent missions, that other measures for restoring contact with the country be investigated. He also asked that urgent consideration be given to the establishment of special squadrons of aircraft (ideally long-range Liberator II bombers) for operation by SOE from either Britain or Egypt.[22]

The military seemed now more favourably disposed towards the Yugoslav revolt than in 1941. General Sir Alan Brooke, the CIGS, stressed to the Chiefs of Staff on 2 March the value of the diversion of Axis forces caused by the resistance, while Portal revealed that two Liberators were being sent to Egypt for use by SOE. (Two Liberators were not many, but they represented a significant proportion of Britain's limited stocks of the precious craft and a big advance over the obsolete Whitleys and Halifaxes.) The Defence Committee nonetheless ignored Eden's suggestion that SOE be provided with its own flight of aircraft and clearly did not see what else was to be done pending restoration of regular communicaions with Mihailović.[23]

Eden appealed to Maisky on 27 March for Soviet help in reestablishing contact with Mihailović.[24] The Russian Ambassador did not reply until 15 April; and then to report that his government had no means of communicating with Yugoslavia.[25] In the meantime, however, the wireless link with Mihailović had become more secure and it was on this basis that a further approach to the military was launched. Sir Frank Nelson, executive director (CD) of SOE under the new Minister, Lord Selborne,[26] addressed a memorandum to the Chiefs of Staff on 30 March informing them that communications had been restored, pointing to the inadequacy of two Liberators for all of SOE's Balkan operations and asking for a reconsideration of Eden's 2 March proposal that more aircraft be allocated to SOE. In view of the fact that 26 Axis divisions were being contained in Yugoslavia, Nelson argued that Mihailović was worthy of support even at the expense of the strategic bombing campaign over western Germany: "General Mihailović's forces provide the only foothold the Allies have on the continent outside Russia and are in a position to threaten the vital Belgrade-Nis railway."[27]

Whatever extra influence SOE may have gained by Selborne's replacement of Dalton, it was not sufficient to override that of Air Marshal A. T. ("Bomber") Harris. The Chiefs of Staff refused to consider "stripping" *Coastal Command* of long-range bombers. (Bomber Command remained inviolable.) SOE would have to find its Liberators from among those already available in the Middle East.[28] How few these were was made clear a few days later when the Chiefs discussed another composite appeal by the Yugoslav government, this time referred to them by the Prime Minister. Auchinleck would be invited to modify for supply duties (by the addition of extra fuel tanks) the *other two* Liberators in his theatre. The Chiefs also decided that the exile government could not be permitted to control its communications with the homeland.[29]

Mihailović's complaints that the communists were sabotaging his work and cooperating with the Axis caused Eden to write to Maisky again on 27 April. He suggested that, even in the absence of direct Soviet links with Yugoslavia, "a word of authority broadcast from Moscow would probably carry considerable influence with the Partisans . . ." The Russians were still unforthcoming. Alexander Bogomolov, Soviet Minister to the exile government, told Rendel that his government did not intend to become involved in the Partisan-

Četnik quarrel, though he felt that Mihailović's policy of conserving his forces in anticipation of a final rising was mistaken and that his reputation as a leader of resistance was undeserved. The Foreign Office was both sceptical of the Russians' claim to have no communications with Yugoslavia and convinced that their seeming refusal to discipline the Partisans was politically motivated.[30] But this did not mean that the Foreign Office was ready to give up appealing to the Soviets to exercise their presumed authority over the Partisans. Nor, for that matter, were the consistent refusals of the Chiefs of Staff to put more aircraft at SOE's disposal to deter future requests that they should do so.[31]

(iii)

Mihailović's reemergence into full-throated volubility in the late spring of 1942 posed as many problems as it promised to solve. Or rather it revealed old difficulties previously masked by silence. Of these Mihailović's antipathy for the Partisans was the most serious politically, but others, including his repeated demands for assistance, also meant that the British could less easily fudge the issue of what sort of resistance they wanted and what sacrifices they were prepared to make to support it. There were in addition various technical, but no less troublesome issues. The dispute over control of communications has already been referred to. The British attempted to represent this as primarily a question of maintaining the necessary security, but the Yugoslavs rightly saw it as a struggle for authority over their War Minister. They disliked, but did not contest, the right of the Commander-in-Chief, Middle East, to issue operational directives to Mihailović. What they did argue was that they should have their own channel for political communications with their Minister. That the issue was largely irrelevant was learnt only by bitter experience. Far distant governments could exercise no more operational or political control over Mihailović than could he over his local chieftains (or *rases,* as their Ethiopian-schooled

Italian allies derisively termed them).[32] But the contention went on throughout 1942.[33] Thereafter it was somewhat attenuated by the Yugoslav exiles' success in developing their own secret courier and wireless links with the homeland.[34] This certainly made them feel better, even if it did nothing to ease their or their leader's by then precarious position.

One of the main concerns of SOE in the spring of 1942 was to restore the credibility of Hudson in Mihailović's camp. On May 26 Mihailović despatched a message which revealed the extent of his distrust of Hudson, his loathing for the communists, his need for arms and his priorities for their use:

> Last autumn I was informed of the British government's view that Yugoslavs must fight for Yugoslavia and not transform the struggle into a rising of communists for Soviet Russia. I repeat, the communists are hated by the people because of their horrible terror. Mark my words, the people will have no truck with them and their end is near. Serbia, Sandžak and eastern Bosnia are completely free of them. In Montenegro the people rose as one against them. I repeat, the people themselves; now Montenegro is also cleansed. Captain Hudson last autumn interfered with my receipt of help in arms and a great crisis ensued. My worry is that through a misunderstanding of our situation he will do so again, when the need is greatest and when the defeat of nazism and fascism and the victory of democracy is at hand. A strike against the enemy cannot be undertaken without arms and munitions. Do not be deceived. The entire populace stands beside the Yugoslav army.[35]

The reply of the British was sent in Jovanović's name on 4 June:

> Report from Major Hudson decided H.M.G. to increase their efforts to send you all possible assistance so as to help you unite the country. He should be treated as your official British liaison officer in which position he can fill most useful role and use should be made of his advice regarding substance of messages as well as codes in which they are sent. We are still most anxious to send you new W/T set so that communications can be established with Cairo

> direct. Please inform Hudson he has been promoted Major and awarded D.S.O.[36]

The report from Hudson referred to in this telegram is not present in the Public Records Office; and it seems that no messages received from Hudson before June have survived.[37] But in a telegram dated 1 November Hudson wrote, "Five months ago I advocated full moral support of Mihailović even at expense of Partisan[s]."[38]

Mihailović had apparently reported Hudson to be with him as early as 29 March. In fact Hudson did not reestablish contact with the Četnik command - and then with Ostojić - until late April.[39] He did not meet with Mihailović until mid-May.[40] Hudson had evidently decided to placate Mihailović lest his uselessness to his superiors and his own internal exile continue indefinitely. Thus Ostojić radioed to Mihailović on 26 April:

> Marko is with me. I explained to him the principles of our work. He is now our great friend and has recognized his mistakes. At my suggestion, Radovan gave him a severe reprimand. His is now soft as cotton and does not get in our way.[41]

That Hudson had become "soft as cotton" was indicated by an obsequious letter which he addressed to Mihailović on 11 June. In it he referred admiringly to the Četniks' recent victories over the Partisans in Montenegro, reported that Britain stood behind them "100%" and asked to be permitted to travel to see Captain Pavle Djurišić and Colonel Bajo Stanišić (Mihailović's commanders in eastern and central Montenegro respectively - and pillars of the Italo-Četnik condominium there).[42] This trip resulted during June and July in reports from Hudson on the deep entanglement of the Montenegrin nationalists with the Italians.[43]

(iv)

In London at mid-year a certain satisfaction was evident both with the way events appeared to be unfolding in Yugoslavia and with the amount of aid which SOE, against formidable obstacles, had succeeded in sending Mihailović. Between 30 March and 3 June 16 sorties were flown. They carried arms, W/T sets and money. While only a proportion of this help had been confirmed as reaching Mihailović, SOE was hopeful that the rest had at least fallen into hands capable of making use of it.[44]

On 2 June the Prime Minister requested the Director of Military Intelligence to provide him with a short report "on patriotic activities in Yugoslavia". The report was compiled and submitted the same day. In its sketchy analysis of the autumn uprising it gave pride of place to Mihailović; in its better-informed description of recent offensives in Bosnia it avoided mention of the Partisans as the objects of Axis attention; while in its conclusions it advocated Mihailović's cause on grounds more political than military:

> (b) The activities of the wilder elements among the "Partisans" or "Communists", against whom Mihailović has often complained, embarrass not only the enemy but ourselves, as they drive the more moderate opponents of the Axis into cooperation with any power that can restore a semblance of law and order. Although the activity of these wild elements in the country will always necessitate considerable Axis garrisons, the policy of Mihailović to curb their activities in order to conserve his potential forces and to wait his time is right.
>
> (c) We are right in backing Mihailović. If we do so successfully not only will we have a certain control over the revolt but we will:
>
> (i) continue to contain at least the present number (i.e. 30) Axis divisions in Yugoslavia,
> (ii) build up a serious threat to the German flank when they are extended in Russia,
> (iii) prepare the way for any operation we may eventually make in the Balkans.
>
> If we do *not* back Mihailović successfully, not only will

> we fail to achieve the above objects, but the military situation will develop into political anarchy and chaos. Not only will British influence and prestige in Yugoslavia be lost, but they will be seriously weakened throughout the rest of the Balkans and the Mediterranean.[45]

The maintenance of military control, the quelling of communist chaos, the preservation of British influence - these were the objectives. But how Mihailović was to pursue his "right" policy of crushing the communists while keeping 30 Axis divisions occupied in Yugoslavia was not explained.

Churchill's minuted reaction to the report was "good". He added in reference to the final paragraph, "Let me know what we can do and are doing."[46] (He did not note the clear implication that arms supplied to Mihailović would, until the time came for the grand finale, be used against those "wild elements" actually resisting the Axis.) The CIGS replied on 16 June that there were two means by which Britain's assistance to Mihailović could be increased: (1) by introducing more W/T sets and operators so as to regularize communications and (2) by providing SOE with more long range aircraft. SOE officials considered that a flight of at least six Liberators based in the Middle East would allow them to do the job. Brooke agreed that everything possible should be done to step up support for Mihailović, but expressed reservations about providing SOE with its own aircraft.[47] The Prime Minister appears to have shown no more interest in Yugoslav resistance until the end of the year.

But for those dealing regularly with Yugoslav affairs the contradictions inherent in exclusive support for Mihailović were beginning to come to the fore. SOE informed the Foreign Office on 3 July that since Mihailović was inactive all recent resistance activity was attributable to the Partisans. Lord Glenconner urged that for public consumption Mihailović continue to receive a portion of the credit. The Foreign Office did not demur.[48]

At the same time Hudson's reports - as translated into SOE appreciations - indicated that the Četniks in Montenegro and Hercegovina were in receipt of Italian arms. But SOE believed, perhaps because Mihailović said so, perhaps because it seemed reasonable given the Italians' interest in fuelling civil war, that the Partisans were also getting Italian help. Hudson's confirmation of the commingling of Mihailović's followers with those of Nedić seemed to pose even fewer problems. SOE accepted Hudson's view that the distinction between those anti-Axis Serbs who formed the majority of Nedić's state guard and those in Mihailović's ranks was one of form only - a distinction without a difference.[49] Mihailović, it was felt, had been candid in the past about his connections with Nedić, even if he sought now to deny them.[50]

Difficulties stemmed from the fact that the Russians were not now inclined to interpret these relations so charitably. The Southern Department was on 13 July in the midst of despatching a new appeal to Moscow to call the Partisans to order when Eden revealed that Maisky had recently informed him that his government was not disposed to intervene with the Partisans because of Mihailović's links with Nedić.[51] The Foreign Office reacted with self-righteous indignation, seeing Maisky's excuse as the flimsiest of pretexts. "The truth of the matter," Dixon wrote, "is that the Soviet government are evidently ready to forego the short-term advantages of a united front to Axis aggression in order to develop their long-term interests in fomenting communism in Yugoslavia." Sargent added that Maisky's allegation against Mihailović was "so specious" as to demand challenge. The Russians must be told that Britain entertained not the slightest suspicion that Mihailović "is double crossing us". Eden concurred.[52]

That the Russians might regard Britain's devotion to Mihailović as a sacrifice of immediate military advantage for the sake of fomenting anti-communism was not considered. The Foreign Office expected the Soviets to share its equation of communism with chaos; and so to a limited extent they had. But if the secrecy of the Comintern's pressure on the Partisans had denied the Soviets any credit with the British, it had also left them free to change their line.

Maisky's aspersions soon began to be aired publicly by the communist press in the west. The Soviet-based "Free

Yugoslavia" radio had broadcast in Serbo-Croat on 16 June the 'news' that a congress of Montenegrin notables in March had denounced Mihailović for collaboration with the Axis and Nedić and had denied his claim to leadership of the resistance. Now, in late July, this story was repeated for the benefit of a wider audience, first in the Stockholm *Ny Dag* and subsequently in the American *Daily Worker*. Since TASS had excised hostile references to Mihailović from its own despatch on the subject, it seemed the Soviets had chosen a somewhat circumspect method for launching their attack.[53]

SOE reacted to this press assault with proprietary zeal. Major J.S.A. Pearson wrote to Dixon on 27 July:

> As you know, in consultation with yourself, we have laid down to our people in the field a definite and clear cut policy that we must support General Mihailović and General Mihailović only, and as far as possible take the Yugoslav government into our confidence and work exclusively with them. This policy, laid down some months ago, has been fully justified by the reports which we are today receiving from all over Yugoslavia. On the other hand, the Partisans are on the wane and, in fact, have almost disappeared except for certain isolated groups in districts of Bosnia.[54]

This was the premise on which Eden carried through his resolve to challenge the Russians' new explanation for their refusal to back Mihailović. Maisky was called to the Foreign Office on 27 July and handed a note proclaiming Britain's continuing faith in Mihailović, dismissing his freely admitted contacts with the Nedić regime as just cause for mistrusting him and asking the Soviet government to reconsider and lend him its support.[55]

The Russians' reply came on 7 August in the form of a copy of a memorandum which had been presented to the Yugoslav Minister in Kuibyshev three days before. It contained eight specific allegations of collaboration by Mihailović with Nedić and the Italians against the Partisans since March. Eden was surprised and confused, telling Maisky that British sources did not bear out such accusations. He promised to look into the matter.[56] The Foreign Office was now compelled to consider seriously those sources, and particularily the many reports, heretofore dismissed (and which have been withheld), that Mihailović was "not playing the game".[57] An obscure Balkan civil war was threatening to become the cause of a serious and public breach in Allied ranks.

A meeting was called by Sargent at the Foreign Office on 8 August at which SOE and SIS were represented. The evidence examined has remained secret, but a summary record is available. Sargent considered that whether or not Mihailović was presently collaborating with the Axis the bitterness of his struggle with the Partisans made such a development possible. It was clear that the Italians and Germans were not being inconvenienced by his activities. This was not the case with the Partisans, whose "opportunistic and short-term policy, with the object of causing the maximum disturbance to the Axis position in Yugoslavia, should therefore entail our support..." But taking the long view, Sargent concluded, it would better serve Britain's interests if the present policy of seeking resistance unity under Mihailović was maintained and a new appeal in this sense addressed to the Russians.[58]

This was the same tired formula invoked in the past, but it now had the appearance of a holding action. SOE's roseate view of Mihailović and his prospects was no longer creditable. And although unrepentant, SOE was constrained to agree that searching questions should be put to Hudson about Mihailović's susceptibility to Anglo-Soviet pressure and that - for the first time - the possibility should be examined of establishing a British mission with the Partisans.[59]

While wrangling went on among the Southern Department, SOE and SIS over the questions that were to be asked of Hudson, Eden replied on 20 August to the Soviets' charge sheet against Mihailović. His defence was less than categorical: allegations of collaboration with the Italians or Germans based on Partisan propaganda could not be considered accurate or objective evidence.[60] Eden dismissed again Mihailović's links with Nedić, but admitted that the General was "devoting at least part of his energies to operations against the Partisans".[61] The Foreign Secretary asked Maisky to seek to cool the war of words - which had now spread to Britain - and to enter into full and frank discussions on the Yugoslav tangle.[62]

Even those without access to the secret intelligence examined at the 8 August meeting were beginning to suspect that in backing Mihailović Britain had chosen the wrong horse. On 19 August Ralph Murray, the Balkan section chief of PWE, submitted to Howard a detailed analysis of resistance based largely on Axis press reports. Murray demonstrated that, far from facing imminent liquidation, the Partisans were active in the two thirds of the country where engagements with the Axis were regularly occurring. Mihailović had not claimed this activity as his own in the past, nor had he shown any readiness to respond to British requests for anti-Axis operations in the future. Murray concluded his covering letter to Howard with a postscript expressing the hope that SOE could refute his attempt from the sidelines to play devil's advocate.[63]

SOE needed to take up only half of this challenge. That the Partisans were making the running militarily was accepted. What required elucidation was whether or not Mihailović possessed a potential military value equivalent to and justifying his assumed political value, and whether or not his collaboration, if proved, rendered him valueless in either case. The Foreign Office was ready to contemplate taking "some heroic action" to discover this. A. V. Coverley-Price suggested on 19 August that Mihailović should be spirited out of Yugoslavia for a confrontation with the British authorities in the Middle East. At best such a meeting would "provide us with the means of convincing the Russians that our opinion about M. is the right one"; at worst it "would enable us to realize that M. is not worthy of our continued support, and we could decide how to dispose of him and what plans to make."[64] There is no trace of the reaction with which this proposal met (it was minuted on RJ 406), but the Foreign Office acquiesced for the time being in merely preparing questions for Hudson.

SOE, claiming the support of SIS, rejected the first Foreign Office draft. Pearson argued in a letter to Howard on 20 August that under no circumstances should Hudson be aksed to jeopardize his shaky relations with Mihailović by broaching the subject of Četnik-Partisan relations. Nor should he be asked questions which would seem to show that all his efforts to explain "the rather subtle inter-relationships" obtaining inside Yugoslavia had been in vain:

> The principal object of Hudson's telegrams has been to try and explain to us what he believes to be Mihailović's policy, i.e. no active attack on the occupying power for the present but concentration upon the restoration of internal order* and the organization of the Serbian forces with the double object of being able to hustle the enemy out of the country as soon as they begin to crack and to maintain order and to prevent a social revolution when this takes place. This has led to a blurring of the line between his forces and those of the gendarmerie of the Nedić government who are also engaged in keeping order in country towns and villages, to the concentration of his principal military effort against Partisans and Ustaše - even perhaps to the extent of accepting some indirect support from the Italians against the Partisans.

Pearson's alternative draft was most notable for containing an assurance that there was "no question" of changing Britain's policy of exclusive support for Mihailović whatever accusations the Soviets might level against him.[65]

The Foreign Office refused to accept that asking *Hudson* to estimate the likely reactions of Mihailović and the Partisans to an Anglo-Soviet appeal for unity posed any of the dire consequences envisaged by SOE. And although agreeing that Hudson's recent reports obviated the need for certain questions, Howard insisted that he be asked point blank if Mihailović's entire military effort consisted of fighting the Partisans. He also succeeded in excising SOE's pledge that Mihailović would enjoy British suport no matter what. SOE,

*Howard noted in the margin: "internal order means, of course, subduing the Partisans."

SIS and the Foreign Office finally agreed on a text on 22 August:

> You may have heard recently that Soviet inspired broadcasts and the communist press in general have been taking a violently anti-Mihailović line. This is in spite of all our efforts with the Soviet government that they should instruct their followers to rally behind Mihailović and thus present a united front to the Axis in Yugoslavia. Nevertheless, the Soviet government claim that they have proof that Mihailović is collaborating with the Italians, the Germans, the Ustaše and with Nedić against the Partisans, while not causing any inconvenience to the Germans and Italians. Your telegrams have given us a very clear picture of the true situation inside the country. We would, however, appreciate your views on the following points:
>
> (1) If the Soviet could be induced to agree, would an Anglo-Soviet appeal to thePartisan leaders to join forces with Mihailović against the Axis have any effect on them and on Mihailović?
>
> (2) Who and where are chief Partisan leaders?
>
> (3) Would you say that the whole of Mihailović's military effort to date has been directed against the Partisans and if so do you think this will continue to be directed against the Partisans until the latter submit or have been exterminated?[66]

Hudson's reply reached London on 6 September. Somewhat mutilated and dealing for the most part with the likely impact of an Anglo-Soviet appeal for unity, it did little to clear the muddied waters of British understanding. Hudson estimated that since the Partisans (whose leaders he did not name) had been harried out of most Serb territory they might respond favourably to an Anglo-Soviet appeal, provided it promised political freedom in post-war Yugoslavia and encouraged the continuation of their active struggle against the Axis. Mihailović, on the other hand, was antipathetic to any discussion of post-war politics, would undertake no action against the occupiers until a Balkan front was opened and was willing to accept in his ranks only those Partisans innocent of crimes against Serbdom and ready to serve him as obedient soldiers. Hudson nonetheless concluded that an appeal for unity should be made.[67]

The Foreign Office agreed; but being unable to follow Hudson's line of reasoning in recommending such action - and indeed it was almost impossible to follow* - decided to discount the formidable stumbling blocks which he had quite clearly listed. Coverley-Price, for example, minuted, "I imagine that in any case the Partisans are not sufficiently homogeneous to be given any sort of political freedom as a party . . ."[68] Hudson did not (or could not) explain that in the Communist Party the Partisans possessed both a centralized leadership and a singleness of purpose far exceeding what Mihailović could provide for his ramshackle agglomeration of junior officers, local chieftains and impressed peasants.

But if communism still spelled chaos, this and subsequent telegrams from Hudson did send the Southern Department off on a tangent of gloomy speculation about Mihailović's own barrack-room beliefs: his scorn for politics and politicians (including those in his own government), his disregard for the niceties of Serb-Croat-Slovene relations, his predilection for work with the Bulgarians and his intention to establish a Četnik dictatorship after the war. Since the Foreign Office, like SOE, continued to assume that Britain could and should "build up" Mihailović as the arbiter of Yugoslavia's destiny such revelations were disquieting.[69] They were also beside the point.

*What Hudson appeared to be getting at was that the Partisans and Četniks should pursue their respective strategies in separate areas. The civil war would be dempened down and Mihailović, as the recognized (if nominal) national leader, would benefit by the reflected glory of the Partisans' continuing fight. This was similar to the solution proposed by Bailey in early 1943.

More immediately threatening to hopes of concerted action with the Russians was the confirmation offered by Hudson that Mihailović had not fought the Axis since December 1941, that his efforts since then had been directed almost exclusively against the Partisans and that, even if some accommodation with them were achieved, the only immediate fighting he was prepared to offer was with the Moslems and Ustaše.[70]

(v)

Policy towards Mihailović remained under intermittent review for six months following the 8 August meeting. During this time more and more evidence damaging to Mihailović accumulated, including in November and December detailed testimony from Hudson on the Četniks' systematic collaboration with the Italians. "This," Howard wrote later, "was the first definite confirmation we had of any serious collaboration between Mihailović and the Italians, although reports to this effect had been coming in for some time."[71] The fact that Mihailović's mythic stature was eroded gradually made it easier for the Foreign Office to maintain its political sangfroid - its determination to keep Britain's long-term interests squarely in view. As Dixon put it in a letter to Pearson on 9 October, "we still feel that we are bound to continue our support for Mihailović because of his potential value, both military and political, at a later stage in the war." This support was to be given "independently of whether or not he continues to refuse to take a more active part in resisting and attacking Axis forces in Yugoslavia."[72] Similar resolve was to be expressed regularly until February 1943.

But no matter how long the view, it was also declared to be provisional, subject both to the eventual decision of the Soviets on a joint approach and, more especially, to the estimation of real Četnik potential provided by a new British emissary to Mihailović.[73] Little was now expected of the Russians since, as Eden noted in late September, "M. Maisky appears to have been more nearly correct than ourselves."[74] And indeed the

Russians remained unhelpfully silent. But British hopes that their new liaison officer, Colonel S. W. Bailey, would quickly show them the way were also disappointed. Bailey contracted malaria soon after arriving in Cairo and his departure was repeatedly postponed.[75] In these circumstances the provisional achieved a sort of permanence.

SOE had apparently decided to supplant Hudson by Bailey well before the Foreign Office became convinced at the beginning of September that an officer of greater authority and more political nous was needed at Mihailović's headquarters. The Foreign Office agreed that Bailey possessed the requisite qualities.[76] SOE's initial decision to relieve Hudson stemmed in part from suspicion that he was operating under duress, but whether this was thought to be exercised by the Axis, the Partisans or "Robertson" is unclear. (Given the substance of Hudson's reports it can be assumed that SOE did not imagine that Mihailović was responsible.) The arrival of the Lofts signals mission at the end of August should have served to assuage any doubts about the authenticity of Hudson's telegrams, but this was not the case.[77]

The Foreign Office also had reservations about Hudson, though these were probably based less on incredulity at his revelation that mihailovic had feet of clay than on the difficulty officials experienced in penetrating his prose. In a letter to Howard on 23 September Rendel referred to Hudson's political views as "innocent" and to the picture conveyed by his telegrams as "unbalanced", but Rendel rarely gave voice to majority opinion.[78] The Foreign Office trusted that Bailey would make the Yugoslav situation intelligible and eagerly awaited his reports.[79] But even before it became apparent that Bailey's departure would be delayed, the Foreign Office and SOE determined not to allow things to hang fire. They decided during September to take action to prod Mihailović into demonstrating that, despite his preoccupation with the Partisan threat and the regrettable alliances into which this had apparently led him, he still possessed real anti-Axis military potential.

In the first half of September SOE Cairo proposed to issue over the signature of General Sir Harold Alexander, the new Commander-in-Chief, Middle East, a request to Mihailović to do all in his power to attack Axis lines of communication. Pearson wrote to Dixon on 15 September seeking Foreign Office approval and proposing that Jovanović be asked to send a supporting message. By giving Mihailović a chance to show what he could do SOE sought both to justify its own policy and to insure against any suggestion that it treat with the Partisans. This Pearson made plain:

> Our view is, as you know, that though the Partisans have fought the Axis and can be said to be engaging the attention of the Axis forces, yet their principal aim is to prosecute a bloody revolution and establish a communist state by eliminating all those members of the educated classes who are opposed to their aims. We suggest that we can never regard them as an effective or organized force for undertaking serious operations against Germany or Italy.[80]

SOE's draft telegram was strengthened by General Alexander and despatched on or about 22 September. Jovanović's supporting message followed shortly thereafter.[81] And perhaps as an added incentive, a team of Yugoslav sappers was dropped over western Serbia at the same time.[82] Mihailović's reply was flowery, but not encouraging. On 30 September he reported that he was already carrying out unspecified acts of sabotage to great effect. He asked, however, that no news of this activity be broadcast for fear of reprisals.[83]

Mihailović's concern on this score was ironic given that the Foreign Office's own contribution to the effort to bestir him was to decide in late September that the BBC might now encourage and laud acts of resistance by all Yugoslav "patriots".[84] But like its predecssor, this formula was soon found wanting. Murray appealed to the Foreign Office at the beginning of October for a less "ostrich-like" propaganda policy, for one which would take into account the escalating virulence with which the Soviet and Yugoslav governments were championing their respective heroes, as well as the contradiction which now beset the BBC itself. While Britain in its official voice praised all 'patriots", the Yugoslavs' military cabinet broadcasts praised only Mihailović and condemned the Partisans as anti-Serb criminals.[85]

Lengthy discussions with PWE and SOE in London during October resulted at the end of the month in a Foreign Office decision that the separate existence and achievements of the Partisans could no longer be publicly ignored. In future the BBC might mention them by name and praise their resistance in the north-western parts of the country. The Yugoslav government would be compelled to toe the line - on the BBC, if not in America. Nothing could be done to impose a similar restraint on the principal source of Partisan propaganda, "Free Yugoslavia", but Dixon hit on the idea of blackening it as "obviously" operating under Axis control with the object of inciting fratricidal strife. Since the Soviets had never admitted the station to be theirs, and since the Foreign Office had never hinted at its suspicions to the contrary, this stratagem seemed workable; until, that is, Murray pointed out that the Germans were doing everything in their power to jam "Free Yugoslavia" broadcasts. The Foreign Office was left with what was admitted to be an unsatisfactory and temporary expedient: the operations of the Partisans would be acknowledged in those areas where Mihailović's writ did not run, but the existence of a civil war between them would go unmentioned.[86]

Also unmentioned - or at least camouflaged - were the sharp disagreements which now beset those who would make British policy. The Foreign Office assumed through late December that it still held the initiative, that the BBC was faithfully propagating the new line (even if this meant in practice that the Partisans and Četniks were usually lumped together as "patriots") and that SOE accepted this approach. When in early December Paul Vellacott of PWE reported from Cairo that SOE, the Minister of State and the Joint Operational Staff objected to any references to the Partisans as being likely to prejudice the success of Bailey's mission, the Foreign Office and SOE London were united in rejecting their counsel.[87] After all, Hudson's telegrams showed what a positive impact the new line was having on Mihailović. On 22 November he wrote,

> I confirm that BBC references to actions by other patriots in Jug is having just that effect on Mvic we hoped for. He protests violently at word *rodoljub* [patriot] which he tells me everyone sees is British way of making love to Communists. He will not tolerate it.

Hudson urged the next day that the "patriot" references should continue, but be limited to one or two per week: "Shall warn you before Mvic breaks off relations with us altogether."[88]

George Taylor and Lord Glenconner professed from Cairo to be aghast at this casual suggestion. Sir Charles Hambro (CD) countered that London regarded it as a joke. Cairo insisted, however, that Hudson's judgment in the matter of pressure was not to be trusted. He was "entirely unfitted" for the responsibility he held, having no political experience and "no full or clear idea of our Yugoslav programme." "The man who is obviously writing most of his telegrams for him," Taylor continued, "is clearly primarily interested in certain political ideas and knows nothing of SOE or our operational plans." Hambro replied that London was well aware of Hudson's background and of the possibility that someone else was writing his messages: "Nevertheless, all here are agreed that his telegrams have been capacious, accurate and of excellent quality and we see no reason to withdraw our confidence."[89]

The real issue dividing the London and Cairo ends of SOE was not Hudson's trustworthiness, but operational control over relations with the resistance. While granting that London had the right to initiate changes in policy, Cairo insisted that it must have the responsibility to judge how these were to be given effect, including their promotion over the BBC. Cairo's challenge was based partly on the assumption that Baker Street had proved cravenly subservient to the Foreign Office on the question of pressuring Mihailović, and partly on the conviction that, as Taylor put it, he and Glenconner "probably know more about SOE work in Yugoslavia today than the rest of the world put together."

In October Glenconner had proposed that Mihailović be prodded into undertaking specific acts of sabotage. But what he had in mind was private pressure - the issuance to Bailey of a mandate from King Peter that would overawe Mihailović and the despatch of British sappers to his headquarters - not goading over the BBC. A public campaign, Cairo felt, would put Bailey's mission at risk, and with it the prospects for acquiring a real hold over Mihailović. And this, more than ever, was what Cairo wanted. For at the same time as SOE London was succumbing (in Cairo's estimation) to the unwarranted initiative of the Foreign Office in lambasting Mihailović, Cairo was concluding that he must be handled far more delicately and realistically.

During November the Cairo officers of SOE decided that it was useless attempting, as both Hudson and London seemed to desire, to make the Četniks behave like the Partisans. They thus repented their earlier advocacy of even private pressure on Mihailović. He and his followers must be accepted for what they were - Serb patriots with limited horizons and all to many unhelpful preoccupations - but at the same time the only people with whom SOE could possibly work in the Serb-inhabited lands. As Taylor endeavoured to explain in a nine-page "note" to Hambro on 14 December,

> What we think is a better way is to accept A.H.31 [Mihailović] as he is, at least for the time being, and to try and get him to do what we want in regard to strategic demolitions by sending in British personnel in the form both of D.H.2's [Bailey's] Mission to A.H.31's H.Q. and other officers, who would be attached, with their own W/T communications, to the leaders of the various bands, who owe him some sort of allegiance (in many cases pretty loose). D.H.2 and these officers will know, (and can be further told from time to time in future) what actual projects for strategic sabotage we want to see carried out. It will be then up to them to try and persuade the General or his various bands to provide the necessary cooperation. It is quite probable that, at least in some cases, they may experience difficulties and that we may be forced to apply pressure, but in my opinion such pressure should not be of a general kind aimed, as it were, at making the leopard change his spots, but should be

> applied for particular limited objects and under the control of the man on the spot who would be in a position to judge what degree and kind of pressure was needed and how far he could go without defeating his object.[90]

What SOE Cairo hankered after was the establishment in the Serb lands of the same sort of limited (but strategically profitable) resistance, directed by British officers, as seemed to be emerging in Greece. And although Cairo's passion for acquiring control seemed to exceed its capacity for discerning the uses to which that control might be put, Glenconner and his colleagues were at least attempting to make themselves useful to the generals. This was evident from the self-satisfied little telegram that Glenconner sent to Hambro in mid-December: "C.G.S. [Alexander] has stated today that SOE already plays an important part in strategy and that in the future he sees us playing an essential part in operations."[91]

All this was apparently too much for SOE London to withstand. But the effect of Cairo's assault was not simply the immediately desired one of causing Baker Street to join with Cairo in seeking to put a stop to any and all broadcasts likely to offend Mihailović, it was also to reverse the tentative steps which SOE London had been taking away from total commitment to the Četnik cause. Despite the vigour and length of Taylor's and Glenconner's explanations, it seems that London failed to appreciate the subtle (or over-subtle) points they had been making: that praising the Partisans *before* entering into relations with them was both useless and dangerous, and that Mihailović was the only man to back *in the Serb lands*. SOE London thus reverted to (or rededicated itself to) the propositions that Mihailović must be regarded as the one national leader and that work with the Partisans was excluded. This was to mean that when Cairo decided in early 1943 that the time had come to send in its long-planned missions to the Partisans in the non-Serb lands it would again have to do battle with its headquarters.[92]

(vi)

Only at the end of December did the Foreign Office discover (1) that orders had been issued (it was assumed by Alexander) that references to the Partisans in British broadcasts should be discontinued and (2) that SOE Cairo had the previous month established a new freedom station, Radio "Karadjordje", dedicated to the exclusive promotion of Mihailović and the Serb cause. The Foreign Office immediately resolved to get the station closed down.[93] Complicating matters further was another belated discovery: that in early December the War Office had on its own initiative sent the Yugoslav government a fulsome message of congratulation for the continuing struggle of Mihailović and his "indomitable Četniks". This the Yugoslavs had been quick to broadcast.[94] The Foreign Office attributed what appeared to be a breakdown in policy coordination to the military's sudden revival of interest in Balkan resistance brought on by the expansion of the war in the Mediterranean.[95]

If, as appears likely, the Foreign Office remained ignorant at year's end of the defeat suffered by SOE London at the hands of its Cairo base, then this was not simply because SOE was naturally reticent about washing its dirty linen in public. Perhaps just as important in militating against any Foreign Office suspicions that SOE stood behind most of the recent pro-Mihailović surprises was the fact that from early November to early December SOE London had not only come to share the Foreign Office's view that Mihailović should be disciplined, but had outpaced the Foreign Office in suggesting that the time had come to consider contacting and helping the Partisans.

On 5 November Pearson forwarded to the Foreign Office a telegram from Hudson dated 1 November and an SOE appreciation based on his very extensive reports during the past two months. The first had already moved SOE to request Jovanović to send another admonition to Mihailović; the second would now cause the Foreign Office to begin another policy review. As noted above, Hudson urged that propaganda pressure on Mihailović be maintained. He suggested that he be authorized to "hold mention of Partisans over Mihailović's head" as a means of combating his "self-jubilant inertia". "It is very difficult to believe", he wrote, "that such elements as so-called Montenegrin Nationalists are more exploiting than exploited by Axis occupation."[96]

Jovanović took exception to SOE's draft telegram to Mihailović, objecting to the suggestion it contained that sabotage undertaken now could prove of greater value to the Allied war effort than a large-scale uprising later on. His objections were generally sustained and the telegram despatched on 6 November.[97] Mihailović's reply on 8 November was diffuse but skilful. He acknowledged the importance of obstructing lines of communication and claimed to have ordered important (but unspecified) acts of sabotage during September and October. These had resulted in (specific) Axis reprisals. He also - and uncannily - reaffirmed the strategic priorities that SOE had sought to question and pointed to the weak spot in Britain's hold over him: "I fear that today's fateful events are not keeping pace with preparations for main action - arms, arms, arms!"[98]

SOE's appreciation was a sober examination of Mihailović's movement and motives which bore little resemblance to earlier exercises in filial pride. The Partisans and Četniks were credited with an equal preoccupation with the post-war order - and with an equal capacity for committing atrocities against each other's supporters. Mihailović was not thought to be in direct contact with the Axis powers, but in indirect relation with the Italians through General Blago Djukanović, described as the quisling governor of Montenegro. SOE estimated that Mihailović tolerated the presence of a British mission only because of the money, supplies and propaganda this connection brought him. He carefully controlled "Robertson's" and Hudson's contacts, and thus the information they were able to send. The report was sceptical of Mihailović's willingness to undertake any anti-Axis operations the British might request and "which may invoke reprisals and incur the odium of the people whose popularity he so anxiously craves."

Despite the direct appeal for sabotage by Alexander in September, "So far no telegram has been received from either of our liaison officers reporting any sabotage undertaken by General Mihailović, nor have we received any reports of fighting against the Axis troops." The appreciation concluded:

> Therefore, while it would be madness to support Partisan elements in a district under the control of General Mihailović, as this might inflame further the internecine feud, there is no reason why the Partisans in districts outside the General's orbit should not be encouraged by judicious propaganda and perhaps at some later date helped in their work. The knowledge that recognition was being given to the patriotism of the Serbs actively engaged against the Axis might spur the General and his followers to emulate their heroism.[99]

The Foreign Office was both impressed and disturbed by this report. Howard and Sargent felt that SOE's suggestion that the Partisans might be helped was, at the very least, premature. As Howard minuted on 20 November, "We all recognize that we may be faced with the awkward dilemma - Mihailović or Partisans - but it would seem to be futile and fatal to try and back both horses and crash between the two." They must await Bailey's report, Sargent ruled, "before trying to thrash out all the questions which are created by the present unsatisfactory situation." Meanwhile SOE must do nothing about "actually helping the Partisans in Croatia." Michael Rose, however, had been far readier to grasp the nettle. He argued that whereas Mihailović represented reaction and pan-Serbianism, the Partisans, for all their excesses and crudeness, "represent the inarticulate aspirations of the greater part of the common people of Yugoslavia - Serbs, Croats, Slovenes all alike and without distinction." He added, "I hope that we will not too easily convince ourselves that our long term interests necessarily lie in supporting Mihailović."[100]

Much as Sargent wished to avoid reopening the question until Bailey's report was in hand, a series of telegrams from Hudson and a letter from Pearson on 3 December necessitated another provisional review. Hudson's telegrams (dated 15-17 November) are available, but Pearson's letter and the resulting minutes have been withheld. Hudson gave details of the mutually dependent relationship of Mihailović, Djurisić and the Italians in Montenegro. Mihailović, he reported, was "merely a name" in Montenegro. He relied upon Djurisić as the most important local leader and "does not interfere but adopts Montenegrin Četniks' compromise with Wops." This included fighting with them against the Partisans even outside Montenegro. Mihailović maintained that his certain inheritance of the Italians' arms and equipment would be jeopardized were he to turn on them. The Germans would intervene "and he will lose forever chance of getting Wop arms and lose people as well. If he sabatoges Wops they will no longer feed Četniks." In Serbia, meanwhile, the Četniks were "little more than symbols of resistance." The peasantry was "Mvic-conscious", but cowed. Hudson was convinced that the Četniks could undertake railway sabotage without undue risk of reprisals: "Actually they have made no serious attempt to see what they can get away with in large sabotage." He repeated his belief that Mihailović could be pressured into action by a threat to deny him the vital support of the BBC, but this would never be more than "half-hearted":

> I am convinced that the mood of the people, as well as the nature of Mihailović's organization and personal ambition, will oblige him to undertake a "grand finale" against the Axis. *When the General is satisfied that victory is certain, blood will not be spared, but until then, I consider him perfectly capable of coming to any secret understanding with either Italians or Germans,* which he believes might serve his purposes without compromising him. Any such understanding would be based on his conviction of an Allied victory and would be directed to the purpose of smashing the hold of the communists on the people.[101]

From the extracts of minutes available it appears that Pearson in his covering letter proposed either a break with Mihailović or direct assistance to the Partisans as a means of forcing him to mend his ways. These, in any case, were the options considered and rejected by the Foreign Office. Sargent wrote, "I do not think that the time has come to break with Mihailović and still less to give direct assistance to the Partisans." Mihailovic might well be Yugoslavia's Darlan, or even its Petain, "but that is not in itself a reason why we should now start building up a Yugoslav de Gaulle out of some unknown communist leader." Sargent seconded Howard's prescribed middle way: continued pressure on Mihailović by means of propaganda, the issuance to him of a stern directive in the name of the British government and a warning to the Yugoslav government that Britain was dissatisfied with him and expected a greater return on its investment. Cadogan and Eden agreed.[102]

(vii)

In addition to the tussle within SOE and the revival of military interest in Balkan resistance, two other factors now made themselves felt. These were a Yugoslav government crisis and the personal involvement of Churchill in policy-making. The former was reaching its climax in December, the latter was just beginning.

Like the first exile government crisis a year before, the 1942 affair was long and involved. It began in early September and ended only on 3 January 1943. The ostensible issue was the need for the cabinet as a whole to confirm the nomination of Konstantin Fotić, the incumbent Minister, as Ambassador in Washington. This meant that ministers otherwise made redundant by the military cabinet's domination of the government were given the chance to vent (and at interminable length) their various distempers: first on the issue of the great-Serb Fotić's suitability as Yugoslav Ambassador given the inflammatory impact he had had on Serbo-Croat relations in the USA and, then, increasingly, on the government's foreign policy and parlous international position.[103]

It was the government crisis that brought Chruchill into the picture. Queen Marie, her son in tow, came to see the Prime Minister on 9 December. They brought two very confused and tendentious documents: the first setting out the reasons for the King's dissatisfaction with the majority of his weak, self-centred and dishonest ministers (as well as with Rendel, who was accused of anti-Orthodox bias); the second, a military cabinet memorandum, arguing for increased and exclusive support for Mihailović and his 200,000 warriors organized throughout two-thirds of Yugoslavia. Both documents evidenced considerable agitation over Britain's propaganda support for all "patriots". The King and Queen Mother asked for Churchill's help and advice. He suggested that they see Eden.[104] Demonstrating how out of touch he was with Yugoslav resistance, the Prime Minister wrote to Eden four days later, "One cannot help being impressed with all this about Mihailović." He asked how the Foreign Secretary had fared with "the Royal Exiles".[105]

The Foreign Office looked upon the luncheon which Eden scheduled with King Peter and Queen Marie for 11 December as an unexpectedly favourable opportunity for informing them of Britain's disenchantment with Mihailović and for taking a discreet hand in the imminent reconstruction of the Jovanović cabinet. The "fantastic" accusations against Rendel could also be refuted.[106] In the event Eden appears to have been more frank about his wish to be rid of Ninčić and Milanović (the Charge d'Affairs) than he was in indicating the depth of British misgivings about Mihailović. He accepted the royal pair's assertion that the General had recently been far more active against the Axis, adding only that this was partly because of British exhortations. He told the King that he would be ready to help and advise him privately in future.[107]

Eden now took the opportunity to acquaint the Prime Minister with recent developments. He sent a five-page memorandum to Churchill on 17 December which dismissed the military cabinet's aide-memoire as presenting "an exaggeratedly favourable idea of Mihailović's strength and general position" and sought to summarize the situation as Hudson had reported it. But Eden referred too to a new Foreign

Office hope - that many of the Croatian Partisans owed their allegiance not to communism, but to Maček. Eden admitted that Mihailović relied upon the Italians for food and arms, that his organization was but a shadow army whose strength it was impossible to estimate and that it was the Partisans who were actively fighting the Axis. Nonetheless, Britain's long-term interests necessitated support for Mihailović "in order to prevent anarchy and communist chaos after the war." Eden reported that he intended to call Mihailović up short, telling him that he was not being supported so that he might fight the Partisans and that more sabotage and a real effort to form a united front were expected of him. The BBC's pressure would meanwhile continue. Churchill merely noted in reply, "good; I agree."[108]

It was at this point that the Foreign Office's plan came unstuck - when it was discovered that the War Office had congratulated Mihailović, that SOE Cairo had started Radio "Karadjordje" to his greater glory and that the BBC had been ordered to cease offending him. In these circumstances the Foreign Office felt that it was impossible to try and call him to order. Instead Sargent suggested that they resort again to the old stand-by - an appeal to the Russians. Maisky had never answered Eden's August letter and the Foreign Office had not pursued the matter. "I think we hoped," Sargent minuted on 26 December, "that if we waited the Partisans might eventually be wiped out by General Mihailović, which unfortunately has not happened." Now, however, military developments had caused the Commander-in-Chief, Middle East, to take a direct interest in Yugoslav resistance and provided a new and better peg on which to hang an appeal to the Soviets to do their part to create resistance unity, "not as a political question, but as a necessary item in joint military planning." Sargent proposed that Clark-Kerr, then on leave in London, should take up the question, if possible with Stalin himself, upon his return to Moscow. Even if such an approach yielded no result, Sargent wrote, the position would be no worse than at present. Meanwhile support for Mihailović should be maintained and nothing more said to the Yugoslav government about British dissatisfaction with him. But the Commander-in-Chief, Middle East, and SOE would have to be restrained "from expressing actual satisfaction". Eden was hardly enthusiastic about trying the Russians ("This may be right."), but adamant on the need to bring the War Office and SOE into line. He proposed to go to the War Cabinet for a ruling if need be.[109]

Contrary to Sargent's expectations, this decision to maintain the appearance of full support for Mihailović pending the result of an approach to Stalin - and, presumably, Bailey's long-awaited report - was in fact to make things much worse. For the British now lost a unique opportunity for divesting themselves of Mihailović in a relatively painless fashion.

It does not seem that Eden's irresolute strictures against Mihailović in the presence of King Peter and Queen Marie had any great impact on the Yugoslav government. Far more worrisome to Jovanovic were the reported comments of Sargent to Milanovic on 22 December and of Major Peter Boughey of SOE to Živan Knežević a week later. According to Milanović, Sargent told him ("with indifference and cynicism") that the Partisans, not Mihailović, were resisting the Axis in Yugoslavia and that, in fact, Mihailović's only serious fighting since October 1941 had been against the Partisans. Milanović expressed amazement that Sargent "could speak with such disdain about the action of General Mihailović, which was the most brilliant exploit in this war . . ."[110] Knežević's record of Boughey's remarks came as an even greater blow to Jovanović. Boughey, described by Knežević as "one of those Englishmen who does not like diplomatic evasion and concealment," reported that the Foreign Office had asked him for his opinion following King Peter's meeting with Churchill. He had recommended that Britain not send arms to Mihailović which he would only use to fight the Partisans. Mihailović, Boughey said, was collaborating openly with the Italians. His units were armed by them and had recently been transported in Italian lorries to western Bosnia for joint operations against the Partisans. Mihailović's reports of anti-Axis sabotage were untrue. Knežević quoted Boughey as declaring, "Draža Mihailović is a quisling just like Nedić, because Nedić works with the Germans and Draza with the Italians." Mihailović would have to fight now, not later; for when the Allies landed in the Balkans it would be all the same to them whether they cooperated with Nedić, Antonescu or Mihailović.[111]

Jovanović summoned Rendel to see him on New Year's eve. He told him that if the British government were actually considering withdrawing support from Mihailović - as Eden's, Sargent's and Boughey's remarks indicated - then he could not possibly recommend to King Peter that Mihailović be retained in the new government. He asked for an immediate clarification of the British attitude. Flustered, Rendel promised to report back the next morning. After meeting with Howard and Sargent, Rendel informed Jovanović that Mihailović still enjoyed British support. There had been no change in policy. Jovanović, reassured, proceeded on 3 January to reshuffle his cabinet, dropping Ninčić and the quarrelsome (and less ardently pro-Mihailović) ministers in America, assuming the foreign affairs portfolio himself and reappointing Mihailović as Minister of War. "The little crisis," Rose minuted on 2 January, "is now over."[112]

The Foreign Office had meanwhile tackled SOE on the question of Boughey's "blundering". Colonels Masterson and Pearson denied roundly that Boughey had made the remarks attributed to him by Knežević. True, Boughey was "hot-headed" and spoke execrable French. Perhaps Knežević had misunderstood or twisted his words for his own ends. Boughey's reported remarks in no way represented his true feelings. Accoring to Rose's record, "Colonel Pearson himself made it quite clear that he rgarded politics as being outside SOE's sphere, and that for his part he had no wish to intrude there."[113] This was so much nonsense. SOE had viewed Yugoslav resistance through political spectacles from the very start and would continue to do so. Boughey's mistake, if mistake it was, had been to be caught out expressing sentiments which the Foreign Office shared, but had now decided it expedient to suppress, and which SOE London had lately repented, at least from the top.

CHAPTER VI

THE END OF THE BEGINNING: CONTACTING THE PARTISANS

(i)

During the first third of 1943 the Partisans won the Yugoslav civil war and the British decided to contact and assist them. There was a connection between these events, but it was not as direct as might be thought. The British heard from Bailey contradictory reports on the fierce fighting between Partisans and Četniks along the Neretva and in Montenegro in these months and overheard from the Germans expressions of confidence that both forces had been or soon would be eliminated in two great offensives - the Fourth and Fifth by Partisan reckoning, "Weiss" and "Schwarz" to the Germans. Only after F. W. Deakin arrived at Tito's headquarters in May, and in the midst of the latter offensive, did the British appreciate that the Partisans were (and remained) a centrally organized power in the land. But they continued to assume for more than a year thereafter that Mihailović was too. And although aware by April that Mihailović had suffered serious reverses, these were thought to have made him a better and less compromised partner in Serbia proper. That the Četnik movement had been mortally wounded by the defeats it sustained in early 1943 was obvious only in retrospect, when in the face of Partisan incursions and Red Army indifference it collapsed in its Serbian heartland in the summer of 1944.

In February 1943 the British decided to contact the Partisans. In April and May, when their first missions arrived, they resolved to aid them in tandem with the Četniks. By December Tito alone had been deemed worthy of military support and the British turned their political attentions towards discharging their obligations to King Peter by means of a deal with Tito. In early 1944 Mihailović and the British liaison officers with his forces possessed only a certain negotiating value: repudiation of Mihailović and the withdrawal of the British missions would be Tito's reward for accepting the King's titular authority. The complicated process by which this transformation took place will be reviewed briefly in the epilogue. Here the focus of attention will be on the first vital steps - the decisions to contact and assist the Partisans.

Various factors of differing importance and uncertain relationship combined to produce these initiatives. The most important was the most obvious: the expansion of the war in the Mediterranean. In January at Casablanca Rosevelt and Churchill approved the British plan to attack Sicily (in the hope of knocking Italy out of the war) as soon as possible after the attainment of complete victory in North Africa. Planning for Operation "Husky" was to begin immediately. With a return to the European continent via a southern back door now in prospect, the importance of containing as many Axis divisions as possible in the Balkans was again apparent to the military strategists. And they, unlike the Foreign Office or SOE headquarters, were not necessarily troubled by long-term political considerations. Moreover, their concern - tying down, harassing and killing the maximum number of Axis soldiers in the Balkans - naturally took precedence. SOE had had in November the great good fortune to demonstrate at the Gorgopotamos viaduct in Greece that its connections with the Balkan resistance movements could prove useful in the wider war effort. With the generals now prepared to take SOE seriously, and eventually to provide it with the aircraft necessary to accomplish objectives important to them, SOE Cairo readily accepted the idea of aiding those elements in

Yugoslavia most likely to serve the immediate needs of the military and the organizational prestige of SOE. SOE Cairo remained sceptical through the spring that the Partisans represented an armed force either capable of or willing to help it fulfil its new brief, but was eager to investigate. In this eagerness it left its London heaquarters trailing behind.

The Foreign Office, meanwhile, had been moving towards acceptance of the Partisans' existence and potential worth for rather different reasons. A few officials, most notably Michael Rose, tended to believe that the Partisans were likely to prove a better bet both for Britain and for Yugoslavia. Others, like Sargent and Howard, were of the opinion that they could not be ignored now that Mihailović had failed to eliminate them. While Eden was particularly sensitive to the issue of collaboration by Mihailović with the Axis and to the dangers which British support of him implied for Anglo - Soviet relations. But whatever the reasons, it was the Foreign Office which took the initiative in the decision to contact the Partisans, mobilizing the Prime Minister and dragging a reluctant SOE headquarters behind. The Foreign Office possessed an ally in SOE Cairo, but did not seem to be aware of the fact.

(ii)

Eden's lukewarm approval of Sargent's proposal on 26 December that, instead of disciplining Mihailović, another appeal should be made to the Soviets had turned to scepticism by early January. The briefing paper prepared by Howard for Clark-Kerr (and affirming the old faith that Mihailović was the man to organize resistance lest anarchy, chaos and the break-up of Yugoslavia follow upon an Axis withdrawal) made Eden uneasy. On 3 January he minuted:

> This seems to me unsatisfactory. The position goes from bad to worse. I have no objection to Sir A. C.-K. taking the matter up with the Russians. That may be useful, but will not happen anyway for another month. Meanwhile we are

> to go back on the decision we had previously taken (because it seems, SOE and C. in-C., Mid-East, don't agree, tho' P.M. does) and give full backing to Mihailović tho' he is not fighting our enemies and is being publicly denounced by our Soviet ally. I can see no sense in such a policy and every likelihood that we and Russians will come to an open clash. I had spoken to Sir A. Cadogan last week on all this and thought he shared my views.

He concluded, "the policy advocated here cannot be right." Cadogan countered by pointing out that Bailey had just arrived in Yugoslavia - making it impolitic to "chide" Mihailović at the moment - and that Britain's faith in the General had been reaffirmed only three days before in the course of Jovanović's cabinet reshuffle. Eden made no comment on this last self-imposed constraint, but agreed that Bailey's report should be awaited.[1]

The first message from Bailey to reach the Foreign Office (on 9 January) was confined to housekeeping matters and to the statement that doubts regarding the authorship of Hudson's telegrams were unfounded. Hudson was healthy, had a keen grasp of all aspects of the situation and enjoyed better relations with Mihailović than expected.[2] But however interesting Bailey's comments on the rough food and drink available in Montenegro "for the benefit of curious fortunates in Cairo," this was not what the Foreign Office so anxiously awaited. When Lord Selborne wrote to Eden on 22 January to offer his agreement on the decision to approach Moscow before sending a stiff message to Mihailović, he reported that Bailey's interim report was now coming in and that such portions of it likely to be of interest to the Foreign Office would be forwarded as received. Eden exploded at the implication that the Foreign Office would not get Bailey's telegrams in their entirety: "SOE treat us like irresponsible children. Perhaps they should know that P.M. considers me fit to see operational telegrams *almost* as important as these."[3] Selborne assured Eden that SOE had nothing to hide; the Foreign Office would receive all Bailey's messages except those of purely routine or domestic interest. The Foreign Office remained wary.[4]

This was understandable, for SOE headquarters remained committed to Mihailović. On 20 January Hambro sent Sargent a report which argued for "unqualified support" for Mihailović on the supposedly realistic grounds which London had accepted from Cairo in December. Even if, as seemed likely, the Soviets proved unwilling to join in backing him, Britain should continue to build up Mihailović as the great national leader:

> Such great men are largely myths, but once they have been created they are a power in the land becoming a centre of attraction and rallying point for the younger generation and all those who may be now undecided as to how they should act. It is within our power to build up Mihailović into such a figure if we are consistent and do not deviate from our policy of giving him the political, propaganda and material backing which he has substantially enjoyed during the past 12 months.

The Foreign Office balked at both the presumption and the desirability of such a policy. Howard noted, "I am not at all sure we want (even if we could) to build up a new dictator." Neither was he impressed by the warning that if Britain faltered Mihailović might turn to the United States for support. There was no sign that the Americans were prepared to offer it.[5]

SOE argued that Mihailović's passivity must be accepted as reasonable given his long-term aims and present circumstances. Rather Britain should seek to make use of his organization for specific operations carried out jointly with SOE officers as in Greece. Private pressure exercised by Bailey and an adequate flow of supplies would make him amenable to cooperation along these lines. Favourable developments in the Mediterranean theatre now made it possible to send him aid on the required scale. In future he would probably succeed in extending his "activities" into Croatia and Slovenia "where guerrillas already exist." The report ended: "In this regard, at the present time, our intention is to make contact with these bodies with a view to endeavouring to induce them to collaborate with him as a first step towards accepting him as the national leader." Howard minuted in the margin, "That's not the point; we are tired of him using his slender resources against the Partisans - and that point is never mentioned in this paper." Collaboration with the Axis likewise went unmentioned.

In his accompanying letter Hambro hinted at the problem which SOE London would now seize upon in arguing against even contacting the Partisans. The six Halifax bombers newly allotted to SOE would permit adequate supply of Mihailović in Serbia, but the Halifax did not possess sufficient range to operate over Croatia and Slovenia. "This," Hambro wrote, "makes it all the more important for us to help and build up General Mihailović to the maximum extent which our facilities will permit."[6] SOE Cairo, meantime, was holding out the enticing prospect of coordinating resistance by the Croats and Slovenes if only enough Liberators were made available.

This, then, was the important difference in perspective: London wished to exclude contact with the Partisans because SOE did not possess sufficient long range aircraft and because Mihailović could in any case be made to serve Britain's purposes, while Cairo argued for more aircraft in order to investigate whether or not good work might also be done with the guerrillas in Croatia and Slovenia who would never accept Mihailović's claims to leadership. The difference in terminology was significant. Whether from conviction or from some calculation of tactical advantage, Cairo insisted that the Croatian and Slovenian guerrillas it longed to contact were not at all the same thing as Tito's Bosnian Partisans. Baker Street appeared to fear - and the Foreign Office to accept - that it might prove otherwise.

Churchill, his interest aroused by the December discussions in London and his attention focused by the decisions of the Casablanca conference, travelled to meet the Turkish President, Ismet Inönü, on 30 January near Adana. He stopped en route in Cairo where he asked to see Brigadier C. M. Keble, Glenconner's chief of staff and SOE's accidental recipient of German intercepts. At Churchill's request Keble prepared a report on SOE operations in Yugoslavia dated 30 January and apparently submitted to the Prime Minister immediately prior to his departure for Turkey. Churchill evidently made use of it in the course of the flight to Adana, including in the "wooing letter" he prepared for the Turks while on board the sentence, "The breaking down of Italy would lead to contact with the western Balkans and with the highly hopeful resistance maintained both by General Mihailović in Serbia and the Partisans in Croatia and Slovenia."[7]

As this implies, Keble's paper advocated both continued support for Mihailović in Serbia (where he was said to be containing three German and six Bulgarian divisions; the six Italian divisions in Montenegro not being counted as 'contained') and the extension of "similar assistance to other resisting elements" (said to be tying down 30 Axis divisions) in Croatia and Slovenia. Whether Bosnia was meant to be included in the rightful domain of Mihailović or the Partisans was not made clear. (An unknown hand amended the copy of the report present in the Foreign Office files to include it in Mihailović's Serbian sphere.)

Keble was insistent that the tasks of contacting and aiding the Partisans must be entrusted to the same organization already maintaining liaison with Mihailović - namely SOE - but that the two operations should be run independently. In this way effective pressure (i.e. withholding supplies) could be brought to bear on the one or the other in order to limit the civil war between them. It is likely that Keble feared that the new and potentially profitable assignment of working with the Partisans might go to SIS or the regular army. It is certain that he professed dread that, if Britain failed to rise to the challenge, the Americans and/or the Russians would - and that Britain (and SOE) would be stuck with the reactionary pan-Serb Mihailović. For unlike his London headquarters, Keble excluded the possibility that Mihailović could expand his operations into Slovenia and Croatia. On the other hand, and like Baker Street, he was tolerant of the Cetniks' collaboration with the Italians in Montenegro. He denied, however, that there was any sign of collaboration with the Germans in the far more important area of Serbia proper.

Keble referred twice to the Partisans by name, but generally described them as "other resisting elements". It was incorrect, he wrote, to label them "Communists", for they were in fact a heterogeneous collection of leftwing leaders (schoolmasters, students and workers), apolitical peasants, refugees, deserters from the Croatian *Domobran* and associated bands led by followers of Maček. Keble stressed that Serbs, as well as Croats and Slovenes, filled their ranks. Nevertheless, Churchill's comment in his letter to Inönü shows that he was willing to accept the one term to cover them all.

After outlining all the advantages which would accrue from working with the Croats and Slovenes, and indicating that SOE was already training missions to undertake the assignment, Keble named the price: two flights of four Liberators each would be required (in addition to SOE's existing four) if operations were to be extended to cover north-west Yugoslavia and if Mihailović were to be supplied to the extent necessary to make him cooperative. "For this reason, and none other," Keble wrote, "we are unable to undertake these operations." Churchill took the point. On his way home he showed Keble's paper to General Eisenhower in Algiers with the object of prising the necessary Liberators out of the Americans. But he did not succeed.[8]

The Prime Minister's intervention must have come like manna from heaven to SOE Cairo. In the previous week Cairo had met with nothing but frustration in its attempts to impress upon London just those points made by Keble's paper. Opening its campaign on 21 January with a lengthy telegram proposing "a far-reaching reconsideration of policy", Cairo sought to convince Baker Street that despite Bailey's "successful debut" at Četnik headquarters (marked by Mihailović's ready acceptance of the idea that British sub-missions should join his local commands in Serbia, and the hope this held out that SOE might use these for working into Bulgaria), Mihailović could never answer all Britain's requirements. In the absence of British officers with both sides, arms supplied to Mihailović would continue to be used against the Partisans. Moreover, if SOE did not expand its operations to cover north-western Yugoslavia, then the resistance there was likely to fall under either Russian or American control. (Cairo pointed ominously in the later case to the highly influential Croat community in the United States.) Cairo also sought to invoke what it saw as the similarly evolving policy of the Foreign Office and PWE, and urged Baker Street to consult with the Foreign Office. Although London's counter-arguments are unavailable, it seems that the Balkan section continued to insist on the superior claims of Mihailović, and to obfuscate the vital issue of more aircraft - all the while paying lip service to the desirability of expanding SOE's operations. The real blow fell on 29 January when Baker Street revealed that it was only beginning to contemplate pressing in high places for the additional Liberators first requested by Cairo in early December. On 31 January and 1 February Cairo responded by accusing London of intentionally misleading the Foreign Office: "it appears to us that we are committed to operations we cannot carry out."[9]

Keble kept up the offensive. On 9 February he wrote to Ralph Murray of PWE proposing amendments to a memorandum on resistance policy which Murray had been compiling in Cairo. Keble and his colleagues were deliberately seeking to make use of PWE in putting over their arguments to London. To that end Keble insisted that references to the Partisans be excised in favour of the more anodyne formulation "Croats and Slovenes". As he pointed out in his conclusion,

> The essential thing for us to do is to make contact with [the] Croats and Slovenes and not to make contact with the straightforward Partisan Forces under Tito in Bosnia, unless it be to move them up into Croat and/or Slovene areas.[10]

This last comment reflected the most recent proposals from Bailey in Montenegro; and it seems, in fact, that Bailey's despatches played the largest part in moving Cairo to reassess its policy. Now the Foreign Office was also to have the benefit of Bailey's considered opinions.

(iii)

Bailey's report reached the Foreign Office on 3 February. Having quickly concluded that the Partisans and Četniks could not be reconciled, Bailey recommended that they be assigned separate spheres of activity. The Partisans should withdraw from their present base in western Bosnia (the "Bihać Republic") into Croatia. Hudson would travel as an emissary to Tito, "who likes and trusts him". Mihailović, meanwhile, would expand his organization to embrace the Serb-inhabited areas of western Bosnia and Hercegovina. Bailey estimated that Tito disposed of 14,000 guerrillas in western Bosnia. Of these, 4,000 were communists and would follow him into Croatia. The remainder were mostly Serbs loyal to the dynasty and likely to prove amenable to service under Mihailović. Bailey reported in a subsequent message that the Partisans wielded "sole and absolute authority" in the Bihać Republic, but that after seven months in a semi-passive region Tito would soon be compelled to move on - because of dearth if not because of Axis pressure:

> Tito and company have so far moved progressively through Serbia, Sandžak, Montenegro, Hercegovina and Bosnia. They have succeeded in every case in winning initially for a certain period the support of the local population. There is no reason to doubt that their technique will be equally successful in Croatia.[11]

Although Bailey's telegrams must have gone a long way towards disabusing the Foreign Office of the notion that the Partisans represented nothing but chaos and disorder, his chief proposal was regarded as both impracticable and impolitic. The most serious objection was that, if implemented, it would contribute greatly to the permanent disintegration of the Yugoslav state, separating Croatia and Serbia and facilitating the establishment of a native communist regime in Croatia and Slovenia. Once established in Croatia, Sargent pointed out to Hambro on 23 February, "the Partisans might establish contact with their comrades in Hungary and Austria and this would strengthen the basis of a spontaneous communist movement in that part of Europe." The transplanting of the Partisans might also lead to the absorption of Maček's followers in their ranks, or to the eruption of a new civil war in Croatia in place of the Partisan-Četnik quarrel in the Serb lands. Either result was undesirable. Last (and no doubt least) Bailey's scheme would entail a rupture with King Peter and his government.[12]

If Bailey's long-awaited proposals offered no way forward and if the prospect that the Soviets would provide some easy escape was increasingly dim (though Clark-Kerr was nonetheless ordered to make his approach), then it remained to decide what else might be done. Eden, Cadogan and Sargent agreed with Howard's suggestion in mid-February that "we should do our best to contact the Partisans in order to bring them into line with Mihailović and to support them, if possible and advisable." However unrealistic the hope on which it was based, the decision had at last been made. As Howard noted later, "This constituted the first step in our policy towards the support of the Partisans."[13]

A meeting was called by Cadogan on 18 February at which SOE was with difficulty prevailed upon to agree to take steps to contact the Partisans.[14] The conclusions of the Foreign Office were summarized in a paper sent to SOE and the War Office two days later. Britain's short-term aim must now be to maximize resistance in Yugoslavia. Mihailović alone would not and could not do this. In the long run British policy should be "the establishment in the areas previously occupied by the Yugoslav state of one or more independent units capable of joining any federal scheme and of contributing [to] a stable settlement of the Balkans." Until now British policy had been based on the assumption that no matter how unsatisfactory Mihailović was as an immediate military asset, and however preferable the Partisans in this respect, "our long-term interests demand[ed] continued support of Mihailović in order to prevent anarchy and communist chaos after the war." This assumption no longer seemed altogether valid. Mihailović's strength in Serbia and Montenegro made it essential that Britain support him there, but not irrevocably and not to the extent of endorsing his pan-Serb ideas. Maintaining relations with, assisting and influencing both sides - Partisans and Četniks - now appeared the best means of reconciling Britain's long and short-term aims.[15]

Thus the Foreign Office grasped in February the implications of the policy which SOE Cairo had been evolving since December: it would - and contrary to Howard's warning in November - attempt to back two horses without crashing between them. SOE London kept its money on one. Hambro's agreement on 18 February to seek to contact the Partisans had been unenthusiastic at best. He did not dispute that opening relations with the Partisans was desirable; in fact he claimed that SOE had always intended to do so and that, therefore, no great modification of policy was implied. But he did raise endless difficulties. He submitted to Sargent on 22 February a commentary on the Foreign Office's paper of 20 February. In it he maintained that SOE had never supported Mihailović out of long-term political considerations, but because his strategy was right. Now Mihailović was showing an increased concern for Slovene and Croat sensibilities and had ordered his units in Bosnia to abstain from attacks on the Partisans. He disputed Keble's calculations that the Partisans were responsible for tying down as many as 30 Axis divisions and asserted that the Cetniks were the more important force:

> It must be remembered that by virtue of numbers, terrain and national character, the Serbian Orthodox population of Yugoslavia is in a position to make a far greater contribution to the war effort in terms of guerrilla activity than are the Croats and Slovenes. It follows from this that support for General Mihailović, as head of the most important para-military organization in Serbia, Montenegro, Hercegovina and south-western Bosnia, should have highest priority in the scale of our encouragement of Yugsolav resistance providing we can develop our collaboration with him as we anticipate.

The Foreign Office rejected virtually all of these assertions and assumptions. If Mihailović was indeed showing signs of abandoning both his struggle with the Partisans and the more extreme elements of his Serb chauvinism (which the Foreign Office doubted), then there could be no better moment for seizing the chance to contact the Partisans. If Mihailović's strategy had always commended itself to SOE, then why had it been urging him to be more active? - "urging pin-pricks" in Howard's words. There was in any case a difference between not embarking upon a mass rising - which Howard agreed was inadvisable - and doing nothing at all against the Axis. He did not mention collaboration.[16]

What most concerned the Foreign Office, however, were the implications of Hambro's continuing belief that Mihailović was capable of making a far greater contribution to the war effort than were the Partisans or any other elements. As Howard observed,

> He may be in a position to do all this but the fact is that the others are doing all the work. I have a feeling that what SOE are driving at . . . is that come what may Mihailović will always rank first and receive nearly all SOE's support however much we may wish, once contact has been made with the Partisans, to give them our support.

Replying to Hambro on 23 February, Sargent wrote that they must not bind themselves to give Mihailović priority in all circumstances. The "other elements" might in future deserve favoured treatment and should get it. It was because of this different understanding of what the decision to contact the Partisans meant that the Foreign Office could not accept Hambro's contention that no great modification of policy was involved. This SOE Cairo appreciated. Responding on 23 February to London's account of the 18 February meeting, Glenconner telegraphed, "I note that ZP [the Foreign Office] pressed case for Partisans." As far as he was concerned, all Cairo's previous proposals - including the despatch of missions to Croatia and Slovenia - had been firmly based on the established policy of improving Mihailović's usefulness and were, therefore, within the legitimate operational prerogatives of SOE. But "support of the Partisans," he wrote, "would be an entirely new policy, which has not been adopted."[17]

(iv)

Clark-Kerr, who returned to Moscow in mid-February, was instructed to make a final appeal to the Russians for a joint policy towards Yugoslavia and if, as expected, this failed "at least to get them to assist us get contact with the Partisans . . ."[18] Elisabeth Barker's suggestion that the British were also in this second respect merely going through the motions may be correct, but there are indications that the Foreign Office badly wanted Russian help. In his letter to Hambro on 23 February Sargent had concluded, "when we get Clark-Kerr's report on his approach to the Russians, we shall be in a better position to know whether there is any hope of obtaining contact with the other elements."[19] This does not suggest great confidence on the part of the Foreign Office that SOE could manage the feat alone. As has been pointed out, SOE London fastened on the shortage of long-range aircraft as an argument against diverting those few available to the less important task of contacting the Partisans. The Foreign Office was probably suspicious of SOE's motives, but accepted that the practical difficulties of entering into relations with the Partisans were formidable.[20]

The whole question of a possible Soviet role in helping the British contact the Partisans remains obscure. The Soviets had in late November asked the Yugoslav government if they might send a mission to Mihailović - and had been turned down with the reply that no mission would be welcome unless and until the Russians called off their propaganda offensive.[21] In January the Russians approached the British for help in infiltrating agents into Yugoslavia. They were again refused, the British assuming that any Soviet mission would in fact be destined for the Partisans. SOE was no doubt unwilling to jeopardize its potential hold over Mihailović by filtering Soviet agents bound for the Partisans through Četnik territory.[22]

On 22 February Clark-Kerr reported from Moscow that he expected the Russians to be suspicious of his forthcoming request for assistance in sending a British mission to the Partisans. He proposed instead to suggest a joint mission. This the Foreign Office rejected, feeling that a fullblown Anglo-Soviet mission to Tito would pre-judge the issue of whether or not the Partisans merited assistance. Howard pointed out that an offer had already been made to facilitate the despatch of a Russian mission and that this ought to still any Soviet suspicions that the British were attempting to manoeuvre behind their backs. Clark-Kerr was informed on 24 February that the only object the Russians could have in denying a British request for help was if they desired for political reasons to prevent British-Partisan contacts. He was authorized, however, to drop the whole matter if he thought it best. In that case action would proceed without the Russians either being informed or asked to help.[23] In the event Clark-Kerr took up the issue of a common policy towards Yugoslav resistance and requested aid in contacting the Partisans when he saw Molotov on 9 March. He got "no change" on either account. Molotov maintained that the question was an internal Yugoslav affair in which the Soviet government could not intervene. It was up to the Yugoslav government to seek to reconcile the Partisans and Četniks. The Soviets had in any case no contacts with the Partisans.[24]

According to Woodward, the Foreign Office concluded that if the Partisans were ignored any longer by Britain they would be forced into total dependence on the USSR.[25] Hambro, on the other hand, reckoned "that now it is not necessary to consider the aspect of possible complications with the Russian government in connection with this group of Yugoslav communists." The Foreign Office regarded this argument, made in a letter to Cadogan on 16 March, as disingenuous. Hambro, it was felt, was interpreting Molotov's response not as permission granted to contact the Partisans, but as a green light to help Mihailović eliminate them without fear of repercussions. Rose minuted that just because Moscow disclaimed any responsibility for the Partisans, that did not mean that "we have a free hand in helping Mihailović to suppress them nor that the Soviet government has disinterested itself entirely in Yugoslavia."[26] As will be shown below, SOE did at this time welcome the prospect that the Partisans would be destroyed. But this attitude was based on Cairo's continuing belief that there was a distinction to be drawn between Tito's Partisans, operating in areas such as Bosnia which rightfully belonged to Mihailović, and the Croatian and Slovenian guerrillas who should be contacted and assisted.

(v)

By mid-February Bailey's telegrams evidenced growing despair at the likelihood of securing effective influence or control over the Četnik movement. Owing to British support Mihailović's standing with his fellow Serbs remained high, but his ability to exert real authority over his local commanders or his shadow army was problematic. The Četniks, Bailey estimated, "can be of great use in final revolt, moderate use in guerrilla activities [and] little use for sabotage or conspiratorial work." He maintained that "the only way to bring the potential Serb army to efficient activity is to run everything ourselves."[27]

But even this limited and contingent usefulness was being vitiated by the British failure to send supplies. Bailey reported on 26 February that Mihailović had received only two sorties during the past four months: "I can no longer convince him that our interest is serious." He was already reneging on his undertaking to accept British liaison officers at his regional commands. In a covering letter to the Foreign Office Boughey wrote that Bailey was in no position to persuade Mihailović to undertake any anti-Axis activity because he could offer so little support. The Cabinet must now decide if Mihailović's movement should be kept alive, or "whether they consider it of such small value that they are prepared for us to lose our grip on what would appear to us to be a most valuable weapon."[28]

Glenconner estimated that to service Mihailović adequately SOE would need to mount a minimum of 28 sorties per month.

To do so would require the allocation to SOE of at least seven new Liberators. As it was Cairo could offer only 12 sorties over the next two months - and the consequent prospect that "our influence over A/H31 [Mihailović] will be so diminished that he may feel he has no alternative but collaboration with the Italians and possibly with Nedić, as indicated in the PLOZ [Hudson] telegrams." In these circumstances Glenconner considered it madness that the BBC should be permitted to laud the Partisans. "If we are to achieve anything worthwhile," he concluded, "our policy must be consistent and sufficient aircraft must be available . . ." Though unshocked by the warning of collaboration ("he's doing that already") and amused by the plea for consistency ("from SOE of all people!"), the Foreign Office agreed that SOE had to have more 'planes.[29]

The Chiefs of Staff Committee met on 4 March to consider both a memorandum from Eden and Selborne stressing the need for more aircraft for SOE's Yugoslav operations and the Foreign Office paper of 20 February outlining the reasons behind the decision to contact the Partisans. The Chiefs refused to give SOE any more Liberators, and thus to sacrifice either Middle East strategic bombing or the anti-U-boat campaign in the Atlantic. But Portal did report that he had allotted SOE four Halifaxes (in addition to the six promised in December). With these he predicted that SOE would be capable of operating effectively over Yugoslavia. In the discussion that followed, however, the Chiefs argued that Britain should decide between Mihailović and the Partisans. There were insufficient aircraft available to attempt to sustain both sides. They agreed, too, that "on balance, taking the long view, it seemed sounder on military grounds to back Mihailović since he could provide some organization and control whereas under the Partisans chaos would probably ensue when the Axis forces were defeated."[30]

This was not, in Howard's words, "a very helpful conclusion". Selborne and Hambro may have thought it just right, but Howard was concerned that the Chiefs seemed to have missed the point: "It was precisely because we have not got sufficient aircraft to help both sides that we asked for more." Neither the Foreign Office nor SOE London was certain whether the Halifax possessed the range necessary to operate over all but north-western Yugoslavia. But if it did, Howard suggested, then the four SOE Liberators might be used exclusively for gaining contact with the Partisans. Sargent ruled that this technical question would have to be answered before a decision was made on "whether we and SOE should or should not make a further appeal to the Chiefs of Staff, or even mobilize the Prime Minister for the purpose."[31]

Cairo's plans for the despatch of two missions composed of Yugoslav-born Canadian communists to Partisan territory in Bosnia and Croatia were well advanced by March.[32] Yet it appeared to the Foreign Office that SOE, even in its Cairo manifestation, remained wedded to Mihailović. This was because the edited versions of Cairo's proposals prepared by Baker Street tended to blur the fine distinction which Cairo attempted to make between the Serbian lands (where Mihailović alone should be supported) and the rest of the country (where another policy might be found appropriate). A long telegram from Glenconner dated 4 March and passed to the Foreign Office a week later as a memorandum from SOE Cairo made this apparent. Baker Street summarized Glenconner's views as follows:

1. Many Partisans are *not* communists.
2. Mihailović is still the best man to back.
3. We must guide him so that he will:
   (a) be discreet in his Italian contacts;
   (b) remove certain undesirables from his entourage;
   (c) adopt a more liberal and constructive policy;
   (d) hold out a hand to the Croats.
4. We should only praise or back the Partisans if he fails to play after we have given him material support.

Neither this summary, nor Howard's minute on the memorandum as a whole, drew attention to the fact that Cairo was advocating wholehearted support for Mihailović in the Serbian lands only. This was understandable since Cairo's continuing concern with increasing Mihailović's appeal to the Croats and Slovenes - "though for the moment it is a counsel of perfection" - rather contradicted this distinction, as did such categorical statements as, "The policy of the Partisans does not suit us, nor would it ever be easy for us to bring them under our control." Faithfully reflecting Bailey's views, Cairo estimated that the remaining Partisans in the Serbian lands (i.e. Bosnia) could be won over to Mihailović if he were both sternly disciplined and adequately supported by Britain: "it is believed that the Partisans under Tito will then lose many of their followers, which constitutes the only practical solution of the existing conflict between him and them."[33]

The means by which this was to be accomplished seemed at hand. On 3 February Bailey had advised Cairo that the Partisans' military circumstances in western Bosnia appeared desperate. Radio "Free Yugoslavia" had adopted an hysterical tone and reports reaching him suggested that Bihać had fallen to the Germans. Bailey guessed that the Italians were keeping the Četniks out of the fray: "This is against their wishes, but even enforced abstinence may [help?] ZP [the Foreign Office] resist Soviet attacks." Thus the situation was promising: "Regrettable as might be Asix success in clearing up Partisans, it may be best solution [for] our long term policy . . . In which case Tito scheme may succeed."[34] By this Bailey meant the transplantation of the remaining Partisans into Croatia and the long-mooted showdown with Mihailović on the basis of adequate arms for adequate action.[35] But the line of retreat forced on the Partisans by Operation "Weiss" decreed otherwise.

At the beginning of March Bailey found himself within earshot of the battle and in little doubt that the Četniks were fighting alongside the Axis as the Partisans attempted to force the Neretva near Konjic. He could not be certain, however, because the rupture in his relations with Mihailović following the latter's anti-British outburst of 28 February (see section vi) left him "cut off from honest information." He asked Cairo to let him know what was happening.[36] The information he did possess suggested that large Četnik formations under Ostojić and Djurišić were meeting with considerable success against the Partisans, though Bailey found the manner in which he received this news as galling as its substance. On 11 March he telegraphed Cairo:

> To me the fact that information which should reach me direct and with accuracy from Mihailović himself, I must seek at third hand from a small-town broadsheet, the property of a local peasant [is intolerable]. We must condone tacitly operation by which arms are taken from those resisting occupiers by those on terms of peace with them. This is a grim revelation of the humiliating position in which the British Mission obviously finds itself and will apparently continue to find itself for some time.[37]

The officials of SOE did not seem to feel a similar chagrin. On the same day as Bailey sent this telegram George Taylor, Hambro's second-in-command, composed a twenty-page report for his chief on the work of the Cairo mission. Taylor was much exercised over defining the proper relations of the mission to head office and of both to the busybodies in the Foreign Office, but half of his report was devoted to what he called the "problem" of Mihailović. That the Partisan problem was about to be solved he took for granted. They were "clearly done for":

> The some thousands of Partisans who are concentrated in their last refuge in Bosnia represent the more or less fanatical core to which the original movement has dwindled, and it is not improbable that a very considerable proportion of these, representing the idealistic, patriotic, young, but non-Communist Serb element, will tend to abandon their Communist leaders as they increasingly see nothing but disaster for Serbia in their tactics, and go over to any alternative national movement which seems to hold out hope of effective resistance and the ultimate re-establishment of Serbia.
>
> From our point of view the vital thing is that it does seem clear that the Partisan movement has shot its bolt, is not carrying out the functions for which we wish to use resistance groups, and has no prospect of effective revival.

It therefore followed (six pages later) that,

> We are quite reconciled to the Partisans being liquidated

> by the Axis, since from a practical resistance point of view they no longer have any interest for us. Indeed, their liquidation has certain advantages. It distracts the Axis and leaves A/H31 [Mihailović] freer to get on with his preparations for short-term operations and eventual rising. Moreover, it would be likely to have the effect of unifying the resistance movement in the *Srpstvo* as the non-Communists in the Bosnia independent State will tend to drift back to A/H31.

Taylor was of two minds as to whether or not SOE ought actively to seek to restrain Mihailović from expediting the Partisans' end. On the one hand, such efforts meant "wasting his substance on other than the true enemies" and brought "him close to the Axis and to collaborationism in general"; but on the other, it was useful that he should stake out a determinedly anti-communist position. It would also be "extremely difficult to prevent the Četniks from endeavouring to assist in the liquidation of the Partisans and in view of the very weak hold which we have on A/H31 [Mihailović] at present I do not think we should press dissuasion too far." Such a policy might annoy the Russians and involve the Foreign Office "in an unpleasant quarter of an hour with M. Maisky," but the advantages that would accrue in the form of a more tractable, effective and discreet Mihailović were worth that small price.[38] Given Hambro's comments in his letter to Cadogan on 16 March, it appears that SOE London concurred.

Two enigmatic telegrams from Bailey in mid-March offer hints - but no more - that SOE may have gone further, and actually decided to facilitate the Četniks' offensive. On 16 March Bailey reported that Djurisic and 4,000 Četniks had left Kolašin the previous day in 80 Italian lorries. The Italians had also provided them with 100,000 rounds of rifle ammunition and 25,000 rounds of machine gun ammunition. It was intended that Djurišić's force would operate along the line Konjic-Prozor-Vakuf and be absent for 15-20 days. After commenting that Cairo's estimate of the situation came near the mark, Bailey noted that, "I offered Djurišić loan of W/T station complete. He accepted, but subsequently did not collect."[39] Three days later Bailey advised Cairo that he had saved 8 million lire for Djurišić and planned to finance him clandestinely should Mihailović object.[40]

These two isolated telegrams may well bear more relation to Bailey's estrangement from Mihailović and to a possible effort on the part of SOE to reinsure with Djurišić - either as an alternative Četnik leader or as a protector for the endangered British mission - than to any deep plot to abet the destruction of the Partisans. But then again they may not. By the end of March SOE Cairo had apparently changed its tune. Wiring London about the demarche being prepared for Mihailović, Cairo insisted that, "Important point is to stop A/H31 [Mihailović] continuing [to] concentrate his own Četniks against Partisans with Axis help."[41] Yet this too was ambiguous. Were the operative phrases "his own Četniks" or "with Axis help"?

SOE's expectation (or hope) that the Partisans were on the point of extinction in the Serb lands had not been shared by SIS. Following closely the progress of "Weiss" since its launching on 20 January, the reports of MI3 to the DMI and CIGS drew attention both to the disarray into which the offensive was throwing the Četniks - torn as they were between the anticipation of smashing the Partisans with the help of the Italians and the fear of what they might suffer thereafter at the hands of the Germans - as well as to the mortal threat which it posed to the Partisans. MI3 predicted on 12 February that if the Partisans managed to survive this largest Axis operation in Yugoslavia since December 1941 - "as has always happened before" - and emerged from it a "coherent organization", however reduced, "then their prestige will be enhanced and their influence enlarged." Through March the military situation was considered to be too confused to warrant intelligent comment, but by April it was apparent to SIS that "Weiss" had failed and that Mihailović had suffered "a disastrous reverse" at the hands of the Partisans in Montenegro and Hercegovina, despite their endurance of "200 miles of running battle with strong German forces" and his importation of reserves from Serbia. As a result, "his Četniks are in danger of becoming even further identified with the Axis."[42]

(vi)

The Foreign Office had been slow to tumble to the distinction which Cairo made between total support for Mihailović in the Serbian lands and possible support for others elsewhere; but once understood it rejected the concept as impossible. It did so at the same time as SOE Cairo was itself abandoning the idea as unworkable given the Partisans' survival of "Weiss" and their consequent penetration of Hercegovina, Montenegro and Sandžak. Rose minuted on 16 April in regard to a report by SOE London that it oversimplified things:

> For instance they talk gaily about "Serbian lands" as if that term were capable of a precise, generally accepted definition. In fact it is, of course, a whole problem in itself. By "Serbian lands" Mihailović understands very much what Fotić means by the term: and it certainly includes the whole of Bosnia. If we now agree that Mihailović has the right to Bosnia, we are in fact selling the Croats straight out to the Serbs. This in itself may not matter from the point of view of the future settlement since there will be no definite commitment on our side. The difficulty arises from the fact that there must be many loyal Croats operating in "Serbian lands", and that these will certainly not relish being virtually handed over to Mihailović who has publicly stated that he would like to hang Maček.

Mihailović, he concluded, was simply "a thoroughly bad choice for the leadership of Yugoslavia."[43]

By April the Foreign Office and both ends of SOE were discussing with greater concord than usual the terms of a stiff directive which they proposed to send to Mihailović. The idea was not new, but the circumstances were. What brought the idea to the fore again was a tirade against the British which an ill and distraught Mihailović had the misfortune to deliver in Bailey's presence on 28 February. This moved the British, first, to protest through the Yugoslav government to Mihailović and, then, to draw up a strict set of terms and conditions which he would have to accept if he were to continue to enjoy British support. There was little question now, however, that this support would be his alone.

Speaking at a semi-public christening ceremony in the house of the mayor of the Montenegrin village of Gornje Lipovo, Mihailović accused the British of seeking to wage war to the last drop of Serb blood. This blood they sought to purchase with an insignificant trickle of arms. He would never be a party to such a "shameful commerce typical of traditional English perfidy." The British not only held the Yugoslav King and government their virtual prisoners, but they had with disgusting cynicism abandoned their support for the sacred Serb cause on the BBC:

> The Allies' lust for fraud was satisfied by the untimely, hypocritical and anti-Yugoslav activity of the Partisans - but let the Allies realize that nothing they could do or threaten could turn the Serbs from their vowed and sacred duty of exterminating the Partisans. *As long as the Italians remained his sole adequate source of benefit and assistance generally,* nothing the Allies could do would make him change his attitude towards them. *His enemies were the Partisans, the Ustaše, the Moslems and the Croats.* When he had dealt with them, he would turn to the Italians and Germans. In conclusion he said that he needed no further contacts with the Western democracies whose sole aim was to win the war at the expense of others.[44]

This, Bailey's text, appears to have reached the Foreign Office during the second week in March. Until then SOE London, fortified by the Chiefs' of Staff decision on 4 March and pleading its own "strong feelings" in the matter, had maintained its dispute with the Foreign Office over whether or not anyone but Mihailović merited British support.[45] Bailey, however, was now reporting that Mihailović had absented himself from headquarters (he rightly guessed in order to direct the battle with the Partisans in eastern Hercegovina) and that he would not be surprised if the Četnik command were to cut and run "without worrying unduly about fate of this mission and abandon[ing] us as they did Major Hudson last year." Echoing also Hudson's recommendation of November 1941, Bailey asked that no supply sorties to the Četniks should be mounted if W/T contact between him and Cairo were to lapse.[46] SOE was evidently struck more by Bailey's unenviable position - and by the reports which now flowed in that the Četniks were having the worst of the fighting - than it was by Mihailović's speech. But its representatives agreed with the Foreign Office at a meeting on 17 March that Mihailović should be disciplined in the strongest possible terms, in the first place through Jovanović.[47]

On 23 March Cadogan sent the Prime Minister, acting for Eden during the Foreign Secretary's absence in America, a memorandum explaining the situation. Attempts to heal the Partisan-Četnik dispute through recourse to the Russians having failed, it was now proposed that SOE establish contact with the Partisans in Croatia and Slovenia:

> It is not going to be easy to do, but if we can learn what is going on in those areas, we shall be able to judge whether we ought to send material assistance to one of these independent bands. As for Mihailović we propose to continue in contact with him pending further developments. And indeed we cannot do otherwise for SOE have two officers living at his headquarters who are more or less hostages. In any case, both SOE and "C" attach importance to the maintenance of direct contact with Mihailović, notwithstanding his misbehaviour. On the other hand, Mihailović's recent anti-British outburst has brought things to a head and we are proposing to take up the matter with the Yugoslav government, in order to see whether they are willing, or indeed capable, of bringing Mihailović into line with our own policy.

Churchill approved both the letter which the Foreign Office was preparing for Jovanović and the despatch of British missions to the Partisans in Croatia and Slovenia. But after signing the letter to Jovanović on 29 March, the Prime Minister minuted to cadogan that while Mihailović's attitude was intolerable, it was perhaps understandable in the absence of real Allied assistance: "He is certainly maltreating us, but I believe that he is also double-crossing the Italians. His position is terrible, and it is not much use preaching to the 'toad beneath the harrow'. We must not forget the very little help we can give."[48]

Rendel presented Churchill's letter to Jovanović on 30 March. It demanded that Jovanović convey to Mihailović the British government's sense of outrage that an Allied minister should give voice to sentiments "so totally at variance with their own." The British government, he was told,

> could never justify to the British public or to their own Allies their continued support for a movement, the leader of which does not scruple publicly to declare that their enemies are his allies - whether temporary or permanent is immaterial - and that his enemies are not the German and Italian invaders of his country, but his fellow Yugoslavs and chief among them men who at this very moment are fighting and giving their lives to free his country from the foreigners' yoke.

The letter concluded with the threat that unless Mihailović changed his policy towards both the Italians and his compatriots, "it may well prove necessary for His Majesty's Government to revise their present policy of favouring General Mihailović to the exclusion of the other resistance movements in Yugoslavia."[49] Shocking as this must have been to Jovanović, the threat understated the change that had already taken place. The British were no longer prepared to guarantee Mihailović exclusive support no matter how contrite and agreeable he might now claim to be.

Jovanović's defence of Mihailović was spirited - and as effective as it could be under the circumstances - combining, as Howard noted, expressions of pained surprise with a counterattack on a broad front. But he agreed with little argument to draft and send a note calling the General to task.[50] He produced a message two days later which took much of its flavour from Churchill's letter. The Foreign Office suggested amendments designed to give emphasis to the total unacceptability of Mihailović's enumeration of his friends and enemies, as well as to dampen the implication of Jovanovic's draft that compliance with British wishes would bring him exclusive support on a grand new scale. Jovanović again proved cooperative.[51] The resulting message was sent on 5 April. It advised Mihailović that "to whatever extent local circumstances might make Italian assistance appear profitable for the time being, it is yet bought dearly if it should jeopardize the much more important help extended to us by Great Britain." Though British assistance may have appeared paltry to him in the past, it was not for want of good will. Now, however, the British were in a position to render assistance on a larger scale "provided they are assured that your policy for dealing with the enemy will conform to theirs . . ."[52]

The Southern Department was rather pleased with itself, feeling that this showdown and Jovanović's forthcoming attitude in producing an "excellent telegram" had cleared the "dangerously foggy" atmosphere between the two governments.[53] The Department thus graciously acceded to Jovanović's plea that the whole affair should remain secret - that the British would inform no other members of the Yugoslav government of their demarche.[54] Eden, back from Washington, was less smug. The telegram for Mihailović, he minuted on 9 April, was "all right", "but I am more interested in Mihailović's actions. Do we hear anything from our representative with him? I have never seen a line of value."[55]

In fact Eden's impatience and frustration at the seeming drift in British policy was no more acute than Bailey's own. On 3 April Bailey reported that he had not seen Mihailović for three weeks. He considered himself "virtually dismissed by him" and asked that Jovanović order Mihailović to receive him. SOE endorsed this request, adding that if the Partisans continued to scatter the Četniks (whom it was now clear that Mihailović was leading at Foča), then Bailey's fears of being deserted appeared well-founded. Jovanović sent this second dictated telegram on 6 April.[56] Until Bailey could see Mihailović and gauge his response to Jovanović's first rebuke, it would not be possible to proceed to the next stage in reordering Britain's relations with him: the issuance of a specific directive containing the terms and conditions that would govern their future work together.

(vii)

There now occurred what Howard described later in the month as "a sudden and unexpected change" in SOE policy which "brought it right into line with our own." During the first week in April SOE received from the Chiefs of Staff a directive on its activities for the remainder of 1943. The Chiefs, according to Howard, urged SOE "to tune up all guerrilla warfare in the Balkans" and required "to know for planning purposes what national forces of resistance were to be relied on in Yugoslavia in the event of operations in that theatre."[57]

Selborne's initial response to this directive was to reaffirm (in a letter to Sargent on 9 April) his faith that Mihailović could be made to serve more activist ends. In any case it would be impossible to consider backing both Četniks and Partisans "unless our resources were increased far beyond anything at present contemplated." If relations with Mihailović could be put on a proper footing and if adequate supplies were sent to him, then the communists would fade into well-deserved insignificance.[58] Three days later Pearson reiterated to Howard that only the Četniks should be backed in the Serbian lands "since there does not seem to be the slightest possibility of running the two movements in double harness and to support them both would merely result in falling between two stools." Nonetheless, "the independent resistance groups" in Croatia and Slovenia must be contacted and assisted for they were doing much valuable work.[59]

In Cairo, however, SOE was now coming to appreciate the scope and implications of the disaster that had overtaken the Četnik movement. On 16 April Glenconner advised London that not only was Mihailović's collaboration with the Italians no longer excusable on grounds of expediency, but that it was part and parcel of his struggle with the Partisans for the leadership of the Serbs. Given the defeats he had just suffered at their hands, the past failure of SOE to lend him adequate aid and the misguided propaganda policy of the BBC, Glenconner considered it likely that Mihailović's movement was destined to become a complete creature of the Axis, which could in any case always outbid the British in terms of "arms and equipment for his services." Glenconner was thus gloomy about the prospects for the forthcoming showdown and reconciled to a less ambitious role for SOE:

> If negotiations should fail, I fear we will have no alternative but to withdraw our support, leaving him to continue on his own way, and give up the attempt to build him into the leader of the Serbs. We should also leave the Partisans to continue their fight against him and the Axis. In other words, whereas in our 959 we urged that we must decide which party we should back so as not to fall between two stools, we would in future back neither and give up the idea of creating a national movement which has involved us in taking sides in an internal dispute which we cannot bring to an end. Our only alternative would be to adopt a much less ostentatious and more opportunist policy of trying to make use of independent groups and bands who may be prepared to work with us for action against the enemy.

Such groups were to be found among the uncompromised Četniks of eastern Serbia (whither Bailey should proceed) and the Partisans in Croatia and Slovenia. Glenconner held out the hope that, by placing British officers with each of these independent bands, some coordination of resistance on the Greek pattern might still be achieved in Yugoslavia.[60]

It was at this point that the British learned something of the Partisans' recent negotiations with the Germans. These had been initiated by the Partisan command in early March - when "Weiss" was still at its height - with the immediate objects of arranging an exchange of prisoners, similar to that which had taken place in August 1942, and of securing for the Partisans and their columns of wounded recognition as belligerents. But

Tito and the Central Committee were also interested in determining whether or not the Germans would be willing to grant them the respite that seemed necessary in order to make good their victory over the Četniks in Hercegovina and Montenegro and their intended advance into Serbia. This last aim was, of course, not mentioned to the Germans by the Partisan negotiators: Djilas, Koča Popović and Vladimir Velebit. They proposed instead to make Sandžak the base from which the Supreme Staff would deal with their main enemy, the Četniks. The Germans proved willing to exchange prisoners, but demanded an end to Partisan sabotage of the Belgrade-Zagreb railway line through Slavonia before proceeding to discussion of a truce. The exchange of prisoners duly took place, but the political talks that began in Zagreb on 26 March got nowhere. Hitler and Ribbentrop vetoed the idea of negotiations with rebels: "rebels must be shot." Tito, meanwhile, had lost interest in a more far-reaching accommodation. "Weiss" had come to its appointed end and Djurisic's Četniks had been defeated. He had, however, ordered a cessation of Partisan operations in Slavonia, apparently so as to guarantee the success of Velebit's second mission to Zagreb: securing the release of Tito's common-law wife, Herta Has.[61]

Mihailović learned of the existence (but not the subject) of Partisan-German talks in Bosnia and naturally informed Bailey, including the information that the chief Partisan negotiator was a Dr. Miloš Marković. This was the pseudonym used by Djilas. Bailey relayed Mihailović's report to Cairo on 22 March and asked for confirmation. Deciphering of this telegram was apparently long-delayed.[62] (This was a chronic problem in SOE Cairo.) In any case, it was not until mid-April that London became aware that something was going on - perhaps because intercepts of German military radio traffic made reference to discussions with the Partisans, perhaps because changes were noticed in the Partisan order of battle. A draft report on "Weiss" dating from mid-April noted in connection with the Partisans' Sixth Brigade operating north of Sarajevo, "It is said that as a result of the negotiations with the Germans these troops will withdraw to the Foča area. See separate Note."[63] Unfortunately this note is no longer attached to the report.

But for whatever reasons - and one of them may simply have been astonishment at the magnitude of the Partisans' victory over the Četniks - SOE London now suspected that the Germans were arming the Partisans. Glenconner was asked to comment. He replied on 19 April that evidence was being sought from Bailey:

> If it is confirmed it would show that the Italians and Germans are arming both sides so as to exploit their mutual hatred and divert attention from themselves. We agree with you that it would also show that the Partisans are no better than A/H31 [Mihailović].

But even if Partisan-German collaboration were proved, Glenconner was convinced that the arguments set out in his telegram of 16 April remained valid. A refusal by Mihailović to accept the terms of the directive now under discussion would mean "we will have reached a stage when if we back either side we are no more than participants in an internal dispute or civil war and playing the same game as the Axis." It could have been different had the Partisans been vanquished. Then Mihailović might have been prevailed upon to turn on the Italians "and join with us in prosecuting the war which we are trying to win." As it was, it was Mihailović who was on the run:

> Our decisions must, therefore, be largely influenced by our estimate of the strength of the Partisans which in turn depends on more intelligence. We have therefore now decided we must improve this by sending a mission to near Sarajevo immediately for D/H2 [Bailey] is chiefly dependent on what he learns from A/H31 [Mihailović] himself and his entourage.[64]

Thus a mission of Yugoslav-Canadians (code-name "Hoathley") was dropped over Javornik in north-eastern Bosnia on the same night - 21 April - as the long-planned mission to the Croatian Partisans (code-name "Fungus") was despatched to Crnačko Polje in the north of Lika. The mission to the Partisans in

Slovenia was put in abeyance until such time as another Liberator became available.[65]

It seems reasonable to conclude that far from deterring the British from seeking contacts with the Partisans, the reports of Partisan-German dealings stimulated their interest in contacting them. Both the circumstances of the decision to mount "Hoathley" and the destination selected for it support this inference. Glenconner testified as much later in May when SOE London apparently rebuked him for his initiative in sending "Hoathley" to an area previously regarded as belonging to Mihailović. Glenconner insisted that the mission was "for the purpose of collecting intelligence only" and referred London to the paragraph of his 19 April telegram relating to the need to get evidence on the Partisans' relations with the Germans.[66]

The policy prescriptions which emerged from SOE Cairo at this time were in anticipation of a meeting which had been called for 21 April in London. At this meeting, chaired by Cadogan, Hambro spelled out for the Foreign Office, PWE and SIS representatives in attendance the terms of his organization's new brief from the Chiefs of Staff. He indicated that he was anxious to force Mihailović to declare himself and to fix British policy accordingly. Howard reported that "he dropped a hint that, if Mihailović refused to collaborate, SOE would be prepared to switch their support to some other resistance group." "This," Howard continued, "was an innovation since SOE had previously never deviated one inch from their blind support of Mihailović." Reviewing several days later the whole history of relations with Mihailović for an Eden angered and confused by what he perceived as a policy of chop and change decreed by SOE, Howard further explained that "SOE doubtless felt that on present showing they could scarcely claim that Mihailović answered their requirements" as now outlined by the Chiefs of Staff.[67]

What the Foreign Office interpreted and welcomed as a volte-face by SOE as a whole was, in fact, another example of London coming belatedly into line with its Cairo base.[68]

Although Baker Street's emotional attachment to Mihailović was to prove remarkably durable, Selborne and his lieutenants were no less susceptible to the blandishments of the military than were Glenconner, Keble and the rest of the Cairo Staff. The Foreign Office's sense of sudden change was however natural in view of a remarkable coincidence of events: the directive by the Chiefs of Staff, the arrival in Cairo of the long-promised Halifaxes and the despatch on 21 April of the first two missions to the Partisans. These events, in combination with the even more important alteration in the balance of power inside Yugoslavia, pointed the way for the future.

The Foreign Office agreed with SOE at the end of April that if Mihailović's response to the proposed directive were unsatisfactory, then it might be necessary to consider dropping him completely. This they wished to avoid. Not only were the Partisans still regarded as chaotic elements with whom it would be difficult to work and impossible to control, but - as Eden minuted on 30 April - "It is clearly desirable to build up our position in that country so far as possible." A communist-controlled Yugoslavia would both thwart this aim and become "a cause of unsettlement to all its neighbours." He thus approved the 'new' SOE policy as set out by Howard:

> To go very slowly with Mihailović, though not to give him up altogether; to contact the Partisans and all other resistance units, and meanwhile to build up our own staff of officers throughout the country with a view to establishing British control over all the various units which go to form the resistance movement, and eventually centralizing the latter under British direction.

Howard concluded that although this plan might appear "far-fetched", he believed there could be "something in it". SOE was in any case resolved to try and should have Foreign Office backing "until and unless it is clearly shown to be impracticable."[69]

SOE Cairo already had a feeling that it might be. On 26 April Glenconner advised London that the civil war could be on the verge of ending in favour of the Partisans. The bulk of the Četniks would go over to the Partisans and Mihailović would be reduced to leading "a remnant of fanatical anti-communists." An agreement with him might therefore be easily achieved, but it would also be useless. The Partisans would constitute the only effective anti-Axis force in the country, numbering between 50,000 and 100,000 men. Glenconner concluded prophetically,

> The situation would be very similar to that which would arise if E.A.M., having waged successful warfare against all other parties, became the only powerful anti-Axis force in Greece, and would have nothing whatever to do with the King and his Government.
>
> This telegram is sent only to prepare you for developments which may be in store and to say that we must be ready to make contact with Tito himself should the need arise. The requisite party is therefore being prepared.

Glenconner warned Baker Street that the time had come to consult both the Foreign Office and the military.[70] It was 45 days since Taylor had predicted the liquidation of the Partisans in the Serb lands.

The first reports from the missions with the Partisans were encouraging. On 25 May the Foreign Office learned that the team sent to Lika had quickly established contact with the Partisan headquarters for Croatia. It had been welcomed with the remark, "We think that you are badly informed of the whole situation." Arrangements were soon made for the reinforcement of the Yugoslav-Canadians by a joint SOE-SIS mission and for the reception at Partisan supreme headquarters in Motnenegro ("with Tito himself!") of an official SOE-SIS mission. This, according to the Partisan invitation, "would be a logical step in synchronizing common plans for the complete and final defeat of the Axis and its quislings."[71]

The mission in Lika reported that the Partisans were strong, well-armed with captured weapons and active against the Axis and its lines of communication. The romantic, enthusiastic and rather simple Major William Jones, who joined "Fungus" on 18 May on behalf of SOE, reported that the Partisans in Croatia were fully organized under central and regional commands: "A high degree of strategic skill, organizational efficiency, military ability and stern discipline characterize the entire force." The Partisan commanders assured Jones "of their trust in British friendship and they enthusiastically welcomed the offer of British cooperation and pledged themselves to reciprocate accordingly."[72] Such effusions followed by less than two months the Partisans' assurances to the Germans that they would fight the British should they land in Yugoslavia. The friendly overtures of the British were in similarly unseemly succession to their hopes in March that the main body of Partisans would be destroyed. As Djilas has written about this change, "In war only the victorious gain a right to hope."[73]

SOE, mindful of the political bias and/or naivete of its first witnesses among the Partisans, was initially sceptical of the rave notices they sent out. But there were no doubts in the minds of SOE officers in Cairo that the Partisans should be actively supported, even in the Serb lands. Endorsing Cairo's view, SOE London reported to the Foreign Office on 31 May "that the Partisan movement must be regarded as a whole, and if we support them in Croatia, as we are now doing, we cannot withhold our support to them further south, provided always, of course, that they do not attack Mihailović's forces."[74] SOE remained hopeful, however, that a significant degree of British control might be established over the Partisans. Only after Churchill's friend and historical collaborator, Captain F. W. Deakin,[75] arrived at Tito's Zabljak headquarters on 28 May was it to be made clear to the British that there was no question of assuming overall command of the Partisan forces or of "centralizing" them with Mihailović. Again, the only solution appeared to be to separate physically the two sides, though on geographical lines now far less generous to the Četniks.

A new phase in Britain's wartime relations with Yugoslavia had opened. Despite the inspiration of 27 March and the promise of Draža Mihailović and his Četniks during 1941 and 1942, Serb nationalism had proved unequal to the threefold task of fighting the Axis, providing a basis for the reconstruction of the Yugoslav state and preserving British influence in the post-war Balkans. It remained to be seen whether or not Tito and the Partisans could be made to serve some or all of these same ends. The inauguration of British relations with the Partisans may not have been - to paraphrase Churchill on El Alamein - the beginning of the end, but it was certainly the end of the beginning.

CHAPTER VII

EPILOGUE

The British had begun in the spring of 1943 to come to grips with the Partisans - with their strength, their unity, their ambition and their military usefulness. But this did not mean that Mihailović - with his many failings - was yet regarded as having been eclipsed as a major factor in Yugoslavia's present and future. Not only did he remain Yugoslav Minister of War and a popular legend of some importance outside Yugoslavia, but he was believed to command the loyalty of the vast majority of Serbs inside the country. The British were determined to make use of this presumed strength if at all possible.

On 7 May the long-planned political directive was sent to Mihailović. It demanded in return for increased British assistance that he: (1) agree that the Axis and not his fellow Yugoslavs should be the objects of his resistance; (2) cease collaboration with Nedić and the Italians; (3) cooperate in future with the directives of the Commanders-in-Chief, Middle East, on operational matters; and (4) undertake no action against the Partisans or Croats except in self-defence and, in fact, make every effort to cooperate with them.

Before Bailey could present this directive to Mihailović the matter was complicated by the decision of the Middle East Defence Committee at the end of May to send its own directive to the General. Cairo's orders, which Bailey then presented to Mihailović simultaneously with those from London, stipulated as a further condition of support that Mihailović must henceforward consider his movement's zone of operations as bounded on the west by the River Ibar. Although this reflected the new military realities - allotting to Mihailović those parts of Serbia in which his movement remained strong and where there were few Partisans against whom he might collaborate with the Axis - it contradicted both the letter and spirit of London's directive. It thus offended the Foreign Office's sense of authority as much as it did Mihailović's pretension to command all Yugoslav resistance.

The General's outrage was mitigated somewhat by the success of the Foreign Office in getting the Ibar order suspended; and he was eventually prevailed upon to send a sweeping acceptance of the terms of the original London directive. But he did not mend his ways, remaining convinced that he would prove indispensable to the British as a bulwark against communism when the inevitable Allied invasion force landed in the Balkans, no matter what he did or did not do in the meantime. Mihailović miscalculated. There was increasingly little prospect of a Balkan invasion. The United States would never participate in one; Britain alone could not mount one. Meanwhile it was the Partisans who were coming to appear indispensable. The favourable reports from the British liaison officers with them found the military authorities both interested in supporting Yugoslav resistance and really able, for the first time, to do so as the Allies' foothold in Italy grew.

For its part the Foreign Office was more aware than ever of Mihailović's disadvantages. Apart from his military uselessness and collaboration, his anti-communist, anti-Moslem and anti-Croat obsessions made it clear that neither Tito nor moderate Croats would ever agree to cooperate with him. He could not be expected to play the stabilizing role in the immediate postwar period for which he had long been cast. His presence on the scene now implied a continuing civil war rather than peace and order. In short, he had come to seem an obstacle to the achievement of any sort of Yugoslav unity, whether in resistance or in the future state.

The Foreign Office remained loath, however, to grant the expanding counter-claims of the Partisans to represent all honest, anti-Axis Yugoslavs. Instead Foreign Office officials looked increasingly to King Peter, substituting him and an assumed devotion to the dynasty on the part of most Yugoslavs (and all Serbs) for the discredited Mihailović in their search for a non-communist unifying factor. In so doing they exaggerated the attraction of the dynasty to most Yugoslavs and minimized the personal limitations of the twenty-year old monarch. Nonetheless, adventuristic plans were discussed for the King either to descend by parachute upon Mihailović's camp and wrest command of the Četnik loyalists from his War Minister, or else to join Tito's Partisans and fight his way back into the hearts of his countrymen along with them.

As 1943 waned the problem of what to do about Mihailović remained unresolved. There was, though, no shortage of proposed solutions and the great Allied conferences in Cairo and Teheran provided the opportunities for discussing them. Brigadier Fitzroy Maclean, who had augmented Deakin at Tito's headquarters in Jajce in early September, came out of Yugoslavia in November to submit his first full report on the Partisans. Maclean's conclusions were discussed at a meeting on 7 November in Cairo with Eden (then en route back to London after the Moscow foreign ministers' conference) and the Middle East Defence Committee. This was an especially interesting meeting because of the sharp contrast it offered between the policies being adopted by the British in two neighbouring countries - Greece and Ygusolavia - where the situations were at least roughly analogous.

At this meeting a decision was reached to step-up support for the communist-led Partisans in Yugoslavia, while doing everything possible to crush the communist side in Greece, beginning with the withdrawal of liaison officers from the Greek communists, EAM/ELAS. Richard Casey, Minister of State in Cairo, concluded his paper on Greece presented at the meeting by affirming that, "British long term interests require that there shall be established in Greece after the war a stable and friendly government."

The military, sceptical of this politically motivated policy in Greece, got something more congenial in Yugoslavia. Ralph Stevenson, the new Ambassador to the exile government, emphasized to the meeting on the basis of Maclean's report that, "The Partisan movement was not only a much more determined military and political force than had been thought, but it appeared that it would be a decisive factor in shaping the future of Yugoslavia." Eden, who had been brutal in his attack on EAM/ELAS, reported in turn how enthusiastic Maclean was about Tito and endorsed his opinion that Britain must expand its support of the Partisans. He drew attention, however, to the vital imortance of bringing King Peter and Tito together lest short-term military interests outweigh completely the long-term political considerations already predominant in the case of Greece. Eden suggested that Mihailović be ordered to carry out a test operation, failing which no more supplies would be sent to him.[1]

At Teheran it was agreed without dissent among the big three Allied powers to increase their support for Tito. Otherwise, inter-Allied discussion of Yugoslav affairs was limited to the question of whether or not the Soviets would soon send a military mission to join the Anglo-American mission at Tito's headquarters. Mihailović entered the discussion only when Molotov suggested, perhaps facetiously (if uncharacteristically), that the Soviet government might be well-advised to send a mission to him rather than to Tito so as to get "better information". Eden thought not and the suggestion was allowed to lapse.[2]

When the leaders of the Western Allies returned to Cairo for further military talks the problems raised by Yugoslavia and Mihailović were high on the British agenda. There was now, however, a vital addition to the equation - and that was the personal interest and involvement of the Prime Minister. Churchill's friend Deakin and the former Tory MP Maclean (who had fought and won the right to send his reports direct to the Prime Minister, bypassing SOE) were both in Cairo to report to him. They convinced him that any weapons given to the Partisans would be well-utilized in killing the maximum number of Germans. They made it plain, however, that the communist-led Partisans were well on the way to becoming Yugoslavia's rulers and would no doubt establish a regime after the war which would be closely allied to the Soviet Union.[3] Mihailović, they told him, was irredeemably compromised by collaboration; King Peter's only chance to regain his throne was to dismiss Mihailović and lend his support to the Partisans' National Liberation Movement. The British should in any case break off all contact with Mihailović.

Churchill accepted these arguments (as did Eden) and Deakin and Maclean were delegated to meet individually with King Peter (whose government had recently been transferred from London to Cairo) to tell him the bad news. The Prime Minister also met with the King and the third Yugoslav Premier of 1943, Božidar Purić, warning them that he might find it necessary to request Mihailović's dismissal from the Yugoslav cabinet by the end of the year. Puric, convinced like Mihailović that the British would never allow the establishment of a communist regime in Yugoslavia, steadfastly defended the General. The Partisans were but a flash in the pan, he asserted, and, in any case, the Serbs would never accept them as their rulers. King Peter, on the other hand, seemed more disposed to accept British advice.

Suffering from pneumonia, Churchill left Cairo for a long convalescence in Marrakesh convinced that the matter had been settled: Mihailović was to be dropped by Britain and King Peter pressed to dismiss him from his government. To this end, the Middle East Defence Committee sent Mihailović a request to carry out the already mooted "test operation" (the blowing up of two bridges on the Belgrade-Salonika railway line) in the certainty that he would fail to do so by the deadline of 29 December and thus provide the British with a pretext for breaking with him. Although sceptical about the need for any "test operation" (what would happen if he carried it out?), the Foreign Office fell in with the new policy laid down by the Prime Minister.

The situation was greatly altered, however, by the announcement of the resolutions adopted by the Partisans at the second congress of their Anti-Fascist Council of National Liberation (AVNOJ) in Jajce on 29 November. These resolutions were broadcast by the ever-cautious Soviets over "Free Yugoslavia" Radio only partially and progressively, so that the full scope of the AVNOJ decisions was not apparent to the Foreign Office until mid-December. Among other things, such as declaring Tito to be Marshal of Yugoslavia and establishing the federative principle as the basis on which the new Yugoslavia would be built, the Jajce congress prohibited the King from returning to Yugoslavia until such time as the people had expressed their will on the question of the monarchy and presumed to deprive the exile government of its right to represent the country's interests abroad. To Cadogan, who carried a confused Foreign Office with him, this seemed to be a political power play on the part of the Partisans which both challenged British policy and significantly worsened the King's prospects. There could now be no question of requiring King Peter to dismiss Mihailović, seemingly his only loyal adherent in Yugoslavia, on the ever more risky supposition that this would endear him to the Partisans. They had now shown their true colours and must be pressed to give specific assurances that if the King were to sack Mihailović they would be prepared to work with him in uniting Yugoslav resistance, ideally by accepting him back in the country.

Maclean's and Stevenson's argument that, more than ever, King Peter's only chance of returning to Yugoslavia lay in dismissing Mihailović "off his own bat", was branded as "appeasement" by the Foreign Office. In this dispute the Foreign Office was eventually able to persuade a highly dubious Prime Minister of the rightness of its demand for a "quid pro quo". The Foreign Office owed its success partly to the fact that Churchill was immobilized in Morocco, and partly to the opportunity which was presented to Churchill to take action himself on a slightly different tack. This opportunity was provided by Tito, who in late December sent the Prime Minister a message wishing him a speedy recovery. Churchill determined to seize the chance to enter into a personal correspondence with Tito - "this important man" as he termed him to Eden - and replied with a letter explaining British obligations to King Peter, the difficulty he felt in asking the King to dismiss Mihailović and concluding with the assurance that, "I am resolved that the British Government will give no further military support to Mihailović and will only give help to you, and that we should be glad if the Royal Yugoslavian Government would dismiss him from their councils."[4]

It was decided to await Tito's response before moving further. His reply, received a month later, was non-committal. He expressed understanding for the Prime Minister's point of view, but did not offer to invite King Peter back to Yugoslavia. Another round of messages and replies was thus felt to be necessary. In this correspondence, as in Anglo-Yugoslav relations in general, the initiative now rested with the Prime Minister. In message after message to Tito he flattered, cajoled and pleaded with the communist revolutionary to accept the King back in the country as his easiest path to national unity and international recognition.

Later Churchill's enthusiasm for Tito - and his briefly held conception of Tito having sunk his communism in nationalism - would begin to fade. This was especially the case after his meeting with Tito in Naples in August 1944 and Tito's "levant" to Russia in September. The Prime Minister would then seek in agreement with Stalin the influence in post-war Yugoslavia which for a brief time he had imagined it possible to gain by means of Tito's friendship and the King's legitimacy. Ironically, it was at this point that the Foreign Office re-emerged as the defenders of the previous policy, arguing that all was not lost and that British influence might still be preserved by cooperating with Tito and not forcing him to rely completely on the Russians.

After the decisions taken in Teheran and Cairo in late 1943 Mihailović had for the British only a certain negotiating value. The Foreign Office and SOE toyed for a time with the possibility of maintaining the Četnik organization under another, less compromised commander as a non-communist, pro-monarchy counterweight to the Partisans. But these dreams of staging a "palace revolution" at Mihailović's headquarters came to naught. As a factor of military significance to the Allies Mihailović had long since been discounted. As a political factor he remained on the scene only so long as it took the British to extract from Tito as many concessions as possible in return for his repudiation. That took place at the end of May 1944. Only then was a surprisingly obdurate King Peter prevailed upon to dismiss the Purić government - and with it, Mihailović - and to call upon the former Ban of Croatia, Ivan Šubašić, to undertake (as a one-man government) the task of reaching an accord with Tito. The last liaison officers had been withdrawn from Mihailović shortly before.

Although the Foreign Office - and then Churchill as well - predicted continuing civil war between the Partisans and Serbs as the former sought to conquer Serbia, these particular premonitions of a bloody conflict in which arms supplied by Britain would be used to suppress the Serbs were not fulfilled. Mihailović's organization was dessicated in the extreme and the Serbs in general did not prove to be so singlemindedly anti-communist as had been imagined. By the time a combined Russo-Partisan force liberated Belgrade in October, Mihailović's Četniks had gone home, rallied to the obviously conquering Partisans, or begun a futile and fatal trek northwards with the retreating Germans.

On several occasions during 1944 the British contemplated evacuating Mihailović from Yugoslavia; or rather asking the Americans to do so in view of their late-developing but long-continuing enthusiasm for this cause. But the United States proved uncooperative and the British themselves were unwilling to risk Partisan anger and the stake in Yugoslavia which they believed their negotiations with Tito (and Stalin) would assure them.

In the summer of 1944 Eden commissioned Hugh Grey of the Foreign Office Library to write a history of relations with Mihailović. Eden was particularly interested in having an account which would absolve Britain of accusations - already rife - that perfidious Albion had sacrificed the noble Mihailović to Soviet friendship and pressure. This survey concluded,

> it may be said that the attitude adopted by Mihailović is understandable and must command a certain amount of sympathy. His position has been difficult in a country in enemy occupation, and at an early stage he left no doubt that his policy was one of not laying his organization open to destruction by premature action, but of keeping it in being until the moment was ripe for him to strike - e.g. when the Allies opened a definite front in the Balkans. Unfortunately for his cause, however, he became more of a politician than a soldier, and not a sufficiently good politician to arrive at a satisfactory understanding with the other elements in Yugoslavia who were conducting active operations against what should have been regarded as the principal enemy - i.e. the occupying forces. His military efforts in the Allied cause were negligible, but this alone would probably have been insufficient to have caused His Majesty's Government to continue to regard him as the when it had been decided to support Tito. He had, however, become a stumbling-block in the way of active operations against the common enemy, and by his open hostility towards other elements in Yugoslavia which were conducting such operations, he made it impossible for His Majesty's Government to continue to rgard him as the central figure of resistance and of the future unity of Yugoslavia which was the original basis of the support given him. Apart from this, and here was the decisive factor, his policy involved certain contacts and collaboration with the occupying forces, and once proof of this was forthcoming His Majesty's Government would have been

placed in an impossible position vis-a-vis their Soviet Ally had they continued to support him.[5]

This weighting of factors - if not the generosity of spirit towards both Mihailović and the British government - seems right. The British did not abandon Mihailović because he collaborated with the Axis, but his collaboration did in the long run make it politically impossible for them to maintain relations with him after it had become apparent that he was not the man to organize either resistance or the future Yugoslav state. The process by which this was realized was painful and prolonged for all concerned; but it was particularly difficult for the British because the unpalatable truths about the Četniks which accumulated - and the startling discoveries about the Partisans which were made - challenged two of the most firmly-held (if unexamined) tenets of British policy: the intrinsic chaos of communism and the natural primacy of traditional Serb nationalism in the Yugoslav context.

That the British should have been predisposed against communism in Yugoslavia or anywhere else seems unremarkable enough. But that they should have feared and reviled it for the reasons they did - as an agent of anarchy and chaos - seems strange some 40 years on. The Foreign Office regarded the communist threat not as an extension of Stalinism (that least disorderly of systems), or even as traditional Russian imperialism (though it might lead to that), but as a plague of disorientating power and unpredictable effect. It was the ghost of Bela Kun and not the living Stalin that inspired such dread. Perhaps one explanation lies in the fact that the USSR had become, for all its ideological pretensions, just another state - a power with which relations could be maintained and bargains struck. Well into 1943 it remained inconceivable to many British decision-makers that they could or should attempt to extend similar recognition to the Partisans. Tito and his followers were - to extend the metaphor - an infection, to be lanced by the experienced Soviet doctors or cauterized by the primitive Četniks of Mihailović; but they were hardly susceptible to the milder remedies available to the British government.

It is equally difficult to understand how the British could have taken Mihailović so seriously for so long. Obviously preconceived expectations, inadequate information, a lack of serious interest and military weakness played a large part; but so too did Yugoslavia's remoteness in time and space, the generally brutalizing impact of war and the arrogant assumption that Balkan chieftains could be made and unmade at will. It seems that, reading Mihailović's often outrageous telegrams, the British were merely confirmed in their beliefs about the normal behaviour of Balkan heroes - and villains. In any case, it was only when Mihailović failed to win the domestic victory which they had assumed must be his that the British began to measure him by the same standards of utility and veracity that they would have applied to an ally in more 'civilized' or important regions. Thus in Mihailović - as in Prince Paul and the Serb officers who made the coup d'état of 27 March - the British were ultimately disappointed. But if in each case their hopes had been based more on illusions than on facts, their subsequent disappointments were real enough.

NOTES

CHAPTER I

1. Sir Alexander Cadogan, Permanent Under-Secretary of State at the Foreign Office, confided to his diary in early 1941, "*All* these Balkan peoples are trash. Poor dears - I know their difficulties. They've got no arms, and no money and no industry. But then they shouldn't have behaved as Great Powers at Geneva . . ." David Dilks, ed., *The Diaries of Sir Alexander Cadogan, 1938-1945* (London: Cassell, 1971), p. 365.

In *Mein Kampf* Hitler had expressed the view that the Balkan peoples were "trash" ("*Gerümpel*") and that their region was a barbaric one infested with "*Serbische Bombenschmeisser*". This was not necessarily to the Serbs' discredit, however, since Hitler respected their highly developed racial self-consciousness. Martin van Creveld, *Hitler's Strategy 1940-1941: The Balkan Clue* (London: Cambridge University Press, 1973), pp. 3-4; Gerhard L. Weinberg, *The Foreign Policy of Hitler's Germany: Diplomatic Revolution in Europe, 1933-1936* (Chicago: University of Chicago Press, 1970), p. 20.

2. British investment in Yugoslavia, principally in mines of nonferrous metals, was estimated by the Board of Trade as totalling 1,364 million dinars in 1937. This represented 18.5% of all foreign investment in the country. FO 371/44358, R19319/5062/92.

On the other hand, only 3.3% of Yugoslav exports went to the U.K. and 8.6% of Yugoslav imports came from the U.K. between 1931 and 1935. Fiscal orthodoxy precluded the British from following the Nazi example and using trade for political ends. An effort was made, however, to take up some of the slack resulting from Yugoslavia's imposition of League of Nations sanctions against Italy (then Yugoslavia's largest trading partner) following Mussolini's invasion of Ethiopia. The British share of Yugoslav exports rose to 8.4%, but that of imports declined to 7.5% during the years 1936-39. By the later year a greater Germany controlled more than 50% of Yugoslav foreign trade. French trade was even less significant than that of the British, despite the fact that France accounted for a quarter of foreign investment in the country. For details see Jozo Tomasevich, "Foreign Economic Relations, 1918-1941," in R. J. Kerner, ed., *Yugoslavia* (Berkeley: University of California Press, 1949).

3. J. B. Hoptner, *Yugoslavia in Crisis, 1934-1941* (New York: Columbia University Press, 1962), pp. 12-14.

4. King Alexander and French Foreign Minister Louis Barthou were murdered by an ex-IMRO (Internal Macedonian Revolutionary Organization) gunman who had been hired by the Croatian separatist and terrorist organization, the Ustaše, trained by the Hungarians and paid by the Italians. Despite abundant evidence of Italian complicity in the plot, only the Hungarians were chastised by the League.

5. The new Foreign Minister, Aleksandar Cincar-Marković, was pro-German. His preferment was intended to reassure the Germans that Yugoslav foreign policy would remain unchanged despite the fall of their favourite. Bogdan Krizman, *Vanjska politika Jugoslavenske države 1918-1941* (Zagreb: Školska knjiga, 1975), p. 103.

The Germans were not convinced. They regarded Stojadinović's departure as a serious blow to their interests. For the Italians, even more, Stojadinović's removal meant a reversion to their usual hostility towards the Yugoslav state. Norman Rich, *Hitler's War Aims: Ideology, the Nazi State and the Course of Expansion* (London: André Deutsch, 1973), p. 199.

6. Prince Paul was so un-Balkan in outlook, preferring as he did the collection of old masters to the direction of a police-state, that one of his English friends, the MP and junior Foreign Office minister "Chips" Channon, even worried that he and his dynasty were losing their vital Serb "*erdgeist.*" Robert Rhodes James, ed., *Chips: The Diaries of Sir Henry Channon* (London: Weidenfeld and Nicolson, 1967), p. 136.

7. FO 371/25033, R7065/415/92.

8. Krizman, *Vanjska politika,* pp. 116-18; Hoptner, *Yugoslavia in Crisis,* pp. 148-49.

9. For a detailed account of the Salonika front/Balkan bloc debate see Elisabeth Barker, *British Policy in South-East Europe in the Second World War* (London: Macmillan, 1976), chapt. II.

10. *Ibid.,* p. 16; Hoptner, *Yugoslavia in Crisis,* pp. 170-71.

11. Krizman, *Vanjska politika,* p. 119.

12. *Ibid.;* Barker, *British Policy,* pp. 14-15.

Between March and May the Foreign Office sought to reassure Prince Paul by supplying him with summaries of secret telegrams relating to Anglo-Italian relations. FO 371/25032, R2389/415/92, R2457/415/92, R3194/415/92.

13. FO 371/25033, R6069/415/92, R6426/415/92.

14. FO 371/25033, R6069/415/92, R6245/415/92.

15. CAB 80/12, COS(40)438(JP).

16. CAB 79/4, COS(40)175.

17. CAB 80/12, COS(40)442.

18. CAB 65/7, WM(40)164.

19. CAB 80/14, COS(40)504(JP); CAB 79/5, COS(40)206; Barker, *British Policy,* p. 19.

NOTES

CHAPTER II

1. Rich, *Hitler's War Aims,* p. 180.
2. Krizman, *Vanjska politika,* pp. 107-08.
3. Van Creveld, *Hitler's Stratgy,* pp. 10-13.
4. FO 371/25031, R7032/415/92. The Serbian Agrarian Party leader, Milan Gavrilović, became the first Yugoslav Minister to Moscow.
5. *Ibid.*
6. FO 371/25032, R6236/415/92; FO 371/25033, R6426/415/92.
7. The Foreign Office was embarrassed by the fact that although Prince Paul had been promised a credit of £1 million for arms purchases in 1939 (with provision for a further credit of £500,000), it had soon been found necessary to halve the total available to £750,000, of which the Yugoslavs had only been allowed to spend £430,000 (mianly for the purchase of transport aircraft and spares) by the end of 1940. Arms were either not available for export, or else went to coutnries with a higher priority - namely Turkey and Greece. FO 371/30227, R343/343/92.

A less straightforward reason for avoiding promises of arms

was advanced by the Foreign Office in May 1940: since the Yugoslavs took it for granted that they would receive British help if attacked, the market value of specific promises had been discounted in advance. FO 371/25032, R5719/415/92.

8. FO 371/25033, R6715/415/92, R7164/415/92.

9. The most notorious of these was a short-lived decree by the anti-Semitic Education Minister (the Slovene priest Anton Korošec) restricting the admission of Jews to secondary schools. FRUS, 1940, I, pp. 518-19.

10. *Ibid.;* FO 371/30216, R2603/115/92.

11. FO 371/25033, R6715/415/92.

12. FO 371/25033, R6426/415/92.

13. FO 371/25033, R6926/415/92.

14. FO 371/25032, R6023/415/92.

15. FO 371/25033, R6629/415/92. It was the French Minister, Brugère, who suggested that an encouraging letter from the King or the Duke of Kent might be well received.

16. FO 371/25033, R6956/415/92.

17. FO 371/25033, R7865/415/92, R7960/415/92.

18. FO 371/25033, R7065/415/92, R8072/415/92.

19. FO 371/25034, R8124/415/92.

20. FO 371/25034, R8144/415/92.

21. FO 371/25034, R8249/415/92.

22. The Yugoslavs were doing both at the time, facts which apparently became known to the Germans and Italians. With the noose tightening about their necks, going to the aid of Greece and/or seizing Salonika appeared to many Serbs to be the only means of maintaining their independence. But either would also mean an early Axis attack. The Serb generals who ran the Yugoslav army were adamant on the importance of Salonika - and some were willing to risk war for its sake. But the Croat politicians were less concerned about defending or acquiring a Greek port and more intent upon avoiding a war in which their people would likely be the first to suffer. Prince Paul decided to split the difference: to attempt to secure Salonika without risking war or abandoning neutrality. A more direct course was advocated by th soon-to-be-sacked War Minister, Milan Nedić: accession to the Axis with Salonika as

the prize. For details see Jozo Tomasevich, *War and Revolution in Yugoslavia 1941-1945: The Chetniks* (Stanford: Stanford University Press, 1975), pp. 29-31.

23. Dragiša N. Ristić, *Yugoslavia's Revolution of 1941* (University Park: Pennsylvania State University Press, 1966), pp. 49-50.

24. FO 371/25034, R8490/415/92. Evidence adduced in support of this sanguine interpretation included the replacement of General Nedić by General Pešić as War Minister. The change was seen as reflecting Prince Paul's healthy anger over the failure of the armed forces to resist the Italian bombardment of Bitola. In fact Nedić was dismissed for a worse offence - advocating accession to the Tripartite Pact - while Pešić owed his appointment less to his martial and pro-British sentiments than to his willingness to obey Prince Paul. Tomasevich, *The Chetniks,* p. 31.

25. FO 371/25034, R8238/415/92.

26. FO 371/25031, R8545/191/92.

27. CAB 80/23, COS(40)977. The Forign Office, which was considering the idea of urging joint staff talks upon the Greeks, Turks and Yugoslavs at the time, was warned by the Joint Planning Staff that such discussions would be unlikely to encourage the Yugoslavs. Neither the Greeks nor the Turks had any arms to spare for Yugoslavia, while the British generals would not wish them to enlarge upon their commitments. The idea was nonetheless pursued by the Foreign Office in subsequent weeks. FO 371/25034, R8631/415/92.

28. FO 371/25031, R8545/191/92.

29. FO 371/25034, R8619/415/92.

30. *Ibid.*

31. Barker, *British Policy,* p. 82.

32. FO 371/25034, R8801/415/92.

33. FO 371/25034, R8611/415/92.

34. General Pešić declared to Campbell in early December that despite the army's deficiencies in arms and equipment - which he realized Britain could not make good - "Yugoslavia asked for nothing and would yield nothing." FO 371/25034, R8611/415/92.

35. MI(R) - Military Intelligence (Research) - was in fact only a cover name for Section "D" and disappeared as a title when "D" became SOE. An etymology of British services is provided by M. R. D. Foot, *Resistance* (London: Eyre Methuen, 1976), pp. 133-41.

36. The memoir literature dealing with secret operations in Yugoslavia in 1940 and 1941 includes: Julian Amery, *Approach March* (London: Hutchinson, 1973); Hugh Dalton, *The Fateful Years: Memoirs 1931-1945* (London: Frederick Muller, 1957); Alexander Glen, *Footholds against a Whirlwind* (London: Hutchinson, 1975); and Bikham Sweet-Escott, *Baker Street Irregular* (London: Methuen, 1965).

Among secondary works, two recent studies offer what is likely to be the most complete picture possible: Barker, *British Policy* (chapters 4 and 9) and David A. T. Stafford, "SOE and British Involvement in the Belgrade Coup d'État of March 1941," *Slavic Review*, XXXVI, no. 3 (September 1977). Also useful, although their focus is on SOE's relations with the resistance, are: Phyllis Auty and Richard Clogg, eds., *British Policy towards Wartime Resistance in Yugoslavia and Greece* (London: Macmillan, 1975); and two works by Sir William Deakin (F. W. D. Deakin), "Britanija i Jugoslavija 1941-1945", *Jugoslovenski istorijski časopis*, no. 2 (1963) and *The Embattled Mountain* (London: Oxford University Press, 1971).

37. The point is well documented in Barker, *British Policy*, chapters 6 and 7.

38. Stafford, "Belgrade Coup d'État", pp. 408, 412-13, 419; C. L. Sulzberger, *A Long Row of Candles: Memoirs and Diaries* (New York: Macmillan, 1969), p. 100.

Besides the most obvious explanation - that Campbell was more sympathetic towards subversive activities in 'his' country than were Owen O'Malley and George Rendel in 'theirs' (Hungary and Bulgaria respectively) - the fact that Belgrade was the Balkan headquarters for Section "D"/SOE and that it operated under the auspices of the Legation may have had something to do with Campbell's indulgent attitude. On the other hand, it seems that Campbell had no very high opinion of SOE's abilities and contacts.

39. Amery, *Approach March,* p. 168; Barker, *British Policy,* p. 43. Slovene irredentists distributed propaganda to their co-nationals in Italy and Austria and worked to sabotage goods trains bound for the Reich. Details of SOE's relations with the Slovenes may be found in WO 202/356, tel. B1/3680, 1/2/42.

40. Deakin, "Britanija i Jugoslavija", p. 44; Barker, *British Policy,* p. 85; Stafford, "Belgrade Coup d'État," pp. 410-11.

41. *Ibid.*; Barker, *British Policy,* pp. 45, 84-85.

According to a former Agrarian Party leader, Mate Ruskovič, the British smuggled small arms and W/T sets into the country in their diplomatic bags and in trains from Greece beginning in November 1940. The arms and radio sets were stored in Gavrilovič's house and in the Party headquarters in Belgrade before being distributed prior to the coup. A secret broadcasting station was organized by Tupanjanin in Belgrade on the eve of the putsch, but it fell silent with the German invasion. The arms, meanwhile, had been surrendered to the Yugoslav army following the success of the coup. Jovan Marjanovič, *Ustanak i Narodno-oslobodilački pokret u Srbiji 1941* (Belgrade: Institut drustvenih nauka, 1963), p. 187. Glen has confirmed that W/T sets and arms (550 submachine guns) were distributed. Glen, *Footholds,* p. 56. A smaller subsidy was paid to the Independent Democratic Party, the party of Serbs from Croatia and Bosnia. Barker, *British Policy,* p. 45; Stafford, "Belgrade Coup d'État", p. 411.

42. FO 371/25033, R6186/415/92.

43. Amery, *Approach March,* pp. 175-79.

44. *Ibid.,* pp. 140-41; FO 371/25031, R5789/298/92, R7039/298/92.

The British attempted to counter the neutralist or pro-Axis bias of the Yugoslav press by founding a news agency of their own in Belgrade in early 1940. Christened *Britanova,* it aimed to place positive reports on the British war effort in the newspapers. The *South Slav Herald,* a fortnightly English-language paper published in Belgrade by the correspondent of the *Daily Mail,* Terence Atherton, was also subsidized. FO 371/25031, R298/298/92.

45. Barker, *British Policy,* p. 45.

46. Sweet-Escott, *Baker Street Irregular,* pp. 22, 52. Hanau was arrested and deported when his efforts to arrange the sabotage of the locks on the Danube below the Iron Gates became known to the Germans. The 60 year-old Masterson had acquired his credentials for special operations by his work in destroying the Romanian oilfields in World War I, oilfields he later returned to manage.

47. Amery, *Approach March,* pp. 175-79; Glen, *Footholds,* pp. 53-54.

48. The Military Attaché was Lt. Col. Charles S. Clarke; the Air Attaché, Wing Commander A. Hugh Macdonald; and the Naval Attaché, Captain Max C. Despard.

49. FO 371/25033, R6186/415/92.

50. Glen, for example, was sent to Belgrade by the Director of Naval Intelligence as Assistant Naval Attaché, but he seems to have worked for SOE once there. That MI(R)'s "Shadow Mission" was not absorbed by SOE after July 1940 is indicated by SOE's subsequent failure to claim the credit for the Air Attachés' involvement in the coup. It was Macdonald and his deputy, not SOE, who identified and maintained contact with the leaders of the putsch. On the other hand, SOE agents Amery and Glen had come to know Col. Draža Mihailović, then Chief of the Operations Bureau of the General Staff and noted for his pro-Allied sentiments and advocacy of guerrilla warfare. Amery. *Approach March,* pp. 179-80; Glen, *Footholds,* pp. 61, 125; Stafford, "Belgrade Coup d'État", pp. 412-17.

51. FO 371/25033, R6426/415/92; Barker, *British Policy,* pp. 85-86.

52. FO 371/25033, R7976/415/92.

53. Barker, *British Policy,* p. 87; Stafford, "Belgrade Coup d'État:, p. 409.

54. FO 371/30205, R131/73/92.

55. *Ibid.* CAB 65/21, WM(41)6.

56. *Ibid.*

57. CAB 65/21, WM(41)7 and WM(41)8.

58. Barker, *British Policy,* p. 87.

59. FO 371/30205, R542/73/92; FO 371/29777, R646/113/67. The Turks, of course, laid the blame on the Yugoslavs.

60. FO 371/29777, R700/113/67.

61. CAB 79/8, COS(41)21; CAB 80/25, COS(41)41.

62. CAB 79/8, COS(41)30.

63. CAB 80/25, COS(41)79; FO 371/30227, R613/343/92. The Yugoslavs' needs can be judged from the shopping list they presented to the American and British governments in late January. It included 50 gun batteries, 100 medium tanks, 100 bombers, 100 fighters, 40,000 tons of aviation spirit and 20,000 tons of petrol. CAB 80/25, COS(41)55.

64. CAB 79/8, COS(41)50; FO 371/30227, R1042/343/92. Although gratified by Donovan's support for Britain's aims in the Balkans, especially his recognition that a foothold there would prove essential when the British grew strong enough to confront the Germans on land, the Foreign Office wanted stronger American diplomatic support in the region and hoped that the U.S. might provide Yugoslavia with arms - so long as there was no corresponding reduction in what was earmarked for Britain. FO 371/29777, R1212/113/67; FO 371/29795, R1005/1003/67.

65. FO 371/30205, R589/73/92. Toynbee was the director of the FRPS, transferred during the war from Chatham House to Balliol College.

66. FO 371/30205, R1524/73/92. Asked now for his opinion, Campbell reported somewhat surprisingly that he was not aware of any great Yugoslav appetite for more territory. He thought, however, that such an offer would serve to scotch fears of a separate peace with Italy at Yugoslavia's expense. FO 371/30205, R1753/73/92.

67. CAB 65/17, WM(41)17, WM(41)18; FO 371/30222, R1230/165/92.

68. FO 371/30240, R960/960/92. The Chatham House recommendations were, in effect, a reaffirmation of the Wilson Line of 1919. All the islands of the Croatian littoral except Lošinj should on ethnographic grounds become part of Yugoslavia, but the cities of Trieste, Zadar, Gorica and Rijeka were deemed properly Italian, as was the west coast of the

Istrian peninsula. While certianly offering an improvement on the patently unfair settlement of the 1920s, a bribe on terms such as these would hardly have inspired the Croats or Slovenes with bellicosity.

69. CAB 65/21, WM(41)20; FO 371/30205; R1770/73/92.

70. CAB 65/17, WM(41)21; CAB 66/15, WP(41)45.

71. CAB 65/18, WM(41)22; FO 371/30205, R1770/73/92. No doubt nervous about possible American reaction, Cadogan advised Churchill that Washington need not be informed, there being no intention to make a definite commitment to the Yugoslavs. The issue nonetheless caused a small contretemps when Roosevelt protested to Churchill on 14 July over "the crazy story that you have promised to set up Yugoslavia again as it formerly existed and the other story that you had promised Trieste to Yugoslavia." What Roosevelt referred to as rumours were, in fact, the assiduously propagated line of the exile government and, as such, roused howls of protest from exiled Italians and Italian-Americans. Cadogan was compelled to reassure Sumner Welles, the American Under-Secretary of State, that Britain had only expressed sympathy for Yugoslav claims, that this did not constitute a firm commitment and that, in any case, there had been no mention of Trieste. F. L. Loewenheim *et al,* eds., *Roosevelt and Churchill: Their Secret Wartime Correspondence* (London: Barrie and Jenkins, 1975), pp. 149-50; FO 371/30240, R9766/960/92.

72. CAB 66/15, WP(41)39.

73. CAB 66/15, WP(41)38.

74. FO 371/29782, R4102/113/67; FO 371/30205, R1487/73/92.

75. FO 371/30205, R1480/73/92.

76. FO 371/30205, R1621/73/92.

77. FO 371/30206, R1834/73/92.

78. FO 371/29779, R2271/113/67. Unfortunately for the British, Prince Paul was no Knez Lazar, Maček no Miloš Obilić.

79. FO 371/29782, R4102/113/67.

80. CAB 65/22, WM(41)24.

81. *Ibid.*

82. CAB 65/22, WM(41)23 and WM(41)24. Cvetković, in his initially combative reaction to the German infiltration of Bulgaria, had indicated to Campbell that Yugoslavia's army would take such action. The Joint Planning Sub-Committee enthusiastically concurred that this would be the Yugoslavs' best strategy in a report to the Chiefs of Staff on 25 February. CAB 84/27, JP(41)155.

83. CAB 65/22, WM(41)25.

84. Hoptner, *Yugoslavia in Crisis,* p. 218.

85. FO 371/30206, R2069/73/92; CAB 65/22, WM(41)25.

86. FO 371/29937, R6661/168/22.

87. Hoptner, *Yugoslavia in Crisis,* pp. 219-21.

88. FO 371/29779, R2131/113/67, R2270/113/67.

89. FO 371/29779, R2133/113/67, R2158/113/67, R2169/113/67.

90. FO 371/29779, R2134/113/67, R2135/113/67, R2208/113/67.

91. FO 371/29779, R2271/113/67.

92. FO 371/29782, R4102/113/67.

93. CAB 79/9, COS(41)90 and JP(41)183.

94. FO 371/29779, R2263/113/67.

95. CAB 65/22, WR(41)28.

96. W. S. Churchill, *The Second World War: The Grand Alliance,* III (New York: Bantam Books, 1962), p. 92. Churchill's emphasis.

97. FO 371/29779, R2289/113/67; CAB 79/9, COS(41)95; CAB 65/22, WM(41)28.

98. *Ibid.*

Tupanjanin's assertion at this time that Prince Paul had decided to fight was discounted by the Foreign Office because of his vested interest in telling the British what they wanted to hear. FO 371/29779, R2274/113/67. But other signs appeared to offer confirmation: the Yugoslav central bank began to transfer its gold reserves abroad (FO 371/30216, R2351/115/92); Prince Paul told his brother-in-law, King George II of Greece, over the telephone that he would "do his duty" (CAB 65/22, WR(41)28); the Yugoslav government authorized the

British to inform the Turks of their military consultations in Athens (FO 371/29780, R2417/113/67, R2473/113/67); the British Naval Attaché in Belgrade reported a more bellicose spirit prevailing in the armed forces (FO 371/30206, R2581/73/92); and the Yugoslavs asked the British to take custody of - and to spirit away to a safe colonial dominion - the ex-strongman and potential quisling, Milan Stojadinović (FO 371/29780, R2477/113/67, R2554/113/67, R2575/113/67).

Some of these occurences could, of course, have been interpreted in an opposite fashion, as, in fact, was a simultaneous flutter over a possible Soviet-Yugoslav alliance. The Foreign Office did not like the look of that at all. FO 371/29779, R2341/113/67, R2360/113/67; FO 371/29780, R2446/113/67.

99. FO 371/29780, R2553/113/67.

100. FO 371/29780, R2490/113/67.

101. FO 371/29780, R2536/113/67, R2538/113/67, R2539/113/67. The British apparently assumed that the violation of a formal treaty would so outrage the legalistic passions of the Croats that they would be willing to fight. The Greeks gave their consent to this stratagem.

102. FO 371/29781, R2679/113/67. Cvetković told Campbell on 16 March that if only the Germans would make an impossible demand he would be ready to stage a frontier incident in Istria - where the Italians were concentrating troops and where Croat and Slovene sentiments would be automatically engaged. Cincar-Marković, however, told Campbell the same day that the Yugoslav generals did not believe it possible for the country to wage war. To counter this "retrogressing", Campbell sought and received Eden's permission to spread the word about Britain's commitment to Greece amongst "robust circles". FO 371/29780, R2540/113/67; FO 371/29781, R2577/113/67.

103. FO 371/30253, R2747/2706/92.

104. FO 371/29780, R2490/113/67.

105. Barker, *British Policy,* p. 90. If Eden did not appreciate the distinction it was not because Campbell failed to draw attention to it. FO 371/29781, R2679/113/67, R2641/113/67.

106. FO 371/29781, R2594/113/67. Shone had been Chargé d'Affaires in Belgrade between 1936 and 1939. On 19 March Eden authorized Shone to remain in Belgrade "to continue his contacts with our friends and others." FO 371/30253, R2743/2706/92.

107. Hoptner, *Yugoslavia in Crisis,* p. 226.

108. FO 371/30253, R2747/2706/92; FO 371/29779, R2271/113/67.

109. FO 371/29782, R4102/113/67.

110. FO 371/29781, R2740/113/67. More realistically, Eden anticipated that staff talks should accompany such a conference. Also indicative of the fact that war was not meant to be kept out of the Balkans for long were the answers provided to a series of Foreign Office questions by the Joint Planning Sub-Committee of the Chiefs of Staff on 20 March. The Joint Planners indicated that they wanted the belligerency of Yugoslavia and Turkey - jointly or separately - at the earliest possible moment.

111. *Ibid.;* CAB 65/22, WM(41)39; FO 371/30206, R2926/73/92.

112. FO 371/29779, R2271/113/67; FO 371/30253, R2828/2706/92.

113. Full details in Hoptner (*Yugoslavia in Crisis,* pp. 227ff.), who suggests that the perverse hope behind the Yugoslavs' stalling efforts was that Germany's invasion of the USSR (plans for which Belgrade learnt from their Military Attaché in Berlin) would take place soon enough to divert Hitler's attention from the Balkans.

Stojan Gavrilović told Campbell after the coup that the Cvetković government had conceded one point to the Germans: they agreed verbally to permit shipments of war materiel and hospital trains to pass through the country. FO 371/30253, R3184/2706/92.

114. Hoptner, *Yugoslavia in Crisis,* pp. 233-40.

115. Stafford, "Belgrade Coup d'État", p. 411; Barker, *British Policy,* p. 90; Tomasevich, *The Chetniks,* p. 39.

116. FO 371/30253, R2830/2706/92. Shone's informant was the faithful Stojan Gavrilović. The complete terms of accession

were confirmed by Campbell the next day. FO 371/30206, R2922/73/92.

117. Stafford, "Belgrade Coup d'État", p. 411; Barker, *British Policy,* pp. 91-92. Since Cvetković did not tell Campbell that the Germans had accepted his government's terms until the evening of 19 March it is uncertain what exactly triggered SOE's change of objective. Although Shone arrived on the 18th, the record of his first conversation with Prince Paul that night shows that he had not yet given up on the Prince Regent. FO 371/30253, R2776/2706/92.

118. Stafford, "Belgrade Coup d'État", p. 411.

119. Barker, *British Policy,* p. 91; Hoptner, *Yugoslavia in Crisis,* pp. 238-39.

120. Stafford, "Belgrade Coup d'État", p. 411.

121. FO 371/30253, R2854/2706/92.

122. FO 371/30253, R2834/2706/92.

123. FO 371/30253, R2855/2706/92.

124. FO 371/30253, R2853/2706/92.

125. FO 371/30253, R2871/2706/92. General Papagos anticipated Eden's concern for the attitude of Yugoslavia's Third Army commander, entering into contact with him in order to promote combined operations on the Albanian front. Papagos urged the British to do likewise - and to be ready to spend some money in the cause. General H. M. Wilson, the British commander in Greece, had qualms about suborning Yugoslav generals, fearing that such attempts would weaken the Yugoslavs' fighting capacity; but he was over-ruled by Eden and Dill and ordered to initiate contacts. FO 371/29782, R2990/113/67, R2992/113/67.

126. FO 371/30253, R2872/2706/92. The Southern Department minuted that, regarding (a), the present government had already been given such assurances and, on (b), they did not know whether or not Campbell had mentioned Istrian revisions to Prince Paul. In fact, he had. Tupanjanin also knew; while Macdonald had been authorized to make the Istrian offer known to General Simović. FO 371/29937, R6661/168/92.

127. FO 371/30206, R2922/73/92, R2924/73/92, R2925/73/92.

128. Hoptner, *Yugoslavia in Crisis,* pp. 237-40; FO 371/30265, R6495/3174/92.

129. FO 371/30206, R2925/73/92. The Southern Department was understandably perplexed about how Shone had acquired a copy of the *Daily Sketch* in Belgrade.

130. Hoptner, *Yugoslavia in Crisis,* p. 240.

131. FO 371/30253, R2854/2706/92.

132. FO 371/30253, R2896/2706/92.

133. FO 371/30253, R2916/2706/92.

134. Barker, *British Policy,* p. 92. "G." was Gladwyn Jebb, seconded to MEW from the Foreign Office and serving as Dalton's chief of staff.

135. FO 371/30253, R2896/2706/92.

136. FO 371/30253, R2916/2706/92. This quotes a summary given in a minute by Nichols. Such a telegram may have supplemented the wire referred to by Dalton, or it may have represented the final version of the same message.

137. Dilks, *The Diaries of Sir Alexander Cadogan,* p. 365. Although the proposal was considered by SOE in Belgrade, it was rejected for fear of imperilling the chances of a coup by provoking an untimely imposition of martial law. Stafford, "Belgrade Coup d'État", p. 412.

138. FO 371/30253, R2916/2706/92.

139. FO 371/33490, R4518/1990/92. Campbell made these points in a letter to Sargent from Washington in July 1942.

140. FO 371/30253, R2987/2706/92. In a following telegram Campbell listed Yugoslavia's immediate needs: 100 anti-tank guns, 54 batteries of anti-air-craft guns, 100 medium tanks, 100 three-ton lorries, 2000 machine guns, 20,000 tons of petrol, etc. FO 371/30253, R2988/2706/92. After the coup d'état Lord Hankey's Committee considered supplies for Yugoslavia and decided that the only offer Britain could make was for 75 75mm guns and 50 155mm guns (to be subtracted from Lend-Lease allocations and delivered in three months). FO 371/30227, R3261/343/92.

141. FO 371/30253, R2987/2706/92.

142. FO 371/30207, R3131/73/92.

143. FO 371/30253, R3032/2706/92.

144. FO 371/30253, R3071/2706/92.

145. Tomasevich (*The Chetniks,* pp. 43-47) summarizes the evidence and cites the relevant literature, including Simović's posthumous memoirs and various depositions by Mirković. SOE - for its own reasons and because of its peripheral perspective - sought after the coup to magnify the role of Radoje Knežević (the "brains" behind the operation) and Trifunović-Birčanin (SOE's one ally amongst the principals). Stafford, "Belgrade Coup d'État, p. 412.

146. Hoptner, *Yugoslavia in Crisis,* pp. 256-57.

147. FO 371/30253, R3071/2706/92.

148. Tomasevich, *The Chetniks,* p. 45; Stafford, "Belgrade Coup d'État", pp. 415-16. T. G. Mapplebeck was a long-time resident of Belgrade, where he had an insurance agency and served as representative of Hawker Aircraft and Rolls Royce. Taken on by Macdonald as Assistant Air Attaché in 1940, Mapplebeck was already assumed locally to be an intelligence agent. Mirković was to claim in 1942 that he too had been a British agent, but his claim is rendered suspect by the fact that he saw fit to make it in the midst of the bitter Cairo Affair. (See Chapter IV.) Campbell discounted Mirković's story. FO 371/33490, R4518/1990/92; Barker, *British Policy,* p. 92.

149. Churchill, *Grand Alliance,* p. 135.

150. FO 371/29803, R7844/3552/67.

151. FO 371/30253, R2962/2706/92, R3032/2706/92.

152. FO 371/30207, R3140/73/92; FO 371/29782, R3072/113/67; CAB 79/10, COS(41)111. Invested seems right: it was felt that the best inducements which could be offered the Yugoslav general to keep his troops mobilized and ready to cooperate with Gen. Wilson were financial.

153. For blow by blow accounts of the coup in English see Hoptner (*Yugoslavia in Crisis*) and Ristić (*Yugoslavia's Revolution of 1941*), a participant's effort to prove Simović responsible. The standard Yugoslav account is Ferdo Čulinović, *Dvadeset sedmi mart* (Zagreb: Jugoslavenska akademija znanosti i umjetnosti, 1965).

154. Stafford, "Belgrade Coup d'État", p. 417.

155. CAB 65/18, WM(41)32.

156. CAB 69/2, DO(41)10. Though undeserved, the accolade was certainly welcome to SOE. Dalton did his best to capitalize on what he referred to as "my Jug achievement." Stafford, "Belgrade Coup d'État", pp. 417-18. For his part, Eden did not neglect to offer congratulations to Campbell for his role in "this most happy turn of events". FO 371/30207, R3133/73/92.

157. *New York Times*, 28/3/41, p. 8.

158. CAB 65/18, WM(41)32. There was in fact no question of recognition since the King gave the coup his blessing, in return for which he was declared to have come of age.

159. FO 371/29782, R3341/113/67.

160. FO 371/30207, R3137/73/92. Eden was shocked to discover that the army was not already mobilized. Anthony Eden, *The Reckoning* (Boston: Houghton Mifflin, 1965), p. 269. Even now the Yugoslavs did not mobilize; rather they accelerated Cvetković's policy of activating reserves. Tomasevich, *The Chetniks*, p. 51.

161. FO 371/30207, R3183/73/92.

162. Among these was not any delay in Hitler's invasion of Russia. This legend has been convincingly exploded by Van Creveld, *Hitler's Strategy*.

163. FO 371/30208, R3387/73/92.

164. FO 371/30225, R3170/297/92. Campbell was probably thinking primarily of Momcilo Ninčić, the elderly, half-deaf and disagreeable Foreign Minister.

165. FO 371/30207, R3110/73/92, R3111/73/92, R3112/73/92.

166. FO 371/29782, R3203/113/67; FO 371/30208, R3305/73/92. The Foreign Office grew sufficiently worried by Maček's week-long delay in joining the government that a broadcast appeal to the Croats which would affirm Britain's intention to see they got Istria after the war was contemplated. FO 371/30208, R3301/73/92, R3494/73/92; FO 371/30225, R3377/297/92.

167. FO 371/30207, R3229/73/92.

168. FO 371/30207, R3235/73/92.

169. FO 371/30208, R3286/73/92.

170. Simović had already advised Ninčić that they must

avoid showing any pro-British sympathies, should undertake to protect the Germans' flank in Bulgaria and the Italians' rear in Albania and ought to occupy Salonika so as to prevent the establishment there of anti-German forces. Tomasevich, *The Chetniks,* p. 51; Barker, *British Policy,* p. 104.

171. FO 371/30207, R3143/73/92, R3186/73/92; CAB 79/10, COS(41)125. The suggestion that King Peter needed a British mentor came from King George II. He reported that King Peter was very young for his 17 years. The officer eventually selected for Simović was the ill-starred General Carton de Wiart, whose similar liaison roles in Poland and Norway hardly inspired confidence. CAB 79/10, COS(41)128; FO 371/30209, R3662/73/92.

172. CAB 79/10, COS(41)114.

173. FO 371/29782, R4102/113/67. The Yugoslavs reneged too on their undertaking to send their Acting Army Chief of Staff, General Milutin Nikolić, and refused to consider Dill's request that they send War Minister Bogoljub Ilić. Instead they proposed to be represented by their Director of Military Operations, General Radivoje Janković.

Simović's state of mind during the much interrupted talks was illustrated by his statement that although a visit by Eden to Belgrade now would provoke the Germans and split his government, the Foreign Secretary might come in two to three months' time! Meanwhile he was determined to keep even Dill's visit secret from his ministers.

Simović did not expect to escape war; in fact he envisaged that Germany would strike at Yugoslavia before Greece. But he believed that Hitler was unprepared for an immediate offensive. (Dill attempted to use this conviction to persuade him to attack Albania immediately.) Given subsequent Serb attribution of their defeat to a Croat stab in the back, it is interesting that Simović recognized that the main thrust of Germany's invasion would come from Bulgaria.

174. FO 371/30208, R3355/73/92.

175. FO 371/29782, R4102/113/67.

176. FO 371/30208, R3387/73/92, R3388/73/92, R3408/73/92, R3465/73/92, R3496/73/92. These reports - many of

which originated with Macdonald - were initially disbelieved, thus adding to London's suspicions of its Air Attaché. When Campbell offered confirmation the Foreign Office was forced to conclude that it was the Simović government, no Macdonald, that was politically naive. Of the Yugoslavs' efforts to find surcease, only that aimed at the Soviets showed promise. A friendship treaty was signed during the night of 5 April in Moscow. It was soon repudiated.

177. FO 371/30208, R3520/73/92.

178. FO 371/30208, R3539/73/92. Simović id not dismiss British warnings only. The Yugoslav Military Attaché in Berlin provided on 2 April forewarning that the attack would begin on 6 April. Hoptner, *Yugoslavia in Crisis,* pp. 281-82.

179. FO 371/30208, R3529/73/92.

180. FO 371/30209, R3746/73/92.

181. FO 371/30208, R3528/73/92.

182. For the best recent account of the April War see Tomasevich, *The Chetniks,* Chapter III. For the partition of the country, the organization of the occupation regimes and their impact on resistance and fratricidal strife see *Ibid.,* Chapter IV: Matteo J. Milazzo, *The Chetnik Movement and the Yugoslav Resistance* (Baltimore: Johns Hopkins University Press, 1975), an abbreviated version of the doctoral dissertation cited subsequently; and Petar Brajović, *et al, Les Systèms d'Occupation en Yougoslavie 1941-1945* (Belgrade: L'Institut pour l'Étude du Mouvement Ouvrier, 1963).

183. The first victim of Britain's unrequited love was Prince Paul. He and his family (carrying some of their favourite pictures) were allowed to leave Yugoslavia for Greece on the morrow of the coup. Once there the Prince asked to see Eden, who snubbed him - much to Churchill's delight. His request to settle in England was also rejected and he was shipped to Kenya as a virtual prisoner of war. As Churchill minuted on 14 April, "The sooner Palsy is interned and out of the way the better". The whole sorry episode is recorded in FO 371/30255.

184. FO 371/30269, R3840/339/92; CAB 69/2, DO(41)13. My emphasis.

185. FO 371/30209, R3964/73/92. A Sunderland flying boat was sent to Kotor to pick up those Yugoslav, Czech and Polish refugees most compromised by their association with the British. A submarine was also sent, but it arrived after the Italians and, more importantly, after the *Luftwaffe*. Glen, *Footholds*, pp. 70-74.

186. FO 371/30213, R3466/114/92. Taylor reported from Belgrade on 31 March on the post-coup prospects for SOE. Radio stations were being established in Sušak (Rijeka), Ljubljana, Maribor, Belgrade, Sarajevo, Niš and Skopje. SOE's principal targets for demolition were the Danube locks, the bridges over the Danube and Sava at Belgrade and over the Drava at Maribor and the road and rail links between Niš and Caribrod (Dimitrovgrad) and Veles and the Greek frontier. Other details in Sweet-Escott, *Baker Street Irregular*, pp. 63-64.

187. FO 371/30209, R3534/73/92.

NOTES

CHAPTER III

1. Michael Howard, *The Mediterranean Strategy in the Second World War* (London: Weidenfeld and Nicolson, 1968), p. 11.

2. *Ibid.*, pp. 12-13; David Stafford, "The Detonator Concept: British Strategy, SOE and European Resistance after the Fall of France", *Contemporary History*, 2 (April 1975), pp. 185-217.

3. The Yugoslav government issued a proclamation on 17 April following the first cabinet meeting in exile which asserted that the country's eventual liberation depended upon the Allies. The government did not consider further armed struggle. Casting the blame for the recent rout on the Croats assumed a higher priority. Dušan Plenča, *Medjunarodni odnosi Jugoslavije u toku Drugog svjetskog rata* (Belgrade: Institut društvenih nauka, 1962), pp. 10-11.

4. FO 371/30291, R7374/4906/92.

5. Jovan Djonović, "Veze s Dražom Mihailovićem sa Srednjeg i Bliskog Istoka i Severne Afrike", *Glasnik Srpskog istorisko-kulturnog društva 'Njegoš'* (Chicago), 1 (July 1958), p. 41. Cited hereafter as *Glasnik.*

6. Marjanović, *Ustanak,* pp. 77-78; Plenča, *Medjunarodni odnosi,* p. 79.

7. Djonović, "Veze s Dražom Mihailovićem", pp. 43-44.

8. Marjanović, *Ustanak,* p. 195.

9. Djonović, "veze s Dražom Mihailovićem", pp. 43-44; Amery, *Approach March,* p. 244. In his acount of the Rakić episode Djonović omits to mention that Mihailović's emissary came in search of contacts with the British, not with the Yugoslav government. He also states incorrectly that the sum sent to Mihailović was 1 million dinars. Finally, the assertion that Mihailović disposed of 100,000 armed men in August 1941 is absurd. He could not have had more than one twentieth that number.

10. John Ehrman, *Grand Strategy,* Vol. 5 (London: HMSO, 1956), p. 77.

11. FO 371/30291, R7641/162/92.

12. FO 371/30214, R7294/114/92; FO 371/30215, R7791/114/92.

13. Marjanović, *Ustanak,* p. 195; Mihailo Marić, *Kralj i vlada u emigraciji* (Zagreb: Epoha, 1966), p. 139.

14. Marjanović, *Ustanak,* p. 195.

15. FO 371/30219, R7968/162/92; Barker, *British Policy,* pp. 157-58. SOE's old friend Trifunović-Birčanin was leader of the Serb nationalists in the Split area.

16. Deakin, *The Embattled Mountain,* p. 126. Churchill apparently interested himself in the Yugoslav revolt after some prompting from Leo Amery. Amery had been urged to intervene by his son, who had been frustrated in his attempts to have a positive decision taken in Cairo on the question of mounting a mission to Mihailović. Amery, *Approach March,* pp. 244-46.

17. Deakin, *The Embattled Mountain,* p. 126.

18. Amery, *Approach March,* pp. 246-49; Milovan Djilas, *Wartime* (London: Secker & Warburg, 1977), p. 68.

19. Deakin, *The Embattled Mountain,* pp. 128-29. Deakin maintains that Hudson was selected to go to Yugoslavia a scant 12 hours before the mission's departure from Egypt, the original intention having been to mount an entirely Yugoslav operation. Hudson, he says, left Cairo never having heard of Mihailović. However, while on Malta, Mihailović's radio operators succeeded in making contact with the British on the island on 14 September, and thus Hudson was appraised of his existence. This does not square with Amery's account of his own participation in the selection, briefing and shepherding of the mission to the Montenegrin beach on which it landed. Amery was certainly aware of Mihailović and, according to him, the whole purpose of the operation was to make contact with Mihailović. Amery, *Approach March,* pp. 244-54 and *passim;* Ante Smith Pavelić, "Britanci i Draža Mihajlović", *Hrvatska revija* (Buenos Aires), VII (1957), p. 236.

20. Deakin, *The Embattled Mountain,* pp. 129-30.

21. Ostojić (who had played a prominent part in the coup d'état) was to become Mihailović's principal deputy. Lalatović (who had helped in the government's evacuation from Nikšić) was to become the chief of Mihailović's operations staff. Hudson thought them an improvement over the original Ravna Gora staff. Later many attempts were made to shore-up Mihailović's command structure by sending in other staff officers. One of them, Nedjeljko Plećaš, has described Lalatović's unfavourable reaction to the instructions given to him and Ostojić by General Ilić prior to their departure from Cairo. They were told to find and kill a certain colonel and to strive to raise the reputation of the exile government and to prepare the people to welcome it back. They considered this part of their assignment an insult given the country's manifold sufferings. Nedjeljko B. Plećaš, "S mora i iz vazduha u porobljenu Otadžbinu", *Glasnik,* 4 (June 1960), pp. 36-37; Deakin, *The Embattled Mountain,* p. 128; Djilas, *Wartime,* pp. 68-72.

22. WO 202/128, tels. 1-24, pp. 118-21.

23. Deakin, *The Embattled Mountain,* pp. 130-31; Plećaš, "S mora i iz vazduha", p. 38.

24. WO 202/128, tel. 25, p. 118. Deakin gives a slightly different version of this telegram and attributes it to Hudson. Both its text and timing lead me to believe that it originated with Lalatović. Deakin, *The Embattled Mountain,* p. 131.

25. For biographies of Mihailović see: Miodrag Al. Purković, "Dragoljub Mihailović: Kratka biografija", *Knjiga o Draži,* ed. R. L. Knežević (2 vols.; Windsor: Srpska narodna odbrana, 1956), I, pp. 1-5; and Lucien Karchmar, "Draža Mihailović and the Rise of the Četnik Movement, 1941-1942" (unpublished Stanford University Ph.d. dissertation, 1973), pp. 69-75.

26. Radoje L. Knežević, "Počeci pokreta otpora", *Knjiga o Draži,* I, pp. 7-14; Matteo Joseph Milazzo, "The Chetnik *Tito's Rise to Power* (London: Cresset Press, 1949); Vladimir of Michigan Ph.D. dissertation, 1971), pp. 24-27; Tomasevich, *The Chetniks,* p. 124.

27. Pavle Mešković, "Od Bosne do Ravne Gore", *Knjiga o Draži,* I, pp. 31-32.

28. Milazzo, "The Chetnik Movement", pp. 30-31.

29. Mešković, *Knjiga o Draži,* I, pp. 31-32.

30. Marjanović, *Ustanak,* pp. 187-89; Vladimir Dedijer *et al, Istorija Jugoslavije* (2nd ed; Belgrade: Prosveta, 1973), pp. 472-73; Tomasevich, *The Chetniks,* Chapter VI.

31. Marjanović, *Ustanak,* pp. 74-75. For a history of the Četnik movement and its ideology see Tomasevich, *The Chetniks,* Chapter V. It was the appearance of the communist-led Partisans that caused Pećanac to abandon any ideas he may have had about offering resistance.

32. Mihailović initially preferred the appellation Ravna Gora Movement. After receiving his government's recognition, however, he styled his forces the Yugoslav Army in the Fatherland.

33. Milazzo, "The Chetnik Movement", p. 34.

34. According to Sir Alexander Glen, Amery had made an effort to learn something of the communist students at Belgrade University in the months before the coup d'état. Glen, *Footholds,* p. 56.

35. There are several biographies of Tito in English. The most important are: Phyllis Auty, *Tito* (London: Longman,

1970); Stephen Clissold, *Whirlwind: An Account of Marshal tito's Rise to Power* (London: Cresset Press, 1949); Vladimir Dedijer, *Tito Speaks* (London: Weidenfeld and Nicolson, 1953); and Fitzroy Maclean, *Disputed Barricade* (London: Jonathan Cape, 1957).

36. Pero Morača contends in his study of KPJ-Comintern relations that from 1938 onwards the Yugoslav Party was able to free itself more and more from direct Comintern control. By concentrating on Yugoslav affairs, the Party sought to gloss over the Hitler-Stalin pact and to maintain a "patriotic" stance. Pero Morača, "Odnosi izmedju Komunističke partije Jugoslavije i Kominterne od 1941 do 1943 godine", *Jugoslovenski istorjiski časopis,* 1-2, (1969), pp. 94-95.

37. Djilas, *Wartime,* p. 4.

38. Dedijer, *Istorija Jugoslavije,* p. 474.

39. The KPJ was not without problems. In one recorded instance a local Party committee in Serbia urged the faithful to support the newly imposed German occupation, reasoning that Hitler and Stalin were still allies. Once the uprising began, the Party had trouble restraining its zealots - those prone to *levačenje* and *sektaštvo,* i.e. left sectarianism. Nationalistic inclinations were also manifest in the Party, especially among Croats, while in Macedonia much of the Party's leadership went over initially to the Bulgarian Party. Marjanović, *Ustanak,* pp. 49, 113-15.

40. Dedijer, *Istorija Jugoslavije,* p. 477.

41. Josip Broz Tito, *Political Report ofthe Central Committee of CPY; Political Report Delivered at the Fifth Congress of the CPY* (Belgrade: 1948), pp. 51-52.

42. Djilas, *Wartime,* pp. 4-8. Even the term Partisan - a Russian borrowing - came later.

43. Marjanović, *Ustanak,* p. 110.

44. Dedijer, *Istorija Jugoslavije,* pp. 478-79; Marjanović, *Ustanak,* pp. 83-85.

45. Djilas, *Wartime,* pp. 22-25.

46. Dedijer, *Istorija Jugoslavije,* p. 479.

47. Marjanović, *Ustanak,* p. 86.

48. *Ibid.,* pp. 85-86.

49. *Ibid.*, pp. 97-98, 110. There were in August approximately 2,000 Party members in Serbia, plus 9,500 members of the youth organization, SKOJ.

50. Walter R. Roberts, *Tito, Mihailović and the Allies, 1941-1945* (New Brunswick: Rutgers University Press, 1973), p. 25.

51. Dedijer, *Istorija Jugoslavije,* p. 487; Marjanović, *Ustanak,* pp. 215-17.

52. *Ibid.*, pp. 127-28; Mešković, *Knjiga o Drazi,* I, pp. 60-62. Mihailović's reference to Pećanac and the Toplica rising against the Bulgarians was ironic. Pećanac was sent to Toplica by the Serbian High Command in order to counsel against a premature uprising. He did so, but was eventually swept along by the popular demand for action. Successful at first, the revolt was later put down with great brutality. In the inter-war years Pećanac parleyed his supposed leading role into a national reputation and leadership of the Četnik Association. The irony was that Mihailović was destined to play an analogous role himself. Tomasevich, *The Chetniks,* pp. 117-19.

53. Hudson emphasized these points in a report submitted to Churchill in the spring of 1944. The communists, he contended, had organized the country for revolt in 1941. Mihailović "was drawn into 'it' by popular feeling coincident with the withdrawal of German troops from Serbia, by a desire to destroy the temporary communist hold on the people, and by the need to divert to himself Allied moral and material support". He therefore exchanged, albeit temporarily, his chosen role as protector of Serbian non-combatants for that of resistance leader. FO 371/44254, R6490/8/92.

54. Milazzo, "The Chetnik Movement", p. 50.

55. Marjanović, *Ustanak,* pp. 208-09.

56. Milazzo, "The Chetnik Movement", pp. 48-49. Djilas, from his vantage point in Montenegro, perceived the Četniks as being more numerous than the Partisans in Serbia at this time. Djilas, *Wartime,* p. 72.

57. Marjanović, *Ustanak,* p. 200.

58. *Ibid.*, pp. 225-26.

59. *Ibid.*, p. 227. Mihailović apparently formed the impression that Tito, whose accent was unfamiliar to him, was a Russian.

He thus spoke candidly of the need to settle accounts with the Croats for their part in the April defeat and the Ustaše massacres.

60. Together the Partisans and the Četniks controlled some 4,500 square miles of mountainous territory in west and central Serbia by the beginning of October. Karchmar, "Draža Mihailović and the Rise of the Četnik Movement", p. 222.

61. Milazzo, "The Cetnik Movement", pp. 34-35, 50. Mihailović's own force then numbered about 1200 men. The total strength of his movement was something under 5000.

62. *Ibid.*, p. 53. Both because they knew far less about the Partisans and because of their traditional respect for the Serbian officer corps, the Germans at this time credited Mihailović with leadership of the entire revolt. This made it more difficult for Mihailović when he subsequently attempted to form an anti-communist alliance with them. Local German commanders and Foreign Office representatives were sometimes willing, but Berlin insisted that there could be no truck with the Serb nationalists.

63. Deakin, *The Embattled Mountain,* pp. 131-34. The last telegram from Montenegro to appear in the register now in the PRO refers to reception arrangements in Radovče for an expected air sortie. It was received in Malta and London on 22 October. Lalatović and Dragićević left for Serbia at about this time. WO 202/128, tel. 31, p. 117.

64. Deakin, *The Embattled Mountain,* pp. 134-35.

65. Josip Broz Tito, *Selected Military Works* (Belgrade: Vojnoizdavački zavod, 1966), p. 82. The journalist mentioned by Hudson was probably Ray Brock, former *New York Times* correspondent in Belgrade. He had cultivated Četnik contacts before the April War and his subsequent despatches from Turkey played a large part in creating the Mihailović legend in the Western press.

66. Deakin, *The Embattled Mountain,* pp. 136-37.

67. Jakša V. Djelević, "Iz prvih meseca," *Knjiga of Draži,* I, p. 185.

68. Albert B. Seitz, *Mihailović - Hoax or Hero?* (Columbus: Leigh House, 1953), p. 12.

69. There is disagreement regarding the orders which the British may have sent to Mihailović either shortly after the establishment of radio links in mid-September or via Hudson in October. At his 1946 trial Mihailović testified that Hudson arrived on Ravna Gora bearing instructions "that in Yugoslavia a rebellion would not be tolerated, but that the struggle should be waged for Yugoslavia and not become a struggle of the communists for the Soviet Union". *The Trial of Dragoljub-Draža Mihailović* (Belgrade: Union of Journalists' Associations, 1946), pp. 123-24.

Mihailović's then adjutant remembered the orders supposedly conveyed by Hudson rather differently: "Hudson brought with him a message that Yugoslavs must fight for their own freedom and not for the aims of the Soviets or the English; he demanded stepped-up activity and close cooperation with the Partisans if they accepted Mihailovic's command." Djelević, *Knjiga o Draži,* I, p. 185.

In that both these versions refer to a British admonition that the struggle be waged by Yugoslavs for Yugoslavia, they resemble orders sent from London on 16 November. (See below.) In other respects, of course, they are contradictory. Mihailović's version seems to correspond with the advice to remain peaceful and unprovocative sent from Istanbul in August; while Djelević's version lends support to suggestions by at least two historians (Marjanović and Karchmar) that the British radioed instructions to Mihailović in early October that he should intensify his anti-Axis activity. Both ascribe this supposed change in British policy to Russian pressure that something be done to ease the situation on the eastern front. As will be described below, consultation had already taken place between the British and Soviet secret services on the Yugoslav uprising. It is likewise known that Stalin appealed to Churchill in September for the opening of a second front-either in France or the Balkans - before the end of the year. Although ordering Mihailović into action would have been one of the few possible responses of the British at the time, it cannot be established whether or not this was done.

According to Marjanović, Mihailović responded to the alleged instructions by simply ascribing to himself the actions and victories of the Partisans. Any change was merely cosmetic. Karchmar, on the other hand, maintains that despite being "horrified by this directive, which was so contrary to all his ideas . . . he carried it out." His commanders were thus "flabbergasted" to receive orders on or about 10 October that they should regard the Partisans as allies and cooperate to the fullest extent with them. Whether cosmetic or real, Mihailović's instructions to his commanders can just as easily be explained as a response to the Partisans' successes as to orders from outside. It is a matter for doubt, too, whether the British would have considered their radio links with Mihailović secure enough to transmit such a message prior to Hudson's arrival with safe ciphers. But whatever the truth of the contention that the British ordered Mihailović into action in October, it is certain that by November both SOE and the Foreign Office had adopted a more aggressive view of the uprising - and that this owed something to Russian prompting. The British were to attempt to turn this responsiveness to good account when they appealed to the Russians in late November to promote resistance unity under Mihailović. Jovan Marjanović, "Prilozi istoriji sukoba Narodnooslobodilačkog pokreta i četnika Daže Mihailovića u Srbiji 1941 godine", *Istorija XX veka: Zbornik radova,* I (Belgrade: Institut društvenih nauka, 1959), pp. 199-200; Karchmar, "Draža Mihailović and the Rise of the Četnik Movement", pp. 220-21.

70. In a telegram sent on 10 October Simović had informed Mihailović, "I agree completely with your work and am taking all measures to provide you with necessary help." Vojmir Kljaković, "Velika Britanija, Sovjetski Savez i ustanak u Jugoslaviji 1941 godine", *Vojnoistorijski glasnik,* 2 (May-August 1970), p. 74.

71. *Ibid.,* pp. 77-78.

72. Many years later Tito told Phyllis Auty that he had offered Mihailović supreme command of the revolt. In the same

year (1968) he told *Paris Match* that he had suggested to Mihailović that he join the Partisan command as chief of staff. The latter version seems more creditable. It remains unclear, however, whether the offer was made at the first meeting between the two men (at Struganik) or later at Brajići. Tomasevich places it at Brajići, Auty and Karchmar at Struganik. The fact that London became aware of the offer in early October indicates that it was certainly made at Struganik, even if later repeated. Auty, *Tito,* pp. 186, 191; Deakin, *The Embattled Mountain,* p. 137; Karchmar, "Draža Mihailović and the Rise of the Četnik Movement", pp. 206-07, 321; Tomasevich, *The Chetniks,* p. 147.

73. Auty, *Tito,* pp. 189-91; Djelević, *Knjiga o Draži,* I, pp. 186-87; Karchmar, "Draža Mihailović and the Rise of the Četnik Movement", pp. 238-40; Marjanović, *Ustanak,* pp. 314-19; Milazzo, "The Chetnik Movement", pp. 59-60.

74. Tomasevich, *The Chetniks,* p. 148.

75. WO 202/128, tel. 118, p. 123. Hudson reported that he had arrived at National Liberation Front headquarters in Užice on 23 October but had moved on to Ravna Gora on 25 October. His telegram was presumably sent on Mihailović's W/T set and perhaps, given its location in the register, in Mihailović's cipher as well.

76. Milazzo, "The Chetnik Movement", p. 60.

77. WO 202/128, tel. received 28/10/41, p. 123.

78. *The Četniks* (Allied Forces Headquarters, Mediterranean Theatre of War, 1944), p. 11.

79. Deakin, *The Embattled Mountain,* p. 140; Christie Lawrence, *Irregular Adventure* (London: Faber and Faber, 1947), pp. 227-28, 230.

80. Djelević, *Knjiga o Draži,* I, p. 187. This plane brought Mihailović 20 machine guns, 10,000 rounds of ammunition, 600 hand grenades, $4556 and £181. Kljaković, "Britanija, Sovjetski Savez i ustanak", p. 83. The Četniks' real needs can be judged by the requests which Mihailović had already put to the Germans. (See below.)

81. FO 371/37584, R3994/2/92.

82. Regarding the bombing proposal, Sargent minuted that it was "typical of the muddled thinking for which General

Simović is becoming famous". FO 371/30220, R9010/162/92.

Djonović (in a telegram to London on 26 September) put the death toll at a scarifying 340,000. His source of information was Dr. Miloš Sekulić, who had lately arrived in Istanbul. Djonović began to urge Simović to expel the Croat ministers from the government. SSIP, MIPKJ, F-3 1941, tel. 485. (See below and Chapter IV.)

83. See note 72 above. This lends credence to Tito's claim that he offered Mihailović a commanding role in the revolt. It was, of course, natural for the exile government to promote Mihailović as the strongest and most unifying element in the resistance.

84. FO 371/30220, R9010/162/92. Djonović also reported that the leader of the communist forces in the Šabac area was the former Counsellor of the Soviet Legation in Belgrade, Lebedev. (See note 96 below.)

85. Marjanović, *Ustanak,* p. 248.

86. Five telegrams were attached to the note. They represented the first few received from both Ravna Gora and Montenegro. The former announced the continued existence of the Yugoslav army in the hills, asked for arms with which to continue the struggle, described the progress of the revolt and gave news of the Ustaše massacres of Serbs. In one telegram, dated 10 October, Mihailović appealed again for help: "We are fighting on all sides. The respectability of the government urgently demands necessary support asked for." CAB 80/31, COS(41)626; Deakin, *The Embattled Mountain,* p. 82.

87. CAB 79/15, COS(41)353.

88. CAB 79/15, COS(41)354.

89. *Ibid.*

90. CAB 79/15, COS(41)363.

91. FO 371/30220, R9331/162/92.

92. *Ibid.*

93. Djonović, "Veze s Dražom Mihailovićem," p. 45; Amery, *Approach March,* pp. 259-60.

94. Kljaković, "Britanija, Sovjetski Savez i ustanak", p. 70.

95. Djonović gives a figure of 1 million dinars. SOE, in the memorandum cited here, put it at 5 million dinars. And Dalton,

in his letter to Churchill, said £20,000. At 1941 official rates of exchange - 200 dinars to the pound - £20,000 would equal 4 million dinars. Since the money was apparently obtained on the Istanbul free market, it is reasonable to assume that 5 million dinars could have been realized from £20,000. Why Djonović, who actually handed the money over to Rakić (and accuses him of creaming off a 100,000 dinar carrying charge), should get the figure wrong is difficult to understand.

96. FO 371/30220, R9505/162/92. V. Z. Lebedev had been Commercial Secretary in the Soviet Legation in Belgrade prior to the April War and was afterwards posted in Sofia. (Deakin, *The Embattled Mountain,* p. 203.) Mention of him as leader of the communist resistance first occurs in the report sent by Djonović to his government in late September and passed on to the Foreign Office by Simovic on 3 October. (See note 84.) He also figures as the communist leader in the Bajloni report received in early November. (See below.) Maisky subsequently informed Eden that Lebedev was not in Yugoslavia, but in Kubibyshev, temporary headquarters of the Soviet Foreign Ministry. FO 371/30220, R9797/162/92.

97. FO 371/30220, R9584/162/92. The Yugoslav government first commended to Mihailović directly the need to await the proper moment for revolt on 18 October. On 28 October Simović wired, "wait and advise everyone of the need for patience and restraint from rash action in order to escape losses. Do not expose yourselves now, but await the order from here for action." General prescriptions of this nature had, of course, been broadcast to the homeland by the government throughout the summer. Kljaković, "Britanija, Sovjetski Savez i ustanak", p. 74.

98. FO 371/30220, R9584/162/92. Although relieved that Simović was now more bellicose in spirit, the Foreign Office felt that his views remained unstable. In this entusiasm for resistance he now seemed to take it for granted that there would be an early British landing on the Adriatic.

99. FO 371/30220, R9436/162/92, R9417/162/92.

100. CAB 65/19, WM(41)107.

101. CAB 69/3, DO(41)24.

102. FO 371/30220, R9520/162/92, R9687/162/92.

103. FO 371/30220, R9506/162/92.

104. CAB 69/3, DO(41)26.

105. CAB 79/55, COS(41)35(0); FO 371/30220, R9547/162/92.

106. FO 371/30220, R9584/162/92.

107. FO 371/30220, R9652/162/92.

108. FO 371/30220, R9715/162/92.

109. Marjanović, *Ustanak,* p. 185; Radoje L. Knežević, "Jugoslovenska vlada i Draža Mihailović", *Poruka* (London), 8 (1 November 1952), pp. 7-8; FO 371/30220, R9797/162/92. The Bajloni report originated with Mihailović. Although suspicious of the reasons behind the Bajlonis' attribution of all resistance to the communists (the family was regarded as pro-Italian), the Foreign Office felt that their report confirmed information received from other sources.

110. Marjanović, *Ustanak,* p. 186.

111. SSIP, MIPKJ, F-1, 1941, tel. Istanbul to London, no. 6734, 29/9/41.

112. FO 371/30220, R9174/162/92, R 9244/162/92. The gist of the Orthodox Church report - which alleged that 180,000 Serbs had been killed in Croatia between April and August - was sent by telegraph from Istanbul, reaching London on 3 October. Sekulić and his information on the resistance did not reach England until a month later. King Peter presented Churchill with a summary of the Church report when he saw him on 13 October. Eden had been sent a copy by Simović on 9 October. In a covering letter Simović estimated that the death toll had then reached 300,000. The Foreign Office was understandably concerned by the deleterious effect the report was likely to have on Serbo-Croat relations inside the government. Serbs saw in the report and its successors evidence that their nation was threatened with literal annihilation. They found it intolerable that their Croat colleagues refused either to credit the reports or to condemn the killings. The Croats feared that to do either to the satisfaction of the Serbs would be to accept national responsibility. By mid-October the alleged death toll had risen to 1,500,000. SSIP,

MIPKJ, F-1, 1941, tel. Ankara to London, no. 138, 30/10/41.

113. FO 371/30221, R10232/162/92.

114. Kljaković, "Britanija, Sovjetski Savez i ustanak", pp. 78-79.

115. See note 80. While the fight went well Mihailović did not inform the outside world about it. But by 4 November he was again appealing for aid - and in desperate terms. On 7 November, when his headquarters was surrounded by the Partisans, he radioed that help must come "now or never." *Ibid.*, p. 82; Marjanović, *Ustanak,* p. 356.

116. Milazzo, "the Chetnik Movement", pp. 63-70; Roberts, *Tito, Mihailović and the Allies,* pp. 34-35; Marjanović, *Ustanak,* pp. 353-54; Jovan Marjanović, ed., *The Collaboration of D. Mihailović's Chetniks with the Enemy Forces of Occupation, 1941-1944* (Belgrade: Arhivski pregled, 1976), pp. 13-27.

Roberts maintains that the initiative for these talks came from the German side: Matl was pursuing his government's policy of dividing the forces of resistance. Milazzo and the published documents, however, are clear that it was Mihailović who sought out the Germans. This is more logical given the pressures to which Mihailović was then subject, and the ultimatum with which he was presented at Divci. Had the Germans simply wished to divide the Četniks and Partisans they would hardly have demanded Mihailović's surrender. This had the opposite effect of forcing him to renew peace talks with Tito.

Addressing his escort just before the start of the Divci meeting, Mihailović is reported to have declared, "I have decided to sacrifice myself for the common good and to try to secure the means for the struggle against the communists and to put an end to [German] punitive expeditions . . ." Kljaković, "Britanija, Sovjetski Savez i ustanak", p. 83.

117. FO 371/30220, R9873/162/92. Mihailović's telegram was dated 10 November, the day before the Divci meeting. In the version of this telegram quoted by Marjanović (*Ustanak,* pp. 358-59) and Deakin (*The Embattled Mountain,* pp. 139-40) the text reads "Germans" where Simović wrote "Nedić". Even

if the exile government had judged it politic to bowdlerize Hudson's views of Četnik proclivities, then SIS (which still handled SOE's communications) would have been in a position to point this out. It should be noted that it is often difficult to tell from surviving paraphrased versions whether Mihailović or Hudson was the author of a given message, or whether they represent - as in this case - amalgamations. Unfortunately, only the first paragraph of this telegram appears in the War Office register. WO 202/128, tel. 23, p. 122.

118. Deakin, *The Embattled Mountain,* p. 139.

119. Marjanović, *Ustanak,* p. 356; Kljaković, "Britanija, Sovjetski Savez i ustanak," p. 82. Mihailović did receive arms from the Užice factory, although perhaps not in the quantities he expected. One of his officers has written that the Partisans provided "only" 600 rifles and 10 cases of ammunition. (Mešković, "Otac i sin," *Knjiga o Draži,* I, p. 174.) Another Četnik officer reports that Tito had promised Mihailović 12,000 rifles at Brajići. (Djelević, "Iz prvih meseca," *Ibid.,* pp. 186-87.) Dedijer, on the other hand, puts the number promised at 500 and Kljaković at 1,200. (Dedijer, *Tito Speaks,* p. 164; Kljaković, *op. cit.,* p. 78.) No note appears to have been taken by the British of this first reference to Tito by name.

120. WO 208/2006, MI3b to DDMI(I), 18/11/41. There are regular situation reports for the period 6/11/41 - 12/2/42. Although they refer occasionally to an "Agent O.L." and once to a Danilovgrad transmitter, they would appear to be based largely on "Ultra" intercepts.

121. Kljaković, "Britanija, Sovjetski Savez i ustanak", p. 88.

122. FO 371/30220, R9872/162/92.

123. Deakin, *The Embattled Mountain,* p. 139.

124. FO 371/30220, R9874/162/92.

125. *Ibid.*

126 CAB 79/15, COS(41)390. London's message to Hudson was: "His Majesty's Government now consider fight should be Yugoslavs for Yugoslavia, and not revolt led by communists for Russia, if it is to prosper. H.M.G. therefore asking Soviet government to urge communist elements to rally Mihailović, collaborating with him against Germans, putting themselves

unreservedly at disposal of Mihailović as national leader. Simovic will also instruct Mihailović to refrain from retaliatory action." (See note 69.) Deakin, *The Embattled Mountain,* p. 140.

127. FO 371/30221, R1009/162/92; Kljaković, "Britanija, Sovjetski Savez i ustanak", p. 90. The difference in the two approaches must have amused the Soviets. This was apparently the first of several attempts by the exile government to instil in the Russians doubts about the Partisans' fealty.

According to Konstantin Fotić, the Yugoslav Ambassador in Washington, the British note requesting intervention with the communists read: "At the particular request of the Soviet government the British government has enouraged the uprising in Yugoslavia, and therefore it is in the interst of the Soviet government to help bring about unity of the insurgents in Yugoslavia." Constantin Fotitch, *The War We Lost*(New York: Viking Press, 1948), p. 170.

128. FO 371/30221, R10016/162/92. Mihailović reported his gratitude for the Anglo-Yugoslav approach to the Soviets and for what seemed to him to be the "right understanding of our internal position" by the British in a telegram received on 19 November. WO 202/128, p. 122.

129. FO 371/30221, R10092/162/92.

130. FO 371/30221, R10336/162/92.

131. WO 202/128, p. 122.

132. CAB 65/20, WM(41)120; Marjanović, *Ustanak,* p. 373.

133. Dedijer, *Tito Speaks,* p. 165.

134. On 25 November Tito sent a message to Zagreb for transmission to the Comintern "because Moscow Radio is announcing horrible nonsense about Mihailović . . . Tell them up there to stop putting out the same foolishness as London radio broadcasts." Kljaković, "Britanija, Sovjetski Savez i ustanak", p. 97.

135. Karchmar, "Draža Mihailović and the Rise of the Četnik Movement", pp. 262-69.

136. Kljaković, "Britanija, Sovjetski Savez i ustanak", pp. 92-93.

137. Hudson reported at this time (i.e. after the first day of negotiations) that, "My attitude to Mihailović has been that he has all qualifications except strength. At present the Partisans are stronger and he must first liquidate them with British arms before turning seriously to the Germans. He told me today that lack of ammunition will force him to retire from Ravna Gora if Partisans continue to fight him. I attended a Četnik-Partisan conference, and conveyed your attitude. The Partisans insist they keep their identity under any joint arrangements with the Četniks. They consider Simović's lack of reference to Partisans' leading part in the revolt shows Yugoslav government's ignorance of the situation. The Partisans consider that the people have lost all confidence in the former Yugoslav officers who were responsible for the collapse. They suspect Mihailović of helping Nedić and other pro-Axis elements in fighting the communists. The Partisans will continue to fight Mihailović unless he combines on their terms." Deakin, *The Embattled Mountain,* p. 141.

138. Kljaković, "Britanija, Sovjetski Svez i ustanak", p. 94.

139. FO 371/30221, R10199/162/92.

140. CAB 65/20, WM(41)120.

141. CAB 80/32, COS(41)705.

142. CAB 80/32, COS(41)390. Intelligence reports at this time may also have contributed to the Chiefs' disinclination to make special efforts. MI3b suggested that the Germans were everywhere scoring successes against the communists; and that although the situation was different in the Italian zone of occupation, "the general picture of the revolt is hardly bright." WO 208/2006, MI3b to DDMI(I), 18/11/41.

143. Marjanović, *Ustanak,* p. 373. The Russians were asked to send a similar message to the Partisans. A greatly heartened Simović replied to Eden on 3 December, assuring the Foreign Secretary that Mihailović had been exhorted to maintain a united front. He also expressed his confidence that Mihailović's movement would succeed owing to the identity of British and Yugoslav views. FO 371/30221, R10248/162/92.

144. FO 371/30221, R10199/162/92; CAB 80/32, COS(41)708; Deakin, *The Embattled Mountain,* p. 144.

145. CAB 79/16, COS(41)402.

146. FO 371/30221, R10257/162/92.

147. CAB 69/3, DO(41)36; PREM 3, 510/1.

148. Vladimir Dedijer, *Dnevnik* (3rd ed.; 3 vols.; Belgrade and Sarajevo: Prosveta and Svjetlost, 1970), I, pp. 61-62.

149. Djelević, *Knjiga o Draži,* I, p. 187; Kljaković, "Britanija, Sovjetski Savez i ustanak", p. 98.

150. *Ibid.*

151. Djelević, *Knjiga o Draži,* I, p. 185; Roberts, *Tito, Mihailović and the Allies,* p. 37. Deakin says that Hudson did manage to lug the W/T set back to Ravna Gora, but that its fate thereafter is unknown. Deakin, *The Embattled Mountain,* p. 146.

152. Milazzo, "The Chetnik Movement," p. 71.

153. WO 202/128, tels. 39 and 43; Kljaković, "Britanija, Sovjetski Savez i ustanak," pp. 98-99; Deakin, *The Embattled Mountain,* p. 145.

154. Tomasevich, *The Chetniks,* p. 199; Deakin, *The Embattled Mountain,* pp. 100, 146.

155. AFHQ, *The Četniks,* p. 17; Deakin, *The Embattled Mountain,* p. 146. Mihailović did not attempt to hide the fact that he had ordered his men to join the Nedić forces. Several weeks later he explained his reasons to an escaped British POW, Captain Christie Lawrence. As is apparent from the admiring tone of Hudson's despatch, he - and the British in general - tended to regard "legalization" as a good ruse. Lawrence, *Irregular Adventure,* pp. 230-31.

156. FO 371/44282, R21295/11/92 (Bailey report, appendix 3, 4/44); Deakin, *The Embattled Mountain,* p. 147. Mihailović apparently wanted to substitute the sympathetic and uncritical Lawrence for the discredited and importunate Hudson as his liaison officer later in 1942, but Lawrence's recapture by the Germans made this impossible.

157. WO 202/128, tel. 43, p. 116.

158. Deakin, *The Embattled Mountain,* pp. 146-47; Tomasevich, *The Chetniks,* p. 199; FO 371/44282, R21295/11/92 (Bailey report).

159. Tomasevich, *The Chetniks,* p. 199.

CHAPTER IV

1. The other ministers and officials destined for London arrived much later - after a sea voyage round the Cape from the Near East.

2. Sir George Rendel, *The Sword and the Olive* (London: John Murray, 1957), p. 210.

3. CAB 65/19, WM(41)91.

4. Ilija Jukić, *The Fall of Yugoslavia* (New York: Harcourt Brace Jovanovich, 1974), p. 90; FO 371/30298 (entire file).

The Soviet government, which had broken diplomatic relations in May, restored contacts with the exile government after 22 June. In July the Russians announced through Maisky that they intended to see Yugoslav independence restored and that they considered the post-war ordering of the country to be the Yugoslavs' affair. Formal diplomatic relations were resumed in September, but the Yugoslav ministers were always suspicious of Soviet intentions (especially after the appearance of the Partisans) and certainly did not look to Moscow to restore them to power in Belgrade. Plenča, *Medjunarodni odnosi,* pp. 28-33.

5. The national composition of the government as a whole - including the ministers in America and the Near East - was more overwhelmingly Serb: two Slovenes, two Croats and 13 Serbs. The Serbs, however, were divided by both party ties and geographical origins. Serbs from Serbia (*Srbijanci*) tended to regard the more Yugoslav-oriented Serbs from former Austria-Hungary as deficient in Serbian feeling.

6. The tasks of the ministers in North America (first in Canada and then in the U.S.A.) were to establish a Yugoslav presence, to maintain contacts with the million-strong Yugoslav-American population, to organize the recruitment of military volunteers from among them and to keep out of the way of the ministers in London.

7. FO 371/30292, R8389/4906/92.

8. FO 371/30265, R6509/3174/92. Queen Marie had lived in England with her British lady-in-waiting since 1939. Her

departure from Yugoslavia had been occasioned by reasons of health, personal and political differences with the Prince Regent and a tempermental lack of sympathy with the Balkan environment. A woman of passing artistic enthusiasms, she lived a self-consciously bohemian existence characterized by irregular hours, chain-smoking, vast tent-like robes of her own design and constant premonitions of her own mortality.

9. FO 371/30265, R6731/3174/92, R7119/3174/92, R7847/3174/92. Seton-Watson submitted a memorandum in August which though based on the same premise as was Forign Office thinking in general - that King Peter's presence offered a great opportunity for indoctrination - was embarrassing in its enthusiasm:

"If his education can be completed on broad and enlightened lines, he might become a model constitutional monarch, who would learn to throw his weight in favour of a sane and balanced democratic development, and whose example might help to rescue the monarchical principle throughout the Balkans at a moment when it is gravely compromised and in danger of total eclipse in South-East Europe. If on the other hand, he should develop learnings (*sic*) towards arbitrary and personal government, the fall of the Karadjordjević dynasty would only be a matter of time, and might easily have repercussions in the neighbouring States. It is not too much to maintain that in the Balkans the choice lies between limited monarchy (perhaps as a link between individual federal units) and some kind of radical Communism (modified, it may be, in some unsuspected direction by the course taken by the regime in Russia)."

After surveying the many educational, personal and familial failings of past Serbian monarchs, Seton-Watson recommended that a supervisory committee be established to watch over King Peter's progress through what was intended to be a lively and unpedantic course of PPE. Although some Foreign Office officials thought this suggestion "idiotic" and a sign of advancing years, no one questioned the central assumption that the choice for the Balkans was between Bolshevism and constitutional monarchy. From this point of view, as from almost every other, King Peter was to prove a grave disappointment. He was immature, impressionable, ignorant and immoderate - and certainly incapable of playing the great historic role for which Seton-Watson, the Foreign Office and Churchill were to cast him.

10. Queen Marie and King George VI were both great grandchildren of Queen Victoria. King George VI was also King Peter's godfather.

11. FO 371/30265, R6587/3174/92, R7119/3174/92. The Foreign Office was also eager that progress be made in re-equipping the Yugoslav soldiers, sailors and airmen in the Near East. King Peter would then have something useful to do, i.e. he could go out to review his troops occasionally. FO 371/30300, R8665/5775/92.

12. FO 371/30292, R8389/4906/92. Ninčić, fearing that Simović was conspiring with the Croats to remove him from office, was successfully fighting to create a counterweight in the court against Simović. For details see: Slobodan Jovanović, *Zapisi o problemima i ljudima, 1941-1944* (London: Udruženje srpskih pisaca i umetnika u inostranstvu, 1976), pp. 15-18.

13. FO 371/33441, R1148/12/92.

14. FO 371/30292, R8389/4906/92, R8571/4906/92. Oxford was already committed to awarding an honorary degree to Emmanuel Tsouderos, Prime Minister of the Greek exile government. When Simović fell, Cambridge gave a degree instead to the American poet and playwright Archibald MacLeish.

15. Slobodan Jovanović is reported to have exclaimed to his fellow Vice-Premier, the Slovene Miha Krek, that, "Yugoslavia no longer exists. The Croats are murdering the Serbs." Jukić, *The Fall of Yugoslavia,* p. 111. Eden minuted on the summary of the report sent to him that if the perpetrators wre really Croats, then "the post-war situation will be terrible." FO 371/30220, R9244/162/92.

16. The Croat ministers attacked the massacres as such, but sought at the same time to question the facts alleged, the soures on which the Church report was based and the form which it

took, i.e. an appeal to the Germans for their intercession. Most of all they sought to dissociate the killings from the Croatian people. They tended to look upon the massacre stories as being more an opportunity for the Serb politicians to indulge their traditionally anti-Croat sentiments than as something so horrible as to require a significantly different response. This politics as usual attitude afflicted the Serbs even more. Rendel, *The Sword and the Olive,* pp. 216-17; Jukić, *The Fall of Yugoslavia,* p. 111; Tomasevich, *The Chetniks,* pp. 265-67; Jovanović, *Zapisi,* p. 22.

17. FO 371/30220, R9244/162/92; FO 371/33441, R1148/12/92.

18. Jukić, *The Fall of Yugoslavia,* p. 112.

19. Djonović, for instance, wrote to Jovanović on 3 November from Jerusalem reporting on the recent commencement of broadcasts from the USSR of a "Free Yugoslavia" radio station. The character of these broadcasts was, he wrote, "purely communist"; they warned the "freedom fighters" against certain "*Mihailovićevci*" who were crossing over to the enemy and advised them to take care in future with whom they worked. Djonović urged the government to intervene with the Russians "so that they stop immediately their unauthorized interference in our internal affairs . . ." "You know," he continued, "how many lives have been lost in our country because of the Bolsheviks and their provocation of armed resistance during the course of the summer, prematurely and without the prospect of any corresponding measure of success." Djonović recommended that action be taken in London before it was too late: "The communist devastation must be nipped in the bud because otherwise any and all resistance by our people will be stamped out and made impossible. We must not be mistaken in this: a large number of our people, because of the terrifying crimes of the communists in our nationally purest regions, or because of weakness in their resolve to stay manfully on the battlefield, have already crossed over to the government of General Nedić. In other words, German collaborators will be made of our people who are loyal to both the King and Fatherland . . . Under such

circumstances one must certainly expect - if the communists are helped further from Moscow - that our people will fail in their struggle and that we will find ourselves before the end of the war in a position from which there is no exit." AJ, Fond 103, F-12, no. 97.

20. Jukić, *The Fall of Yugoslavia,* p. 112; Kosta St. Pavlovic, "Pad Simovićeve vlade", *Glasnik,* 2 (December 1958), p. 68.

21. Jukić, *The Fall of Yugoslavia,* pp. 112-14; FO 371/33441, R1292/12/92. The draft policy declaration was brought to London from the United States by a Slovene minister, Franc Snoj. His proposal contained an emotional account of the trials and tribulations of the Yugoslav peoples, as well as suggestions for the future ordering of the country on the basis of local autonomy and for its expansion to embrace Slovene irredenta.

22. Jovanović, *Zapisi,* p. 21; Jukić, *The Fall of Yugoslavia,* pp. 112-14; FO 371/33441, R1148/12/92. The Minister of Court, Radoje Knežević, and his brother, Major Živan Knežević, became the principal spokesmen for the younger officers who had participated in the coup d'état and resented the stranglehold kept by Simović and the senior officers on the levers of power and promotion. They succeeded in convincing the King and Queen Mother that Simović was both inept and ill-disposed towards the dynasty. Simović's attempt to cut their civil list cemented royal opposition to him. This was illustrated by a speech of King Peter's on 17 December in which he gave credit for the putsch to the younger officers without mentioning Simović or Mirković. Responsibility for the coup was to remain a major issue in exile politics throughout the war and beyond. Tomasevich, *The Chetniks,* pp. 267-69.

23. FO 371/30295, R10545/4906/92.

24. AJ, Fond 103, F-1, no. 3. Meanwhile Rendel warned Simović that any attempt to unseat Ninčić would only worsen his relations with the court and thus hasten his fall. FO 371/30295, R10850/4906/92.

25. *Ibid.;* Rendel, *The Sword and the Olive,* p. 213.

26. FO 371/30295, R10545/4906/92. Ninčić gave Rendel the

impression in late December that he had flip-flopped into the pro-Simovic camp in order to protect himself from Gavrilović. (If so, he soon flopped back again.) Ninčić favoured a confederation joining Greece and Yugoslavia and had made this the centrepiece of his foreign policy. Gavrilović, seemingly Ninčić's most likely successor, turned out upon arrival in London to be dangerously pan-Slav in sentiment, i.e. he favoured a confederation linking Bulgaria and Yugoslavia. This was, of course, profoundly unsettling to the traditional sensibilities of the Foreign Office. FO 371/33133, R57/43/67. (See below, section iv.)

27. FO 371/33440, R127/12/92.

28. Jukić, *The Fall of Yugoslavia,* p. 115; Pavlović, "Pad Simovićeve vlade", p. 80; Jovanovic, *Zapisi,* pp. 21-22.

29. FO 371/33440, R58/12/92.

30. The rest of the cabinet was reappointed with the exception of General Ilić, a supporter of Simović. His successor as War Minister was Draža Mihailović. (See below.)

Simović regarded the manner of his dismissal as unconstitutional. At the ceremony marking the transfer of the mandate on 12 January he told Jovanović that he, the country's not say for he had now relinquished the study of law for the study trespass on the constitution. Jovanović replied that he could not say, for he had now reliquished the study of law for th study of military affairs. On the other hand, he (General Simović) could now concentrate on the study of constitutional law. Pavlović, "Pad Simovićeve vlade," pp. 77-78, 80.

Simović, too, was capable of some wit on the subject of the new government. It consisted, he told Bob Dixon, of a King who was too young, a premier who was too old and a foreign minister who was far too clever. FO 371/33440, R521/12/92.

31. FO 371/33440, R58/12/92, R210/12/92.

32. This was the exile government's intention. According to Jukić, Mihailović was named War Minister "primarily to ensure British recognition of the new government." Jukić, *The Fall of Yugoslavia,* p. 116.

33. FO 371/33440, R210/12/92.

34. FO 371/33441, R2569/12/92.

35. Rendel, *The Sword and the Olive,* pp. 218-19. Describing Jovanović's combination of brilliance and naivete, wit and bemused detachment, Rendel related that, "He could never comprehend how we conducted our politics, since there were no cafes in London where people could sit and argue about them." He exercised little authority over his government because, in part, "his sense of humour led him almost to enjoy watching the foibles of more foolish men - so that it was often difficult to get him to take politics sufficiently seriously to reach any conclusion." For an analysis of Jovanović's political career see Dimitrije Djordjević, "Historians in Politics: Slobodan Jovanović," *Journal of Contemporary History,* VIII, 1 (January 1973), pp. 21-40.

36. Although he became Foreign Minister in name only in January 1943, the British tended to deal with him in preference to Ninčić. There was no Yugoslav minister to the Court of St. James, the reason being that the government could come to no decision on whether a Serb or a Croat should get the job once the pre-coup Minister (Subotić) had been reassigned. The long-running wrangle over this appointment provided the occasion for Jovanović to tell Rendel in July 1942 that when he came to write his memoirs after the war he proposed to adopt the title of a recent Russian novel published in France as *En Mauvaise Compaigne.* FO 536/4, 3000/11/42.

37. Michael Rose of the Southern Department wrote in late 1942 that, "In his position as Chief of the Military Cabinet to the Prime Minister, who is also Deputy Minister of War, Major Knežević is able to exercise an almost dictatorial control over all Yugoslav military matters." FO 371/33464, R8632/151/92.

38. The three majors were also referred to as "the three musketeers." Besides serving in the military cabinet, Roždjalovski and Vohoska were aids-de-camp to the King. According to Tomasevich, the Majors' League had its origins in the days prior to 27 March and embraced a goodly number of officers. Other members in London were Major Zobenica (also an ADC to the King) and Lt. Col. Lozić. The group also had adherents in Cairo. Tomasevich, *The Chetniks,* p. 272.

39. Although formally Yugoslav Consul in Istanbul, Nikola

Kneževič spent a part of 1941 and 1942 working in London in the cipher section of the Foreign Ministry and came to be regarded as his brothers' confidential agent there. His influence was, however, very much less than theirs. He was sent back to Istanbul in the course of 1942 and later served as Consul in Beirut. In both posts he concerned himself primarily with gathering intelligence and establishing contacts with Mihailović. Communication from Mr. Kosta St. Pavlowitch, 17/5/75.

40. The Foreign Office did not include Radoje Kneževič as being among those whose influence on King Peter was undesirable - at least in an extrapolitical sense. Nor, according to one government official, did Radoje and Živan Kneževič always see eye to eye. (Communication from Mr. K. St. Pavlowitch, 20/5/75.) The British view, however, was that the brothers acted in concert. In the "Handbook of Jugoslav Personalities" prepared by the Political Branch of Allied Forces Headquarters, Mediterranean Theatre, in 1944 the brothers were described "as the most powerful forces in the exiled Yugoslav Government and the most instrumental in carrying through its chauvinistic Great Serb and anti-Partisan policy."

41. Tomasevich, *The Chetniks,* p. 279.

42. Simović had tried in December to bring an unwilling Mirković to London to serve as first ADC to the King and principal prop to himself. As the man who put him in power, Simović apparently hoped that Mirković would contrive to keep him there. Jovanović's renewal of the invitation no doubt came from different motives, i.e. Živan Kneževič's desire to separate th formidable Mirković from his air force supporters. SSIP, Iz arhive Kr. Poslanstva u Londonu, 1940-45 (Fragmenti arhive Poslanstva Kr. Jug. u Kairu, 1940, 1942-44), F-1, tel. 29.

According to Jovanović, it was Mirković whom the younger officers disliked most of all. Jovanović, *Zapisi,* p. 24.

43. Lozić was outranked by four generals, eight colonels and one lieutenant colonel in exile. Tomasevich, *The Chetniks,* p. 279.

44. Jovanović, *Zapisi*, p. 24.

45. *Ibid.*, pp. 24-25; Tomasevich, *The Chetniks*, p. 279; FO 371/33441, R2569/12/92; FO 371/33451, R1008/151/92, R1061/151/92; AVII, Pretsednistvo vlade Kr. Jug.: Vojni kabinet, kutija 171, 16/1-1, 25/1-1; SSIP, Iz arhive Kr. Poslanstva u Londonu, 1940-45 (Fragmenti arhive Poslanstva Kr. Jug. u Kairu, 1940, 1942-44), F-1, tel. Popović to Jovanović (no number), 9/2/42. Popović protested that the disputed orders nullified the glorious past of the armed forces and he threatened dire repercussions.

46. FO 371/33441, R2569/12/92; FO 371/33451, R972/151/92.

47. This was reinforced by the fact that the men charged with maintaining liaison with the Yugoslav forces - Squadron Leader Mapplebeck and Captain Hatch - had formerly served in Belgrade as agents of SOE and/or SIS. They had thus come under Mirković's spell in the heady days surrounding the coup. Jovanović, for his part, believed that Mirković was also an agent of British intelligence. FO 371/33451, R1226/151/92; Jovanović, *Zapisi*, p. 30.

48. Tomasevich (*The Chetniks*, p. 280) gives the total number of rebels as 430. They were separated from their comrades in a British detention camp.

49. Mirković referred to a promise made to him by Wing Commander Macdonald before the coup d'état that Yugoslav officers who fled the country rather than serve a pro-Axis government would be received into the RAF. FO 371/33451, R1393/151/92, R1467/151;92.

50. FO 371/33451, R1505/151/92.

51. FO 371/33452, R1598/151/92.

52. In fact the Foreign Office then thought that by bringing the crisis to a head the Yugoslav government would be compelled to withdraw Lozić. FO 371/33452, R1703/151/92.

53. FO 371/33452, R1718/151/92.

54. Both as an historian and as a personal friend of Colonel Dragutin Dimitrijević ("Apis"), Jovanović was well aware of the prominent part played by the military in Balkan politics.

Ironically, he now found himself cast in the same role in relation to Mirković as Nikola Pašić had played in Salonika in regard to Prince Alexander's scheme to eliminate "Apis". Djordjević, "Historians in Politics: Slobodan Jovanović," pp. 35-36.

55. FO 371/33453, R1780/151/92, R1917/151/92, R2061/151/92.

56. FO 371/33454, R2105/151/92, R2106/151/92.

57. FO 371/33454, R2128/151/92. A formal inquiry never took place.

58. FO 371/33441, R2569/12/92, R3092/12/92. Most of the missions sent into Yugoslavia by SIS during 1942 were composed of pro-Mirković Yugoslav officers. FO 371/33456, R3518/151/92; Tomasevich, *The Chetniks,* p. 279.

59. FO 371/33454, R2296/151/92.

60. FO 371/33454, R2384/151/92. Dixon certainly underestimated the appeal which the fleshpots of Cairo would - and later did - have for King Peter.

61. FO 371/33454, R2389/151/92, R2427/151/92; R2430/151/92, R2582/151/92.

62. FO 371/33455, R2773/151/92. When the Minister of State revived the proposal that King Peter travel to Cairo in order to induce the dissidents to return to the fold, Eden minuted sadly in mid-May that, "King Peter is not King George." The far more serious Greek mutinies of 1943 and 1944 suggest that Eden overrated the Greek King's powers. FO 371/33456, R3177/151/92.

63. FO 371/33455, R2794/151/92; FO 371/33456, R3207/151/92.

64. FO 371/33455, R3011/151/92, R3070/151/92; FO 371/33456, R3220/151/92.

65. FO 371/33455, R2794/151/92; FO 371/33456, R3328/151/92.

66. FO 371/33456, R3632/151/92.

67. Howard summarized the Foreign Office view of the interminable crisis when he wrote on 28 May that "the Yugoslav Government were stupid beyond belief in the first place in dismissing their C. in C. Middle East, Colonel (*sic*) Ilić,

and in trying to impose an unpopular and incompetent officer, Colonel Lozić, in his place. There is no doubt that the effect of this was to lose for the Yugoslav Government the support of their best officers and men in the Middle East such as General Mirković, etc. In the first instance General Auchinleck and the military authorities in the Middle East were our chief advisers - perforce - since it was a question of military security within their zone. It soon became clear that our military authorities favoured, not unnaturally, the more competent, agreeable and friendly elements, i.e. the dissidents." When brought into the affair the Minister of State's office, Howard continued, either took the same pro-Mirković line without appreciating the political issues at stake, or else found itself powerless to oppose the wishes of GHQ. FO 371/33456, R3287/151/92, R3421/151/92; FO 371/33460, R6040/151/92.

68. FO 371/33456, R3715/151/92. The Yugoslav government responded to the disintegration of both its forces and reputation in the middle East by transferring the seat of the Yugoslav Supreme Command from Cairo to occupied Yugoslavia on 8 June. Wedding the legitimist cause even more firmly to the Četniks, Mihailović was named Chief of Staff of the Supreme Command and promoted (for the third time in less than a year) to Army General. The former Supreme Command Headquarters in Cairo was downgraded to Middle East Command Headquarters with Rakic as Chief of Staff. Explaining the changes to the Yugoslav Military Attache in Turkey, Živan Knežević pointed out that the force that would play the decisive part, both now and "at the fateful hour", was already operating in the Fatherland. Compared to Mihailović, the forces available abroad were insignificant. But most importantly, according to Knežević, "Up to now our Supreme Command in Cairo has been subjected in the most literal sense to the English Near East Command. Recent events in Cairo and the forcible changing of our Supreme Command on 5 March of this year have shown what a complete disaster it was to place an important institution such as the Headquarters of the Supreme Commander His Majesty the King under the command of the English commanding officer on one of the numerous

battlefronts of the British Empire. With the formation of the Supreme Command from the headquarters staff of General Mihailović all these unfortunate consequences of the subjugation of this Headquarters to whatever Allied headquarters will be avoided." SSIP, Vojni izaslanik Kr. Jug. u Turskoj, F-1, referat 34, 8/6/42.

69. CAB 72(42)6; FO 371/33456, R3825/151/92; FO 371/33457, R3941/151/92.

70. FO 371/33457, R4046/151/92, R4140/151/92.

71. FO 371/33458, R4498/151/92, R4544/151/92, R4642/151/92, R4628/151/92.

72. FO 371/33458, R4701/151/92, R4736/151/92.

73. FO 371/33458, R4829/151/92, R4858/151/92.

74. FO 371/33459, R5414/151/92, R5567/151/92.

75. FO 371/33460, R5977/151/92, R6010/151/92. Rendel wrote on 10 September in a telegram distributed to the War Cabinet that, "It would be difficult to exaggerate the deplorable effect which this affair is having on our relations with the Yugoslav government. All Yugoslav Ministers are convinced that we are supporting General Mirković against the Yugoslav government here for political reasons. They refuse to believe that we have been genuinely unable to remove him from Egypt or bring any pressure to bear upon him - particularly as we were apparently able to remove the bulk of the loyal forces without difficulty. Their disbelief in our sincerity has brought out all their worst qualities (like all Balkan governments they have a native leaning towards tortuous methods), and until we can convince them that we are not simply out to do them down it is likely to be impossible to re-establish any mutual confidence or obtain satisfaction on any other issue." Rendel clinched the argument - at least for Eden - when he further observed that, "If General Miailović begins, rightly or wrongly, to believe that we are using the latter [i.e. Mirković] to undermine the position of the Yugoslav government and monarchy here he can hadly fail to become uncertain as to our policy towards Yugoslavia, and may, it seems to me, easily be tempted to throw in his hand." Eden minuted on this telegram, "If it is as bad as this surely Cabinet should issue an order to the Minister of State?"

76. According to a letter written to Howard on 31 August by Henry Hopkinson, the great pro-Mirković enthusiasm in GHQ Cairo was largely the creation of Captain Hatch and a few others, but that it had faded considerably by late August. The sympathy of which he was the heir because of the coup d'etat melted away after months of "bitter experience" of the man. Most people in Cairo were now convinced that he was no better than Rakić or the other pro-Knežević officers; only Colonel Prosen of the guards Battalion retained their respect. (It was Hopkinson who came to London in mid-September to work out the details of the settlement with the Foreign Office.) FO 371/33460, R6040/151/92.

77. FO 371/33460, R6022/151/92, R6144/151/92, R6146/151/92, R6273/151/92.

78. FO 371/33461, R6608/151/92, R6778/151/92; Jovanovic, *Zapisi*, pp. 28-29.

79. FO 371/33462, R7197/151/92, R7198/151/92, R7393/151/92.

Neither the Foreign Office nor Cairo was happy with the nomination of Putnik. They would have preferred Prosen, but were told by Jovanović that Prosen - as a Slovene - would have been unacceptable to Mihailović. There was also some regret on the part of the British that they had not contrived to rid themselves of Živan Knežević, perhaps by bringing Putnik to London as his replacement in the military cabinet. The Foreign Office felt that the removal of Knežević would facilitate the necessary binding up of the wounds suffered in the Cairo Affair. The returning dissidents would have less fear of victimization - a course on which it seemed obvious Knežević was bent. It also came to light at this time that Knežević regarded Rendel as an enemy and had asked Jovanović to secure his removal. Although confirming the long-held Foreign Office opinion that Živan Knežević was a thoroughly unsavoury character, no effort was made to unseat him - despite a formal request in this sense from MI5. The reason was that the Foreign Office doubted whether any effort they might make could possibly succeed. FO 371/33463, R7988/151/92, R7989/151/92; FO 371/33464, R8403/151/92.

80. FO 371/33461, R6895/151/92. This had been another contentious issue between the British and the Yugoslavs. The ex-Italian POWs had been promised when enrolled that they would not be compelled to fight their former comrades in arms and thus risk frightful consequences if captured. The British military authorities had disregarded this condition.

81. FO 371/33462, R7022/151/92; FO 371/33463, R7855/151/92. Jovanović's interpretation (*Zapisi,* p. 31) was that the British realized by autumn that the prolongation of the crisis was likely to destroy their hold over King Peter. They thus put an end to it.

82. FO 371/33453, R1883/151/92.

83. Rendel, *The Sword and the Olive,* p. 215.

84. FO 371/33134, R3793/43/67.

85. FO 371/29782, R4932/113/67.

86. FO 371/30210, R4621/72/92.

87. FRUS, 1941, Vol. II, pp. 979-80; Roberts, *Tito Mihailović and the Allies,* p. 18.

88. FO 371/30210, R4452/73/92.

89. FO 371/30210, R6732/73/92.

90. FO 371/33443, R6876/12/92.

91. Both the Americans and the Russians came to consider the exile government a British plaything. The 'policy' of the State Department was to avoid any discussion of the reordering of Europe beyond pious intonations of the principles of the Atlantic Charter and the virtues of free trade. Roosevelt was not so punctilious. He often expressed his opinion to the pan-Serb Yugoslav Minister in Washington that Serbia (with which he equated Yugoslavia - allegedly because of his boyhood philatelism) would be stronger if shorn of her "western provinces". The future of the Croats he held to be "cloudy". Fotitch, *The War We Lost,* pp. 85, 128-29, 189-90.

The Soviets for their part expressed themselves in favour of Yugoslavia's restoration, but because of the Partisans were rarely taken at their word. (See below.)

92 FO 371/33441, R1292/12/92.

93. The Declaration of Corfu, signed in July 1917 by Nikola Pašić for the exiled Serbian government and by Ante Trumbić

for the Yugoslav Committee from Austria-Hungary, provided for the union of Serbs, Croats and Slovenes in a single constitutional monarchy under the Karadjordjević dynasty. Details were left to a constituent assembly, but "local autonomies in accordance with national, social and economic conditions" were to be established and freedom and equality for the three principal religions and two alphabets guaranteed. Since the vague provisions of the Declaration had not prevented the Serbs from imposing a centralistic and Serb-dominated constitutional framework, it is hard to see how the Croats and Slovenes (let alone the still-unrecognized nationalities and minorities) could have been expected to rise to the bait a second time.

94. FO 371/33441, R2156/12/92.

95. FO 371/33441, R2788/12/92.

96. *Ibid.* and R3348/12/92.

97. FO 371/33456, R3261/151/92, R3345/151/92.

98. FO 371/33441, R3482/12/92, R3765/12/92; FO 371/33443, R6875/12/92. Seton-Watson's participation would hardly have served to recommend the project to the Serbs, who considered him irredeemably pro-Croat in sympathy. Rendel increasingly laboured under the same handicap, in part because he was a Roman Catholic.

99. The Pact of Rome was an agreement between the Yugoslav Committee and the Italians which resulted from the convocation of a Congress of Oppressed Nationalities of Austria-Hungary in Rome in April 1918. It represented a short-lived Italian interest in promoting South Slav union following their defeat at Caporetto.

100. FO 371/33443, R6875/12/92.

101. FO 371/33442, R4603/12/92. What, in fact, the Serbs were refusing to do was to reaffirm the *Sporazum* for a *second* time. The government had done so once in Jerusalem; but that was before they knew of the mass murders of Serbs in the Ustaše state. Stevan K. Pavlowitch, "Out of Context: The Yugoslav Government in London, 1941-1945" (unpublished paper presented at the Conference on Exiled Governments in London during the Second World War, October 1977).

102. FO 371/33442, R4603/12/92.

103. FO 371/33442, R4717/12/92, R4811/12/92. Rendel, on the other hand, felt that not only had the Foreign Office expected too much, but that it had expected it too quickly. He wrote later that the Yugoslavs had been given "hopelessly short notice" of the British desire for a policy statement: "I had not had time to prepare the ground, and I doubt whether in any case he [Jovanović] would have agreed. As it was the proposal went off so to speak at half-cock and the document which emerged was of little value." Rendel, *The Sword and the Olive,* p. 217.

104. FO 371/33443, R6875/12/92, R7069/12/92. Grol had now been converted to the proposition that the Serbs must come to terms with the Croats.

105. Jovanović's commitment to federalism was equivocal at best. A Serb nationalist at heart, he feared that Serb interests would suffer even in a tripartite federation. On the other hand, like many in the pre-war opposition, he judged that Alexandrine centralism had been most harmful to the Serbs. Djordjević, "Historians in Politics: Slobodan Jovanović", p. 27ff.

106. FO 371/33443, R6875/12/92, R7069/12/92, R7778/12/92.

107. FO 371/33443, R7970/12/92. In the same minute Rose wrote that, "Within the Cabinet the great disruptive force seems to be Ninčić, supported by Gavrilović and to a lesser extent Trifunović. The Pan-Serbs seem, however, to have their headquarters outside the Cabinet in the Prime Minister's Military Cabinet where they are ruled by that source of all Yugoslav troubles, Major Knežević. As this group seems also to have the ear of the King and probably of the Queen Mother, and to be in control of the main organs of the executive, it is in a position to frustrate the good intentions of the rest of the government. The villain of the piece is Ninčić, but the fool Jovanović who seems utterly incapable of exercising the least control over his subordinates." Rendel had proposed on 30 October that the Foreign Office seek to unseat Ninčić who, besides his many other faults, was "one of the main niggers in the wood-pile" on the declaration question.

108. FO 371/33443, R6810/12/92. It had never been part of British wartime policy to seek to recreate a centralized Yugoslavia in the mould of King Alexander. Sargent's apparent confusion on this point indicates that he either did not pay very close attention to Yugoslav affairs, or that his strong personal commitment to the idea of Balkan confederation - as opposed to South Slav federation - caused him to impute this object to his juniors' efforts to put Yugoslav unity on a firmer foundation.

109. *Ibid.*

110. FO 371/33443, R8023/12/92.

111. Vladimir Milanović, the Yugoslav Chargé d'Affaires and one of the most chauvinistic Serbs, spelled out for Rendel the extent of his territorial ambitions at this time. In the future Yugoslavia Croatia would be limited to its old Austrian (*sic*) frontiers. All of Bosnia, Hercegovina, the former Habsburg Military Frontier and the Adriatic littoral south of Metković (at the mouth of the Neretva) would be incorporated in a greater Serbia (which, of course, already included Montenegro, Sandžak, Vojvodina and Vardar Macedonia). FO 371/33443, R8197/12/92.

112. The Partisans were by the autumn of 1942 committed to such a solution. The British also came to appreciate that this might offer a way forward. Rendel requested Robin Laffan (a Cambridge history don then working for Toynbee at Balliol College) for a paper on the Bosnian ethnographic tangle on 15 December. His paper (dated 31 December and later expanded into a formal FRPS handbook) envisaged two practicable solutions: (1) a Bosnian unit within a Yugoslav federation, or (2) an east-west partition along lines of geographical convenience and accompanied by exchanges of population. The latter would be best, he felt, were Serbia and Croatia to emerge as separate states. FO 371/37601, R84/84/92.

On the debates within the exile government on these questions see Vojmir Kljaković's two articles: "Jugoslavenska vlada u emigraciji i Saveznici prema pitanju Hrvatske 1941-1944" (*Časopis za suvremenu povijest*, II-III, 1971, pp. 97-138) and "Jugoslavenska emigrantska vlada prema pitanju Bosne i Hercegovina" (*Prilozi*, IV, 1968, pp. 307-15).

113. FO 371/33443, R8286/12/92; FRUS, 1942, Vol. III, pp. 827-31. Credit for this pronouncement was claimed not by Rendel and the Foreign Office, but by A. J. Drexel Biddle, Jr., the American Ambassador to the London exile governments. He had been endeavouring to convince the Yugoslav ministers that they must adopt a "liberal, forward-looking policy" and had pushed King Peter to declare himself for "equal economic, social and political equality for all". Biddle's efforts had come at the instance of the current moderates, Jukić and Grol, and were not part of a concerted campaign with the British. Rendel, in fact, was disgusted by FDR's playboy diplomat - terming him "a complete humbug as well as a most irritating *faux bonhomme*" - and essayed to avoid all "assignations" with him. FO 371/33443, R8023/12/92, R8912/12/92; Jukić, *The Fall of Yugoslavia,* p. 134.

114. This assessment, made by an unnamed former British consul in the Balkans, occasioned a study by the FRPS on German and Soviet ambitions in South-Eastern Europe. FO 371/29782, R4932/113/67.

115. Sir Llewellyn Woodward, *British Foreign Policy in the Second World War* (London: HMSO, 1962), pp. 190-96; Herbert Feis, *Churchill-Roosevelt-Stalin: The War They Waged and the Peace They Sought* (Princeton: Princeton University Press, 1967), pp. 23-28. In return for accepting his "algebra", Eden offered the Russians a prominent role in the planing of post-war confederations and economic reconstruction.

116. FO 371/33133, R474/43/67.

117. *Ibid.*

118. *Ibid.*

119. *Ibid.* Gavrilović, Ninčić, Krnjević and Krek all added their voices to this chorus. Krek told Rendel in March that if the Western Allies did not occupy South-Eastern Europe upon the German withdrawal, "its situation would be like that of the man from whom the unclean spirit had departed, but who was an easy prey to seven other devils." FO 371/33134, R2211/43/67.

120. FO 371/33133, R474/43/67. Regarding the particular fears of the Croat and Slovene politicians, Rendel wrote on 1

January: "The fact that, since Germany's attack on Russia, the communists have been the most active elements in these areas in carrying on the fight against the German occupying forces has, according to them, in many cases deterred other anti-German but non-communist elements from cooperating as fully as they might have done in the common resistance to the invader. They have more than once expressed the hope that it might be possible for His Majesty's Government to give the people of Slovenia and Croatia some assurance that His Majesty's Government do not intend to disinterest themselves from the future fate of these countries or allow them to fall under Soviet control."

121. *Ibid.;* FO 371/33142, R396/387/67.

122. FO 371/33133, R216/43/67.

123. SSIP, MIPKJ, F-1, 1941, report Jukić to Ninčić, br. B687, 27/9/41; Stephen G. Xydis, *Greece and the Great Powers 1944-1947* (Thessaloniki: Institute for Balkan Studies, 1963), pp. 19-20.

124. For an account of Polish-Czechoslovak confederation plans see Piotr S. Wandycz, "Recent Traditions of the Quest for Unity: Attempted Polish-Czechoslovak and Yugoslav-Bulgarian Confederations, 1940-1948", in Jerzy Lukaszewski (ed.), *The Peoples' Democracies after Prague: Soviet Hegemony, Nationalism, Regional Integration?,* Cahiers de Bruges, no. 25 (Bruges: De Tempel, 1970).

125. FO 371/33133, R142/43/67, R207/43/67. The desire for Britain's official stamp of approval no doubt reflected the traditional - and not unfounded - Balkan belief that little of consequence can take place in the region without the midwifery of a great power, as well as the Greeks' special concern lest the project offend the Russians.

126. FO 371/33133, R211/43/67; Xydis, *Greece and the Great Powers,* p. 20.

127. FO 371/33133, R216/43/67. Lampson also suggested (modestly enough) that the opportunity be taken by Britain to pledge to insure social justice and internal security in the post-war Balkans!

128. *Ibid.* and R735/43/67. Sargent argued for a pro-

confederation campaign on the somewhat curious premise that if the Russians did thereupon come out in opposition, "it can only be because they wish to exploit the Balkans in their own interests by playing off Romania against Hungary and by fomenting a mixture of Pan-Slavism and Communism in Yugoslavia and Bulgaria." This overlooked the possiblity that the confederation schemes might themselves arouse Soviet fears of encirclement and so provoke expansionist moves. Sargent, however, felt that Stalin had not yet worked out any definite plans about the future European settlement and that therefore Britain had a chance to impose its own vision of the post-war order.

Dixon and Rose argued for a British propaganda campaign in favour of confederations on the contrary assumption that Stalin had certainly laid his own plans and that it was therefore useless to attempt to mask the developing clash of interests. The matter would be settled by the military balance at war's end. As Rose minuted, "Stalin is too suspicious and too much of a realist to allow his conduct of the war to be influenced by any hypothetical plans about the future settlement of Eruope on which the exiled governments in this country may agree."

The Greek government, for its part, disliked this tendency to view Balkan union as an anti-Soviet strategem and was alarmed by Yugoslav statements referring to possible cooperation between a future Balkan union and a future Polish-Czechoslovak confederation. SSIP, MIPKJ, F-5, 1941-43, letter from Tsouderos to Ninčić, br. 151, 4/2/42; Xydis, *Greece and the Great Powers,* p. 21.

129. FO 371/33133, R216/43/67. Answering a question in the Commons on 4 February, Eden did go so far as to say that the Graeco-Yugoslav treaty was regarded as the basis for a larger Balkan confederation. Barker, *British Policy,* p. 131.

130. FO 371/33142, R396/387/67.

131. FO 371/32481, W1823/81/67.

132. *Ibid.* One Foreign Office official characteristically pointed out that no confederation had endured since the Athenians seized control of the Confederation of Delos in the

fifth century B.C. This may not have been reported to the modern Athenians.

133. FO 371/33142, R396/387/67.

134. FO 371/33133, R687/43/67, R735/43/67, R817/43/67.

135. FO 371/33133, R979/43/67.

136. FO 371/33133, R817/43/67.

137. FO 371/33490, R1990/1990/92. The Yugoslavs also hoped that by putting their relations with the Soviets on a friendlier footing they might both move Moscow to call the Partisans to heel (FO 371/33490, R3643/1990/92) and lessen their dependence on the British (FO 371/33490, R3806/1990/92).

138. Barker, *British Policy,* p. 132; Woodward, *British Foreign Policy* (1962), pp. 195-96.

139. FO 371/33490, R3620/1990/92. In Sargent's revised version the proper object of East European confederations was markedly less anti-Soviet in inspiration. Confederations, he now maintained, must be directed against Germany, not only because they could hardly be expected to withstand pressure from both sides, but also because the victorious Soviets would only tolerate confederations with which they were closely allied. The way to keep Russian influence to a minimum was to exclude any tinge of pan-Slavism from them, i.e. Serbo-Bulgarian union.

Other points made by Sargent were: (1) that confederation rather than federation was as much as could be hoped for; (2) that there should be two confederations, one in Central Europe (composed of Poland, Czechoslovakia, Hungary and probably Austria) and one in South-Eastern Europe (consisting of Yugoslavia, Greece, Bulgaria, Romania and Albania); (3) that border regions such as Transylvania, Slovenia and Croatia might exist militarily and politically within the Balkan confederation, but economically within the Central European unit; and (4) that such problems of split affinity emphasized the need for close links between the two confederations.

Regarding Yugoslavia in particular, Sargent wrote that "it may prove the best solution for Serbs, Croats and Slovenes each to form a separate unit in the confederation, the experiment of uniting into one kingdom three peoples joined by racial and linguistic affinities, but separated by divergent interests and outlooks, having proved a conspicuous failure."

140. FO 371/33490, R2367/1990/92, R2691/1990/92.

141. FO 371/33490, R3620/1990/92.

142. FO 371/33490, R3643/1990/92.

143. *Ibid.*

144. FO 371/33490, R3977/1990/92, R4036/1990/92. Formal Soviet agreement to a self-denying ordinance was communicated to Eden by Maisky on 14 July. The British later made it clear to the Russians that they did not object to a Soviet-Yugoslav mutual assistance pact, provided that it related only to the war-time period. (In fact, the British welcomed the idea as perhaps providing a lever with which to counter the Soviets' hostility to Mihailović.) Maisky was told, however, that a Soviet guarantee of Yugoslavia's territorial integrity would be unwise since Britain had refrained from going so far. FO 371/33490, R4693/1990/92, R5031/1990/92.

145. The Greek and Yugoslav ministers agreed in late September to coordinate their foreign policies on the basis of fortnightly consultations. They were particularly determined not to negotiate with any "free movement", nor with any neighbour of the USSR whose borders remained undefined, i.e. Poland and Romania. The fortnightly meetings continued until the end of the year, but became infrequent thereafter and finally lapsed altogether. From the Greek perspective, the Yugoslav government was an increasingly feeble and dubious partner; while the Yugoslavs, for their part, disliked the Greeks' preoccupation with territorial acquisitions from Albania and Bulgaria. SSIP, MIPKJ, F-5, 1941-43, Minutes of Greek-Yugoslav Discussions, br. 538, 26/9/42; Xydis, *Greece and the Great Powers*, pp. 21-22; FO 371/33134, R6626/43/67.

146. FO 371/33154, R8820/8820/67. Rendel deprecated this tendency to think that all could be sorted out with the Soviets. He believed that the threat in the Balkans (and especially in its "crux", Bulgaria) came not from Russian intervention, but from spontaneous communist revolution. His solution, argued

so persistently and at such length that the Foreign Office ultimately declared the controversy "sterile", was South Slav confederation. In this, of course, he was at one with Milan Gavrilović. FO 371/33154, R8821/8820/67; FO 371/37173, *passim.* Rendel also proposed consultations with the Turks on the subject of confederations. This was tried by the Foreign Office, but with disasterous consequences. For the Turks quickly began promoting an anti-Soviet bloc among the Axis states of South-Eastern Europe. Barker, *British Policy,* p. 135.

147. For details, *Ibid.,* pp. 134-35.

148. FO 371/37173, R13912/214/67.

NOTES

CHAPTER V

1. Deakin, *The Embattled Mountain,* p. 177. The same evaluation is made in Deakin's "Britanija i Jugoslavija, 1941-1945", p. 48, and by Sweet-Escott in *Baker Street Irregular,* pp. 161-62, and in his contribution to Auty and Clogg, *British Policy towards Wartime Resistance,* pp. 12-13.

2. These factors are explored in detail by Elisabeth Barker in "Fresh Sidelights on British Policy in Yugoslavia, 1942-3", *Slavonic and East European Review,* LIV, 4 (October 1976), pp. 572-85; as well as by her and other contributors to Auty and Clogg, *British Policy towards Wartime Resistance,* pp. 22-58 and *passim.* See also Sweet-Escott, *Baker Street Irregular,*p. 73ff, and Karchmar, "Draža Mihailović and the Rise of the Četnik Movement", pp. 721-98.

The exile government was aware of the organizational inadequacy of Britain's approach to the resistance, and particularly of the gulf that divided SIS and SOE. The Jovanović government was frustrated by the inability of the Foreign Office to convince MI5 that it should have direct radio communications with Mihailović and angered by the unseemly competition in Cairo between SIS and SOE for Yugoslav military bodies suitable for infiltration into the country. Apparently the latter led to a general refusal on the part of Yugoslav soldiers in Cairo to go back at either organization's behest. Radoje L. Knežević, "Organizovanje otpora", *Poruka,* 13 (16 June 1953), pp. 10-11; AVII, kutija 171, br. 13/3(1-5), Vojni kabinet referat 104, 24/2/42.

3. That this was the case is illustrated by Captain Michael Maclagan's report for MI3b, "A Short History of the Revolt in Yugoslavia", dated 27 April 1943. FO 371/37586, R4765/2/92. The SIS presence in Slovenia is affirmed by SOE's appeal in December 1942 for the assistance of SIS agents on the ground in gathering intelligence and preparing reception committees for a planned SOE mission. WO 202/356, tel. B1/3754.

4. Auty and Clogg, *British Policy towards Wartime Resistance,* pp. 12-13, 210-15; Barker, "Fresh Sidelights", p. 574.

5 Deakin, *The Embattled Mountain,* pp. 155-76. Deakin does refer to an "SOE mission" composed of two Yugoslavs carrying four million lire to Mihailović in July. This may have been the "Robertson" mission. See note 6.

6. Plećaš, "S mora i iz vazduha u porobljenu Otadžbinu", pp. 39-45. The author gives what appear to be reliable details about all the missions despatched from Egypt during 1942, including his own. But he does not distinguish their provenance as between SOE and SIS. Of the nine missions not accounted for by Deakin, all but one were sent to areas either known to be in Četnik hands or over which the Partisans and Četniks had recently fought, e.g. Majevica, Sandžak and central Montenegro. The exception was a Yugoslav team destined for Jagodina (Svetozarevo) and designed to make contact with Nedić - obviously an SIS assignment. This mission was, however, dropped over Hercegovina by mistake and was quickly captured. Two missions went to Mihailović's Montengrin headquarters: that of Captain "Charles Robertson" (a Yugoslav ex-communist named Dragi Radivojević) in July and that of Plećaš himself in September.

According to Bailey's 1944 report, the presence of the "freelance Robertson" and the "sinister Vemić" (evidently the other surviving member of the four-man Plećaš team) on Sinjajevina with their own W/T sets, mysterious briefs and undefined relationships to Hudson seriously impaired the latter's recently reestablished authority with Mihailović. On the other hand, the arrival in late August of a signals mission headed by Lieutenant P. H. A. Lofts eased Hudson's communications problems. Since SOE secured from SIS during 1942 the right to operate its own signals service, the Lofts mission may have been a fruit of this change. FO 371/44282, R21295/11/92.

By mid-November Hudson had been granted some limited authority over "Robertson", SOE referring to the latter as Hudson's assistant in communications with the Foreign Office. It seems, however, that "Robertson's" attempts to disseminate communist propaganda among the Četniks and his apparent wish to cross over to the Partisans made him something less than a help to Hudson. WO 202/356, tels. GESH 151, 161, 192 and Villa Resta 967; FO 371/33469, R7571/178/92. Further details on "Robertson" may be found in Amery, *Approach March,* p. 261, and Deakin, *The Embattled Mountain,* pp. 150-54.

Bailey's references to Vemić following his own arrival at Mihailović headquartrs on Christmas Day 1942 made it plain that Vemić was an SIS body: e.g. W0202/357, tels. EMBODY 136 and 137 of 24-26/1/43 and 169 of 5/2/43.

7. *Post hoc* evidence of this is offered by the sole Foreign Office minute on the aforementioned Maclagan report. Rose noted only - and three months after its receipt - that it provided "a useful summary". Had the Southern Department not seen such things before, the report would have come as a blockbuster. The reaction of SOE London may have been stronger. FO 371/37586, R4705/2/92.

8. Barker, "Fresh Sidelights," p. 572.

9. For example: FO 371/33465, R1144/178/92, R1375/178/92.

10. FO 371/33135, R2472/75/67. Directive of 11/4/42.

11. Karchmar, "Draža Mihailović and the Rise of the Četnik Movement", p. 873.

12. AVII, kutija 175, br. 4/1-5, tel. 22. Though signed by Jovanović, operational orders such as this originated with SOE.

13. AVII, kutija 175, br. 11/1(5-6), Ostojić to Mihailović, tel. 1002. This is a typical example of Četnik prose, though the meaning - that Atherton threatened to undermine the Serb nationalist cause by promoting wasteful resistance - is clear enough. For a full examination of Atherton's strange and fatal behaviour, and its impact on the Partisans, see Deakin, *The Embattled Mountain,* pp. 155-76.

14. AVII, kutija 172, br. 25/2-1, tel. 197; also WO 202/128 for a much mutilated version.

15. AVII, kutija 175, br. 11/1-8, tel. 121.

16. Bailey report, FO 371/44282, R21295/11/92.

17. Communications with Mihailović were erratic rather than non-existent in this period. Mihailović sent no telegrams between 2 December and 2 January. On 6 January, however, three telegrams arrived bearing the date 2 December. The British doubted the authenticity of these; for in a further message (dated 8 January, but only received on 24 January) Mihailović explained that they had been erroneously dated December instead of January and attested to their authorship. He also reported that he was located once more on Suvobor and accompanied by Lalatović and Ostojić. Several more messages bearing January dates were received at the end of the month. In February, March and April the gaps between telegrams generally ranged from several days to a week. There was, however, one long break between 24 February and 18 March. During this period Mihailović transferred his headquarters from Suvobor to Takovo. He moved southwards twice more in April - from Takovo to Čemerno and then to Golija in Sandžak - each time causing another short lapse in communications. By May the steady trickle of messages had become a torrent. According to Mihailović's own numbering, he sent 101 telegrams between 2 January and 5 May, but 60 in the next three weeks. By no means all these messages were received by

the British. Those that were may be found in the Villa Resta file, WO 202/128. The accounts of Mihailović's long silence by Deakin (*The Embattled Mountain,* p. 149) and Roberts (*Tito, Mihailović and the Allies,* p. 53) are exaggerated.

18. AVII, kutija 175, br. 18/3-5, tel. 107; also WO 202/128 for a slightly different translation.

19. FO 371/33465, R178/178/92; PREM 3, 510/1; FO 371/33440, R462/12/92. In his January messages (the authenticity of which the British suspected) Mihailović had however reported that, "The communists although broken up are again beginning to appear sporadically and are hindering my work. They should be called to obedience through Moscow." WO 202/128, tel. 64.

20. FO 371/33465, R1394/178/92.

21. FO 371/33465, R890/178/92; AVII, kutija 171, br. 36/1-1 (Jovanović to Cairo, tel. 82, 31/1/42) and br. 13/3(1-5) (Vojni kabinet referat 104, 24/2/42); Knežević, "Organizovanje otpora", p. 11.

22. FO 371/33465, R1351/178/92. The Liberator was the only bomber with sufficient range to operate the 2000 mile round trip from Egypt or Britain to central Yugoslavia with a useful payload. None of the six aircraft (five Whitleys and one Halifax) allocated to supply duties over the 1200 mile route from Malta in December remained operational. Meanwhile enemy action and serious congestion had rendered Malta unusable for supply flights.

23. FO 371/33465, R1589/178/92, R1590/178/92.

24. FO 371/33466, R2079/178/92.

25. FO 371/33467, R2515/178/92. The Russians did, of course, have wireless links with the Partisans and - from February - directly with Tito's headquarters. Messages no longer had to be relayed by courier to and from Zagreb. *Zbornik,* Tom II, knjiga 2, p. 429.

26. Dalton (whose relations with Eden were bad) was replaced in February by the Earl of Selborne (a personal friend of Churchill's) as Minister of Economic Warfare. But like Dalton he remained outside the War Cabinet. Nelson was

forced by ill-health to retire in May. He was succeeded by his second-in-command, Sir Charles Hambro. Foot, *Resistance,* p. 138, and *SOE in France,* p. 16; Barker, "Fresh Sidelights", pp. 577-78.

27. CAB 80/62, COS(42) 80(0). The Axis order of battle was estimated to comprise 17 Italian, 5 German and 4 Bulgarian divisions. Nelson implied - but did not explain how Mihailović's operations could account for them all.

28. CAB 79/20, COS(42)102.

29. CAB 79/20, COS(42)117.

30. FO 371/33466, R2855/178/92; FO 371/33467, R3008/178/92. The published Yugoslav documents reveal how assiduous the Russians in fact were at this time in attempting to guide the Partisans privately in ways inoffensive to the British, e.g. *Zbornik,* II, 3, pp. 104, 131-32, 210.

31. Given the constant stream of Yugoslav petitions it could not have been otherwise. Jovanović appealed to Churchill and King Peter to King George in late April; Ninčić to Eden in early May. Aid for and communications with Mihailović were the subjects. The result on 6 May was another refusal by the Chiefs of Staff to consider withdrawing aircraft from Coastal Command, fortified at that moment by a new (but temporary) break in radio links with Mihailović while he transferred headquarters. (Deakin's explanation for the lapse, however, is that London had put questions to Mihailović about the Partisans' leadership and strength which he was disinclined to answer.) FO 371/33467, R2972/178/92; FO 371/33493, R2976/2345/92; SSIP, MIPKJ, F-3, Jovanović to Churchill, letter 341 of 23/4/42; CAB 79/20, COS(42)141; Deakin, *The Embattled Mountain,* p. 150.

32. Karchmar, "Draža Mihailović and the Rise of the Četnik Movement", p. 536.

33. The Yugoslavs were aware, as were the other exile governments, of the privileged position accorded the Poles in the matter of communications - and resented the fact. AVII, kutija 171, br. 33/4-2, Vojni kabinet referat 217, 20/3/42.

34. See Dušan Petković, "Kako je uspostavljena veza sa djen. Mihailovićem iz Carigrada", *Glasnik,* 5 (June 1960), pp. 49-55;

as well as various articles by Jovan Djonović, also in *Glasnik:* "Veze s Dražom Mihailovićem sa Srednjeg i Bliskog Istoka i Severne Afrike", pp. 49-54; "Moje veze s Dražom Mihailovićem sa Srednjeg Istoka", 2 (December 1958), pp. 82-98; "Telegrami Draže Mihailovića o Engleskim misijama u svom stabu i Engleskoj politici na terenu", 5, 6, 7 (June and December 1960, June 1961), pp. 24-35, 53-57, 63-80.

35. AVII, kutija 175, br. 18/3-5, tel. 209; also WO 202/128, p. 80.

36. AJ, Fond 103, F-8, no. 68 (English text submitted to Jovanović 1/6/42); AVII, kutija 175, br. 29/1-2, tel. 31 (Serbo-Croat text as despatched 4/6/42). The Lofts signals mission (see note 6) was no doubt the solution envisaged for continuing communications vagaries. The British rightly suspected that Mihailović's codes were compromised and wished to put some order into his chaotically run signals section. PREM 3, 510/3.

37. Deakin, *The Embattled Mountain,* pp. 149-50.

38. FO 371/33445, R7445/21/92.

39. Deakin, *The Embattled Mountain,* p. 149. I have not found the message quoted by Deakin in the Villa Resta file.

40. Roberts, *Tito, Mihailovic and the Allies,* p. 57.

41. Tomasevich, *The Chetniks,* p. 285. "Radovan" was Ronald H. Jones, an Australian Officer who had escaped with Christie Lawrence from a German POW train passing through Serbia the previous year. The Četniks proved more adept at winning to their cause these and other accidental liaison officers than they were with their official guests. The recapture of Lawrence in June and of Jones in July may have stimulated Mihailović's interest in restoring tolerable relations with Hudson. Lawrence, *Irregular Adventure,* pp. 226ff.

42. Hudson's letter is reproduced in *The Trial of Dragoljub-Draža Mihailović,* p. 122. On the Montenegrin situation see AFHQ, *The Četniks,* chapt. 3, and Milazzo, *The Chetnik Movement,* pp. 43-48, 81-86.

43. Deakin, *The Embattled Mountain,* pp. 149-50.

44. FO 371/33455, R3139/151/92; PREM 3, 510/12.

45. *Ibid.*

46. *Ibid.*

47. *Ibid.* Brooke also reported that after his long silence Hudson was now sending interesting messages, and he gave

details of aid thus far sent to Mihailović. This included 43 machine guns, 24 submachine guns, 880 grenades, 50,000 rounds of ammunition, 15,500 gold sovereigns, $12,000, 5 million lire and 7 W/T sets.

48. FO 371/33467, R4516/178/92. Neither SOE nor the Foreign Office placed a high premium on truth in the making of effective propaganda. PWE and the BBC did; and this entailed battles with their political masters. (See Elisabeth Barker's sardonic reflections in Auty and Clogg, *British Policy towards Wartime Resistance,* pp. 27-29.)

The Foreign Office saw propaganda as the handmaiden of high policy; SOE as a means of soothing (or not upsetting) its liaison officers' relations with Mihailović. He of course was quick to express outrage at the mention of any Yugoslav "patriots" other than himself. Typical was a telegram of 26 May, well before the BBC dared mention the Partisans by name: "Radio emissions which apostrophize the Partisans seriously harm the reputation of both the English and our government among the people. Nowhere are they fighting the occupiers. They kill only distinguished nationalists . . . Theirs is a war in the rear and not at the front. Nor do the Germans pursue them." AVII, kutija 175, br. 18/3-5, tel. 211.

The Partisans were just as sensitive about their image and, by May, happy to be getting a look-in. Moša Pijade wrote to Tito on 6 May, "It seems now that various radio stations (Ankara, Switzerland, America) are talking more about the Partisans in Yugoslavia. That Stalin has mentioned us in his orders of the day I interpret as the best sign and perspective." *Zbornik,* II, 4, p. 43.

49. FO 371/33467, R4144/178/92.

50. On 15 July Mihailović telegraphed: "Nedić and company always say that they are cooperating with me . . . I again reject with disgust any suggestion of collaboration with traitors in either thought or deed." AVII, kutija 175, br. 35/3-3, tel. 310. Yet earlier in July Mihailović had noted, "Nedic has no army of his own. All of it is secretly with us. Unfortunately there are some officers who serve him as well as the Germans. . . . I have plenty of officers infiltrated in his ranks." AVII, kutija 175, br.

14/4-3, tel. 165. There was no necessary contradiction, but something approaching a leap of faith was required to avoid one.

51. FO 371/33467, R4400/178/92.

52. FO 371/33468, R4788/178/92.

53. FO 371/33468, R4873/178/92, R4975/178/92; Louis Adamic, *My Native Land* (New York: Harper & Brothers, 1943), pp. 63-65.

54. FO 371/33468, R5018/178/92. The information on which such expectations were based was illustrated by a report on Croatia sent to the Yugoslav government by its Istanbul intelligence agent in mid-June and no doubt shared with SOE: "It is considered that the Partisans are being dispersed and had they not been helped by the Četniks they would have been completely annihilated. The Partisans are everywhere weak and factionalized and are trying to join with General Mihailović." SSIP, MIPKJ, F-1, 1940-44, br. 107, 12/7/43.

55. FO 371/33468, R4788/178/92.

56. FO 371/33490, R5212/1990/92.

57. FO 371/33458, R5165/178/92. Minute by A. V. Coverley-Price, 5/8/42. Similar sentiments were expressed by him on R5143/178/92.

58. FO 371/44276, R12712/11/92. This is a short history of relations with Mihailović which Eden commissioned in July 1944 from Hugh Grey of the Foreign Office Library. Its purpose was to demonstrate that Britain had not betrayed Mihailović for sake of the Russians.

59. *Ibid.;* Llewellyn Woodward, *British Foreign Policy in the Second World War,* Vol. 3 (London: HMSO, 1971), p. 287.

60. FO 371/44276, R12712/11/92.

61. FO 371/33469, R5577/178/92. As quoted by Rendel in a protest to Howard on 22 August that Eden had gone so far in impugning Mihailović.

62. FO 371/44276, R12712/11/92. Eden was particularly exercised over the 12 August issue of *Soviet War News* which named Tito as the real leader of Yugoslav resistance. FO 371/33468, R5334/178/92.

63. FO 371/33469, R5474/178/92. Murray did not, however,

challenge the prevailing assumption that the Partisans possessed no centralized command, nor did he discuss the issue of collaboration.

64. FO 371/33469, R5427/178/92.

65. FO 371/33469, R5538/178/92.

66 *Ibid.*

67. FO 371/33470, R5973/178/92.

68. *Ibid.*

69. *Ibid.;* and R6363/178/92.

70. FO 371/33470, R5973/178/92; FO 371/33471, R6882/178/92.

71. FO 371/37584, R3994/2/92. Dated 29/4/43, this memorandum by Howard surveying the Četnik-Partisan conflict cities many documents otherwise withheld.

72. FO 371/33470, R5973/178/92. Dixon's letter expressed the conclusions of a late September policy review (RJ 484). Sargent felt that although Mihailović should continue to get token material support, no effort should be made to increase its scale "merely in order to enable him to fight the Partisans." FO 371/37584, R3994/2/92. A month later, however, Eden expressed pleasure at the increased support for Mihailović reported by SOE. FO 371/33471, R6695/178/92.

73. FO 371/33470, R5973/178/92.

74. FO 371/37584, R3994/2/92.

75. Auty and Clogg, *British Policy towards Wartime Resistance,* p. 212.

76. *Ibid.*, pp. 69, 212; FO 371/37584, R3994/2/92. Bill Bailey - a mining engineer long resident in Yugoslavia, fluent in Serbo-Croat and steeped in Balkan history - had served Section "D" and SOE since 1939 in Belgrade, Istanbul, Cairo and North America. He had also incurred the enmity of the Yugoslav military cabinet; and SOE Cairo feared that the Knežević brothers would seek to undermine his authority with Mihailović. WO 202/356, tel. B1/3393 of 22/11/42.

77. Auty and Clogg, *British Policy towards Wartime Resistance,* pp. 34, 212; Barker, "Fresh Sidelights", p. 573; Taylor papers, AD to CD (Taylor to Hambro), tel. 687/89 of 4/12/42. See below.

78. FO 371/33470, R6363/178/92.

79. FO 371/33470, R5973/178/92.

80. FO 371/33470, R6253/178/92.

SOE apparently took at face value the long lists of distinguished Serbs murdered by the Partisans that Mihailović was sending to his government and which it, in turn, was using as ammunition in its counterattack on the Russians. After first approving this strategy ("This has probably given the Russians a headache," wrote Coverly-Price), the Foreign Office soon came to the conclusion that it was counter-productive - it showed just how hopeless the prospect of resistance unity really was. The Foreign Office seemed not to react at all to the concomitant Yugoslav attempt to convince the Soviets that the Partisans' ranks were - besides Hungarians, Jews and international criminals - rife with Trotskyites who worked for the Gestapo. FO 371/33469, R5479/178/92, R5798/178/92; FO 371/33470, R5961/178/92, R6220/178/92; AVII, kutija 172, br. 23/6-5 and 30/6-2.

Mihailović saw no contradiction in accusing the Partisans of serving the Germans and the Ustaše while at the same time denouncing them for provoking horrible reprisals by their resistance. (He also accused them of every sexual perversion his limited imagination could run to, though the presence of women in Partisan units meant that he could manage quite a few.) He reported his own reprisals with relish (e.g. the massacre of 2000 Croat and Moslem inhabitants of Foča) and expected his allies to undertake others for him. The British engaged in a running battle with the military cabinet over the issue of broadcasting Mihailović's infamous "Z" notices (for *zaklati,* to slaughter) whereby "traitors" were marked out for execution by his "trojkas". He repeatedly asked that Zagreb be bombed and on 15 October demanded that Roosevelt execute two German-Americans for every Serb murdered by the Nazis and Ustaše in Yugoslavia. For a sampling see: FO 371/33472, R7571/178/92; WO 202/ 355; AVII, kutija 174.

81. FO 371/33470, R6315/178/92. Whereas SOE had written, "Small but constant sabotage would make an appreciable difference . . ." to the Axis war effort, Alexander omitted the

"small but" and specified his interest in the interdiction of railways.

Unhappy at Jovanović's quick compliance with British desires in this matter, Živan Knežević protested against both unreserved acceptance of British operational authority over Mihailović and the suggestion that yet more sacrifices should be asked of the Serbs, whose losses already totalled a million dead. AVII, kutija 172, br. 30/9-1, referat 845, 25/9/42.

82. Plećaš, "S mora i iz vazduha u porobljenu Otadžbinu", p. 43. The mission was dropped over Suvobor on 22/23 September.

83. FO 371/33471, R6801/178/92.

84. FO 371/33470, R6303/178/92.

85. FO 371/33471, R7027/178/92; AVII, kutija 172, br. 13/8(1-5), kutija 173, br. 9/1(1-5).

86. FO 371/33471, R7027/178/92; FO 371/33472, R7336/178/92. The new line had in fact been anticipated by H. D. Harrison, the BBC's Balkan editor. On 18 October he broadcast a commentary (based on recent recommendations from Hudson) which praised resistance "no matter under whose leadership" and mentioned the Partisans as fighting for the same ideals of freedom and a new Yugoslavia as was Mihailović. This naturally outraged both sides. FO 371/33445, R7177/21/92, R7178/21/92.

87. FO 371/33473, R8377/178/92.

88. WO 202/356, tels. GESH 197 and 199. Hudson had already reported that the new line was prompting Mihailović to claim more (and more specific) anti-Axis operations. Hudson insisted, however, that besides the pressure of broadcasts, he must also have the carrot of increased aid with which to bargain. FO 371/33445, R7445/21/92.

89. Taylor papers, tels. 687/9 (AD to CD) of 4/12/42, A/608/9 (CD to AD) of 7/12/42, 694 (AD 3 to CD) of 6/12/42; WO 202/356, tel. G/3516 (AD3 to London) of 26/11/42. Taylor, Hambro's chief of staff, was on an inspection tour of the Cairo mission.

90. Taylor papers, letter (AD to CD) of 14/12/42; Barker, "Fresh Sidelights", pp. 579-80. The contention was not just

between the London and Cairo ends of SOE. On 18 November Glenconner wrote to his chief of staff, Brigadier C. M. Keble, arguing against a proposal from inside the Cairo mission that Mihailović should be dropped in favour of the Partisans. To do so, Glenconner wrote, would be both to betray the Yugoslav government and to deprive SOE of any viable instrument inside the country: "it is more than doubtful whether the Communists would ever agree to work with us even if we turned completely round and gave them our full support." WO 202/132A, G/JU198 (AD to DSO/B) of 18/11/42.

91. Taylor papers, tel. 717 (AD3 to CD) of 12/12/42.

92. Taylor papers, *passim;* Barker, "Fresh Sidelights", pp. 579-80; Auty and Clogg, *British Policy towards Wartime Resistance,* pp. 229-33. Glenconner travelled to London - bearing Taylor's note - with the object of clearing up the "misunderstanding".

93. FO 371/33474, R8721/178/92. Radio "Karadjordje" began operations on 20 November in Jerusalem, but under the guise of broadcasting from inside Serbia. It was until the last weeks of its short life - through 27 March 1943 - vigourously anti-Croat in tone. Dušan Petković, "Četnička radio stanica 'Karadjordje'", *Glasnik,* 3 (June 1959), p. 43. Mihailović thought many of the station's broadcasts were "brilliant." WO 202/356, tel. GESH 221 of 1/12/42.

94. FO 371/33474, R8805/178/92. The message originated with the Deputy DMI and was meant merely to commemorate the Yugoslav national day, 1 December.

95. FO 371/33474, R8721/178/92.

96. FO 371/33445, R7445/21/92.

97. FO 371/33472, R7426/178/92, R7496/178/92.

98. AVII, kutija 174, br. 33/3(15-16), tel. 946.

99. FO 371/33472, R7571/178/92.

100. FO 371/33472, R7756/178/92. In his reply to Pearson on 21 November Howard queried some of the terminology used in a recent OSS report received by the Foreign Office. What was meant, he asked, by the term "Green Army" (*Zeleni kadar*)? This may have been the beginning of Foreign Office hopes that the Partisans might turn out to be more green Croats than red Bolsheviks.

101. FO 371/33473, R8181/178/92 (FO emphasis); WO 202/356, tels. GESH 171-83. Hudson's telegrams were edited for Foreign Office consumption. Those dealing with specific aspects of Mihailović's relations with the Italians have been expurgated from the Foreign Office files, but the whole series is available in the War Office file cited here.

102. FO 371/37584, R3994/2/92.

102. FO 371/33443, R7970/12/92; FO 371/33477, *passim;* SSIP, F-1, Pretsedništvo vlade K. J., 1941-44. (This file contains the minutes of the autumn's marathon cabinet meetings.)

104. FO 371/33474, R8720/178/92.

105. FO 371/33474, R8721/178/92.

106. FO 371/33474, R8720/178/92.

107. FO 371/33503, R8605/5606/92. King Peter had a heart to heart chat with Howard on 15 December regarding the composition of his new government and asked if he might see him regularly in place of Rendel - and as a second best to Eden or Cadogan. The King subsequently embarrassed Eden by representing the Foreign Secretary as having demanded Ninčić's exclusion from the government. This was, of course, the point of Eden's comments, but a violation of confidence and an exaggeration. Rendel inclined to the view that either MI5 or SOE had it in for Ninčić and worked to secure his removal. FO 371/33433, R8699/12/73, R8733/12/92, R9091/12/92.

108. PREM 3, 510/5. It was by this line of reasoning that Mihailović convinced himself that he could ignore British expressions of dissatisfaction: he would be far too important to them in the long run as a force against communism.

109. FO 371/33474, R8721/178/92.

110. SSIP, Pretsednistvo ministarskog saveta - Kabinet, 1941-45, F-1, br. 2500, 26/12/42.

111. AVII, kutija 173, br. 33/9(1-3), Vojni kabinet referat br. 1057, 30/12/42. Knežević also wrote that he had led Boughey into a discussion of possible replacement leaders for Mihailović. Boughey opined that perhaps Pavle Djurišić was the best candidate. See Chapter VI, section v.

112. FO 371/37578, R2/2/92. Jovanović made it a condition of entry into his new government that each minister swear his

loyalty to Mihailović and his opposition to the Partisans. FO 371/37606, R121/121/92.

113. FO 371/37578, R2/2/92.

NOTES

CHAPTER VI

1. FO 371/37578, R3/2/92.
2. FO 371/37578, R335/2/92.
3. FO 371/37578, R745/2/92.
4. FO 371/37608, R1097/143/92.
5. FO 371/37607, R614/143/92.
6. *Ibid.*
7. Churchill, *The Hinge of Fate,* p. 616; Michael Howard, *Grand Stategy,* Vol. IV (London: HMSO, 1972), p. 389; Auty and Clogg, *British Policy towards Wartime Resistance,* p. 103. It was apparently this manifestation of the Prime Minister's interest that converted the ambitious Keble to avid pursuit of the Partisans. Barker, *British Policy,* p. 162; Auty and Clogg, *op. cit.,* p. 239.
8. FO 371/37579, R1513/2/92; Howard, *Grand Strategy,* pp. 390-91. As has been noted above, six Halifaxes were promised to SOE in December. Their addition to SOE's flight of four Liberators would mean that SOE disposed of 20% of the total bomber force in the Middle East. The planes did not arrive until April.
9. WO 202/357, tels. B1/3323/6 of 21/1/43, B1/3550 of 28/1/43, B1/3577 of 28/1/43, B1/3585 of 29/1/43, B1/3619 of 30/1/43, B1/3658 of 31/1/43 and B1/3662 of 1/2/43. This assault was initiated by Cairo while Glenconner was still (or again) in London.
10. WO 202/132A, COS/100/1A/547 (letter from Keble to Murray of 9/2/43), B/MDH/1/630 (memo from DSO(b) to COS of 8/2/43), B1/55/18/315 (memo from B1 to DSO(b) of 7/2/43).

11. The Bailey report was dated 22 January and entered by the Foreign Office as R978, but has been withheld. It is, however, summarized by both Deakin (*The Embattled Mountain,* pp. 179-80) and Howard (FO 371/37584, R3994/2/92). Bailey's follow-up message is contained in FO 371/37579, R1384/2/92 and WO 202/357, tel. B1/3979/80 of 7/2/43. SOE Cairo argued to London on 1 February that "without operations to Croatia, D/H2's [Bailey's] Tito plan certain failure." WO 202/357, tel. B1/3662. Woodward's contention (*British Foreign Policy,* III, p. 289) that Bailey advocated exclusive support for Mihailović and no dealings with the ruthless and cruel Partisans cannot be credited.

Bailey later wrote that he and Hudson realized that their scheme for a territorial division was almost "a counsel of despair." His description of the demarcation line proposed (from the Yugoslav-Bulgarian frontier on the Danube in the northeast to the Montenegrin-Albanian border in the southwest) is wrong. He apparently confused his first spheres proposal with the line of the River Ibar which Cairo attempted to impose in May. Auty and Clogg, *British Policy towards Wartime Resistance,* p. 73.

12. FO 371/37579, R1521/2/92. Most of these points were first made by Rendel in a letter to Sargent on 3 February. FO 371/37579, R1141/2/92. Deakin lists another important Foreign Office objection to Bailey's scheme: the potential embarrassment for the Allies of encountering a hostile Partisan force were there to be a landing on the Dalmatian or Croatian coasts later in the war. Deakin, *The Embattled Mountain,* pp. 180-81.

13. FO 371/37584, R3994/2/92.

14. *Ibid.* Representatives of SIS also attended this meeting, the specific record of which (on R1503/2/92) has been withheld.

15. Howard, *Grand Strategy,* p. 390; FO 371/37579, R1521/2/92; FO 371/37584, R3994/2/92; WO 202/357, *passim.*

16. FO 371/37579, R1521/2/92.

17. *Ibid.;* WO 202/357, tel. G/611 (AD3 to London). Rose was quick to urge (on 19 February) explicit propaganda support for

the Partisans over the BBC. FO 371/37579, R1345/2/92. Yet when SOE Cairo pointed at the end of the month to the deleterious effect which mention of the Partisans was having on Bailey's relations with Mihailović, compounding the basic weakness of his position produced by the absence of supply sorties, Rose investigated. He discovered that there had been a 6:1 ratio in favour of the Partisans in the BBC's news bulletins during the first three weeks of February. While he felt that this reflected accurately the relative activity of the two forces, he recommended that an effort be made to 'right' the balance. On 2 March the BBC was asked to mention the Četniks more frequently, if necessary by inventing 'news' about their actions. FO 371/37580, R1719/2/92.

18. FO 371/37584, R3994/2/92. Clark-Kerr had been told on 2 February that if the Soviets agreed to exert pressure on the Partisans, Britain would tackle Mihailović with the object of ending hostilities. The Foreign Office was right to discount the attraction this would have for the Russians. FO 371/37578, R3/2/92.

19. Barker, *British Policy,* p. 163; FO 371/37579, R1521/2/92.

20. FO 371/37583, R3031/2/92. Although the 18 February meeting apparently accepted Bailey's suggestion that Hudson should travel to Tito's headquarters to open talks, this idea was soon dropped, presumably because of the battles between Partisans and Četniks that accompanied Operation "Weiss." Deakin, *The Embattled Mountain,* p. 181.

21. FO 371/33473, R8236/178/92; AVII, kutija 173, br. 22/6(1-4), Lozić to Jovanović tel. 579, 23/11/42, and Jovanović to Lozić tel. 983, 30/11/42; Stephen Clissold (ed.), *Yugoslavia and the Soviet Union 1939-1973: A Documentary Survey* (London: RIIA / Oxford University Press, 1975), pp. 140-41.

22. FO 371/37578, R3/2/92; Barker, *British Policy,* p. 163.

23. FO 371/37579, R1609/2/92. According to Roberts (*Tito, Mihailović and the Allies.* p. 91), the British had proposed a simultaneous - not a joint - mission to the Partisans.

24. FO 371/37584, R3994/2/92; FO 371/37583, R3031/2/92.

25. Woodward, *British Foreign Policy,* III, p. 290.

26. FO 371/37582, R2496/2/92.

27. FO 371/37581, R1988/2/92; WO 202/357, tel. EMBODY 218 of 14/2/43 and 386 (AD to London) of 17/2/43.

28. FO 371/37580, R1847/2/92.

29. FO 371/37580, R1848/2/92; WO 202/357, tels. G/742/4 (AD3 to London) of 27/2/43 and G/779/80 (AD3 to London) of 28/2/43.

30. CAB 79/59, COS(43)34(0). The Chiefs' conclusion reflected the advice received from the Middle East Defence committee on 22 February. WO 202/357, tel. G/641 (AD3 to London) of 23/2/43; Howard, *Grand Strategy,* p. 391.

31. FO 371/37581, R2091/2/92. London was not alone in its confusion over aircraft. Glenconner's immediate reaction to the news that SOE would get four more Halifaxes was to express satisfaction. Once modified by the addition of extra fuel tanks and added to SOE's existing four Halifaxes, they would permit adequate supply of Mihailović, leaving SOE's four Liberators free "for Croatia and Slovenia." WO 202/359, tel. G/918/19 (AD3 to London) of 3/3/43. A few days later, however, Glenconner had changed his mind - and lost four Halifaxes in the process: "I am glad that Chiefs of Staff agree that it is best to back A/H31 and not the Partisans *in Serbia*... The Chiefs are under a complete misapprehension, however, if they think that the four existing Liberators and the four new Halifaxes which have now been allotted to us will suffice to back A/H31 in Serbia as well as the Croat and Slovene guerrillas who are sometimes also referred to as Partisans which has led to much confusion." SOE must have at least *four more Halifaxes* for use in supporting Mihailović (eight Halifaxes representing the carrying capacity of three Liberators over the distance) before it could contemplate diverting the existing Liberators to work over Croatia and Slovenia. The six Halifaxes allocated to SOE in December - and finally en route to Egypt - were reserved for Greece. WO 202/359, tel. 1049/51 (AD3 to D/HV) of 7/3/43. (My emphasis.) It seems that the latter acounting was the correct one. A new problem was soon posed by the fact that SOE's Liberators were

ageing rapidly and only 50% serviceable by the spring. Taylor papers, letter Taylor to Casey, 6/3/43.

32. SOE Cairo had proposed to London in late November 1942 the recruitment of up to 100 Yugoslav-Canadians of NCO potential for infiltration into Yugoslavia. The first consignments of men arrived in Egypt in early February. By the end of the month Cairo had called a halt on further shipments, not because of any dissatisfaction with the calibre of the men selected, but because the aircraft shortage necessitated a downward revision of SOE's targets. WO 202/356, tel. B1/3438 of 24/11/42; WO 202/357, tels. B1/15/16 of 9/2/43 and B1/555 of 21/2/43. More details in Deakin, *The Embattled Mountain,* pp. 207-11.

33. FO 371/37581, R2221/2/92; WO 202/359, tel. G/959/62 (AD3 to London) of 4/3/43. One of the most significant excisions made by Baker Street from Glenconner's original telegram was its conclusion: "In short, we must get into the country and run it ourselves as far as our resources permit and the more the Serbs, Croats and Slovenes can be made to depend on us, the more will we be able to control events. Until we have done this, we are hardly entitled to complain if they are recalcitrant and misguided."

In a commentary on Glenconner's telegram Bailey pointed out that although the Partisans' tactics against the Axis were exhausting the country, so in a different way was Mihailović's inactivity. Both represented extremes undesirable from the British point of view. Mihailović argued against anti-Axis operations on the grounds of conserving Serb blood, but meanwhile he "does not hesitate to shed [it] extravagently against the Partisans." The time had come to treat Mihailović firmly: "He must be made to realize that we can make or break him." FO 371/37582, R2655/2/92.

34. WO 202/357, tel. EMB 156 of 3/2/43. In fact the Italians had already decided to ignore the Germans' instructions not to make use of the Četniks in the operation. The ferocity of the struggle owed much to the conviction shared by all those involved that an Allied landing in the Balkans was in prospect.

For full details of "Weiss" see Milazzo, *The Chetnik Movement*, chapter 6.

35. WO 202/357, tels. EMB 176 of 6/2/43 and EMB 218 of 12/2/43.

36. WO 202/357, tels. EMB 226 of 10/3/43, EMB 273 of 3/3/43, Special series tel. of 8/3/43.

37. WO 202/359, tels. EMB 290 of 10/3/43, EMB 292 of 11/3/43; FO 371/37582, R2664/2/92. Far from meeting with success, the Četniks were already in total strategic and physical disarray. See Milazzo. *The Chetnik Movement*, chapter 6.

38. Taylor papers, "Report on Visit to Cairo Mission" (AD to CD), 11/3/43. For Elisabeth Barker's comments on the Taylor report see "Fresh Sidelights," pp. 583-84.

At a later date Taylor noted in the margin alongside his prediction of the Partisans' liquidation: "This appreciation of position in Serbian lands has proved quite wrong." It is worth emphasizing yet again, lest Taylor and his colleagues appear more cynical than in fact they were, that the Partisans as such were still thought to exist (and to be on the point of destruction) only in what SOE was pleased to regard as the Serb lands.

39. WO 202/359, tel. EMB 302 of 16/3/43.

40. WO 202/359, tel. EMB 307 of 19/3/43.

41. WO 202/359, tel. B1/1857 of 31/3/43.

42. WO 208/2026, MI3/6968/2; also see WO 208/2019. The appreciations of MI3 were presumably based on German intercepts, as well as on reports from Bailey. Italian intercepts would have been of far greater value. On the other hand, a vastly detailed survey entitled "Guerrilla Warfare in Yugoslavia" (available only in draft form and undated, but evidently prepared in mid-April) shows the extent of information that was available from German intercepts. WO 202/132A.

43. FO 371/37584, R3368/2/92.

44. Tomasevich, *The Chetniks*, p. 292. This is the text communicated by Churchill to Jovanović on 29 March. The emphasis is therefore the Prime Minister's. The Foreign Office files relating to the speech have been withheld, though the full Anglo-Yugoslav correspondence on the subject has been published by Pavelić, "Britanci i Draža Mihajlović," pp. 242-

51. Bailey's report of the speech (as relayed to London in several parts on 3-4 March) is also available, including his explanation for Mihailović's tirade: a heart complaint brought on by overwork and the toll exacted by two years in the mountains. WO 202/359, tels. EMB 268 and 278, B1/920/22, B1/948/49, B1/968.

45. FO 371/37581, R2330/2/92.

46. FO 371/37582, R2705/2/92, R2823/2/92.

47. WO 202/359, tels. B1/1808 of 29/3/43, B1/1857 of 31/3/43. These telegrams reflect Cairo's reaction to the reports from London of the decision.

48. FO 371/37584, R3994/2/92; Woodward, *British Foreign Policy*, III, p. 290.

49. Tomasevich, *The Chetniks*, pp. 292-93; FO 371/37584, R3994/2/92.

50. FO 371/37582, R2937/2/92.

51. FO 371/37583, R3030/2/92, R3105/2/92.

52. FO 371/37583, R3107/2/92; AVII, kutija 178, br. 21/1(1-2), tel. 33.

53. FO 371/37582, R2937/2/92. Minutes by Howard.

54. FO 371/37583, R3146/2/92. And secret it remained. Krnjević apparently learned of the episode only 13 years later. Tomasevich, *The Chetniks*, p. 293.

55. FO 371/37583, R3107/2/92.

56. FO 371/37583, R3124/2/92. The contradictory nature of Bailey's reports on the course of the fighting was illustrated by his report on 6 April that "there is no doubt that Mihailović will ultimately disperse Partisans by weight of numbers", though he would be weakened considerably for a period thereafter. FO 371/37584, R3382/2/92. Ten days later, however, he telegraphed that Mihailović (with shom he was reunited) was encamped eight kilometres from Berane (Ivangrad) so that the Italians could protect him from the Partisans. FO 371/37584, R3753/2/92. Meanwhile Glenconner in Cairo was fearful that Bailey was losing his grip and that SOE's unserviceable Liberators would preclude both adequate supply of Mihailović (should he prove repentant) and work with the Partisans. He again reproached London for having failed to get the

necessary Liberators months ago. WO 202/359, tel. 2412/14 (AD3 to London) of 15/4/43.

57. FO 371/37584, R3994/2/92.

58. FO 371/37583, R3246/2/92. Selborne reflected advice received from Glenconner. The latter wrote on 31 March that Mihailović - once prevailed upon to respect Bailey, to refrain from collaboration with the Italians, to avoid clashes with the Partisans in the Serb lands (except in self-defence) and to adopt a more warlike attitude - "will go far to terminate this movement", i.e. the Partisans. It was a tall order. WO 202/359, tel. 1863 (AD3 to London) of 31/3/43.

59. FO 371/37584, R3368/2/92.

60. WO 202/359, tel. G/2501/5 (AD3 to London) of 16/4/43.

61. Djilas, *Wartime,* pp. 229-45; Roberts, *Tito, Mihailović and the Allies,* pp. 106-12.

62. FO 371/37586, R4598/2/92. This telegram did not reach the Foreign Office until May. What Mihailović had in fact learned about was the first phase of the prisoner exchanges and Djilas's attendant movements between Sarajevo and Konjić. It was near the latter town that the Partisans handed over their dozen or so German prisoners on 23 March. According to Djilas, there were Četniks with the Germans in this area. Djilas, *Wartime,* pp. 229-45.

63. WO 202/132A, "Draft: Guerrilla Warfare in Yugoslavia", undated. The British were right about the movements of the Sixth Brigade (the Eastern Bosnian Brigade) and Foca was, of course, en route to Sandžak. Vlado Strugar, *Rat i revolucije naroda Jugoslavije* (Belgrade: Vojnoistorijski institut, 1962), pp. 152-54.

64. WO 202/359, tel. 2572/3 (AD3 to London) of 19/4/43. According to Djilas, there was never any question of the Partisans receiving weapons or other help from the Germans. They sought only a respite. Djilas, *Wartime* pp. 242-44.

65. WO 202/359, tel. G/2600 of 20/4/43, tel. 2787 of 26/4/43; Deakin, *The Embattled Mountain,* pp. 211-13. Sub-missions to the Četniks on Homolje and near Pristina were sent during the three nights preceding these flights to the Partisans.

66. WO 202/358, tel. G/476/7 (AD3 to London) of 17/5/43. The "Hoathley" mission had an eventful initiation, but does not seem to have discovered anything about Partisan-German relations. Nor could it raise Cairo by radio before 11 May. Deakin, *The Embattled Mountain,* pp. 53-54, 213.

67. FO 371/37584, R3994/2/92. Memoranda by Howard of 23 and 29 April. The record of the meeting itself remains secret. Eden had written on 25 April, "This is all thoroughly unsatisfactory. The Department write all the time as if it were for SOE to decide these matters. It isn't, it is for the Dept. to advise me and frankly they never give me any coherent account or intelligible advice. Therefore we must have a meeting, for I am responsible for all this to War Cabinet and must know where we are and whither we travel." Howard's seven-page history ("Mihailović-Partisan Conflict"), which has often been cited here, satisfied Eden in every respect. He minuted on 30 April, "I think I could be forgiven for not having guessed at SOE's recent change of policy."

68. Barker, "Fresh Sidelights", p. 584.

69. FO 371/37584, R3994/2/92.

70. WO 202/358, tel. G/2790 (AD3 to London) of 26/4/43.

71. FO 371/37586, R4708/2/92. Tito, remembering the Atherton affair, was initially very wary of these missions. The development of the Partisans' attitude towards their new allies - and their growing recognition of the benefits which relations with the British could bring - can be traced in *Zbornik,* II, 9, pp. 159-62, 176, 283, 287, 291, 293, 397-410.

72. FO 371/37586, R4708/2/92. The SIS representative with Jones was Captain Anthony Hunter.

73. Djilas, *Wartime,* p. 228.

74. FO 371/37586, R4794/2/92.

75. The SIS officer who accompanied Deakin, Captain W. F. Stuart, was killed within a few days of their arrival. Stuart had been coveted for some months by SOE. He was fluent in both Serbo-Croat and Hungarian and much versed in the region. SIS had proposed in January to send Stuart (then in New York) to join Bailey. SOE Cairo was of the opinion that Stuart would

be wasted at Mihailović headquarters. Cairo proposed instead to share Bailey with SIS and to hold Stuart in reserve for the first mission to Croatia, where he would serve both organizations. WO 202/357, tel. B1/3042 (AD3 to London) of 14/1/43. Stuart's death deprived the "Typical" mission of its expert, but not of its connections.

NOTES

CHAPTER VII

1. FO 371/37184, R11941/6780/67.
2. FRUS, *Cairo and Tehran,* pp. 574-75.
3. This was the occasion for Maclean's famous exchange with Churchill on whether or not either of them intended to make his home in Yugoslavia after the war. Since they did not, Churchill told Maclean, "the less you and I worry about the form of government they set up, the better. That is for them to decide. What interests us is, which of them is doing most harm to the Germans?" Fitzroy Maclean, *Eastern Approaches* (London: Jonathan Cape, 1949), pp. 402-03. But worry Churchill did.
4. Churchill, *Closing the Ring,* pp. 402-03.
5. FO 371/44276, R12712/11/92.

BIBLIOGRAPHY

I. *Unpublished Collections of Documents*

A. Public Record Office, Kew, Richmond, Surrey

1. Foreign Office Papers

FO 371 - General Political Correspondence of the Southern European Department (R); documents on Yugoslavia (92) and General Southern (67).

FO 536 - Correspondence of the British Embassy to Yugoslavia in London and Cairo.

2. War Cabinet Papers

CAB 65 - War Cabinet Minutes

CAB 66 - War Cabinet Memoranda

CAB 67 - War Cabinet Memoranda

CAB 69 - War Cabinet Defence Committee (Operations)

CAB 79 - Chiefs of Staff Committee, Minutes of Meetings

CAB 80 - Chiefs of Staff Committee, Memoranda

CAB 88 - Combined Chiefs of Staff Committee and Sub-Committees

PREM 3 - Prime Minister's Office, Operational Papers

PREM 4 - Prime Minister's Office, Confidential Papers

3. War Office Papers

WO 201 - Military Headquarters Papers: Middle East Forces

WO 202 - Military Headquarters Papers: Military Missions (contains partial records of SOE Cairo)

WO 208 - Directorate of Military Intelligence

B. Archives of the Federal Secretariat for Foreign Affairs (Savezni sekretarijat za inostrane poslove SFRJ: Diplomatski arhiv - SSIP), Belgrade

Ministry of Foreign Affairs of the Kingdom of Yugoslavia in London (Ministarstvo inostranih poslova KJ, Izbeglicka vlada), 1941-1943

Presidency of the Government of the Kingdom of Yugoslavia in London (Pretsednistvo vlade KJ u Londonu), 1941-1945

Presidency of the Council of Ministers of the Kingdom of Yugoslavia in London (Pretsednistvo ministarskog saveta KJ - Kabinet - u Londonu), 1941-1945

Ministry of Internal Affairs of the Kingdom of Yugoslavia, London - Cairo (Ministarstvo unutrasnjih poslova KJ, London-Kairo), 1940-1945

Miscellaneous Files from the Yugoslav Legation in London and other Diplomatic Posts, 1940-1945

C. Archives of Yugoslavia (Arhiv Jugoslavije - AJ), Belgrade

Fond 103 - Cabinet Papers of the Exile Government (Fond emigrantske vlade), 1941-1945

D. Archives of the Military History Institute of the Yugoslav People's Army (Vojno-istorijski institut JNA - Arhiv - AVII), Belgrade

Ministry of International Affairs; Army, Navy and Air Force Attache in Great Britain (Ministarstvo inostranih poslova; Vojni, pomorski i vazduhoplovni izaslanik u Velikoj Britaniji), 1942-1943

Presidency of the Government of the Kingdom of Yugoslavia - Military Cabinet (Pretsednistvo vlade KJ - Vojni kabinet), 1942-1943

E. King's College Library, University of London

George Taylor Papers

II. *Published Documentary Material*

Allied Force Headquarters, Mediterranean Branch. *Handbook of Jugoslav Personalities*. Bari (?), 1944 (?)

Allied Force Headquarters, Mediterranean Theatre. *Handbook of Personalities of the National Liberation Movement*. Caserta (?), 1944-45.

Allied Force, Mediterranean Headquarters. *The Četniks: A Survey of Četnik Activity in Yugoslavia, April 1941-July 1944*. Bari (?), September 1944.

Clissold, Stephen. (ed.) *Yugoslavia and the Soviet Union 1939-1973: A Documentary Survey*. London: Royal Institute of International Affairs/Oxford University Press, 1975.

Djonović, Jovan. "Izveštaji djenerala Mihailovića iz kraja 1943 i 1944 godine." *Glasnik SIKD 'Njegoš'*. 3(June 1959), pp. 63-80, 94-96.

Djonović, Jovan. "Telegrami Draže Mihailovića o engleskim misijama u svom štabu." *Glasnik SIKD 'Njegoš'*. 5(June 1960), pp. 24-35.

Djonović, Jovan. "Telegrami Draže Mihailovića o engleskim misijama u svom stabu i engleskoj politici na terenu." *Glasnik SIKD 'Njegos'*. 6 and 7 (December 1960 and June 1961), pp. 53-57, 33-38.

Knezevich, Zivan L. *General Mihailovich and USSR with Official Memoranda and Documents.* Washington (?), 1945.

Loewenheim, F.L., Langley, H.D., and Jonas, M. (eds.) *Roosevelt and Churchill: Their Secret Wartime Correspondence.* London: Barrie & Jenkins, 1975.

Marjanović, Jovan. (ed.) *The Collaboration of D. Mihailović's Chetniks with the Enemy Forces of Occupation* (1941-1944). Belgrade: Arhivski pregled, 1976.

Martin, David. (ed.) *Patriot or Traitor: The Case of General Mihailovich. Proceedings and Report of the Comission for a Fair Trial for Draja Mihailovich.* Stanford: Hoover Institution Press, 1978.

Middle East Headquarters. *National Liberation Movement of Yugoslavia.* Cairo (?), 1944.

Pijade, Moša. *About the Legend that the Yugoslav Uprising Owed its Existence to Soviet Assistance.* London, 1950.

The Trial of Dragoljub-Draža Mihailović: Stenographic Record and Documents. Belgrade: Union of the Journalists' Associations of the Federative People's Republic of Yugoslavia, 1946.

Tito, Josip Broz. *Political Report of the Central Committee of the Communist Party of Yugoslavia - Report Delivered at the Fifth Congress of the CPY.* Belgrade, 1948.

Tito, Josip Broz. *Selected Military Works.* Belgrade: Vojnoizdavački zavod, 1966.

United States Department of State. *Foreign Relations of the United States; Diplomatic Papers, 1940-1945.* Washington: US Government Printing Office, 1958-1967.

United States Department of State. *Foreign Relations of the United States; Diplomatic Papers, the Conferences at Malta and Yalta, 1945.* Washington: US Government Printing Office, 1955.

Zbornik dokumenata i podataka o Narodno-oslobodilackom ratu naroda Jugoslavije. Tom II, knjige 1-12: *Dokumenta Centralnog komiteta KP Jugoslavije.* Belgrade: Vojnoistorijski institut JNA, 1949-1971.

III. *Articles, Diaries, Memoirs and Monographs*

Adamic, Louis, *My Native Land.* New York: Harper & Brothers, 1943.

Alexandra, Queen of Yugoslavia. *For a King's Love: The Intimate Recollections of Queen Alexandra of Yugoslavia.* London: Odhams Press, 1956.

Amery, Julian. *Approach March.* London: Hutchinson, 1973.

Auty, Phyllis. *Tito — A Biography.* London: Longman, 1970.

Auty, Phyllis and Clogg, Richard. (eds.) *British Policy towards Wartime Resistance in Yugoslavia and Greece.* London: Macmillan, 1975.

Avakumović, Ivan. *History of the Communist Party of Yugoslavia.* Aberdeen: Aberdeen University Press, 1964.

Avon, Earl of. *The Memoirs of Anthony Eden: The Reckoning.* Boston: Houghton Mifflin, 1965.

Barker, Elisabeth. *British Policy in South-East Europe in the Second World War.* London: Macmillan, 1976.

Barker, Elisabeth. "British Wartime Policy towards Yugoslavia." *The South Slav Journal.* II (April 1979), pp. 3-9.

Barker, Elisabeth. "Fresh Sidelights on British Policy in Yugoslavia, 1942-3." *Slavonic and East European Review.* LIV (October 1976), pp. 572-85.

Barker, Elisabeth. "Serbia 1944." Unpublished article, 1978.

Božić, I., Ćirković, S., Ekmečić, M., Dedijer, V. *Istorija Jugoslavije.* Second edition. Belgrade: Prosveta, 1973.

Brajović, Petar (*et al*) *Les Systmes d'Occupation en Yougoslavie 1941-1945.* Belgrade: Institut radnickog pokreta, 1963.

Churchill, Winston S. *The Second World War.* Six volumes. New York: Bantam Books, 1962.

Clissold, Stephen. "Britain, Croatia and the Croatian Peasant Party, 1939-1945. Unpublished article, 1978.

Clissold, Stephen. *Whirlwind: An Account of Marshal Tito's Rise to Power.* London: Cresset Press, 1949.

Čolaković, Radoljub. *Winning Freedom.* London: Lincolns-Prager, 1962.

Creveld, Martin van. *Hitler's Strategy 1940-1941: The Balkan Clue.* London: Cambridge University Press, 1973.

Creveld, Martin van. "The German Attack on the USSR: The Destruction of a Legend." *European Studies Review.* II (January 1972), pp. 69-86.

Cruickshank, Charles. *Greece 1940-1941.* London: Davis-Poynter, 1976.

Čubrilović, Vasa. (ed.) *Ustanak u Jugoslaviji 1941 godine i Evropa.* Belgrade: Srpska akademija nauka i umetnosti, Odeljenje istorijskih nauka, 1973.

Dalton, Hugh. *The Fateful Years: Memoirs 1931-1945.* London: Frederick Muller, 1957.

Davidson, Basil. *Partisan Picture.* Bedford: Bedford Books, 1946.

Deakin, F.W.D. "Britanija i Jugoslavija 1941-45." *Jugosolovenski istorijski časopis.* II (no. 2, 1963), pp. 43-58.

Deakin, F.W.D. *The Embattled Mountain.* London: Oxford University Press, 1971.

Deakin, F.W.D. "Great Britain and European Resistance." *European Resistance Movements 1939-1945: Proceedings of the Second International Conference on the History of the Resistance Movements held at Milan, 26-29 March 1961.* Oxford: Pergamon Press, 1964.

Dedijer, Vladimir. *The Battle Stalin Lost: Memoirs of Yugoslavia 1948-1953.* New York: Viking, 1971.

Dedijer, Vladimir. *Dnevnik.* Three volumes, third edition, Belgrade and Sarajevo: Prosveta and Svjetlost, 1970.

Dedijer, Vladimir. (*et al*) *History of Yugoslavia.* New York: McGraw-Hill. 1974.

Dedijer, Vladimir. *On Military Conventions: An Essay on the Evolution of International Law.* Lund: C. W. K. Gleerup, 1961.

Dedijer, Vladimir. *Tito Speaks.* London: Weidenfeld and Nicolson, 1953.

Dilks, David. (ed.) *The Diaries of Sir Alexander Cadogan, O.M., 1938-1945.* London: Cassell, 1971.

Dixon, Piers. *Double Diploma: The Life of Sir Pierson Dixon.* London: Hutchinson, 1968.

Djilas, Milovan. *Conversations with Stalin.* New York: Harcourt, Brace & World, 1962.

Djilas, Milovan. *Memoir of a Revolutionary.* New York: Harcourt Brace Jovanovich, 1973.

Djilas, Milovan. *Wartime.* London: Martin Secker & Warburg, 1977.

Djonović, Jovan. "Moje veze sa Drazom Mihailovicem sa Srednjeg Istoka." *Glasnik SIKD 'Njegos'.* 2 (December 1968), pp. 82-98.

Djonović, Jovan. "Veze sa Dražom Mihailovićem sa Srednjeg i Bliskog Istoka i Severne Afrike." *Glasnik SIKD 'Njegoš'.* 1 (July 1958), pp. 41-65.

Djonović, Jovan. "Veze sa generalom Mihailovićem sa Srednjeg Istoka." *Glasnik SIKD 'Njegoš'.* 4 (December 1959), pp. 17-25.

Djordjević, Dimitrije. "Historians in Politics: Slobodan Jovanović." *Journal of Contemporary History.* VIII (January 1973), pp. 21-40.

Drasković, Milorad. "Komunistička internacionala i 'narodnooslobodilačka akcija' Komunističke partije Jugoslavije u 1941-1942 godine." *Glasnik SIKD 'Njegoš'.* 13 and 16 (June 1964 and December 1965), pp. 42-56, 29-46.

Ehrman, John. *Grand Strategy,* Vols. V and VI. London: HMSO, 1956.

Feis, Herbert. *Churchill, Roosevelt, Stalin: The War They Waged and the Peace They Sought.* Princeton: Princeton University Press, 1967.

Foot, M. R. D. *Resistance: European Resistance to Nazism 1940-1945.* London: Eyre Methuen, 1976.

Foot, M. R. D. *SOE in France: An Account of the work of the British Special Operations Executive in France 1940-1944.* London: HMSO, 1966.

Fotitch, Constantin. *The War We Lost: Yugoslavia's Tragedy and the Failure of the West.* New York: Viking Press, 1948.

General Mihailovich: The World's Verdict; A Selection of Articles on the First Resistance Leader in Europe Published in the World Press. Gloucester: John Bellows, 1947.

Glen, Alexander. *Footholds Against a Whirlwind.* London: Hutchinson, 1975.

Hamilton-Hill, Donald. *SOE Assignment.* London: William Kimber, 1973.
Hart, B. H. Liddell. *History of the Second World War.* London: Cassell, 1970.
Hoettl, Wilhelm. *The Secret Front: The Story of Nazi Political Espionage.* London: Weidenfeld and Nicolson, 1953.
Hoptner, J. B. *Yugoslavia in Crisis, 1934-1941.* New York: Columbia University Press, 1962.
Howard, Michael. *Grand Strategy,* Vol. IV. London: HMSO, 1972.
Howard, Michael. *The Mediterranean Strategy in the Second World War.* London: Weidenfeld and Nicolson, 1968.
Hull, Cordell. *The Memoirs of Cordell Hull,* Vol. II. New York: Macmillan, 1948.
Huot, Louis. *Guns for Tito.* New York: L. B. Fischer, 1945.
Jones, William. *Twelve Months with Tito's Partisans.* Bedford: Bedford Books, 1946.
Jovanović, Slobodan. *Zapisi o problemima i ljudima, 1941-1944.* London: Udruženje srpskih pisaca i umetnika u inostranstvu, 1976.
Jukić, Ilija. *The Fall of Yugoslavia.* New York: Harcourt Brace Jovanovich, 1974.
Karchmar, Lucien. "Draža Mihailović and the Rise of the Četnik Movement, 1941-1942." Two volumes. Unpublished Ph.D. dissertation, Stanford University, 1973.
Kemp, Peter. *No Colours or Crest.* London: Cassell, 1958.
Kerner, Robert J. (ed.) *Yugoslavia.* Berkeley: University of California Press, 1949.
King, F. P. *The New Internationalism: Allied Policy and the European Peace, 1939-1945.* Newton Abbot: David and Charles, 1973.
Kljaković, Vojmir. "Jugoslavenska emigrantska vlada prema pitanju Bosne i Hercegovine." *Prilozi.* 4(1968), pp. 307-15.
Kljaković, Vojmir. "Jugoslavenska vlada u emigranciji i Saveznici prema pitanju Hrvatske, 1941-1944." *Časopis za suvremenu povijest.* III(2-3, 1971), pp. 97-138.
Kljaković, Vojmir. "Promena politike Velike Britanije prema

Jugoslaviji u prvoj polovici 1943 godine." *Jugoslovenski istorijski časopis.* VIII (3, 1969), pp. 25-57.

Kljaković, Vojmir. "Velika Britanija, Sovjetski Savez i ustanak u Jugoslaviji 1941 godine." *Vojnoistorijski glasnik.* XXI (May-August 1970), pp. 69-103.

Knežević, Radoje L. (ed.) *Knjiga o Draži.* Two volumes. Windsor: Srpska narodna odbrana/Avala Printing and Publishing Company, 1956.

Knežević, Radoje L. "Jugoslovenska vlada i Draža Mihailović." *Poruka.* Numbers 8(1/11/52), pp. 5-14; 10(1/2/53), pp. 5-13; 13(16/6/53), pp. 9-19; 18(1/2/54), pp. 5-15; 23(16/10/54), pp. 5-15; 24(1/11/54), pp. 11-15.

Kofos, Evangelos. *Nationalism and Communism in Macedonia.* Thessaloniki: Institute for Balkan Studies, 1964.

Kolko, Gabriel. *The Politics of War: The World and United States Foreign Policy, 1943-1945.* New York: Random House, 1968.

Krizman, Bogdan. *Vanjska politika Jugoslavenske države 1918-1941.* Zagreb: Školska knjiga, 1975.

Lawrence, Christie. *Irregular Adventure.* London: Faber & Faber, 1947.

Leverkuehn, Paul. *German Military Intelligence.* London: Weidenfeld and Nicolson, 1954.

Lockhart, R. H. Bruce. *Comes the Reckoning.* London: Putnam, 1947.

Maček, Vladko. *In the Struggle for Freedom.* New York: Robert Speller and Sons, 1957.

Maclean, Fitzroy. *Disputed Barricade: The Life and Times of Josip Broz-Tito.* London: Jonathan Cape, 1957.

Maclean, Fitzroy. *Eastern Approaches.* London: Jonathan Cape, 1949.

Maclean, Fitzroy. *The Battle of Neretva.* London: Panther Books, 1970.

Macmillan, Harold. *The Blast of War, 1939-1945.* London: Macmillan, 1967.

Marić, Mihailo. *Kralj i vlada u emigraciji.* Zagreb: Epoha, 1966.

Marjanović, Jovan. "Prilozi istoriji sukoba Narodnooslobodilačkog pokreta i Četnika Draže Mihailovića u Srbiji 1941 godine." *Istorija XX veka: Zbornik radova.* I (1959), pp. 153-230.

Marjanović, Jovan. *Ustanak i Narodnooslobodilački pokret u Srbiji 1941 godine.* Belgrade: Institut društvenih nauka, 1963.

Marjanović, Jovan. "Velika Britanija i Narodnooslobodilački pokret u Jugoslaviji, 1941-1945." *Jugoslovenski istorijski časopis.* II (2, 1963), pp. 31-42.

Martin, David. *Ally Betrayed: The Uncensored Story of Tito and Mihailovich.* New York: Prentice-Hall, 1946.

Matloff, Maurice. Strategis Planning for Coalition Warfare *1943-1944.* Washington: Department of the Army, 1959.

Medlicott, W. N. *The Economic Blockade,* Vol. II. London: HMSO and Longmans, Green, 1959.

Michel, Henri. *The Shadow War: Resistance in Europe, 1939-1945.* London: Andre Deutsch, 1972.

Milazzo, Matteo Joseph. *The Chetnik Movement and the Yugoslav Resistance.* Baltimore: Johns Hopkins University Press, 1975.

Milazzo, Matteo Joseph. "The Chetnik Movement in Yugoslavia, 1941-1945." Unpublished Ph.D. dissertation, University of Michigan, 1971.

Molony, C. J. C. *(et al) The Mediterranean and Middle East,* Vol. V. London: HMSO, 1973.

Morača, Pero. "Odnosi izmedju Komunističke partije Jugoslavije i Kominterne od 1941 do 1943 godine." *Jugoslovenski istorijski časopis.* VIII (1-2, 1969), pp. 94-132.

Murphy, Robert. *Diplomat Among Warriors.* Garden City: Doubleday, 1964.

Nešović, Slobodan. *Inostranstvo i nova Jugoslavija 1941-1945.* Belgrade and Ljubljana: Prosveta and Državna založba Slovenije, 1964.

Nicolson, Harold. *Dairies and Letters 1939-1945.* Edited by Nigel Nicholson. London: Collins, 1967.

Novak, Bogdan C. *Trieste 1941-1954: The Ethnic, Political and Ideological Struggle.* Chicago: University of Chicago Press, 1970.

Ostović, P. D. *The Truth about Yugoslavia.* New York: Roy, 1952.

Pavelić, Ante Smith. "Britanci i Draža Mihajlović." *Hrvatska revija.* VII (September 1957), pp. 235-53.

Pavlović, Kosta St. "Obrazovanje namesništva." *Glasnik SIKD 'Njegoš'.* 9 (June 1962), pp. 26-42.

Pavlović, Kosta St. "Pad Jovanovićeve vlade." *Glasnik SIKD 'Njegoš'.* 4 (December 1959), pp. 1-16.

Pavlović, Kosta St. "Pad Purićeve vlade." *Glasnik SIKD 'Njegoš'.* 7 (June 1961), pp. 7-32.

Pavlović, Kosta St. "Pad Simovićeve vlade." *Glasnik SIKD 'Njegoš'.* 2 (December 1958), pp. 67-81.

Pavlović, Kosta St. "Pad Trifunovićeve vlade." *Glasnik SIKD 'Njegoš'.* 6 (December 1960), pp. 58-70.

Pavlowitch, K. St. "Yugoslav-British Relations 1939-1941 as seen from British Sources." *East European Quarterly.* XII (Fall and Winter 1978), pp. 309-39, 425-41.

Pavlowitch, Stevan K. *Yugoslavia.* London: Ernest Benn, 1971.

Pavlowitch, Stevan K. "Out of Context: The Yugoslav Government in London, 1941-1945." Unpublished article, 1977.

Peter II, King of Yugoslavia. *A King's Heritage.* New York: G. P. Putnam's Sons, 1954.

Petković, Dušan. "Četnicka radio stanica 'Karadjordje'." *Glasnik SIKD 'Njegoš'.* 3 (June 1959), pp. 43-48.

Petković, Dušan. "Kako je upostavljena veza sa djen. Mihailovićem iz Carigrad." *Glasnik SIKD 'Njegoš'.* 5 (June 1960), pp. 49-55.

Playfair, I. S. O. (*et al*) *The War in the Mediterranean and Middle East.* Two volumes, London: HMSO, 1954-1955.

Plećaš, Nedjeljko B. "S Mora i iz vazduha u porobljenu Otadžbinu." *Glasnik SIKD 'Njegoš'.* 5 (June 1960), pp. 36-48.

Plenča, Dušan. *Medjunarodni odnosi Jugoslavije u toku Drugog svjetskog rata.* Belgrade: Institut društvenih nauka, 1962.

Putnik, Dimitrije. "Radio vese sa zemljom un prošlom ratu." *Glasnik SIKD 'Njegoš'.* 7 (June 1961), pp. 39-43.

Rendel, Sir George. *The Sword and the Olive: Recollections of Diplomacy and the Foreign Service, 1913-1954.* London: John Murray, 1957.

Rich, Norman. *Hitler's War Aims: Ideology, the Nazi State and the Course of Expansion.* London: Andre Deutsch, 1973.

Ristić, Dragiša N. *Yugoslavia's Revolution of 1941.* University Park: Pennsylvania State University Press, 1966.

Roberts, Walter R. *Tito, Mihailović and the Allies, 1941-1945.* New Brunswick: Rutgers University Press, 1973.

Rootham, Jasper. *Miss-Fire: The Chronicle of a British Mission to Mihailovich, 1943-1944.* London: Chatto and Windus, 1946.

St. John, Robert. *From the Land of the Silent People.* London: Harrap, 1942.

Seitz, Albert B. *Mihailović - Hoax or Hero?* Columbus: Leigh House, 1953.

Seton-Watson, Hugh. *The East European Revolution.* New York: Frederick A. Praeger, 1951.

Shoup, Paul, *Communism and the Yugoslav National Question.* New York: Columbia University Press, 1968.

Smith, R. Harris. *OSS: The Secret History of America's First Central Intelligence Agency.* Berkeley: University of California Press, 1972.

Smodlaka, Josip. *Partizanski dnevnik.* Belgrade: Nolit, 1972.

Stafford, David. "The Detonator Concept: British Strategy, SOE and European Resistance after the Fall of France." *Journal of Contemporary History.* X (April 1975), pp. 185-217.

Stafford, David. "SOE and British Involvement in the Belgrade Coup d'État of March 1941." *Slavic Review.* XXXVI (September 1977), pp. 399-419.

Stavrianos, Leften S. *Balkan Federation: A History of the Movement toward Balkan Unity in Modern Times.* Northampton: Smith College Studies in History. Vol. XXVI, 1944.

Strugar, Vlado, *Rat i revolucija naroda Jugoslavije 1941-1945.* Belgrade: Vojnoistorijski institut, 1962.

Strutton, Bill. *Island of Terrible Friends*. London: Hodder and Stoughton, 1961.

Sudjić, Milivoj J. *Yugoslavia in Arms*. London: Lindsay Drummond, 1942.

Sulzberger, Cyrus L. *A Long Row of Candles: Memoirs and Dairies, 1934-1954*. New York: Macmillan, 1969.

Sweet-Escott, Bickham. *Baker Street Irregular*. London: Methuen, 1965.

Thayer, Charles W. *Hands Across the Caviar*. London: Michael Joseph, 1953.

Todorovich, Borislav J. *A Forgotten Army*. Washington: Constantin Fotitch for the Central National Committee, 1945.

Tomasevich, Jozo. *War and Revolution in Yugoslavia 1941-1945: The Chetniks*. Stanford: Stanford University Press, 1975.

Topalovic, Živko. *Pokreti narodnog otpora u Jugoslaviji 1941-1945*. Paris: Izdanje jugoslovenskih sindikalista, 1958.

Toynbee, Arnold and Veronica (eds.) *The Initial Triumph of the Axis*. London: Royal Institute of International Affairs / Oxford University Press, 1958.

Tributes to General Mihailovich. Windsor: Avala Printing and Publishing Company, 1966.

Velebit, Vladimir. "Naša diplomatija u Narodnooslobodilačkoj borbi." *Narodna armija*. XIII (no. 958, 28/11/57), p. 3.

Vucinich, Wayne S. (ed.) *Contemporary Yugoslavia: Twenty Years of Socialist Experiment*. Berkeley: University of California Press, 1969.

Wandycz, Piotr S. "Recent Traditions of the Quest for Unity: Attempted Polish-Czechoslovak and Yugoslav-Bulgarian Confederations 1940-1948." *The People's Democracies after Prague: Soviet Hegemony, Nationalism, Regional Integration?* Edited by Jerzy Lukaszewski. Cahiers de Bruges 25. Bruges: De Tempel, 1970.

Weinberg, Gerhard L. *The Foreign Policy of Hitler's Germany: Diplomatic Revolution in Europe, 1933-1936*. Chicago: University of Chicago Press, 1970.

Wilson, Field Marshal Lord Wilson of Libya. *Eight Years Overseas, 1939-1947.* London: Hutchinson, 1948.

Wolff, Robert Lee. *The Balkans in Our Time.* Cambridge: Harvard University Press, 1956.

Woodhouse, C. M. *The Struggle for Greece 1941-1949.* London: Hart-Davis, MacGibbon, 1976.

Woodward, Sir Llewellyn. *British Foreign Policy in the Second World War.* London: HMSO, 1962.

Woodward, Sir Llewellyn. *British Foreign Policy in the Second World War,* Volume III. London: HMSO, 1971.

Xydis, Stephen G. *Greece and the Great Powers, 1944-1947.* Thessaloniki: Institute for Balkan Studies, 1963.

INDEX

EAST EUROPEAN MONOGRAPHS

The *East European Monographs* comprise scholarly books on the history and civilization of Eastern Europe. They are published in the belief that these studies contribute substantially to the knowledge of the area and serve to stimulate scholarship and research.

1. *Political Ideas and the Enlightenment in the Romanian Principalities, 1750–1831.* By Vlad Georgescu. 1971.
2. *America, Italy and the Birth of Yugoslavia, 1917–1919.* By Dragan R. Zivojinovic. 1972.
3. *Jewish Nobles and Geniuses in Modern Hungary.* By William O. McCagg, Jr. 1972.
4. *Mixail Soloxov in Yugoslavia: Reception and Literary Impact.* By Robert F. Price. 1973.
5. *The Historical and National Thought of Nicolae Iorga.* By William O. Oldson. 1973.
6. *Guide to Polish Libraries and Archives.* By Richard C. Lewanski. 1974.
7. *Vienna Broadcasts to Slovakia, 1938–1939: A Case Study in Subversion.* By Henry Delfiner. 1974.
8. *The 1917 Revolution in Latvia.* By Andrew Ezergailis. 1974.
9. *The Ukraine in the United Nations Organization: A Study in Soviet Foreign Policy. 1944–1950.* By Konstantin Sawczuk. 1975.
10. *The Bosnian Church: A New Interpretation.* By John V. A. Fine, Jr., 1975.
11. *Intellectual and Social Developments in the Habsburg Empire from Maria Theresa to World War I.* Edited by Stanley B. Winters and Joseph Held. 1975.
12. *Ljudevit Gaj and the Illyrian Movement.* By Elinor Murray Despalatovic. 1975.
13. *Tolerance and Movements of Religious Dissent in Eastern Europe.* Edited by Bela K. Kiraly. 1975.
14. *The Parish Republic: Hlinka's Slovak People's Party, 1939–1945.* By Yeshayahu Jelinek. 1976.
15. *The Russian Annexation of Bessarabia, 1774–1828.* By George F. Jewsbury. 1976.
16. *Modern Hungarian Historiography.* By Steven Bela Vardy. 1976.
17. *Values and Community in Multi-National Yugoslavia.* By Gary K. Bertsch. 1976.
18. *The Greek Socialist Movement and the First World War: the Road to Unity.* By George B. Leon. 1976.

19. *The Radical Left in the Hungarian Revolution of 1848.* By Laszlo Deme. 1976.
20. *Hungary between Wilson and Lenin: The Hungarian Revolution of 1918–1919 and the Big Three.* By Peter Pastor. 1976.
21. *The Crises of France's East-Central European Diplomacy, 1933–1938.* By Anthony J. Komjathy. 1976.
22. *Polish Politics and National Reform, 1775–1788.* By Daniel Stone. 1976.
23. *The Habsburg Empire in World War I.* Robert A. Kann, Bela K. Kiraly, and Paula S. Fichtner, eds. 1977.
24. *The Slovenes and Yugoslavism, 1890–1914.* By Carole Rogel. 1977.
25. *German-Hungarian Relations and the Swabian Problem.* By Thomas Spira. 1977.
26. *The Metamorphosis of a Social Class in Hungary During the Reign of Young Franz Joseph.* By Peter I. Hidas. 1977.
27. *Tax Reform in Eighteenth Century Lombardy.* By Daniel M. Klang. 1977.
28. *Tradition versus Revolution: Russia and the Balkans in 1917.* By Robert H. Johnston. 1977.
29. *Winter into Spring: The Czechoslovak Press and the Reform Movement 1963–1968.* By Frank L. Kaplan. 1977.
30. *The Catholic Church and the Soviet Government, 1939–1949.* By Dennis J. Dunn. 1977.
31. *The Hungarian Labor Service System, 1939–1945.* By Randolph L. Braham. 1977.
32. *Consciousness and History: Nationalist Critics of Greek Society 1897–1914.* By Gerasimos Augustinos. 1977.
33. *Emigration in Polish Social and Political Thought, 1870–1914.* By Benjamin P. Murdzek. 1977.
34. *Serbian Poetry and Milutin Bojic.* By Mihailo Dordevic. 1977.
35. *The Baranya Dispute: Diplomacy in the Vortex of Ideologies, 1918–1921.* By Leslie C. Tihany. 1978.
36. *The United States in Prague, 1945–1948.* By Walter Ullmann. 1978.
37. *Rush to the Alps: The Evolution of Vacationing in Switzerland.* By Paul P. Bernard. 1978.
38. *Transportation in Eastern Europe: Empirical Findings.* By Bogdan Mieczkowski. 1978.
39. *The Polish Underground State: A Guide to the Underground, 1939–1945.* By Stefan Korbonski. 1978.
40. *The Hungarian Revolution of 1956 in Retrospect.* Edited by Bela K. Kiraly and Paul Jonas. 1978.
41. *Boleslaw Limanowski (1835–1935): A Study in Socialism and Nationalism.* By Kazimiera Janina Cottam. 1978.
42. *The Lingering Shadow of Nazism: The Austrian Independent Party Movement Since 1945.* By Max E. Riedlsperger. 1978.
43. *The Catholic Church, Dissent and Nationality in Soviet Lithuania.* By V. Stanley Vardys. 1978.

44. *The Development of Parliamentary Government in Serbia.* By Alex N. Dragnich. 1978.
45. *Divide and Conquer: German Efforts to Conclude a Separate Peace, 1914–1918.* By L. L. Farrar, Jr. 1978.
46. *The Prague Slav Congress of 1848.* By Lawrence D. Orton. 1978.
47. *The Nobility and the Making of the Hussite Revolution.* By John M. Klassen. 1978.
48. *The Cultural Limits of Revolutionary Politics: Change and Continuity in Socialist Czechoslovakia.* By David W. Paul. 1979.
49. *On the Border of War and Peace: Polish Intelligence and Diplomacy in 1937–1939 and the Origins of the Ultra Secret.* By Richard A. Woytak. 1979.
50. *Bear and Foxes: The International Relations of the East European States 1965–1969.* By Ronald Haly Linden. 1979.
51. *Czechoslovakia: The Heritage of Ages Past.* Edited by Hans Brisch and Ivan Volgyes. 1979.
52. *Prime Minister Gyula Andrássy's Influence on Habsburg Foreign Policy.* By János Decsy. 1979.
53. *Citizens for the Fatherland: Education, Educators, and Pedagogical Ideals in Eighteenth Century Russia.* By J. L. Black. 1979.
54. *The History of the "Proletariat": The Emergence of Marxism in the Kingdom of Poland, 1870–1887.* By Norman M. Naimark. 1979.
55. *The Slovak Autonomy Movement, 1935–1939: A Study in Unrelenting Nationalism.* By Dorothea H. El Mallakh. 1979.
56. *Diplomat in Exile: Francis Pulszky's Political Activities in England, 1849–1860.* By Thomas Kabdebo. 1979.
57. *The German Struggle Against the Yugoslav Guerrillas in World War II: German Counter-Insurgency in Yugoslavia, 1941–1943.* By Paul N. Hehn. 1979.
58. *The Emergence of the Romanian National State.* By Gerald J. Bobango. 1979.
59. *Stewards of the Land: The American Farm School and Modern Greece.* By Brenda L. Marder. 1979.
60. *Roman Dmowski: Party, Tactics, Ideology 1895–1907.* By Alvin Marcus Fountain II. 1980.
61. *International and Domestic Politics in Greece During the Crimean War.* By Jon V. Kofas. 1980.
62. *Fires on the Mountain: The Macedonian Revolutionary Movement and the Kidnapping of Ellen Stone.* By Laura Beth Sherman. 1980.
63. *The Modernization of Agriculture: Rural Tranformation in Hungary, 1848-1975.* Edited by Joseph Held. 1980.
64. *Britain and the War for Yugoslavia, 1940-1943.* By Mark C. Wheeler. 1980.